The Annotated VRML 2.0 Reference Manual

Rikk Carey
and
Gavin Bell

ADDISON–WESLEY

Boston • San Francisco • New York • Toronto • Montreal
London • Munich • Paris • Madrid
Capetown • Sidney • Tokyo • Singapore • Mexico City

Many of the designations used by manufacturers and sellers to distinguish their products are claimed as trademarks. Where those designations appear in this book, and we were aware of a trademark claim, the designations have been printed in initial capital letters or in all capitals.

The author and publisher have taken care in the preparation of this book, but make no expressed or implied warranty of any kind and assume no responsibility for errors or omissions. No liability is assumed for incidental or consequential damages in connection with or arising out of the use of the information or programs contained herein.

Images of "O2 Out of Box Experience" (color plate section) courtesy of Sam Chen, Silicon Graphics, Inc., and Construct Internet Design.

The publisher offers discounts on this book when ordered in quantity for special sales. For more information, please contact:

Pearson Education Corporate Sales Division
One Lake Street
Upper Saddle River, NJ 07458
(800) 382-3419
corpsales@pearsontechgroup.com

Visit AW on the Web: www.awl.com/cseng/

Library of Congress Cataloging-in-Publication Data
Carey, Rikk.
    The annotated VRML 2.0 reference manual / Rickk Carey and Gavin Bell.
        p. cm.
    Includes index.
    ISBN 0-201-41974-2
    1. VRML (Document markup language). I. Bell, Gavin. II. Title.
    QA76.76.H94C368 1997
    006—dc21   97–6495
                                                                    CIP

Sponsoring Editor: Mary Treseler (marytr@aw.com)
Project Manager: John Fuller
Production Coordinator: Melissa Lima
Cover image courtesy of Sam Chen
Text design: Octal Publishing, Inc.
Set in 10.5-point Berkeley by Octal Publishing, Inc.

3 4 5 6 7 8 9 10—MA—0403020100
3rd printing, May 2000

Readers are encouraged to contact the authors with questions or comments. Rikk Carey can be reached via e-mail at rikk@best.com; his web page is located at http://www.best.com/~rikk. Gavin Bell's e-mail address is gavin@acm.org; his web page can be found at http://www.mailbag.com/users/gavin.

To Heather, my love and light
                    —RC

To my beautiful wife Michele
                    —GB

Contents

Chapter 3: Node Reference

Chapter 4: Field and Event Reference.....351

Chapter 5: Conformance and Minimum Support Requirements.....361

Acknowledgments

This book would not be possible without the dedication and help of many people. The following is a short list of some of those people. We cannot possibly thank everyone (although we would like to); please forgive us if we've neglected to mention you here.

Special thanks to Paul Strauss for his pioneering efforts on Open Inventor, which eventually led to VRML. Thanks to the rest of the Open Inventor engineering team for laying the groundwork that VRML is based on: Thad Beier, Alain Dumesny, Dave Immel, Paul Isaacs, Howard Look, David Mott, Nick Thompson, and Helga Thorvaldsdóttir. Thanks to Chris Marrin for his work on the Java and JavaScript appendices, as well as a variety of other important areas of the VRML Specification.

Thanks to Mark Pesce and Tony Parisi for writing the first prototype of a 3D web browser, *Labyrinth*, and for their tireless contribution and dedication to VRML.

Thanks to Mitra, Kouichi Matsuda, Rodger Lea, and Yasuaki Honda for their work on the Moving Worlds proposal and the Java appendix. Thanks to the many unnamed people who contributed ideas and work to the VRML Specification—you know who you are.

Thanks to Silicon Graphics, Inc., for creating a fantastic work environment and for taking a risk on VRML.

Thanks to Mary Treseler, John Fuller, Keith Wollman, and the Addison Wesley Longman staff for guidance and support. Thanks to our book reviewers: Scott S. Ross, Stephen Chenney, Len Bullard, Cindy Reed-Ballreich, Jan C. Hardenbergh, Chet Murphy, Jai Natarajan, Matt O'Donnell, David Story, and Mason Woo. Thanks to Sam Chen and Silicon Graphics, Inc., for providing the cover image for this book. Thanks also to Sam Chen, Silicon Graphics, Inc. and Construct Internet Design for the *O2 Out of Box Experience* images used in the color plates.

And last, but not least, thanks to the members of the *www-vrml* mailing list for your ideas, passion, and hard work.

About This Book

The *Annotated VRML 2.0 Reference Manual* contains the complete specification of the Virtual Reality Modeling Language, version 2.0, as of February 1997. In addition, throughout this book you will find a variety of technical annotations, authoring tips, and illustrative examples. While the VRML specification is technically accurate and precise, it is not intended to address questions on why it is designed the way it is, what's the best way to use it, what to avoid, or how to implement it. These issues and more are featured throughout this book. The annotations relate the various separate parts of VRML into a coherent whole. The contents of this book are relevant to implementors of the VRML specifications as well as to authors and users of VRML.

This book is not a tutorial on VRML. There are a variety of books that teach basic and advanced VRML concepts, and serve as excellent companions to this book (see Appendix F, Recommended Reading).

This book does not rely on or describe any single specific implementation of VRML, rather it presents the ideal definition of VRML and suggests typical implementation pitfalls and difficulties to watch out for. See Appendix E, VRML Compendium, for a summary of the browser and authoring tools available for you to choose from.

What This Book Contains

The first chapter, Introduction, describes the motivation, history, and basis for VRML. Chapter 2, Key Concepts, presents a technical overview of the VRML file format and underlying architecture. This chapter introduces you to the file format syntax and goes on to discuss a variety of important architectural fundamentals of VRML, such as prototypes, routing, scripting, execution model, and binding node behavior. The third chapter, Node Reference, contains the largest and most significant aspect of the book. It defines the syntax and semantics of every node in the specification, as well as complete working examples for each node, and a variety of annotations and tips. Chapter 4, Field and Event Reference, describes the syntax and semantics of the VRML data types—fields and events. The fifth chapter, Conformance and Minimum Support Requirements, specifies the baseline requirements to which VRML implementations must adhere. This chapter is useful to authors and implementors alike, as a benchmark of which features are required in

a conforming VRML application. Appendix A, VRML Grammar Definition, provides a precise grammar definition of the VRML file format. Appendix B, Examples,
includes the revised sample files found in the VRML specification. Appendix C,
Java Scripting Reference, describes the integration of the Java programming language with VRML. This appendix defines the specific classes and methods that may
be invoked from a VRML **Script** node using Java. Appendix D, JavaScript Scripting
Reference, defines the integration of the JavaScript scripting language with VRML.
It includes a detailed specification of the JavaScript objects and functions available
to a VRML **Script** node. Appendix E, VRML Compendium, lists a variety of Uniform Resource Locators (URLs) to VRML-related sources and topics. Appendix F,
Recommended Reading, lists a variety of books that supplement the material contained in this book. Appendix G, Summary of Java Scripting API, provides a quick
reference to the Java classes and methods. Appendix H, Summary of JavaScript
Scripting API, provides a quick reference to the JavaScript objects and methods.

How to Use This Book

There are several ways to use this book. First you can read Chapter 1, Introduction,
and Chapter 2, Key Concepts, for an in-depth description of the fundamentals of
VRML, and use Appendix E, VRML Compendium, to find a variety of references on
VRML-related information sources. Advanced technical readers should have no
problem using these chapters as their introduction to VRML, while novices may
wish to start with an introductory book before reading these chapters. The second
way to use this book is as an everyday reference guide. It is organized for fast access
and daily use: specification text is easily distinguished from the annotations; reference topics are alphabetized and tabbed; and notes, tips, and examples are located
in the section containing the relevant topic. The third way to use this book is to
read the notes, tips, and examples to enhance your knowledge and gain new
insight into VRML. The fourth way to use this book is to access the on-line World
Wide Web (WWW) site, which includes most of the book, including live versions
of the examples:

`http://www.aw.com/devpress/titles/41974.html`

The examples included in this book conform to the VRML specification and are
accurate to the best of our knowledge, but may not work in all browsers (see the
browser's release notes for supported features and known bugs).

This book contains references to a variety of URLs. Note that it is possible that
URLs may change or become inactive after the publication of this book, and that it
may be necessary to employ a search engine to find a more up-to-date URL.

Getting Started

There are only two things needed to get started with VRML: a VRML browser and a text editor. When choosing from the wide variety of VRML browsers available, keep in mind which system you are using, which system(s) you expect your users to have, and the essential VRML features that you intend to use (not all browsers support all features in the specification). VRML files are plain text files, so you can create them using any text editor. Most word processors can read and write text files; be sure to "Save As" plain text. Special-purpose programming editors are even better for editing VRML files because they support features such as matching opening and closing braces and automatically indenting each line.

There are also VRML authoring tools available. These range from file converters to single-task utilities to full-fledged authoring environments. VRML has become so popular as a three-dimensional (3D) file exchange format that many 3D applications output VRML. File converters from most 3D formats are also readily available. Note that there is a big difference between an authoring system that *outputs* VRML and one that *authors* VRML. Typically, native VRML systems support more features and produce better results, but some of the systems that output VRML are just as good.

Conventions Used in This Book

1. There are three types of annotations in the book: technical notes, authoring tips, and examples. Each annotation type is labeled with an icon in the margin for easy recognition:

DESIGN NOTE

This is an example technical note. It may contain historical footnotes concerning the design of VRML, advanced technical notes, or implementation details. These notes are typically of interest to implementors and advanced authors.

TIP

This is an example of an authoring tip. Tips range from suggestions on proper usage to warnings on problem areas to nonobvious ideas for combining and using VRML.

EXAMPLE

This is an example of a VRML example file. Most of the examples start with an explanatory introduction; some include an image illustrating the results on screen. Most of the examples are complete, but some may include "**. . .**" to imply that valid VRML syntax goes here:

```
#VRML V2.0 utf8
Transform { children [
  ...
]}
```

2. Node types are printed in bold type:

   - A **TouchSensor** node . . .
   - The **Sphere** node . . .

3. New terms, field names, and event names are printed in italic type:

   - A *prototype* is a . . .
   - The *radius* field . . .
   - The *isActive* eventOut . . .

4. *Node definitions* specify the complete set of events and fields for a given node
   type. The parts of the definition that correspond to the file format are given in
   a bold, fixed-space font, while the rest of the definition is given in a plain,
   fixed-space font:

```
Collision {
   eventIn        MFNode      addChildren
   eventIn        MFNode      removeChildren
   exposedField   MFNode      children       []
   exposedField   SFBool      collide        TRUE
   field          SFVec3f     bboxCenter     0 0 0
   field          SFVec3f     bboxSize       -1 -1 -1
   field          SFNode      proxy          NULL
   eventOut       SFTime      collideTime
}
```

5. Programming interfaces, VRML file examples, and URLs are printed in a
   plain, fixed-space font:

   - `void createVrmlFromString( String vrmlSyntax );`
   - `Cylinder { radius 3 height 5 }`
   - `http://www.aw.com/`

6. DEF and USE names are usually chosen as an abbreviation of the node type and are numbered if there are more than one of the same type in the file. For example, if an example file contains two **ProximitySensors,** the first one would be named `PS1` and the second one `PS2`:

```
#VRML V2.0 utf8
Transform { children [
  DEF PS1 ProximitySensor {...}
  ...
  DEF PS2 ProximitySensor {...}
  ...
]}
```

7. **Background** nodes have been added to most of the examples to produce white backgrounds for printing.

8. The colors in most of the examples were chosen to be in gray scale since the images are printed in gray scale.

9. Field values and closing braces and brackets are often combined on one line to compress the examples in the book:

```
#VRML V2. utf8
Transform { children [
  Sphere { radius 4 }
  Cylinder { height 5 radius 3 }
  Transform {
    children [
      ...
]}]}
```

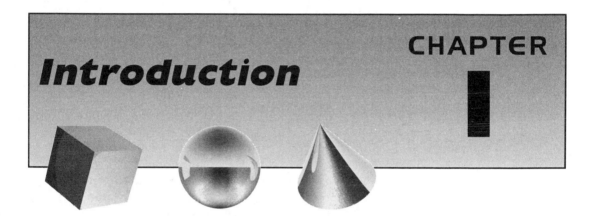

Introduction

CHAPTER

1

This chapter provides an introduction to VRML. It includes an overview of VRML, the goals and constraints used in designing VRML, a brief history of the specification, how VRML fits into the WWW, predictions on the future of the specification, and an overview of the VRML language.

1.1 What Is VRML?

VRML, sometimes pronounced *vermal*, is an acronym for the Virtual Reality Modeling Language. Technically speaking, VRML is neither *virtual reality* nor a *modeling language*. Virtual reality typically implies an immersive 3D experience (such as a head-mounted display) and 3D input devices (such as digital gloves). VRML neither requires nor precludes immersion. Furthermore, a true modeling language would contain much richer geometric modeling primitives and mechanisms. VRML provides a bare minimum of geometric modeling features and contains numerous features far beyond the scope of a modeling language.

So if VRML is not virtual reality or a modeling language, what is it? There are several answers to this question. At its core, VRML is simply a 3D interchange format. It defines most of the commonly used semantics found in today's 3D applications such as hierarchical transformations, light sources, viewpoints, geometry, animation, fog, material properties, and texture mapping. One of the primary goals in designing VRML was to ensure that it at least succeeded as an effective 3D file interchange format.

The second answer is that VRML is a 3D analog to HTML. This means that VRML serves as a simple, multiplatform language for publishing 3D Web pages. This is motivated by the fact that some information is best experienced three dimensionally, such as games, engineering and scientific visualizations, educational experiences, and architecture. Typically these types of projects require intensive interaction, animation, and user participation and exploration beyond what is capable with a page-, text-, or image-based format (i.e., HTML).

Another answer is that VRML provides the technology that integrates three dimensions, two dimensions, text, and multimedia into a coherent model. When these media types are combined with scripting languages and Internet capabilities, an entirely new genre of interactive applications are possible. A 3D metaphor presents a natural user experience that supports classic two-dimensional (2D) desktop models as well as extends into broader contexts of *space* and *place*. Many have speculated that the 3D world model will supersede and thus replace the popular 2D desktop model as the primary user interface paradigm in the next decade. Of course, there are a variety of challenges that need to be overcome before this is possible, such as 3D user interface and navigation, user training, and ubiquitous 3D graphics performance.

A fourth answer, and the one most publicized and debated, is that VRML is the foundation for *cyberspace* and the on-line *virtual communities* that were painted and popularized by science fiction writers William Gibson in *Neuromancer* and Neal Stephenson in *Snow Crash*. Critics have accurately pointed out that VRML does not yet define the networking and database protocols necessary for true multiuser simulations. However, the strategy behind VRML has been

- evolve the standard one step at a time
- keep it simple
- standardize only on problems that are completely understood and reasonably solved
- encourage experimentation and extensions on the frontiers
- don't reinvent technologies that can be solved outside of VRML (e.g., HTTP)

There are already several working, multiuser systems implemented on top of VRML—proof that the incremental approach is working.

So the answer to "What is VRML?" is actually "All of the above" and will most likely never be a simple one-sided answer. However, there are a few misconceptions or "wrong" answers. For example, VRML is *not* a programming library for application developers. Since VRML is based on the Open Inventor file format, many people assume that it also provides the rich programming interfaces and tools included in the Open Inventor toolkit. In actuality, VRML is an extended subset of Open Inventor's *file format* and does not define an application programmer interface (API). The fact that VRML includes scripting language integration tends to promote this misconception. Scripting language capabilities are predominantly intended for authors who need more power or integration.

1.2 Design Goals and Constraints for VRML 2.0

VRML 2.0 was created to extend the capabilities of VRML 1.0. VRML 1.0 specified static objects and scenes, and although it is very successful as a file format for 3D objects and worlds, objects and worlds that don't do anything aren't very interesting. The overall goal for VRML 2.0 was fairly modest: to allow objects in the world to move and to allow the user to interact with the objects in the world, allowing the creation of more interesting user experiences than those created with VRML 1.0. It was decided that more ambitious features—such as multiuser interaction or autonomous creatures that can sense and react to their environment—would not be a standard part of VRML 2.0. It is expected that many extensions to VRML 2.0 will be implemented and tested, with the best extensions incorporated into a future version of the standard.

The goals for VRML 2.0 might be modest, but the constraints placed on the design were very ambitious. The technical notes scattered throughout this book give examples of how and why specific design decisions were made. The entire VRML 2.0 design was profoundly influenced by several general design philosophies arising from the constraints put on the design by the VRML standardization process and the intended uses of VRML.

Simplicity was an important design constraint. The success of the HTML file format motivated this constraint. The simplicity of HTML fueled the explosive growth of the WWW. Because it is possible to create Web pages with any generic text editor, and because it is relatively easy to create an HTML browser, small organizations and individuals quickly created thousands of Web pages and a multitude of browsers. Even though VRML 2.0 is significantly more complex than VRML 1.0, there are at least a half a dozen different VRML 2.0 browsers available, with more under development. A simple specification encourages the development of more browsers, which leads to competition, which will encourage the development of higher quality implementations.

Another important design constraint was allowing implementations to be highly optimized. The performance ramifications of every feature were considered. If a fast implementation of something didn't seem possible, the feature was rejected. Features were also rejected if they made a "typical" implementation slower even when the feature was not being used. It is surprisingly easy to add a "little" feature that causes all implementations to be a little bit slower and is surprisingly hard to remove any feature once it is part of the specification. Good performance still requires a lot of work from world creators to create optimizable VRML files and requires a lot of work from VRML implementors to optimize their implementations, but VRML 2.0 is designed to make that work as easily as possible.

VRML 1.0 has gained widespread support as a file interchange format, and another constraint on the VRML 2.0 design was to make it an even better interchange format. This means that it must be easy for applications to both read and write VRML files. One of the critical design decisions was whether it would be best to add animation and interaction capabilities to VRML by making VRML a full-fledged programming language. Programming languages are very powerful, but they make poor file interchange formats. For example, Adobe's PostScript and HTML are both used to define 2D documents and both could be used as file interchange formats. However, HTML is much more common, even though it was introduced long after PostScript and is much less powerful. One of the reasons HTML is so successful as a file interchange format is the wide variety of HTML editors that can read, modify, and write any HTML file. Because PostScript is a programming language, it is almost impossible to do the same for PostScript files. The needs of both VRML browsers and VRML editors are considered in the VRML 2.0 design.

Another property of a good file interchange format is composability. It should be relatively easy to take files created by various people or tools and compose them together to create a new document. This is another property that VRML shares with HTML: It is easy to cut and paste text from several HTML documents using either a generic text editor or a specialized editing tool, just as it is easy to cut and paste objects between VRML worlds.

Finally, scalability is a constraint on the VRML 2.0 design. VRML is designed to scale in three ways. First, it should be theoretically possible for a VRML browser to handle a world distributed across the Internet that contains millions or billions of objects. Second, VRML should work well when used with both very powerful and very inexpensive machines, allowing the VRML browser to trade off image or simulation quality for improved performance and to scale well with increased hardware performance. And third, VRML worlds should scale with network performance, from the 14.4K modems that are common today to multigigabit connections that might become common in the future. Scalability profoundly influenced the entire design of VRML 2.0, and although there are still many unsolved problems, the infrastructure defined by VRML 2.0 should continue to scale as worlds get larger and machines and networks get faster. The ultimate test of any design is a working, practical implementation, and at the time of this writing the scalability limits of the VRML 2.0 design have not been tested because none of the currently available browsers are designed to handle very large worlds.

1.3 History of the VRML Specification

In 1989 a new project was started at Silicon Graphics, Inc., by Rikk Carey and Paul Strauss (code name: *Scenario*) to design and build an infrastructure for interactive 3D graphics applications. The two original goals were to build a development environment that enabled the creation of a wide variety of interactive, distributed 3D applications and to use this environment to build a new 3D desktop interface. The first phase of the project concentrated on designing and building the semantics and mechanism for the foundation framework. The distributed applications issues were used as design goals throughout the work, but were beyond the scope of the first phase implementation. In 1992 the Iris Inventor 3D toolkit was released as the first product of these efforts. Iris Inventor was a C++ toolkit that defined many of the semantics found in VRML today. An important part of the Inventor toolkit was the file format used to store application objects. From the very beginning, the Inventor file format was designed to be lightweight and easy to use. In 1994 the second major revision of Inventor was released. It was called *Open Inventor* because it was portable to a variety of platforms and because it was based on Silicon Graphics' *OpenGL*. The reference manual describing the objects and file format in the Open Inventor toolkit were eventually used by Gavin Bell to write the first draft of the VRML 1.0 specification.

In 1994 Mark Pesce and Tony Parisi built an early prototype of a 3D browser for the WWW, called *Labyrinth*. Later that year, Mark and Brian Behlendorf created the VRML mailing list, *www-vrml*, and issued a call for proposals for a formal specification for 3D on the WWW. Gavin Bell saw the obvious suitability of Inventor and quickly put together a proposal based on Open Inventor by choosing the fundamental elements of the Inventor file format (leaving out the tricky stuff), adding a couple of necessary WWW features (**WWWAnchor** and **WWWInline** nodes), and using the Inventor reference manual as the starting point for the text. After a stimulating debate on the mailing list, the Inventor proposal was voted in as the working document for the specification. Gavin, with help from Tony, Rikk, and a variety of Inventor engineers, revised and finalized the first draft of the VRML 1.0 specification. In October 1994 at the Second International Conference on the World Wide Web in Chicago, the specification was published.

During the first half of 1995 the VRML 1.0 specification underwent a variety of fixes and clarifications, but was functionally unchanged. By August 1995 there was a lot of discussion on the mailing list concerning the creation of a VRML 1.1 or a

VRML 2.0. Some people thought that VRML needed only a few incremental features, while others felt that it needed a complete overhaul. But, everyone agreed that VRML 1.0 was missing key features (animation, interaction, and behavior) and that a significant revision was needed. The debates raged from September to December with no clear outcome. In January 1996 a request for proposals for VRML 2.0 was issued to the VRML mailing list. The *Moving Worlds* proposal led by Silicon Graphics, Inc. (`http://www.sgi.com`), in collaboration with Sony Corporation (`http://www.sony.com`) and Mitra (`http://earth.path.net/mitra`), received a strong majority of the votes and became the working document for the VRML 2.0 specification. In August 1996 at SIGGRAPH 96 in New Orleans, the first version of the VRML 2.0 specification was released.

At its July 1996 meeting in Kyoto, the International Standards Organization's (ISO) JTC1/SC24 committee agreed to publish the August 1996 version of VRML 2.0 as Committee Draft (CD) 14772. The Draft International Standard (DIS) text was submitted to ISO in April 1997. An ISO vote will take place after the mandatory four-month DIS ballot. If VRML receives enough votes it will be forwarded for publication as an ISO standard. The text will be published electronically as an HTML document and will mark the first time that an ISO standard has been so published.

1.4 VRML and the WWW

VRML is designed to fit into the existing infrastructure of the Internet and the WWW. It uses existing standards wherever possible, even if those standards have some shortcomings when used with VRML. Using existing standards instead of inventing new, incompatible standards makes it much easier for the Web developer, who can use existing tools to help create VRML content. It also makes it much easier for somebody implementing the VRML standard, since libraries of code for popular standards already exist.

VRML files may contain references to files in many other standard formats. JPEG, PNG, GIF, and MPEG files may be used as texture maps on objects. WAV and MIDI files may be used to specify sound that is emitted in the world. Files containing Java or JavaScript code may be referenced and used to implement programmed behavior for the objects in your worlds. Each of these is an independent standard, chosen to be used with VRML because of its widespread use on the Internet. This book (and the VRML 2.0 specification) describes how they are used with VRML; it does not attempt to define these other standards or describe how to create files in these other file formats.

The definition of how VRML should be used with other standards is generally done by the organizations that define those standards. For example, the World Wide Web Consortium (W3C) is standardizing an <OBJECT> tag for HTML that will be used to embed VRML, Java, or other file types into HTML documents (replacing the currently used, pseudostandard <EMBED> and <APPLET> tags). Using VRML with HTML pages and Java applets can be very effective. Combining both 2D and 3D information is often much better than either 2D or 3D alone.

There are at least six different ways that VRML, HTML, and Java may be combined, making it easy to get confused about whether or not some particular combination is required by the HTML, Java, and/or VRML standards. The following list summarizes the possibilities:

- *VRML file inside an HTML file:* This is a semistandard part of HTML using the <EMBED> or <OBJECT> HTML tag, although HTML does not require that HTML browsers support embedding of VRML files (or any other type of file) into HTML documents.

- *Java code inside a VRML file:* This is a standard (although not required) part of VRML 2.0, using a **Script** node that refers to the compiled Java code.

- *Java applet communicating with a VRML browser.* This is a not-yet-standard extension to VRML 2.0 known as the *External Authoring Interface* (EAI). At some time in the future it will probably become a standard (but perhaps not required) part of VRML.

- *Java classes corresponding to VRML nodes:* Several companies are developing programming toolkits that define in-memory representations of VRML nodes that can be used in any way the programmer wishes. These can be extremely useful when implementing VRML browsers or VRML tools, but none are yet a standard part of either VRML or Java.

- *HTML file inside a VRML file:* Using an HTML file as a texture map to display it inside a 3D world would be an interesting extension to VRML, but it is not yet supported by any VRML browser and is not part of VRML 2.0.

- *Java applet inside a VRML file:* Using a Java applet as a texture map to display the Java program inside the 3D world would also be an interesting extension. Interaction with the Java program could also be supported by projecting pointing device motion onto the applet. However, this also is not supported and is not part of VRML 2.0.

1.5 Versions

The April 1997 revised VRML 2.0 specification (ISO DIS) contains numerous editorial fixes and several technical changes from the original August 4, 1996, version. With the exception of changes to the Java and JavaScript interfaces, VRML files are backward compatible. Therefore, VRML files based on the August 1996 version should read successfully into implementations based on the April 1997 revision.

1.6 Future of the VRML Specification

There are several obvious short-term issues for the VRML specification. A binary file format for VRML has been discussed and debated since the early days of VRML. At present, standard file compression tools, such as gzip, are used to compress VRML files. This yields, on average, about a 5:1 compression ratio and requires no extra implementation by the VRML browser. However, many users and developers have requested even more compression. A binary format for VRML could produce much higher compression ratios (e.g., 10:1 to 50:1). Therefore, a request for proposals was issued to the VRML community in September 1996 (`http://vag.vrml.org/binrfp.html`). The only submitted proposal was by IBM, Apple, and Paragraph International, Inc. (`http://www.rs6000.ibm.com/vrml/binary/`). This proposal has been adopted as the working document for VRML's binary file format and will continue to be reviewed and revised, and eventually ratified as an addendum to the VRML specification.

The second obvious short-term issue for VRML is the External Authoring Interface (EAI). Many users have requested that a standard programmer interface to VRML browsers be defined. This feature allows technical users to write external programs that communicate with a VRML browser. In October 1996 a request for proposals for an EAI was issued (`http://vag.vrml.org/esipoll/index.html`). Two proposals were received and the proposal by Chris Marrin of Silicon Graphics, Inc., won the voting and was selected as the working document (`http://vrml.sgi.com/moving-worlds/spec/ExternalInterface.html`). This work will continue to be reviewed and revised, and eventually ratified as an addendum to the VRML specification.

Many feel that the most important long-term issue for VRML is adding multiuser capabilities. At present there are several groups working on related research and proposals, such as *Living Worlds* (`http://www.livingworlds.com`), *Open Community* (`http://www.merl.com/opencom/opencom.htm`), and *Universal Avatars* (`http://www.chaco.com/avatar/avatar.html`). The first implementations of these proposals will appear in 1997 and should be interesting to see.

1.7 An Overview of VRML

The following is a brief overview that describes the major features of VRML.

1.7.1 Scene Graph Structure

VRML files describe 3D objects and worlds using a hierarchical *scene graph*. Entities in the scene graph are called *nodes*. VRML 2.0 defines 54 different node types, including geometry primitives, appearance properties, sound and sound properties, and various types of grouping nodes. Nodes store their data in *fields*, and VRML 2.0 defines 20 different types of fields that can be used to store everything from a single number (the SFFloat field type) to an array of 3D rotations (the MFRotation field type).

The VRML scene graph is a *directed acyclic graph*. Nodes can contain other nodes (some types of nodes may have "children") and may be contained in more than one node (they may have more than one "parent"), but a node must not contain itself. This scene graph structure makes it easy to create large worlds or complicated objects from subparts.

1.7.2 Event Architecture

VRML 2.0 defines an event or message-passing mechanism by which nodes in the scene graph can communicate with each other. Each node type defines the names and types of events that instances of that type may generate or receive, and ROUTE statements define event paths between event generators and receivers.

1.7.3 Sensors

Sensors are the basic user interaction and animation primitives of VRML. The **TimeSensor** node generates events as time passes and is the basis for all animated behaviors. Other sensors are the basis for all user interaction, generating events as the viewer moves through the world or when the user interacts with some input device. Sensors only generate events; they must be combined with other nodes via ROUTE statements to have any visible effect on the scene.

1.7.4 Scripts and Interpolators

Script nodes can be inserted between event generators (typically sensor nodes) and event receivers. **Scripts** allow the world creator to define arbitrary behaviors, defined in any supported scripting language. The VRML 2.0 specification defines **Script** node bindings for the Java and JavaScript languages.

Interpolator nodes are essentially built-in **Scripts** that perform simple animation calculations. They are usually combined with a **TimeSensor** and some node in the scene graph to make objects move.

1.7.5 Prototyping: Encapsulation and Reuse

VRML 2.0 includes a prototyping mechanism for encapsulating and reusing a scene graph (the PROTO statement). Geometry, properties, and animations or behaviors can be encapsulated, either separately or together. Prototyping allows the definition of a new node type in terms of a combination of existing node types, which can make VRML easier to use and can reduce the size of VRML files.

1.7.6 Distributed Scenes

VRML 2.0 includes two primitives that allow a single VRML world definition to span the WWW. The **Inline** node allows the inclusion of another VRML file stored anywhere on the Web and the EXTERNPROTO statement allows new node definitions to be fetched from anywhere on the WWW. More generally, EXTERNPROTO allows nodes to be defined external to the VRML file and it is the basic extensibility mechanism for VRML.

Key Concepts

CHAPTER 2

This chapter describes key concepts related to the definition and use of the VRML specification. This includes syntax fundamentals, how nodes are combined into scene graphs, how nodes receive and generate events, how to create new node types using prototypes, how to distribute and share new nodes, how to incorporate user-programmed scripts into a VRML file, and various general topics on nodes.

TIP

This chapter quickly jumps into technical details. If you are looking for an overview or introduction, read Chapter 1, Introduction, or one of the recommended tutorial books listed in Appendix F.

2.1 File Syntax and Structure

2.1.1 Syntax Basics

Every VRML file must begin with the following characters:

```
#VRML V2.0 utf8
```

The identifier `utf8` allows for international characters to be displayed in VRML using the UTF-8 encoding of the ISO 10646 standard (see `ftp://ds.internic.net/rfc/rfc2044.txt`). *Unicode* is an alternate encoding of ISO 10646. UTF-8 is explained under the **Text** node.

Any characters on the same line of the header are ignored. The line is terminated by either the ASCII newline or carriage-return characters.

DESIGN NOTE

Extra characters on the first line after the mandatory `#VRML V2.0 utf8` are allowed so that tools have a convenient place to store tool-specific information about the VRML file. For example, a program that generates VRML files might append information about which version of the program generated the file:

```
#VRML V2.0 utf8 Generated by VRML-o-matic V1.3
```

However, like other comments in the VRML file, the extra information on the first line may not be preserved by tools that read and write VRML files. A more reliable technique is to save the tool-specific information in a **WorldInfo** node (see section Chapter 3, Node Reference, WorldInfo).

The # character begins a comment; all characters until the next newline or carriage return are ignored. The only exception to this is within double-quoted SFString and MFString fields, where the # will be part of the string.

Commas, blanks, tabs, newlines, and carriage returns are whitespace characters wherever they appear outside of string fields. One or more whitespace characters separate the syntactical entities in VRML files, where necessary.

> *Note:* Comments and whitespace may not be preserved. In particular, a VRML document server may strip comments and extra whitespace from a VRML file before transmitting it. **WorldInfo** nodes should be used for persistent information such as copyrights or author information. To extend the set of existing nodes in VRML 2.0, use prototypes or external prototypes rather than named information nodes.

DESIGN NOTE

Commas are treated as whitespace characters to ease the transition from the VRML 1.0 file format syntax. Equating commas to whitespace does not hamper parsing and allows both the VRML 1.0 syntax for multiple-valued fields (which required commas) and the VRML 1.0 syntax for MFNode child lists (which were a special case in VRML 1.0 and required that the children be separated by blank/tab/newline).

After the required header, a VRML file can contain any combination of the following:

- Any number of prototypes (see Section 2.6, Prototypes)
- Any number of children nodes (see Section 2.3.1, Grouping and Children Nodes)
- Any number of ROUTE statements (see Section 2.4.1, Routes)

See Appendix A, VRML Grammar Definition, for precise grammar rules.

Field, event, prototype, and node names must not begin with a plus (0x2b: +), a minus (0x2d: –), or a digit (0x30–0x39), but may otherwise contain any characters except for nonprintable ASCII characters (0x0–0x20), double or single quotes (0x22: ", 0x27: '), pound sign (0x23: #), comma (0x2c: ,), period (0x2e: .), square brackets (0x5b, 0x5d: []), backslash (0x5c: \), or curly braces (0x7b, 0x7d: {}).

Characters in names are as specified in ISO 10646 and are encoded using UTF-8. VRML is case sensitive: "Sphere" is different from "sphere" and "BEGIN" is different from "begin."

TIP

The following table summarizes the illegal character rules for names:

TABLE 2-1 *Illegal characters for names*

First character	All other characters
+ - 0-9 " ' # , . [] \ {} 0x0-0x20 (nonprintable)	" ' # , . [] \ {} 0x0-0x20 (nonprintable)

The following reserved keywords shall not be used for node, PROTO, EXTERN-PROTO, or DEF names:

- DEF
- EXTERNPROTO

- FALSE
- IS
- NULL
- PROTO
- ROUTE
- TO
- TRUE
- USE
- eventIn
- eventOut
- exposedField
- field

DESIGN NOTE

All of these rules make it easier to write a parser that reads VRML files using traditional parsing technology such as YACC and Lex. The public domain VRML 2.0 file format parser donated by Silicon Graphics is an example of such a parser (see `http://vrml.sgi.com/`).

DESIGN NOTE

The VRML 2.0 file syntax grew out of the VRML 1.0 file syntax, which came directly from the Open Inventor ASCII file format. The original goals for the Open Inventor file format were simplicity, ease of use, ease of parsing, and small file size.

The VRML 2.0 syntax was changed from the VRML 1.0 syntax in a number of ways based on feedback from VRML 1.0 implementors. Most of the changes make the format more regular and easier to parse, sometimes at the expense of making it more difficult to edit VRML files with a text editor. Deciding where to draw the line between ease of parsing and ease of text editing was one of the many controversial issues debated during the VRML 2.0 design process.

At the time of this writing, a binary, compressed file format for VRML is being defined (`http://vag.vrml.org/BinaryRFP.html`).

2.1.2 File Syntax vs. Public Interface

In this document, the first item in a node specification (Chapter 3, Node Reference) is the public interface for the node. The syntax for the public interface is the same as that for that node's prototype (see Section 2.6, Prototypes). This interface is the definitive specification of the fields, events, names, types, and default values for a given node. Note that this syntax is not the actual file format syntax. However, the parts of the interface that are identical to the file syntax are in bold. For example, the following example defines the **Collision** node's public interface and file format:

```
Collision {
    eventIn       MFNode   addChildren
    eventIn       MFNode   removeChildren
    exposedField  MFNode   children       []
    exposedField  SFBool   collide        TRUE
    field         SFVec3f  bboxCenter     0 0 0
    field         SFVec3f  bboxSize       -1 -1 -1
    field         SFNode   proxy          NULL
    eventOut      SFTime   collideTime
}
```

Fields that have implicit *set_* and *_changed* events are labeled exposedField. For example, the *collide* field has an implicit *set_collide* input event and *collide_changed* output event. Exposed fields may be connected using ROUTE statements, and may be read and/or written by **Script** nodes. Also, any exposedField name can be prefixed with *get_* to indicate a read of the current value of the eventOut. This is used only in **Script** nodes or when accessing the VRML world from an external API.

Note that this information is arranged in a slightly different manner in the actual file syntax. The keywords "field" or "exposedField" and the types of the fields (e.g., SFColor) are not specified when expressing a node in the file format. An example of the file format for the **Collision** node is

```
Collision {
    children    []
    collide     TRUE
    bboxCenter  0 0 0
    bboxSize    -1 -1 -1
    proxy       NULL
}
```

The rules for naming fields, exposedFields, eventOuts, and eventIns for the built-in nodes are as follows:

1. All names containing multiple words start with a lower case letter and the first letter of all subsequent words is capitalized (e.g., *bboxCenter*), with the exception of *get_* and *_changed* described later.

2. All eventIns have the prefix *set_*, with the exception of the *addChildren* and *removeChildren* eventIns.

3. All eventOuts have the suffix *_changed*, with the exception of eventOuts of type SFBool. Boolean eventOuts begin with the word *is* (e.g., *isFoo*) for better readability.

4. Most eventIns and eventOuts of type SFTime do not use the *set_* prefix or *_changed* suffix; these events and exposedFields use a *Time* suffix instead (e.g., **ProximitySensor**'s *exitTime* and **TimeSensor**'s *startTime*).

It is recommended that these naming conventions be followed in user-defined field names found in **Script**, PROTO, and EXTERNPROTO.

TIP

> Note that the names of exposedFields do not include a prefix or suffix. For example, the **PointLight** node's *on* exposedField is not named *isOn*. However, the *set_* and *_changed* conventions may be used when referring to the eventIn and eventOut of the exposedField respectively. See Section 2.4.1, Routes, for details.

2.1.3 URLs

A URL specifies a file located on a particular server and accessed through a specified protocol (e.g., `http`).

All URL fields are of type MFString. The strings in the field indicate multiple locations to look for data, in decreasing order of preference. If the browser cannot locate the first URL or doesn't support the protocol type, then it may try the second location and so on. Note that the URL field entries are delimited by " " and, due to the data protocol (see Section 2.1.4, Data Protocol) and the scripting language protocols (see Section 2.1.5, Scripting Language Protocols), are a superset of the standard URL syntax (IETF RFC 1738). Browsers may skip to the next URL by searching for the closing, unescaped ". See Section 4.9, SFString and MFString, for details on the string field.

URLs are described in "Uniform Resource Locator," IETF RFC 1738, `http://ds.internic.net/rfc/rfc1738.txt`.

Relative URLs are handled as described in "Relative Uniform Resource Locator," IETF RFC 1808, `http://ds.internic.net/rfc/rfc1808.txt`.

DESIGN NOTE

Allowing multiple locations to be specified wherever a VRML file refers to some other file adds some useful features:

- forward and backward compatibility between browsers as new protocols are created and deployed across the Internet. You can specify the new protocol as the first (most desirable) string in the *url* field and specify a more standard protocol as a backup in case the new protocol isn't understood by the browser. For example:

  ```
  url [ "new://www.vrml.org/foo.wrl" "http://www.other.org/foo.wrl" ]
  ```

- "fault-tolerant" URLs. You can store a file on several different servers around the Web, then have the *url* field point to all of them. If one of the servers goes down, the VRML browser will simply use one of the other servers. For example:

  ```
  url [ "http://server1.com/foo.wrl" "http://server2.com/foo.wrl" ]
  ```

2.1.4 Data Protocol

The IETF is in the process of standardizing a `data:` URL to be used for inline inclusion of base64 encoded data, such as JPEG images. This capability should be supported as specified in IETF's work in progress, *Data: URL scheme,* found at `http://www.internic.net/internet-drafts/draft-masinter-url-data-01.txt`. Note that this is an Internet draft, and the specification may (but is unlikely to) change.

DESIGN NOTE

The `data:` URL scheme is meant to be used for small pieces of data when the overhead of establishing a network connection is much greater than the time it takes to send the data. Some other uses for `data:` URLs include

- low-resolution stand-ins. Using the multiple-strings URL feature, specify the full-resolution URL first and give an inline low-resolution version of the data as the second URL. Smart VRML browsers can display the low-resolution version to the user while the full-resolution version is being fetched across the network.

- stand-alone VRML files. Sometimes it is convenient to bundle up a VRML world into one single file. This can be done by recursively replacing any URLs in the main VRML file with inline `data:` URLs. This is generally a bad idea if the VRML file will be delivered by a network, since it is much better if the user doesn't have to wait for a huge file to download before interacting with a world, but it can be very convenient for moderate-size VRML worlds distributed on (for example) CD-ROM.

2.1.5 Scripting Language Protocols

The **Script** node's *url* field may also support a custom protocol for the various scripting languages. For example, a **Script** *url* prefixed with `javascript:` shall contain JavaScript source, with newline characters allowed in the string. A **Script** prefixed with `javabc:` shall contain Java byte codes using base64 encoding. The details of each language protocol are defined in the appendix for each language. Browsers are not required to support any specific scripting language, but if they do then they shall adhere to the protocol for that particular scripting language. The following example illustrates the use of mixing custom protocols and standard protocols in a single URL (order of precedence determines priority):

```
#VRML V2.0 utf8
Script {
    url [ "javascript: ...",          # custom protocol JavaScript
          "http://bar.com/foo.js",     # std protocol JavaScript
          "http://bar.com/foo.class" ]# std protocol Java byte
}
```

DESIGN NOTE

These new VRML-specific "protocols" were added to make it easier to create behaviors with a text editor and they don't follow the strict URL syntax as specified by the IETF (which requires certain common punctuation to be encoded, for example).

2.1.6 File Extension and MIME Type

The file extension for VRML files is .wrl (for world). The official MIME type for VRML files is defined as

> `model/vrml`

where the MIME major type for 3D data descriptions is `model` and the minor type for VRML documents is `vrml`.

For historical reasons (VRML 1.0) the following MIME type must also be supported

> `x-world/x-vrml`

where the MIME major type is `x-world` and the minor type for VRML documents is `x-vrml`.

IETF documentation on this subject can be found in *The Model Primary Content Type for Multipurpose Internet Mail Extensions* (`ftp://ds.internic.net/ internet-drafts/draft-nelson-model-mail-ext-01.txt`).

DESIGN NOTE

MIME types do not encode file format version information, so both the MIME type and the file extension were not changed between VRML 1.0 and VRML 2.0. Changing the MIME type would avoid cryptic error messages like "Not a VRML file" from VRML 1.0 tools that do not understand VRML 2.0. However, this would require that every Web server in the world be configured to support the new file suffix. The most frequently encountered problem with VRML 1.0 files is that Web servers are not configured to serve VRML files. Therefore, changing the MIME type of the suffix would cause more problems than it solved.

TIP

Almost all VRML 1.0 files can be transparently converted into VRML 2.0. There are VRML 1.0-to-VRML 2.0 file translators available from both Silicon Graphics (`http://vrml.sgi.com`) and Sony (`http://vs.sony.co.jp/VS-E/vstop.html`). Also, if you are using VRML 1.0, it is recommended that you avoid **Matrix Transform** and **Transform Separator** since both of these nodes do not translate into VRML 2.0 very well.

2.1.7 Uniform Resource Names (URNs)

A URN is a special form of URL that provides a more abstract way to refer to data than is provided by typical URLs. URNs are location-independent names to a file or to different representations of the same content. In most ways they can be used like URLs, except that when fetched a smart browser should fetch them from the closest source. While URN resolution over the Net has not been standardized yet, they may be used now as persistent, unique identifiers for files, prototypes, textures, and so forth. For more information on the standardization effort see `http://services.bunyip.com:8000/research/ietf/urn-ietf/`. VRML 2.0 browsers are not required to support URNs; however, they are required to ignore them if they do not support them.

URNs may be assigned by anyone with a domain name. For example, if company Foo owns `foo.com`, it may allocate URNs that begin with `"urn:inet:foo.com:"`, such as `"urn:inet:foo.com:texture/wood01"`. No special semantics are required of the string following the prefix, except that they should be lower case and characters should be URL encoded as specified in RFC 1738.

To reference a texture, prototype, or other file by URN it should be included in the *url* field of another node. For example

```
ImageTexture {
  url [ "http://www.foo.com/textures/woodblock_floor.gif",
        "urn:inet:foo.com:textures/wood001" ]
}
```

specifies a URL file as the first choice and URN as the second choice. Note that until URN resolution is widely deployed, it is advisable to include a URL alternative whenever a URN is used. For more details and recommendations, see `http://earth.path.net/mitra/papers/vrml-urn.html`.

> *Note:* The term *URL* is used throughout this book and is intended to include both URLs and URNs.

DESIGN NOTE

It is hoped that eventually there will be a standard set of VRML data files that will be widely distributed and frequently used by world creators—a standard library of objects, textures, sounds, and so forth. If a common set of resources are agreed on, they could be distributed and loaded from a CD-ROM or hard disk on a user's local machine, resulting in much faster load times. The world creator would merely refer to things by their standard URN name. The VRML browser will know the location of the "nearest" copy, whether already loaded into memory, on a CD in the local CD-ROM drive, or located somewhere on the network.

2.2 Nodes, Fields, and Events

2.2.1 Introduction

At the highest level of abstraction, VRML is simply a file format for describing objects. Theoretically, the objects can contain anything—3D geometry, MIDI data, JPEG images, and so on. VRML defines a set of objects useful for doing 3D graphics, multimedia, and interactive object/world building. These objects are called *nodes* and contain elemental data that is stored in *fields* and *events*.

DESIGN NOTE

VRML's object model doesn't really match any of the object models found in formal programming languages (object oriented, delegation, functional, etc.). This is because VRML is not a general-purpose programming language; it is a persistent file format designed to store the state of a virtual world efficiently and to be read and written easily by both humans and a wide variety of tools.

2.2.2 General Node Characteristics

A node has the following characteristics:

1. A type name—This is a name like **Box, Color, Group, Sphere, Sound, Spot-Light,** and so on.

2. The parameters that distinguish a node from other nodes of the same type—For example, each **Sphere** node might have a different radius, and different **SpotLights** have different intensities, colors, and locations. These parameters are called *fields*. A node can have zero or more fields. Each node specification defines the type, name, and default value for each of its fields. The default value for the field is used if a value for the field is not specified in the VRML file. The order in which the fields of a node are read does not matter. For example, `Cone { bottomRadius 1 height 6 }` and `Cone { height 6 bottomRadius 1}` are equivalent. There are two kinds of fields: *field* and *exposedField*. Fields define the initial values for the node's state, but cannot be changed and are considered private. ExposedFields also define the initial value for the node's state, but are public and may be modified by other nodes. Each field or exposedField may be defined once within a specific node instance; results are undefined if a field or exposedField is defined more than once for a given node instance (e.g., `Sphere { radius 1 radius 2 }`).

3. A set of associated events that nodes can receive and send—Nodes can receive a number of incoming *set_* events (such as *set_position, set_color,* and *set_on*), denoted as *eventIn,* that change the node. Nodes can also send out a number of *_changed* events (for example, *position_changed, color_changed, on_changed*), denoted as *eventOut,* that indicate that something in the node has changed. The *exposedField* keyword may be used as shorthand for specifying that a given field has a *set_* eventIn that is directly wired to a field value and a *_changed* eventOut. For example, the declaration

```
exposedField foo
```

is equivalent to the declaration

```
eventIn set_foo
field foo
eventOut foo_changed
```

where *set_foo*, if written to, automatically sets the value of the field *foo* and generates a *foo_changed* eventOut.

DESIGN NOTE

Nodes in general may have a couple of other characteristics:

1. **A name assigned using the DEF keyword**—See Section 2.3.2, Instancing, for details.

2. **An implementation**—The implementations of the 54 nodes in the VRML 2.0 specification are built in. The PROTO mechanism (see Section 2.6, Prototypes) can be used to specify implementations for new nodes (specified as a composition of built-in nodes) and the EXTERNPROTO mechanism (see Section 2.6.4, Defining Prototypes in External Files) may be used to define new nodes with implementations that are outside the VRML file (see Section 2.8, Browser Extensions). Implementations are typically written in C, C++, or Java, and use a variety of system libraries for 3D graphics, sound, and other low-level support. The VRML specification defines an abstract functional model that is independent of any specific library.

The file syntax for representing nodes is as follows:

```
nodetype { fields }
```

Only the node type and braces are required; nodes may or may not have field values specified. Unspecified field values are set to the default values in the specification.

TIP

The most commonly used values have been selected as the default values for each field. Therefore, it is recommended that you do not explicitly specify fields with default values since this will unnecessarily increase file size.

2.3 The Structure of the Scene Graph

This section describes the general scene graph hierarchy, how to reuse nodes within a file, coordinate systems and transformations in VRML files, and the general model for viewing and interacting within a VRML world.

2.3.1 Grouping and Children Nodes

Grouping nodes contain a *children* field, *addChildren* and *removeChildren* eventIns, and *bboxCenter* and *bboxSize* fields (see Section 2.3.6, Bounding Boxes, for details). The MFNode *children* field specifies a list of nodes that is encapsulated and managed by the grouping node. **Anchor** and **Collision** nodes assign interaction behaviors to the nodes contained by the group. **Group** composes the list of children into a container for instancing and file organization purposes. **Transform** and **Billboard** nodes define a transformed coordinate system for their children.

Grouping Nodes

- Anchor
- Billboard
- Collision
- Group
- Transform

Children nodes (nodes that are allowable in the *addChildren* eventIn) are restricted to the following node types

Legal Children Nodes

- Anchor
- Background
- Billboard
- Collision
- ColorInterpolator
- CoordinateInterpolator
- CylinderSensor
- DirectionalLight
- Fog
- Group
- Inline
- LOD
- NavigationInfo
- NormalInterpolator
- OrientationInterpolator
- PlaneSensor
- PointLight
- PositionInterpolator
- ProximitySensor
- ScalarInterpolator
- Script
- Shape
- Sound
- SpotLight
- SphereSensor
- Switch
- TimeSensor
- TouchSensor
- Transform
- Viewpoint
- VisibilitySensor
- WorldInfo
- PROTO'd child nodes

DESIGN NOTE

Unlike VRML 1.0, the VRML 2.0 scene graph serves only as a transformation and spatial-grouping hierarchy. The transformation hierarchy allows the creation of jointed, rigid-body motion figures. The transformation hierarchy is also often used for spatial grouping. Tables and chairs can be defined in their own coordinate systems, grouped to form a set that can be moved around a house, which in turn is defined in its own coordinate system and grouped with other houses to create a neighborhood. Grouping things in this way is not only convenient, it also improves performance in most implementations.

The VRML 1.0 scene graph also defined an object property hierarchy. For example, a texture property could be placed at any level of the scene hierarchy and could affect an entire subtree of the hierarchy. VRML 2.0 puts all properties inside the hierarchy's lowest level nodes—a texture property cannot be associated with a grouping node; it can only be associated with one or more **Shape** nodes.

This simplified scene graph structure is probably the biggest difference between VRML 1.0 and VRML 2.0, and was motivated by feedback from several different implementors. Some rendering libraries have a simpler notion of rendering state than VRML 1.0, and the mismatch between these libraries and VRML was causing performance problems and implementation complexity.

VRML 2.0's ability to change the values and topology of the scene graph over time makes it even more critical for the scene graph structure to match existing rendering libraries. It is fairly easy to convert a VRML file to the structure expected by a rendering library *once;* it is much more difficult to come up with a conversion scheme that efficiently handles a constantly changing scene.

VRML 2.0's simpler structure means that each part of the scene graph is almost completely self-contained. An implementation can render any part of the scene graph if it knows

- what part of the scene graph to render (which children nodes)
- the transformation for that part of the scene graph (the accumulated transformation of all **Transform** and **Billboard** nodes above that part of the scene graph)
- the currently bound **Fog** parameters and all light sources that might affect this part of the scene graph

For example, this makes it much easier for an implementation to render different parts of the scene graph at the same time or to rearrange the order in which it decides to render the scene (e.g., to group objects that use the same texture map, which is faster on some graphics hardware).

The *addChildren* event appends the node(s) passed in to the grouping node's *children* field. Any nodes passed to the *addChildren* event that are already in the group's children list are ignored. The *removeChildren* event removes the node(s) passed in from the grouping node's *children* field and adjusts the list so that the empty space remains. Any nodes passed in the *removeChildren* event that are not in the grouping nodes' children list are ignored.

DESIGN NOTE

The order of a grouping node's children has no effect on the perceivable result; the children can be rearranged and there will be no change to the VRML world. This was a conscious design decision that simplifies the Open Inventor scene graph by eliminating most of the traversal state and enabling easier integration with rendering libraries (very few rendering libraries today support Inventor's rich traversal state). The net effect of this decision is smaller and simpler implementations, but more burden on the author to share attributes in the scene graph. It is important to note that the order of children is deterministic and cannot be altered by the implementation, since **Script** nodes may access children and assume that the order does not change.

DESIGN NOTE

The **LOD** and **Switch** nodes are *not* considered grouping nodes because they have different semantics from the grouping nodes. Grouping nodes display all of their children, and the order of children for a grouping node is unimportant, while **Switch** and **LOD** display, at most, one of their "children" and their order is *very* important.

2.3.2 Instancing

A node may be referenced in a VRML file multiple times. This is called *instancing* (using the same instance of a node multiple times; called *sharing, aliasing,* or *multiple references* by other systems) and is accomplished by using the DEF and USE keywords.

The DEF keyword defines a node's name. The USE keyword indicates that a reference to a previously named node in the file is inserted into the scene graph. This has the effect of sharing a single node in more than one location in the file. If the node is modified, then all instances of that node are modified. DEF/USE name scope is limited to a single file. If multiple nodes are given the same name, then the most recent DEF encountered during parsing is used for USE definitions.

DESIGN NOTE

DEF was an unfortunate choice of keyword, because it implies to many people that the node is merely being defined. The DEF syntax is

```
DEF nodeName nodeType { fields }
```

For example:

```
DEF Red Material { diffuseColor 1 0 0 }
```

A vote was taken during the VRML 2.0 design process to see if there was consensus that the syntax should be changed, either to change the keyword to something less confusing (like NAME) or to change the syntax to

```
nodeType nodename { fields }
```

For example:

```
Material Red { diffuseColor 1 0 0 }
```

VRML 1.0 compatibility won out, so DEF is still the way you name nodes in VRML 2.0.

The rules for scoping node names in VRML also seem to cause a lot of confusion, probably because people see all of the curly braces in the VRML file format and think it must be a strange dialect of the C programming language. The rules are actually pretty simple: When you encounter a USE, just search backward from that point in the file for a matching DEF (skipping over PROTO definitions; see Section 2.6.3, Prototype Scoping Rules, for prototype scoping rules). Choosing some other scoping rule would either make VRML more complicated or would limit the kinds of graph structures that could be created in the file format, both of which are undesirable.

Tools that create VRML should either not allow the user to create more than one node with the same name (i.e., DEF) or modify all redundant node names to ensure that there is no confusion or ambiguity when the file is read by a browser. The recommended way of doing this is to append an underscore followed by an integer to the user-defined name. These tools should remove these automatically generated suffixes when VRML files are read back into the tool, presenting only the user-defined names.

DESIGN NOTE

Similarly, if an authoring tool allows users to multiply instance unnamed nodes, the tool will need to generate a name automatically in order to write the VRML file. The recommended convention for such names is an underscore followed by an integer (e.g., _3).

DEF/USE is in essence a simple mechanism for writing out pointers. The Inventor programming library required its file format to represent in-memory data structures that included nodes that pointed to other nodes (grouping nodes that contained other nodes as children, for example). The solution chosen was DEF/USE. One algorithm for writing out any arbitrary graph of nodes using DEF/USE is

1. Traverse the scene graph and count the number of times that each node needs to be written out

2. Traverse the scene graph again in the same order. At each node, if the node has not yet been written out *and* it will need to be written out multiple times, it is written out with a unique DEF name. If it has already been written out, just USE and the unique name are written. If it only needs to be written once, then it does not need to be DEF'ed and may be written without a name.

This algorithm writes out any arrangement of nodes, including recursive structures.

A simple way of generating unique names is to increment an integer every time a node is written out and give each node written the name "_integer": The first node is written as `DEF _0 Node { ... }` and so on. Another way of generating unique names is to write out an underscore followed by the address where the node is stored in memory (if you're using a programming language such as C, which allows direct access to pointers).

The DEF feature also serves another purpose—you can give your nodes descriptive names, perhaps in an authoring tool that might display node names when you select objects to be edited, and thus allow you to select things by name and so on. The two uses for DEF—to give nodes a name and to allow arbitrary graphs to be written out— are orthogonal, and the conventions for generating unique names suggested in the specification (appending an underscore and an integer to the user-given name, if any) essentially suggest a scheme for separating these two functions. Given a name of the suggested form

```
DEF userGivenName_instanceID ...
```

The first part of the name, `userGivenName`, is the node's "true" name—the name given to the node by the user. The second part of the name, `instanceID`, is used only to ensure that the name is unique, and should never be shown to the user. If tools do not follow these conventions and come up with their own schemes for generating unique DEF/USE names, then after going through a series of read/write cycles a node originally named Spike might end up with a name that looks like %3521%Spike$83EFF*952—not what the user expects to see!

2.3.3 Standard Units

VRML provides no capability to define units of measure. All linear distances are assumed to be in meters and all angles are in radians. Time units are specified in seconds. Colors are specified in the red-green-blue (RGB) color space and are restricted to the 0.0 to 1.0 range.

DESIGN NOTE

The VRML convention that one unit equals one meter (in the absence of any scaling **Transform** nodes) is meant to make the sharing of objects between worlds easier. If everyone models their objects in meters, objects will be the correct size when placed next to each other in the virtual world. Otherwise, a telephone might be as big as a house, which is very inconvenient if you are trying to put the telephone on a desk inside the house.

Put a scaling **Transform** node on top of your objects if you want to work in some other units of measure (e.g., inches or centimeters). Or, if compatibility with objects other people have created is not important for your use of VRML, then nothing will break if you disregard the one-unit-equals-one-meter convention. For example, if you are modeling galaxies then it probably isn't important that a telephone be the proper real-world scale, and you might just assume that one unit equals one light-year.

Radians were originally chosen for Open Inventor's file format to be compatible with the standard C programming language math library routines. Although another angle representation might be more convenient (e.g., 0.0 to 1.0 or 0.0 to 360.0), the benefits of compatibility have always outweighed the minor inconvenience of doing an occasional multiplication by 2 × pi.

Times are expressed as double-precision floating point numbers in VRML, so nanosecond accuracy is possible. Although there are no time transformation functions built into VRML, time values may be manipulated in any of the scripting languages that work with VRML.

2.3.4 Coordinate Systems and Transformations

VRML uses a Cartesian, right-handed, 3D coordinate system. By default, objects are projected onto a 2D display device by projecting them in the direction of the positive Z-axis, with the positive X-axis to the right and the positive Y-axis up. A modeling transformation (**Transform** and **Billboard**) or viewing transformation (**Viewpoint**) can be used to alter this default projection.

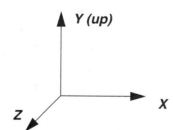

FIGURE 2-1 *Right-handed Coordinate System*

TIP

> Coordinate systems are a fundamental and difficult topic to understand. There are a variety of books that provide excellent explanations and tutorials on this subject. One that stands out is *The OpenGL Programming Guide* by Mason Woo, Jackie Neider, and Tom Davis (see Chapter 3, Viewing and Modeling Transformations, in their book).

DESIGN NOTE

The VRML convention of the Y-axis pointing in the up direction is intended to make it easier to share objects. Not only will objects be the right size (assuming they obey the units-equals-meters convention), but they will also be oriented correctly. Walking around worlds is also easier if your VRML browser and the world you load agree about which direction is up; if they disagree, you'll find yourself climbing the walls.

Deciding which way is up was perhaps the longest of all of the debates that happened on the *www-vrml* mailing list during both the VRML 1.0 and the VRML 2.0 design processes. There are two common conventions: the *Y*-axis is up (the convention in mathematics and many of the sciences) or the *Z*-axis is up (the convention for architects and many engineering disciplines). It is easy to convert from one to the other. Putting the following **Transform** as the root of your VRML files will switch the file from the Z-is-up convention to the VRML-standard Y-is-up:

```
Transform { rotation 1 0 0  -1.57 children [...] }
```

Scenes may contain an arbitrary number of local (or object-space) coordinate systems, defined by the transformation fields of the **Transform** and **Billboard** nodes.

Conceptually, VRML also has a world coordinate system. The various local coordinate transformations map objects into the world coordinate system, which is where the scene is assembled. Transformations accumulate downward through the scene graph hierarchy, with each **Transform** and **Billboard** inheriting the transformations of their parents. (Note, however, that this series of transformations takes effect from the leaf nodes up through the hierarchy. The local transformations closest to the **Shape** object take effect first, followed in turn by each successive transformation upward in the hierarchy.)

2.3.5 Viewing Model

This specification assumes that there is a real person viewing and interacting with the VRML world. The VRML author may place any number of viewpoints in the world—interesting places from which the user might wish to view the world. Each viewpoint is described by a **Viewpoint** node. Viewpoints exist in a specific coordinate system, and both the viewpoint and the coordinate system may be animated. Only one **Viewpoint** may be active at a time (see the description in Section 2.9.1, Bindable Children Nodes). When a viewpoint is activated, the browser parents its view (or camera) into the scene graph under the currently active viewpoint. Any changes to the coordinate system of the viewpoint have an effect on the browser view. Therefore, if a user teleports to a viewpoint that is moving (one of its parent coordinate systems is being animated), then the user should move along with that viewpoint. It is intended, but not required, that browsers support a user interface by which users may "teleport" themselves from one viewpoint to another..

TIP

Viewpoints are a powerful feature for improving usability of your worlds. You can create guided tours by binding the user to a viewpoint and then animating the viewpoint along a predefined path (automatic navigation through the virtual world). Keep in mind that many users will have difficulty navigating through 3D spaces; combining viewports with the other interaction features in VRML creates "point-and-click" worlds that are very easy to navigate.

2.3.6 Bounding Boxes

Several of the nodes in this specification include a bounding box (*bbox*) field. This is typically used by grouping nodes to provide a hint to the browser about the group's approximate size for culling optimizations. The default size for bounding boxes, (−1, −1, −1), implies that the user did not specify the bounding box and the browser must compute it or assume the most conservative case. A *bboxSize* value of (0, 0, 0) is valid and represents a point in space (i.e., infinitely small box). Note that the bounding box of a grouping node may change as a result of changing children. The *bboxSize* field values must be ≥ 0.0 or equal to (−1, −1, −1), otherwise results are undefined. The *bboxCenter* field specifies a translation offset from the local coordinate system and may be in the range −infinity to +infinity.

DESIGN NOTE

Why does VRML use axis-aligned bounding boxes instead of some other bounding volume representation such as bounding spheres? The choice was fairly arbitrary, but tight bounding boxes are very easy to calculate, easy to transform, and they have a better "worst-case" behavior than bounding spheres (the bounding box of a spherical object encloses less empty area than the bounding sphere of a long, skinny object).

The *bboxCenter* and *bboxSize* fields may be used to specify a maximum possible bounding box for the objects inside a grouping node (e.g., **Transform**). These are used as hints to optimize certain operations such as determining whether or not the group needs to be drawn. If the specified bounding box is smaller than the true bounding box of the group, results are undefined. The bounding box should be large enough to contain completely the effects of all sound and light nodes that are children of this group. If the size of this group may change over time due to animating children, then the bounding box must also be large enough to contain all possible animations (movements). The bounding box should typically be the union of the group's children bounding boxes; it should not include any transformations performed by the group itself (i.e., the bounding box is defined in the local coordinate system of the group).

TIP

See the illustration in Figure 2-2 of a grouping node and its bounding box. In this figure the grouping node contains three shapes: a **Cone,** a **Cylinder,** and a **Sphere.** The bounding box size is chosen to enclose the three geometries completely.

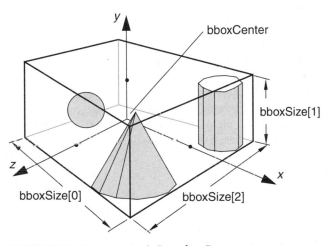

FIGURE 2-2 *Grouping Node Bounding Boxes*

DESIGN NOTE

Prespecified bounding boxes help browsers do two things: avoid loading parts of the world from across the network and avoid simulating parts of the world that can't be sensed. Both of these rely on the "out-of-sight-out-of-mind" principle: If the user cannot see or hear part of the world, then there's no reason for the VRML browser to spend any time loading or simulating that part of the world.

For many operations, a VRML browser can automatically calculate bounding volumes and automatically optimize away parts of the scene that aren't perceptible. For example, even if you do not prespecify bounding boxes in your VRML world, browsers can compute the bounding box for each part of the world and then avoid drawing the parts of the scene that are not visible. Since computing a bounding box for part of the world is almost always faster than drawing it, if parts of the world are not visible (which is usually the case), then doing this "render culling" will speed up the total time it takes to draw the world. Again, this can be done automatically and should not require that you prespecify bounding boxes.

However, some operations cannot be automatically optimized in this way because they suffer from a "chicken-and-egg" problem: The operation could be avoided if the bounding box is known, but to calculate the bounding box requires that the operation be performed!

Delaying loading parts of the world (specified using either the **Inline** node or an EXTERNPROTO definition) that are not perceptible falls into this category. If the bounding box of those parts of the world is known, then the browser will know if those parts of the world might be perceptible. However, the bounding box cannot be automatically calculated until those parts of the world are loaded.

One possible solution would be to augment the standard Web protocols (such as HTTP) to support a "get bounding box" request; then, instead of asking for an entire .wrl file to be loaded, a VRML browser could just ask the server to send it the bounding box of the .wrl file. Perhaps, eventually, Web servers will support such requests, but until VRML becomes ubiquitous it is unlikely there will be enough demand on server vendors to add VRML-specific features. Also, often the network bottleneck is not transferring the data, but just establishing a connection with a server, and this solution could worsen that bottleneck since it might require two connections (once for the bounding box information and once for the actual data) for each perceptible part of the world.

Extending Web servers to give bounding box information would not help avoiding simulating parts of the world that aren't perceptible, either. Imagine a VRML world that contained a toy train set with a train that constantly traveled around the tracks. If the user is not looking at the train set, then there is no reason the VRML browser should spend any time simulating the movement of the train (which could be arbitrarily complicated and might involve movement of the train's wheels, engine, etc.). But the browser can't determine if the train is visible unless it knows where the train is; and it won't know exactly where the train is unless it has simulated its movement, which is exactly the work we hoped to avoid.

The solution is for the world creator to give the VRML browser some extra information in the form of an assertion about what might possibly happen. In the case of the toy train set, the user can give a maximum possible bounding box for the train that surrounds all the possible movements of the train. Note that if the VRML browser could determine all the possible movements of the train, then it could also do this calculation. However, calculating all possible movements can be very complicated and is often not possible at all because the movements might be controlled by an arbitrary program contained in a **Script** node. Usually it is much easier for the world creator (whether a computer program or a human being) to tell the browser the maximum possible extent of things.

Note also that the world's hierarchy can be put to very good use to help the browser minimize work. For example, it is common that an object have both a "large" motion through the world and "small" motions of the object's parts (e.g., a toy train moves along its tracks through the world, but may have myriad small motions of its wheels, engine, drive rods, etc.). If the object is modeled this way and appropriate maximum bounding boxes are specified, then a browser may be able to optimize away the simulation of the small motions after it simulates the large motion and determines that the object as a whole cannot be seen.

Once set, maximum bounding boxes cannot be changed. A maximum bounding box specification is an assertion; allowing the assertion to change over time makes implementations that rely on the assertion more complicated. The argument for allowing maximum bounding boxes to be changed is that the world author can often easily compute the bounding box for changing objects and thus offload the VRML browser from the work. However, this would require the VRML browser to execute the code continually to calculate the bounding box. It might be better to extend the notion of a bounding box to the more general notion of a bounding box that is valid until a given time. World authors could give assertions about an object's possible location over a specific interval of time, and the browser would only need to query the world-/creator-defined **Script** after that time interval had elapsed. In any case, experimentation with either approach is possible by extending a browser with additional nodes defined with the EXTERNPROTO extension mechanism (see Section 2.8, Browser Extensions).

2.4 Events

Most nodes have at least one eventIn definition and thus can receive events. Incoming events are data messages sent by other nodes to change some state within the receiving node. Some nodes also have eventOut definitions. These are used to send data messages to destination nodes that some state has changed within the source node.

If an eventOut is read before it has sent any events (e.g., *get_foo_changed*), the initial value as specified in Chapter 4, Field and Event Reference, for each field/event type is returned.

DESIGN NOTE

Events are the most important new feature in VRML 2.0. Events make the world move; the only way to change something in a VRML world is to send an event to some node. They form the foundation for all of the animation and interaction capabilities of VRML, and more effort was put into the event model design than any of the other new features in VRML 2.0. VRML's event model design is a result of collaboration between the Silicon Graphics team, the Sony team, and Mitra.

2.4.1 Routes

The connection between the node generating the event and the node receiving the event is called a *route*. A node that produces events of given type can be routed to a node that receives events of the same type using the following syntax:

```
ROUTE NodeName.eventOutName TO NodeName.eventInName
```

DESIGN NOTE

Note that the only way to refer to a node in a ROUTE statement is by its name, which means that you must give a node a name if you are establishing routes to or from it. See Section 2.3.2, Instancing, for the recommended way of automatically generating unique (but boring) names.

The prefix *set_* for eventIn names and the suffix *_changed* for eventOut names are recommended conventions, not strict rules. Thus, when creating prototypes (see Section 2.6, Prototypes) or scripts, the names of the eventIns and the eventOuts may be any legal identifier name. Note, however, that exposedFields implicitly define *set_xxx* as an eventIn, *xxx_changed* as an eventOut, and *xxx* as a field for a given exposedField named *xxx*. It is strongly recommended that developers follow these guidelines when creating new types. See the exceptions to field naming conventions in Section 2.1.2, File Syntax vs. Public Interface.

Routes are not nodes; ROUTE is merely a syntactic construct for establishing event paths between nodes. ROUTE statements may appear at either the top level of a .wrl file or prototype implementation, or may appear inside a node wherever fields may appear. The node names referenced in the ROUTE must be DEF'ed *before* the ROUTE statement.

DESIGN NOTE

ROUTE statements are usually put at the end of the VRML file (or the end of a PROTO definition if you are defining routes inside a prototype; see Section 2.6, Prototypes), but it is often convenient to put them in the middle of the file. For example:

```
DEF T Transform {
  translation 1 1 1
  ROUTE T.translation_changed TO T.set_center
  center 1 1 1
}
```

Allowing ROUTE statements inside nodes makes it easier to create VRML files using a text editor and doesn't make implementing VRML much harder. Implementing parsing of ROUTE statements is essentially equivalent to implementing USE statements, and since USE statements can appear inside nodes that have SFNode/MFNode fields it is not difficult to also implement ROUTE statements inside nodes.

Tools that read and write VRML files are not required to maintain the position of ROUTE statements in the file. They will usually either put all ROUTE statements at the end of the file or will put them in either the source or destination node, depending on which is written last (since a ROUTE statement must appear after both the source and destination nodes have been DEF'ed).

The types of the eventIn and the eventOut must match exactly. For example, it is illegal to route from an SFFloat to an SFInt32 or from an SFFloat to an MFFloat.

DESIGN NOTE

Automatic type conversion along routes would often be convenient. So would simple arithmetic operations along SFFloat/SFInt32/SFVec* routes, and simple logical operations for SFBool routes. However, one of the most important design criteria for VRML 2.0 was to keep it as simple as possible. Therefore, since the ROUTE mechanism is such a fundamental aspect of the browser implementation and even simple type conversions require significant amounts of code and complexity, it was decided not to include any data modification along routes.

If type conversion is required, it is easy (although tedious) to define a **Script** that does the appropriate conversion. Standard prototypes for type conversion nodes have already been proposed to the VRML community. If they are used often enough, browser implementors may begin to provide built-in, optimized implementations of these prototypes, which will be a clear signal that they should be added to a future version of the VRML specification.

Routes may be established only from eventOuts to eventIns. Since an exposedField implicitly defines a field, an eventIn, and an eventOut, it is legal to use the exposedField's defined name when routing to and from it, rather than specifying the *set_* prefix and *_changed* suffix. For example, the following **TouchSensor**'s *enabled* exposedField is routed to the **DirectionalLight**'s *on* exposedField. Note that each of the four following routing examples are legal syntax:

```
DEF CLICKER TouchSensor { enabled TRUE }
DEF LIGHT DirectionalLight { on FALSE }
#...
ROUTE CLICKER.enabled TO LIGHT.on
```

or

```
ROUTE CLICKER.enabled_changed TO LIGHT.on
```

or

```
ROUTE CLICKER.enabled TO LIGHT.set_on
```

or

```
ROUTE CLICKER.enabled_changed TO LIGHT.set_on
```

Furthermore, ROUTE statements allow an abbreviation that drops the *set_* prefix for eventIn names and drops the *_changed* suffix for eventOut names. Therefore, when an unresolved ROUTE eventIn name is detected, apply a *set_* prefix to eventIn names and a *_changed* suffix to eventOut names to test for the shorthand case.

Redundant routing is ignored. If a file repeats a routing path, the second (and all subsequent identical routes) are ignored, and likewise for dynamically created routes via a scripting language supported by the browser.

DESIGN NOTE

Three different architectures for applying changes to the scene graph were considered during the VRML 2.0 design process. The key considerations were how much information the VRML browser knows about the world, how little reinvention of existing technology needed to be done, and how easy it would be for nonprogrammers to create interactive worlds. The architecture chosen is a compromise between these conflicting desires.

One extreme would be to keep all behaviors out of VRML and perform all behaviors in an existing language such as Java. In this model, a VRML file looks very much like a VRML 1.0 file, containing only static geometry, and instead of loading a .wrl VRML file into your browser, you would load an applet that referenced a VRML file and then proceed to modify the objects in the world over time. This is similar to conventional programming; the program (applet) loads the data file (VRML world) into memory and then proceeds to make changes to it over time. The advantages of this approach are that it would make the VRML file format simpler and it matches the traditional way applications are created.

There are several disadvantages to this approach, however. Tools meant to help with the creation of interactive worlds would either have to be able to parse and understand the code for an applet (since all of the interactive code would be contained inside an applet) or would be forced to use their own proprietary format for representing behaviors, which were then "published" into the required applet+VRML world form. This would severely limit the interoperability between tools and would make it very difficult for tools or world creators to update the geometry of a VRML world without breaking the behaviors that affect the world.

In addition, it isn't clear that the scalability and composability goals for VRML could be met if all behaviors were performed outside the VRML world. Architectures for composing arbitrary applets (such as Microsoft's ActiveX or Netscape's LiveConnect) have only recently been defined and are designed for the case of a small number of applets on a Web page. The vision for VRML is a potentially infinite, continuous landscape containing an arbitrary number of interacting entities; a very different environment than a Web page!

Another extreme would be to redefine VRML to be a complete programming language, allowing any behavior to be expressed completely in VRML. In this model, a VRML browser would act as a compiler and runtime system, much like the Java runtime reads in Java byte codes and runs them. This approach has all of the disadvantages just described. Defining a specialized language just for VRML would make it possible to do many VRML-specific optimizations, but the disadvantages of defining Yet Another Programming Language probably outweigh the potential gains.

The architecture chosen treats behaviors as "black boxes" (**Script** nodes) with well-defined interfaces (routes and events). Treating behaviors as black boxes allows any scripting language to be used without changing the fundamental architecture of VRML. Implementing a browser is much easier because only the interface between the scene and the scripting language needs to be implemented, not the entire scripting language.

Expressing the interface to behaviors in the VRML file allows an authoring system to deal intelligently with the behaviors and allows most world creation tasks to be done with a graphical interface. A programming editor only need appear when a sophisticated user decides to create or modify a behavior—opening up the black box. The authoring system can safely manipulate the scene hierarchy (add geometry, delete geometry, rename objects, etc.) and still maintain routes to behaviors, and yet the authoring system does not need to be able to parse or understand what happens inside the behavior.

The VRML browser also does not need to know what happens inside each behavior to optimize the execution and display of the world. Since the possible effects of a **Script** are expressed by the routes coming from it (and by the nodes it may directly modify, which are also known), browsers can perform almost all of the optimizations that would be possible if VRML were a specialized programming language. Synchronization and scheduling can also be handled by the browser, making it much easier for the world creator since they can express their intent rather than worry about explicit synchronization between independent applets. For example, giving a sound and an animation the same starting time synchronizes them in VRML. Performing the equivalent task with an architecture that exposes the implementation of sounds and animations as asynchronous threads is more difficult.

2.4.2 Sensors

Sensor nodes generate events. Geometric sensor nodes (**ProximitySensor, Visibility-Sensor, TouchSensor, CylinderSensor, PlaneSensor, SphereSensor,** and the **Collision** group) generate events based on user actions, such as a mouse click or navigating close to a particular object. **TimeSensor** nodes generate events as time passes. See Section 2.9.7, Sensor Nodes, for more details on the specifics of sensor nodes.

DESIGN NOTE

They are called *sensors* because they sense changes to something. Sensors detect changes to the state of an input device (**TouchSensor, CylinderSensor, Plane-Sensor, SphereSensor**), changes in time (**TimeSensor**), or changes related to the motion of the viewer or objects in the virtual world (**ProximitySensor, VisibilitySensor,** and **Collision** group).

Some often-requested features that did not make it into VRML 2.0 could be expressed as new sensor types. These are object-to-object collision detection, support for 3D input devices, and keyboard support.

Viewer-object collision detection is supported by the **Collision** group, but object-to-object collision detection is harder to implement and much harder to specify. Only recently have robust, fast implementations for detecting collisions between any two objects in an arbitrary virtual world become available, and efficient algorithms for object-to-object collision detection is still an area of active research. Even assuming fast, efficient algorithms are widely available and reasonably straightforward to implement, it is difficult to specify precisely which nodes should be tested for collisions and what events should be produced when they collide. Designing a solution that works for a particular application (e.g., a game) is easy; designing a general solution that works for a wide range of applications is much harder.

Support for input devices like 3D mice, 3D joysticks, and spatial trackers was also an often-requested feature. Ideally, a world creator would describe the desired interactions at a high level of abstraction so that users could use any input device they desired to interact with the world. There might be a **Motion3DSensor** that gives 3D positions and orientations in the local coordinate system, driven by whatever input device the user happened to be using.

In practice, however, creating an easy-to-use experience requires knowledge of the capabilities and limitations of the input device being used. This is true even in the well-researched world of 2D input devices; drawing applications treat a pressure-sensitive tablet differently than a mouse.

One alternative to creating a general sensor to support 3D input devices was to create many different sensors, one for each different device or class of devices. There were two problems with doing this: First, the authors of the VRML 2.0 specification are not experts in the subtleties of all of the various 3D input device technologies and second, it isn't clear that many world creators would use these new sensors since they would restrict the use of their worlds to people that had the appropriate input device (a very small percentage of computer users). It is expected that prototype extensions that support 3D input devices will be available and proposed for future revisions of the VRML specification.

Unlike 3D input devices, keyboards are ubiquitous in the computing world. However, there is no **KeyboardSensor** in the VRML 2.0 standard. Virtual reality purists might argue that this is a good thing since keyboards have no place in immersive virtual worlds (and we should have **SpeechSensor** and **FingerSensor** instead), but that isn't the reason for its absence from the VRML specification. During the process of designing **KeyboardSensor** several difficult design issues arose for which no satisfactory solution was found. In addition, VRML is not designed to be a stand-alone, do-everything standard. It was designed to take advantage of the other standards that have been defined for the Internet whenever possible, such as JPEG, MPEG, Java, HTTP, and URLs.

The simplest keyboard support would be reporting key-press and key-release events. For example, a world creator might want a platform to move up while a certain key is pressed and to move down when another key is pressed. Or, different keys on the keyboard might be used to "teleport" the user to different locations in the world. Adding support for a single **KeyboardSensor** of this type in a world would be straightforward, but designing for just a single **KeyboardSensor** goes against the composability design goals for VRML. It also duplicates functionality that is better left to other standards. For example, Java defines a set of keyboard events that may be received by a Java applet. Rather than wasting time duplicating the functionality of Java inside VRML, defining a general communication mechanism between a Java applet and a VRML world will give this functionality and much more.

Java also defines *textArea* and *textField* components that allow entry of arbitrary text strings. Designing the equivalent functionality for text input inside a 3D world (e.g., fill-in text areas on the walls of a room) would require the definition of a 2D windowing system inside the 3D world. Issues such as input methods for international characters, keyboard focus management, and a host of other issues would have to be reimplemented if a VRML solution were invented. Again, rather than wasting time duplicating the functionality of existing windowing systems, it might be better to define a general way of embedding existing 2D standards into the 3D world. Experimentation along these lines is certainly possible using the current VRML 2.0 standard. The **ImageTexture** node can point to arbitrary 2D content, and although only the PNG and JPEG image file formats are required, browser implementors could certainly support **ImageTexture** nodes that pointed to Java applets. They could even map mouse and keyboard events over the texture into the 2D coordinate space of the Java applet to support arbitrary interaction with Java applets pasted onto objects in a 3D world.

Each type of sensor defines when an event is generated. The state of the scene graph after several sensors have generated events must be as if each event is processed separately, in order. If sensors generate events at the same time, the state of the scene graph will be undefined if the results depend on the ordering of the events (world creators must be careful to avoid such situations).

DESIGN NOTE

Events generated by sensor nodes are given time stamps that specify exactly when the event occurred. These time stamps should be the exact or ideal time that the event occurred and *not* the time that the event happened to be generated by the sensor. For example, the time stamp for a **TouchSensor**'s *isActive* TRUE event generated by clicking the mouse should be the actual time when the mouse button was pressed, even if it takes a few microseconds for the mouse-press event to be delivered to the VRML application. This isn't very important if events are handled in isolation, but can be critical in cases when the sequence or timing of multiple events is important. For example, the world creator might set a double-click threshold on an object. If the user clicks the mouse (or, more generally, activates the pointing device) twice rapidly enough, an animation is started. The browser may happen to receive one click just before it decides to rerender the scene and the other click after it is finished rendering the scene. If it takes the browser longer to render the scene than the double-click threshold and the browser time stamps the click events based on when it gets around to processing them, then the double-click events will be lost and the user will be very frustrated. Happily, modern operating and windowing systems are multithreaded and give the raw device events reasonably accurate time stamps that can be retrieved and used by VRML browsers.

It is possible to create dependencies between various types of sensors. For example, a **TouchSensor** may result in a change to a **VisibilitySensor**'s transformation, which may cause its visibility status to change. World authors must be careful to avoid creating indeterministic or paradoxical situations (such as a **TouchSensor** that is active if a **VisibilitySensor** is visible and a **VisibilitySensor** that is not visible if a **TouchSensor** is active).

TIP

If you create a paradoxical or indeterministic situation, your world may behave differently on different VRML browsers. Achieving identical (or at least almost-identical) results on different implementations is the primary reason for defining a VRML specification, so a lot of thought was put into designs that removed any possibilities of indeterministic results. For example, two sensors that generated events at exactly the same time could be given a well-defined order, perhaps based on which was created first or their position in the scene graph. Requiring implementations to do this was judged to be unreasonable, because different implementations will have different strategies for delaying the loading of different parts of the world (affecting the order in which nodes are created) and because the scene graph ordering can change over time. The overhead required to make all possible worlds completely deterministic isn't worth the runtime costs. Indeterministic situations are easy to avoid, can be detected and reported at runtime (so the world creator knows that they have a problem), and are never useful.

2.4.3 Execution Model

Once a sensor or **Script** has generated an initial event, the event is propagated along any route to other nodes. These other nodes may respond by generating additional events and so on. This process is called an *event cascade*. All events generated during a given event cascade are given the same time stamp as the initial event (they are all considered to happen instantaneously).

Some sensors generate multiple events simultaneously. In these cases, each event generated initiates a different event cascade.

DESIGN NOTE

The task of defining the execution model for events is simplified by breaking it down into three subtasks:

1. Defining what causes an initial event

2. Defining an ordering for initial events

3. Defining exactly what happens during an event cascade

The only nodes in the VRML 2.0 specification that can generate initial events are the sensor nodes, **Collision** group, and **Script** nodes. ExposedFields never generate initial events (they are always part of the event cascade) and neither do the interpolator nodes. So the first subtask, defining what causes an initial event, is satisfied by precisely defining the conditions under which each sensor or **Script** node will generate events. See Section 2.7, Scripting, for a discussion of when **Script** nodes generate initial events, and see the description for each sensor node for a discussion of when they generate initial events.

The second subtask, defining an ordering for initial events, is made easier by introducing the notion that all events are given time stamps. We can then guarantee determinism by requiring that an implementation produce results that are indistinguishable from an implementation that processes events in time stamp order, and defining an order for events that have the same time stamp (or declare that the results are inherently indeterministic and tell world creators, "Don't do that!"). Defining the execution model becomes manageable only if each change can be considered in isolation. Implementations may choose to process events out of order (or in parallel, or may choose not to process some events at all!) only if the results are the same as an implementation that completely processes each event as it occurs. VRML 2.0 is carefully designed so that implementations may reason about what effects a particular event might possibly have, allowing sophisticated implementations to be very efficient when processing events.

The third subtask, defining what happens during an event cascade, is made easier by not considering all possible route topologies at once. In particular, event cascades that contain loops and fan-ins are difficult to define and are considered separately (see Sections 2.4.4, Loops, and 2.4.5, Fan-in and Fan-out).

Processing an event cascade ideally takes no time, which is why all events that are part of a given event cascade are given the same time stamp. ROUTE statements set up explicit *dependencies* between nodes, forcing implementations to process certain events in an event cascade before others.

For example, given nodes A, B, and C in the arrangement in Figure 2-3, where A is a **TouchSensor** detecting the user touching some geometry in the world, B is a **Script** that outputs TRUE and then FALSE every other time it receives input, and C is a **Time-Sensor** that starts an animation, the ROUTE statements would be

```
ROUTE A.touchTime TO B.toggleNow
ROUTE A.touchTime TO C.set_startTime
ROUTE B.toggle_changed TO C.set_enabled
```

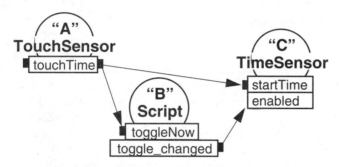

FIGURE 2-3 *Routing Example*

In this case, whether or not **TimeSensor** C will start generating events when **TouchSensor** A is touched depends on whether or not it is enabled, so an implementation must run **Script** B's script before deciding which events C should generate. If B outputs TRUE and C becomes active, then C should generate *startTime_changed, enabled_changed, isActive, fraction_changed, cycleTime,* and *time* events. If B outputs FALSE and C becomes inactive, then it should only generate *startTime_changed, enable_changed,* and *isActive* events.

Paradoxical dependencies (when, for example, results of A depend on B and results of B depend on A) can be created, and implementations are free to do whatever they wish with them—results are undefined. See Section 2.4.5, Fan-in and Fan-out, for an explanation of what happens when more than one event is sent to a single eventIn.

2.4.4 Loops

Event cascades may contain loops where an event, E, is routed to a node that generated an event that eventually resulted in E being generated. Loops are broken as follows: implementations must not generate two events from the same eventOut or to the same eventIn *with identical time stamps.* Note that this rule also breaks loops created by setting up cyclic dependencies between different sensor nodes.

TIP

> In general, it is best to avoid route loops. There are some situations in which they're useful, however, and the loop-breaking rule combined with the dependencies implied by the routes are sufficient to make loops deterministic, except for some cases of cyclic dependencies (which are inherently indeterministic and must be avoided by world creators) and some cases of fan-in (which must also be avoided and are discussed later).
>
> One simple situation in which a route loop might be useful is two exposedFields, A.foo and B.foo, with values that you want to remain identical. You can route them to each other, like this:
>
> ```
> ROUTE A.foo_changed TO B.set_foo
> ROUTE B.foo_changed TO A.set_foo
> ```
>
> First, note that no events will be generated unless either A or B is changed. There must be either another route to A or B or a **Script** node that has access to and will change A or B, or neither A nor B will ever change. A route is a conduit for events; it does not establish equality between two fields. Or, in other words, if A.foo and B.foo start out with different values, then establishing a route between them will not make their values become equal. They will not become equal until either A receives a *set_foo* event or B receives a *set_foo* event. See Section 2.7, Scripting, for a description of how to write a script that generates initial events after the world has been loaded, if you want to guarantee equality between exposedFields.
>
> The loop-breaking rule prevents an infinite sequence of events from being generated and results in "the right thing" happening. If A receives a *set_foo* event from somewhere, it sets its value and sends a *set_foo* event to B. B then sets its value and sends A another *set_foo* event, which A ignores since it has already received a *set_foo* event during this event cascade.

2.4.5 Fan-in and Fan-out

Fan-in occurs when two or more routes write to the same eventIn. If two events with different values but the same time stamp are received at an eventIn, then the results are undefined. World creators must be careful to avoid such situations.

DESIGN NOTE

Like loops, in general it is best to avoid fanning into a single eventIn, since it is possible to create situations that lead to undefined results. Fan-in can be useful if used properly, though. For example, you might create several different animations that can apply to a **Transform** node's *translation* field. If you know that only one animation will ever be active at the same time and all of the animations start with and leave the objects in the same position, then routing all of the animations to the *set_translation* eventIn is a safe and useful thing to do. However, if more than one animation might be active at the same time, results will be undefined and you will likely get different results in different browsers. In this case, you should insert a **Script** that combines the results of the animations in the appropriate way, perhaps by adding up the various translations and outputting their sum. The **Script** must have a different eventIn for each animation to avoid the problem of two events arriving at the same eventIn at the same time.

While designing VRML 2.0, various schemes for getting rid of ambiguous fan-in were considered. The simplest would be to declare all fan-in situations illegal, allowing only one route to any eventIn. That solution was rejected because it makes some simple things hard to do. Other possibilities that were considered and rejected included determining a deterministic ordering for each connection to an eventIn (rejected because determining an order is expensive and difficult) and built-in rules to automatically combine the values of each eventIn type, such as logical "OR" for SFBool events (rejected because it would make implementations more complex and because some event types [e.g., SFNode] don't have obvious combination rules). World creators are given the power to create ambiguous situations and are trusted with the responsibility to avoid such situations.

Fan-out occurs when one eventOut routes to two or more eventIns. This case is perfectly legal and results in multiple events sent with the same values and the same time stamp.

DESIGN NOTE

Fan-out is very useful and, by itself, can never cause undefined results. It can also be implemented very efficiently, because a node can't modify the events it receives. Only one event needs to be created for any eventOut, even if there are multiple routes leading from that eventOut.

2.5 Time

2.5.1 Introduction

The browser controls the passage of time in a world by causing **TimeSensors** to generate events as time passes. Specialized browsers or authoring applications may cause time to pass more quickly or slowly than in the real world, but typically the times generated by **TimeSensors** will roughly correspond to "real" time. A world's creator must make no assumptions about how often a **TimeSensor** will generate events, but can safely assume that each time event generated will be greater than any previous time event.

DESIGN NOTE

The sampling of time is controlled by the VRML browser. This makes it much easier for the world creators, since they don't have to worry about synchronization of events, writing a "main loop," and so on. It also makes it much easier to create VRML authoring systems. If VRML had a model of time where independent applets each ran in a separate thread and made asynchronous changes to the world, then it would be very difficult for the user to "freeze time" and make necessary adjustments to the virtual world. Because time events all come from a single place— **TimeSensor** nodes—it is easy for a world creation system to control time during the authoring process.

Time (0.0) starts at 00:00:00 GMT January 1, 1970.

DESIGN NOTE

Defining an absolute origin for time isn't really necessary for proper functioning of VRML worlds. Absolute times are very rare in VRML files; they are almost always calculated during execution of the world relative to the occurrence of some event ("start this animation 2.3 seconds after the viewer walks into this room").

If you know where in the real world the VRML file will be viewed, then the absolute origin for time allows you to synchronize the real world and the virtual world. For example, if you know that your world will be viewed in California, then you can create a day-to-night animation that is driven by a **TimeSensor** and will match the sunrises and sunsets in California. VRML does not include a **RealWorldPositionSensor** that outputs the real-world position of the real-world VRML viewer, but if it did (perhaps when every computer includes a Global Positioning System satellite receiver, . . .) many very interesting applications merging the virtual and real worlds would become possible.

A frequently asked question is how can something be scheduled to start some amount of time "after the world is loaded." If time were defined to start "when the world is loaded," then this would be easy—the world creator would just give a **TimeSensor** an appropriate absolute *startTime*. One problem with this is defining precisely what is meant by "when the world is loaded." VRML browsers may load different parts of the world at different times or may preload parts of the world before they're actually needed. If the browser decides to preload part of the world because it knows that the user is traveling at a certain speed in a certain direction and will arrive there in 20 seconds, the world creator probably doesn't want a 5-second welcome animation to be performed before the user is anywhere near that part of the world. In this case, it is better for the world creator to use a **ProximitySensor** or a **VisibilitySensor** to generate an event that can then be used as the basis for starting animations, sounds, and so forth. Instead of thinking in terms of "when the world is loaded," it is better to think of "when the user enters my world" (**ProximitySensor**) or "when the user first sees . . ." (**VisibilitySensor**). Worlds created this way will be composable with other worlds, allowing the creation of the potentially infinite cyberspace of the future.

Events that are "in the past" cannot be generated. Processing an event with time stamp *t* may only result in generating events with time stamps greater than or equal to *t*.

DESIGN NOTE

The rule that "events in the past cannot be generated" means that browsers are not responsible for simulating anything that occurred before the VRML file was loaded. The mental model is that a VRML file expresses the complete state of a virtual world at a given point in time. If the VRML browser knows exactly when the VRML file was written, then it could theoretically simulate all of the events that occurred between when the file was written and when it was read back into memory, just as if it had been simulating the world all along. However, VRML files do not record the time the world was written, and it is not always possible or convenient for the VRML browser to retrieve that information from the underlying operating system or transport mechanism. In addition, requiring the VRML browser to simulate the passage of an arbitrary amount of time after reading in every VRML file would be an unnecessary burden.

2.5.2 Discrete and Continuous Changes

VRML does not distinguish between discrete events (like those generated by a **TouchSensor**) and events that are the result of sampling a conceptually continuous set of changes (like the fraction events generated by a **TimeSensor**). An ideal VRML implementation would generate an infinite number of samples for continuous changes, each of which would be processed infinitely quickly.

Before processing a discrete event, all continuous changes that are occurring at the discrete event's time stamp should behave as if they generate events at that same time stamp.

DESIGN NOTE

This follows from the premise that an ideal implementation would be continuously generating events for continuous changes. A simple implementation can guarantee this by generating events for all active **TimeSensors** whenever a discrete event occurs. More sophisticated implementations can optimize this by noting dependencies and ensuring that if a node depends on both a discrete event and a continuous event, then it will always receive a continuous event along with the discrete event.

Beyond the requirements that continuous changes be up-to-date during the processing of discrete changes, implementations are otherwise free to sample continuous changes as often or as infrequently as they choose. Typically, a **TimeSensor** affecting a visible (or otherwise perceptible) portion of the world will generate events once per "frame," where a *frame* is a single rendering of the world or one time step in a simulation.

DESIGN NOTE

Thinking in terms of the ideal VRML implementation is a useful exercise and can resolve many situations that may at first seem ambiguous. It is impossible to implement the ideal, of course, but for well-behaved worlds the results of a well-implemented browser will be identical to the theoretical results of the ideal implementation. "Well behaved" means that the world creator didn't rely on any undefined behavior, such as assuming that **TimeSensors** would generate 30 events per second because that happened to be how quickly a particular browser could render their world on a particular type of machine.

In its quest to be machine- and implementation-neutral, the VRML specification tries to avoid any notion of rendering frames, pixels, or screen resolution. It is hoped that by avoiding such hardware-specific notions the VRML world description will be appropriate for many different rendering architectures, both present and future.

2.6 Prototypes

2.6.1 Introduction

Prototyping is a mechanism that allows the set of node types to be extended from within a VRML file. It allows the encapsulation and parameterization of geometry, attributes, behaviors, or some combination thereof.

DESIGN NOTE

Prototypes have many possible uses and can be thought of as

- An extensibility mechanism that allows a new node type to be defined in terms of other, predefined nodes. Prototypes replace the VRML 1.0 extension features (*isA* and *fields*[]) with a single, more general mechanism.

- A protection mechanism that allows an author to limit what can be done to an object. The only way to violate the interface defined by a prototype is to make a copy of its implementation and modify the copy.

- A method of defining a library of reusable objects

- An object-definition mechanism that allows someone to impose application-specific policies on top of the general VRML scene structure

- A convenience mechanism that allows geometry and/or behavior to be packaged in an easy-to-use way

- An optimization mechanism that allows browsers to reason about which objects can and cannot be changed

- A bandwidth-saving mechanism that allows the definition of a world structure to be defined once and reused multiple times, and allows the creation of abbreviations for commonly used nodes

- An alternative to DEF/USE instancing

Prototypes give VRML 2.0 much of its flexibility. Many arguments about the details of the VRML design were ended by pointing out that the feature in question can be implemented using the prototyping mechanism and the built-in nodes.

A prototype definition consists of the following:

- the PROTO keyword
- the name of the new node type

DESIGN NOTE

The convention used for all nodes defined in the VRML 2.0 standard (which should be thought of as PROTO's with built-in implementation) is that each word in a node type name begins with a capital letter (e.g., **Box, OrientationInterpolator**). Although not enforced, you are encouraged to follow this convention when defining your own node types using PROTO.

- the prototype declaration, which contains

  - a list of public eventIns and eventOuts that can send and receive events
  - a list of public exposedFields and fields, with default values

DESIGN NOTE

The prototype declaration defines its *interface*—how the prototype communicates with the rest of the scene and what parameters may be set for each instance of the prototype.

- the prototype definition, which contains a list of one or more nodes, and zero or more routes and prototypes (The nodes in this list may also contain the IS syntax, which associates field and event names contained within the prototype definition with the events and fields names in the prototype declaration.)

DESIGN NOTE

The prototype definition is the implementation of the prototype, defining exactly what the prototype does in terms of other prototypes and built-in nodes.

Square brackets enclose the list of events and fields, and braces enclose the definition itself:

```
PROTO PrototypeName [
   eventIn       eventtypename name
   eventOut      eventtypename name
   exposedField fieldtypename name defaultValue
   field         fieldtypename name defaultValue
   ... ]
{
 # Zero or more prototypes
 # First node (defines the node type of this prototype)
 # Zero or more nodes (of any type), routes, and prototypes
}
```

The names of the fields, exposedFields, eventIns, and eventOuts must be unique for a single prototype (or built-in node). Therefore, the following prototype is illegal because the name *foo* is overloaded:

```
PROTO BadNames [ field        SFBool   foo
                 eventOut     SFColor  foo
                 eventIn      SFVec3f  foo
                 exposedField SFString foo ] {...}
```

Prototype and built-in node field and event name scopes do not overlap. Therefore, it is legal to use the same names in different prototypes, as follows:

```
PROTO foo  [ field    SFBool   foo
             eventOut SFColor  foo2
             eventIn  SFVec3f  foo3 ] {...}
PROTO bar  [ field    SFBool   foo
             eventOut SFColor  foo2
             eventIn  SFVec3f  foo3 ] {...}
```

DESIGN NOTE

Allowing nonunique field and event names in different node types makes it much easier to reuse PROTOs defined by different people in the same scene and doesn't make parsing VRML significantly more difficult (because parsers must keep track of the fields and events that are declared for each PROTO type anyway). Forcing all field and event types to be unique between all node types would be very annoying, even just for the nodes defined in the VRML 2.0 standard. For example, all interpolator nodes have *set_fraction, key, keyValue, and value_changed* fields/events. Defining slightly different names for fields that perform the same function would be confusing and error prone.

A prototype statement does not define an actual instance of a node in the scene. Rather, it creates a new node type (named **PrototypeName**) that can be created later in the same file as if it were a built-in node. It is thus necessary to define a node of the type of the prototype to create an object. For example, the following file is an empty scene with a **FooSphere** prototype that by itself produces nothing:

```
#VRML V2.0 utf8
PROTO FooSphere [ field SFFloat fooRadius 3.0 ]
{ Sphere { radius IS fooRadius } }
```

In the following example, a **FooSphere** is actually created and thus produces a visible result:

```
#VRML V2.0 utf8
PROTO FooSphere [ field SFFloat fooRadius 3.0 ]
{ Sphere { radius IS fooRadius } }
Shape { geometry FooSphere { fooRadius 42.0 } }
```

The first node found in the prototype definition is used to define the prototype's node type. This first node's type determines how instantiations of the prototype are used in a VRML file. An instantiation is created by filling in the parameters of the prototype declaration and inserting the first node (and its scene graph) wherever the prototype instantiation occurs. When the prototype is instantiated only the first node is inserted into the scene graph and it is the only node directly affected by the scene's transformation hierarchy.

For example, if the first node in the prototype definition is a **Material** node, then instantiations of the prototype can be used wherever **Material** can be used. Any other nodes and accompanying scene graphs are not rendered, but may be referenced via routes or scripts (and thus cannot be ignored). The following example defines a **RampMaterial** prototype that animates a **Material**'s *diffuseColor* continuously and may be used wherever **Material** can be used in the file (i.e., within an **Appearance** node):

```
#VRML V2.0 utf8
PROTO RampMaterial [
  field MFColor colors [ ]
  field MFFloat keys [ ]
  field SFTime cycle 1 ]
{
  DEF M Material {}
  DEF C ColorInterpolator {
    keyValue IS colors
    key IS keys
  }
  DEF T TimeSensor {
    enabled TRUE
    loop TRUE
    stopTime -1
    cycleInterval IS cycle
  }
  ROUTE T.fraction_changed TO C.set_fraction
  ROUTE C.value_changed TO M.diffuseColor
}
Transform {
  children Shape {
    geometry Sphere {}
    appearance Appearance {
      material RampMaterial {
        colors [ 1 0 0, 0 1 0, 1 0 0 ] # red to green to red
        keys [ 0.0 0.5 1.0 ]
        cycle 3.0
      }
    }
  }
}
```

DESIGN NOTE

VRML's prototyping mechanism is not equivalent to the object-oriented notion of inheritance. The **RampMaterial** of the previous example may be used anywhere a **Material** node may be used, but it can't really be considered a subclass of **Material** because it doesn't support all of the operations (eventIns, eventOuts, and exposedFields) that the **Material** node supports. In fact, object-oriented notions such as superclass and subclass are consciously kept out of the VRML specification, although many of the node classes are designed to make an object-oriented implementation straightforward. For example, the **Transform** node can be implemented as a subclass of the **Group** node, and all of the interpolator nodes can share much of their code in a common base class. Anticipating implementation needs but not requiring any particular implementation was another of the many design constraints on VRML.

Because the second and subsequent root nodes in a PROTO definition are *not* part of the scene's transformation hierarchy, only the following node types should be used there: **Script, TimeSensor,** and interpolators. Using any of the other node types as the second or subsequent root of a PROTO is never useful, but is not prohibited because there were no compelling reasons to do so.

The next example defines a **SphereCone** (fused **Sphere** and **Cone**) and illustrates how the first node in the prototype definition may contain a complex scene graph:

```
#VRML V2.0 utf8
PROTO SphereCone [ field SFFloat radius    2.0
                   field SFFloat height    5.0
                   field SFNode  sphereApp NULL
                   field SFNode  coneApp   NULL ]
{
  Transform { children [
    Shape {
      appearance IS sphereApp
      geometry Sphere { radius IS radius }
    }
    Shape {
      appearance IS coneApp
      geometry Cone { height IS height }
    }
  ]}
}  # end of PROTO
Transform {
  translation 15 0 0
  children SphereCone {
    radius 5.0
    height 20.0
```

```
      sphereApp Appearance { material Material {...} }
      coneApp Appearance { texture ImageTexture {...} }
   }
}
Transform {
   translation -10 0 0
   children SphereCone {
      sphereApp Appearance { texture ImageTexture {...} }
      coneApp Appearance {  material Material {...} }
   }
}
```

PROTO and EXTERNPROTO (see Section 2.6.4, Defining Prototypes in External Files) statements may appear anywhere ROUTE statements may appear—either at the top level of a file or a prototype definition, or wherever fields may appear. Prototypes define a DEF/USE name scope that begins at the PROTO keyword and ends at the prototype's closing brace, }. Therefore, names defined within a prototype cannot be used outside of the prototype, and names defined outside of a prototype cannot be used inside the prototype.

DESIGN NOTE

Like ROUTE statements, the position of a PROTO definition in a file is irrelevant; the only constraint is that the PROTO appear in the file before any instance of the prototype. Tools that read and write VRML files will typically put all PROTO definitions at the top of the file.

2.6.2 IS Statement

The eventIn and eventOut prototype declarations receive and send events to and from the prototype's definition. Each eventIn in the prototype declaration is associated with zero or more eventIns and exposedFields defined in the prototype's node definition via the IS syntax. If there are no IS statements for a given eventIn, then the events sent to that eventIn are ignored. The eventIn declarations define the events that the prototype can receive. Each eventOut in the prototype declaration is associated with zero or more eventOuts and exposedFields defined in the prototype's node definition via the IS syntax. If there are no IS statements for a given eventOut, then that eventOut is ignored. The eventOut declarations define the events that the prototype can send. For example, the following statement exposes a **Transform** node's *set_translation* event by giving it a new name, *set_position*, in the prototype interface:

```
PROTO FooTransform [ eventIn SFVec3f set_position ] {
   Transform { set_translation IS set_position }
}
```

DESIGN NOTE

Allowing multiple eventIns to be mapped to the same prototype parameter is a convenient way to do ROUTE fan-out transparently. For example, you might want a prototype that starts several **TimeSensors** when it receives a *set_startTime* eventIn:

```
PROTO Animations [ eventIn SFTime set_startTime ] {
  DEF ANIM1 TimeSensor {
    set_startTime IS set_startTime
    cycleInterval 4.5
  }
  DEF ANIM2 TimeSensor {
    set_startTime IS set_startTime
    cycleInterval 11.3
  }
}
```

Instantiating and ROUTE-ing to an **Animations** object, like this:

```
DEF ANIMS Animations { }
DEF SENSOR TouchSensor { }
ROUTE SENSOR.touchTime TO ANIMS.set_startTime
```

is equivalent to doing this:

```
DEF ANIM1 TimeSensor { cycleInterval 4.5 }
DEF ANIM2 TimeSensor { cycleInterval 11.3}
DEF SENSOR TouchSensor { }
ROUTE SENSOR.touchTime TO ANIM1.set_startTime
ROUTE SENSOR.touchTime TO ANIM2.set_startTime
```

Similarly, allowing multiple eventOuts to be mapped to the same prototype parameter allows implicit fan-in and, like regular ROUTE fan-in, care must be taken to ensure that indeterministic situations are not created. For example, events from this PROTO's *out* eventOut are undefined:

```
PROTO BAD [
  eventIn SFTime set_startTime
  eventOut SFFloat out ]
{
  DEF ANIM1 TimeSensor {
    set_startTime IS set_startTime
    cycleInterval 4.5
    fraction_changed IS out
  }
  DEF ANIM2 TimeSensor {
    set_startTime IS set_startTime
    cycleInterval 11.3
    fraction_changed IS out
  }
}
```

Although legal syntactically, such a construction makes no sense semantically. In general, it is best to avoid associating multiple eventOuts with a single prototype parameter.

Fields (exposedField and field) specify the initial state of nodes. Defining fields in a prototype's declaration allows the initial state of associated fields in the prototype node definition to be specified when an instance of the prototype is created. The fields of the prototype are associated with fields in the node definition using the IS keyword. Field default values must be specified in the prototype declaration. For example,

```
PROTO BarTransform [ exposedField SFVec3f position 42 42 42 ] {
  Transform {
    translation IS position
  }
}
```

defines a prototype, **BarTransform**, that specifies the initial values (42, 42, 42) of the *position* exposedField in the prototype's declaration. The *position* field is associated with the *translation* field of the **Transform** node in the prototype definition using the IS syntax. Note that it is illegal to specify both the field values and an IS statement for a field. Therefore in the following example the field values in the prototype node definition for *translation* (100, 100, 100) are illegal and conflict with the IS statement:

```
PROTO BarTransform [ exposedField SFVec3f position 42 42 42 ] {
  Transform {
    translation IS position     # It is illegal to
    translation 100 100 100     # have both!
  }
}
```

Note that in some cases it is necessary to specify the field defaults inside the prototype definition. For example, the following prototype associates the prototype definition's **Material** node *diffuseColor* (exposedField) to the prototype declaration's eventIn *myColor* and also defines the default *diffuseColor* values:

```
PROTO foo [ eventIn myColor ] {
  Material {
    diffuseColor 1 0 0
    diffuseColor IS myColor
    # or set_diffuseColor IS myColor
  }
}
```

DESIGN NOTE

ExposedFields are really just a shorthand notation for the combination of an eventIn, an eventOut, and a field, along with the semantics that eventOuts are generated whenever eventIns are received. Allowing the eventIn portion of an exposedField to be referred to without its *set_* prefix and the eventOut portion without its *_changed* suffix makes it easier to create VRML files in a text editor, but makes both the specification and implementations a little more complicated.

Each exposedField in the prototype declaration is associated with zero or more exposedFields defined in the prototype's node definition via the IS syntax. If there are no IS statements for a given exposedField, the exposedField may ignore *set_* events to itself (not generate *_changed* events).

IS statements may appear inside the prototype definition wherever fields may appear. IS statements must refer to fields or events defined in the prototype declaration. Conversely, if an IS statement refers to a nonexistent declaration, results are undefined. Also, if the type of the field or event being associated does not match the type declared in the prototype's interface declaration, results are undefined. If a node in a prototype definition specifies more than one IS statement for a field, exposedField, or event, results are undefined. For example, it is illegal to associate an SFColor with an SFVec3f, and it is also illegal to associate an SFColor with an MFColor, and vice versa. Table 2-2 defines the rules for mapping between the prototype declarations and the primary scene graph's nodes (*yes* denotes a legal mapping, *no* denotes an error).

TABLE 2-2 *Legal field/event prototype mapping*

	Prototype declaration			
Node	**exposedField**	**field**	**eventIn**	**eventOut**
exposedField	yes	yes	yes	yes
field	no	yes	no	no
eventIn	no	no	yes	no
eventOut	no	no	no	yes

Specifying the field and event types both in the prototype declaration and in the node definition is intended to prevent user errors and to provide consistency with EXTERNPROTOs (see Section 2.6.4, Defining Prototypes in External Files).

When associating an exposedField in a prototype node definition with an eventIn or an eventOut in the prototype declaration, it is valid to use either the shorthand exposedField name (e.g., *translation*) or the explicit event name (e.g., *set_translation* or *translation_changed*) because the type is unambiguously defined by the prototype declaration. For example, both of the following prototype definitions are valid syntax:

```
PROTO Paul [ eventIn SFVec3f translateIn
             eventOut SFVec3f translateOut
             field translateValue ]
{
  Transform {
    translation IS tranlateIn   # eventIn shorthand
    translation IS tranlateOut  # eventOut shorthand
    translation IS tranlateValue
  }
}

PROTO Paul2 [ eventIn SFVec3f translateIn
              eventOut SFVec3f translateOut
              field translateValue ] {
  Transform {
    set_translation IS tranlateIn       # explicit name
    translation_changed IS tranlateOut  # explicit name
    translation IS tranlateValue
  }
}
```

2.6.3 Prototype Scoping Rules

A prototype is instantiated as if **PrototypeName** was a built-in node. The prototype name must be unique within the scope of the file and cannot rename a built-in node or prototype.

Prototype instances may be named using DEF and may be multi-instanced using USE as any built-in node. A prototype instance can be used in the scene graph wherever the first node of the primary scene graph can be used. For example, a prototype defined as

```
PROTO MyObject [ ... ] {
  Box { ... }
  ROUTE ...
  Script { ... }
  ...
}
```

may be instantiated wherever a **Box** may be used (e.g., the **Shape** node's *geometry* field), since the first node of the prototype definition is **Box**.

DESIGN NOTE

Each prototype instance is, conceptually, a completely new copy of the prototype's definition inserted into the scene. Each instance of a prototype must act independently of any other instance. The USE keyword, on the other hand, inserts the same object into the scene again. If it weren't for this key difference, PROTO could replace the USE statement. The following DEF/USE statements

```
DEF Something Transform { ... }
USE Something
```

are almost equivalent to the following:

```
PROTO Something [ ] { Transform { ... } }
Something { }
Something { }
```

The first two statements define and create a **Something** node, very much like the previous DEF statement. And, instantiating another **Something** node is very much like the USE statement. The key difference is that in the first example there is only one **Transform** node, while in the second example there are two different nodes.

Smart implementations can determine which parts of a prototype instance can't possibly change and can automatically share those parts of the prototype definition between instances. For example, the **Transform** node of the **Something** prototype can never change because none of its eventIns are exposed in the prototype's interface, and **Transform** is not given a name so there cannot be any ROUTE statements inside the prototype that refer to it. If none of **Transform**'s children can change either, then implementations can create just one **Transform** node to save memory. In VRML, there is no way to tell the difference between two copies of a node if the copies are identical and cannot change, which allows implementations to optimize and create just one copy.

A prototype's scene graph defines a DEF/USE name scope separate from the rest of the scene. Nodes DEF'ed inside the prototype may not be USE'd outside of the prototype's scope, and nodes DEF'ed outside the prototype scope may not be USE'd inside the prototype scope.

Prototype statements appearing inside a prototype definition (i.e., nested) are local to the enclosing prototype. For example:

```
PROTO One [...] {
  PROTO Two [...] { ... }
  ...
  Two { } # Instantiation inside "One":  OK
}
Two { } # ERROR: "Two" may only be instantiated inside "One".
```

The second instantiation of **Two** is illegal. IS statements inside a nested prototype statement may refer to the prototype declarations of the innermost prototype. Therefore, IS statements in **Two** cannot refer to declarations in **One.** Note that IS statements may not appear inside of prototype declarations.

A prototype may be instantiated in a file anywhere after the completion of the prototype definition. A prototype may not be instantiated inside its own definition (i.e., recursive prototypes are illegal). The following example produces an error:

```
PROTO Foo [] {
  Foo {}
}
```

DESIGN NOTE

A PROTO definition is almost like a completely separate VRML file inside the VRML file. The only communication between the main file and the nodes in the PROTO definition must occur through the parameters defined in the prototype declaration, which is why it is not possible to DEF a node in the main file and USE it inside the prototype's definition or vice versa. However, prototypes can be defined in terms of other prototypes. PROTOs defined before the PROTO definition may be used inside the PROTO's definition, although the converse is not true (PROTOs defined inside a prototype definition are not available outside of that definition).

2.6.4 Defining Prototypes in External Files

The syntax for defining prototypes in external files is as follows:

```
EXTERNPROTO ExternPrototypeName [
   eventIn        eventtypename name
   eventOut       eventtypename name
   field          fieldtypename name
   exposedField fieldtypename name
   ... ]
"URL" or [ "URL", "URL", ... ]
```

The external prototype is then given the name **ExternPrototypeName** in this file's scope. It is an error if the eventIn/eventOut/field/exposedField declaration in the EXTERNPROTO is not a pure subset (names and types) of the eventIn/eventOut/field/exposedField declarations specified in the PROTO referred to by the URL. If multiple URLs are specified, the browser searches in the order of preference (see Section 2.1.3, URLs).

DESIGN NOTE

The syntax for EXTERNPROTO was carefully chosen so that VRML browsers can continue to parse the VRML file without fetching the EXTERNPROTO's definition. This was done for two reasons: First, because the Internet is not a reliable network, and broken or temporarily unavailable links are commonplace, and second, because it is important that VRML browsers be able to delay loading pieces of the world that are not yet needed. Interacting with a partially loaded world while the rest of the world is being sent across the network is an important usability feature.

VRML browsers need to know the field/event names and types for a node type before being able to parse node types that aren't part of the standard. Therefore, you must use a PROTO or EXTERNPROTO declaration before instantiating any new node type.

Several other file formats deal with the problem of new types by defining a syntax that allows them to be skipped during parsing by defining delimiting characters or writing a byte count as the first part of any type. However, the existence of SFNode/MFNode fields along with DEF/USE and ROUTE makes it difficult to use such a scheme with VRML. For example:

```
UnknownNode {
    children [ DEF T Transform { ... } ]
}
Group {
    children [ USE T ]
}
```

If a parser skipped everything inside the new **UnknownNode** type, then it would generate a syntax error when it later encountered the USE T statement in the **Group** node since the DEF T statement had been skipped. It would be possible to redesign the node reference mechanisms completely (by requiring all nodes be predefined and referred to via a table of contents structure, for example), but doing so would complicate VRML and make it significantly harder to use. Besides, declaring all of the events and fields for new node types is good style and makes it much easier to implement authoring systems that can deal with new node types.

Unlike a prototype, an external prototype does not contain an inline implementation of the node type. Instead, the prototype implementation is fetched from a URL. The other difference between a prototype and an external prototype is that external prototypes do not contain default values for fields. The external prototype references a file that contains the prototype implementation, and this file contains the field default values.

The external prototype's URL specifies valid VRML files in which the first PROTO statement (not EXTERNPROTO) found in the files is used to define the external prototype's definition. Note that **PrototypeName** does not need to match **Extern-PrototypeName**. The following example illustrates how an external prototype's declaration may be a subset of the prototype's declaration (*diffuse* vs. *diffuse* and *shiny*) and how the external prototype's typename may differ from the prototype's typename (e.g., FooBar !=SimpleMaterial):

`foo.wrl:`

```
#VRML V2.0 utf8
EXTERNPROTO FooBar [ eventIn SFColor diffuse ]
  "http://foo.com/NewMaterial.wrl"
FooBar {}
...
```

`http://foo.com/NewMaterial.wrl:`

```
#VRML V2.0 utf8
PROTO SimpleMaterial [
  exposedField SFColor diffuse 1 0 0
  eventIn      SFFloat shiny   0.5  ]
{
  Material {
    diffuseColor IS diffuse
    shininess IS shiny
  }
}
```

DESIGN NOTE

Allowing the user to give the EXTERNPROTO a different type name than the type name defined in the prototype definition file makes it possible always to compose together prototypes created by different people. For example, suppose you wanted to use two different prototypes both named **House,** but defined by different people (Helga and Jackie). The requirement that node type and prototype names be unique in any file would be a problem if EXTERNPROTO did not allow a renaming to occur. In this case, you could create the following file

```
# Reference to file containing PROTOHouse
EXTERNPROTO HelgaHouse [ ... ] "http://helga.net/House.wrl"
# Reference to file containing PROTO House
EXTERNPROTO JackieHouse [ ... ]  "http://jackie.net/House.wrl"
```

`http://helga.net/House.wrl:`

`PROTO House [...] { ... }  # Helga's def for a House proto`

`http://jackie.net/House.wrl:`

`PROTO House [...] { ... }  # Jackie's def for a House proto`

and then instantiate as many **HelgaHouses** and **JackieHouses** as you wish.

To allow the creation of libraries of small, reusable PROTO definitions, browsers shall recognize EXTERNPROTO URLs that end with "#name" to mean the prototype definition of "name" in the given file. For example, a library of standard materials might be stored in a file called materials.wrl that looks like the following:

```
#VRML V2.0 utf8
PROTO Gold   [] { Material { ... } }
PROTO Silver [] { Material { ... } }
...etc.
```

A **Material** from this library could be used as follows:

```
#VRML V2.0 utf8
EXTERNPROTO Gold [] "http://.../materials.wrl#Gold"
...
Shape {
  appearance Appearance { material Gold {} }
  geometry   ...
}
...
```

The advantage is that only one `http` fetch needs to be done if several things are used from the library; the disadvantage is that the entire library will be transmitted across the network even if only one prototype is used in the file.

TIP

Note that the file materials.wrl described here is a perfectly valid VRML file, but will not render anything if loaded into a browser directly. This is because the file contains only prototype statements and does not instantiate any nodes.

DESIGN NOTE

Even though you can put several PROTO definitions into one file, you can't "#include" that entire file and have all of the definitions available. You must have an EXTERNPROTO statement for each prototype you use. The reasons there is no "#include" feature for VRML are the same reasons that EXTERNPROTO requires you to declare the fields and events of the prototype—because it is assumed that VRML will be used on the Internet, where there are no guarantees that auxiliary files will be available. A C compiler can simply report an error and stop compilation if it can't find an include file. A VRML browser must be more robust; it shouldn't give up if some small part of a large world cannot be loaded.

2.7 Scripting

2.7.1 Introduction

Decision logic and state management is often needed to decide what effect an event should have on the scene: *"If the vault is currently closed* and *the correct combination is entered, then open the vault."* These kinds of decisions are expressed as **Script** nodes (see Chapter 3, Nodes Reference, Script) that receive events from other nodes, process them, and send events to other nodes. A Script node can also keep track of information between executions (i.e., manage internal state over time). This section describes the general mechanisms and semantics that all scripting languages must support. See the specific scripting language appendix for the syntax and details of any language (see Appendix C, Java Scripting Reference, and Appendix D, JavaScript Scripting Reference).

Event processing is done by a program or script contained in (or referenced by) the **Script** node's *url* field. This program or script can be written in any programming language that the browser supports. Browsers are not required to implement any specific scripting languages in VRML 2.0.

DESIGN NOTE

The lack of a *required* scripting language for VRML is a problem for content creators who want their content to run on all VRML browsers. Unfortunately, the VRML community was unable to reach consensus on a language to require. The leading candidates were Java, JavaScript (or possibly a subset of JavaScript), and both Java *and* JavaScript. The scripting language situation isn't completely chaotic, however. Appendix C, Java Scripting Reference, and Appendix D, JavaScript Scripting Reference, define the language integration specifications if a browser chooses to implement one of these two.

A **Script** node is activated when it receives an event. At that point the browser executes the program in the **Script** node's *url* field (passing the program to an external interpreter if necessary). The program can perform a wide variety of actions: sending out events (and thereby changing the scene), performing calculations, communicating with servers elsewhere on the Internet, and so on. See Section 2.4.3, Execution Model, for a detailed description of the ordering of event processing.

DESIGN NOTE

Scripts are also activated when the file is loaded (see Section 2.7.3, Initialize and Shutdown). Some scripting languages allow the creation of asynchronous threads of execution, allowing scripts to be continuously active (see Section 2.7.6, Asynchronous Scripts). But it is expected that most scripts will act as "glue" logic along routes and will be executed only when they receive events.

2.7.2 Script Execution

Script nodes allow the world author to insert logic into the middle of an event cascade (see Section 2.4.3, Execution Model). Scripts also allow the world author to generate events when a **Script** node is created or, in some scripting languages, at arbitrary times.

Script nodes receive events in time stamp order. Any events generated as a result of processing an event are given time stamps corresponding to the event that generated them. Conceptually, it takes no time for a **Script** node to receive and process an event, even though in practice it does take some amount of time to execute a script.

DESIGN NOTE

Creating **Script** nodes that take a long time to process events (e.g., half a second) is a bad idea, since one slow **Script** node might slow down the entire VRML browser. At the very least, slow scripts will cause browsers problems as they try to deal with events with out-of-date time stamps, since even if the script takes three seconds to process an event, the events it generates will have time stamps equal to the original event.

If you want a **Script** node to perform some lengthy calculation, it is best to use a language like Java that allows the creation of separate threads, and perform the lengthy calculation in a separate thread. The user will then be able to continue interacting with the world while the calculation is proceeding.

2.7.3 Initialize and Shutdown

The scripting language binding may define an `initialize()` method (or constructor). This method is called before any events are generated. Events generated by the `initialize()` method must have time stamps less than any other events that are generated by the **Script** node.

DESIGN NOTE

Note that the specification is fuzzy about exactly when `initialize()` is called. The only requirement is that it be called before the **Script** generates any events (which can happen only after either an event has been received or `initialize()` is called). However, implementations should call the `initialize()` method as soon as possible after the **Script** node is created. For example, you might write a script that has an `initialize()` method that starts a thread that establishes and listens to a connection to a server somewhere on the network. Such a **Script** might not generate any events until it receives a message from the server, so an implementation that never called its `initialize()` method in the first place would, technically, be compliant with the requirements of the VRML specification.

Requiring that the `initialize()` method be called "as soon as possible" may not be desirable, either. Implementations may have prefetching strategies that call for loading part of the world into memory but not initializing it until the user performs some action (e.g., walks through the teleportation device). In this case, browser implementors are trusted to make reasonable decisions.

TIP

It is sometimes useful to create **Scripts** that have *only* an `initialize()` method. This technique can be used to ensure that exposedFields along an event cascade route start out with reasonable values. The **Script** simply generates an initial event (with a value that might be specified as a field of the **Script,** for example) in its `initialize()` method. The same technique is also useful for generating geometry or textures at load time; transmitting code that generates nodes rather than specifying the nodes explicitly, can save lots of bandwidth.

DESIGN NOTE

If a **Script** has no eventIns and doesn't start up an asynchronous thread, then it can safely be deleted as soon as its `initialize()` method has been called. There is no way for such a **Script** to ever generate events after the `initialize()` method is finished.

Likewise, the scripting language binding may define a `shutdown()` method (or destructor). This method is called when the corresponding **Script** node is deleted or the world containing the **Script** node is unloaded or replaced by another world. This can be used as a cleanup operation, such as informing external mechanisms to remove temporary files.

DESIGN NOTE

Again, the specification doesn't precisely specify when `shutdown()` is called. Unless you are writing a script that starts separate threads, you probably won't need a `shutdown()` method.

2.7.4 EventsProcessed

The scripting language binding may also define an `eventsProcessed()` routine that is called after one or more events are received. It allows scripts that do not rely on the order of events received to generate fewer events than an equivalent script that generates events whenever events are received. If it is used in some other way, `eventsProcessed()` can be nondeterministic, since different implementations may call `eventsProcessed()` at different times.

For a single event cascade, a given **Script** node's `eventsProcessed()` routine must be called, at most, once. Events generated from an `eventsProcessed()` routine are given the time stamp of the last event processed.

DESIGN NOTE

Sophisticated implementations may determine that they can defer executing certain scripts, resulting in several events being sent to a script at once. The `events-Processed()` routine is an optimization that lets the script creator be more efficient in these cases. For example, if you create a simple **Script** that receives *set_a* and *set_b* events and generates *sum_changed* events where sum = a + b, it is more efficient to calculate the sum and generate the *sum_changed* event in an `eventsProcessed()` routine, after all *set_a* and *set_b* events have been received. The end result is the same as generating *sum_changed* events whenever a *set_a* or *set_b* event is received, but fewer events will be generated.

Of course, if it is important that events for *all* of the changes to sum are generated, `eventsProcessed()` should *not* be used. For example, you might create a script that recorded the time and value of each event it receives, which could be used to generate a history of the sum over time. Most of the time, however, only the most current result is of interest.

2.7.5 Scripts with Direct Outputs

Scripts that access other nodes (via SFNode or MFNode fields or eventIns) and that have their *directOutput* field set to TRUE may directly post eventIns to those nodes. They may also read the last value sent from any of the node's eventOuts.

When setting a value in another node, implementations are free either to set the value immediately or to defer setting the value until the script is finished. When getting a value from another node, the value returned must be up-to-date; that is, it must be the value immediately before the time of the current time stamp (the current time stamp is the time stamp of the event that caused the **Script** node to execute).

The order of execution of **Script** nodes that do not have routes between them is undefined. If multiple true **Scripts** with *directOutput* all read and/or write the same node, the results may be undefined. Just as with ROUTE fan-in, these cases are inherently nondeterministic and it is up to the world creator to ensure that these cases do not happen.

DESIGN NOTE

The *directOutput* field is a hint to the browser that the **Script** may directly read or write other nodes in the scene, instead of just receiving and sending events through its own eventIns and eventOuts. When *directOutput* is FALSE (the default), several optimizations are possible that cannot be safely performed if the **Script** might directly modify other nodes in the scene. If we assumed that browsers could examine the **Script**'s code and look at the calls it makes before execution, then this hint wouldn't be necessary. However, it is assumed that scripts are black boxes and browsers may **not** be able to examine their code. For example, Java byte code may be passed directly to a Java interpreter embedded in the computer's operating system, separate from the VRML browser.

If a **Script** node, with its *directOutput* set to FALSE, directly modifies other nodes, results are undefined. Browsers are not required to check for this case because it would slow down scripts that have set the field correctly (slowing down execution of the common case to test for a rare error condition would violate the design principle that VRML should be high performance). Errors due to incorrectly setting the *directOutput* flag are likely to be hard to find, since they will cause some browsers to make invalid assumptions about what optimizations they can perform and have no effect on other browsers that perform different optimizations.

Scripts that have their *directOutput* field set to TRUE can only read or write nodes to which they have access. There are four ways for scripts to get access to other nodes:

- Scripts with SFNode or MFNode fields have access to the nodes in those fields.
- Scripts with SFNode or MFNode eventIns have access to the nodes in those events.
- Scripts that create nodes using the `createVrmlFromString()` routine (see Section 2.7.10, Browser Script Interface) have access to the nodes they create.

- If a script has access to a node, and that node has SFNode or MFNode eventOuts, then the script has access to all of the nodes in those eventOuts. This means that if a **Script** node has access to a **Group** node, for example, it has access to (and may read or write to) any of the **Group**'s children.

Since browsers know whether or not a script might directly modify other nodes (from the *directOutput* field), and because browsers know which nodes scripts may access (from their fields, events received, etc.), they can determine which parts of the scene cannot possibly change. And, knowing that, browsers may decide to perform certain optimizations that are only worthwhile if the scene doesn't change. For example, a browser could decide to create texture map "imposters"—images of the object from a particular point of view that can be drawn less expensively than the object itself—for objects that cannot change. It is best to limit the number of nodes to which a script has access so that browsers have maximum opportunity for such optimizations.

Often the same task can be performed either using a ROUTE or by giving a script direct access to a node and setting its *directOutput* field to TRUE. In general, it is better to use a ROUTE, since the ROUTE gives the browser more information about what the script is doing and, therefore, gives the browser more potential optimizations.

2.7.6 Asynchronous Scripts

Some languages supported by a VRML browser may allow **Script** nodes to generate events spontaneously, allowing users to create **Script** nodes that function like new sensor nodes. In these cases, the **Script** is generating the initial event that causes the event cascade, and the scripting language and/or the browser will determine an appropriate time stamp for that initial event. Such events are then sorted into the event stream and processed like any other event, following all of the same rules for looping and so forth.

TIP

Java, for example, allows the creation of separate threads. Those threads can generate eventOuts at any time, essentially allowing the **Script** containing the Java code to function as a new, user-defined sensor node.

If you want to create scalable worlds, you should be careful when creating asynchronous threads. You can easily swamp any CPU by creating a lot of little scripts that are all constantly busy. Make each script as efficient as possible, and make each thread inactive (blocked and waiting for input from the network, for example) as much of the time as possible.

2.7.7 Script Languages

The **Script** node's *url* field may specify a URL that refers to a file (e.g., **http:**) or directly inlines scripting language code (e.g., **javabc:**). The MIME type of the returned data defines the language type. Additionally instructions can be included inline using either the **data:** protocol, which allows a MIME-type specification (see Section 2.1.4, Data Protocol), or a scripting language protocol (see Section 2.1.5, Scripting Language Protocols), defined for the specific language (in which the language type is inferred).

For example, the following **Script** node has one eventIn field named *start* and three different URL values specified in the *url* field: JavaScript, Java, and inline JavaScript:

```
Script {
  eventIn SFBool start
  url [ "http://foo.com/fooBar.class",
        "http://foo.com/fooBar.js",
        "javascript:function start(value, timestamp) { ... }" ]
}
```

In this example when a *start* eventIn is received by the **Script** node, one of the scripts found in the *url* field is executed. The Java code is the first choice, the Java-Script code is the second choice, and the inline JavaScript code the third choice (see Section 2.1.3, URLs, for a description of order of preference for multivalued URL fields).

DESIGN NOTE

An earlier design of the **Script** node had a *languageType* SFString field and a *script* SFString field that either contained or pointed to the script code. Using the same URL paradigm for the script code as is used for other media types that aren't part of VRML (images, movies, sounds) is a much better design and had several unexpected benefits:

- Scripts can be placed either inline (using the `data:`, `javabc:`, or `javascript:` protocols) or can be placed in separate files.

- The desire to put script code inline inside the VRML file led to investigation and the discovery of the `data:` protocol proposal (see Section 2.1.4, Data Protocol). That, in turn, allows *any* media type (images, sounds, movies, or script code) to be put inline in the VRML file—a feature that was often requested.

- All of the functionality of the MIME and URL standards can be used with script code (e.g., server-client content-type negotiation or automatic decompression of script code via the standard content-encoding mechanisms).

2.7.8 EventIn Handling

Events received by the **Script** node are passed to the appropriate scripting language function in the script. The function's name depends on the language type used. In some cases it is identical to the name of the eventIn, while in others it is a general callback function for all eventIns (see Appendix C, Java Scripting Reference, and Appendix D, JavaScript Scripting Reference, for details). The function is passed two arguments: the event value and the event time stamp.

DESIGN NOTE

Passing the event time stamp along with every event makes it easy for script authors to generate results that are consistent with VRML's ideal execution model. If time stamps were not easily available, then script authors that wished to schedule things relative to events (e.g., start animations or sounds two seconds after receiving an event) would be forced to schedule them relative to the time the script happened to be executed. That wouldn't be a problem for an ideal implementation that processed all events the instant they happened, but it could cause synchronization problems for real implementations, since two scripts triggered by the same event will be executed at slightly different times (ignoring multiprocessor implementations, which are possible and could execute scripts in parallel).

There is no way for a **Script** node to find out what nodes are sending it events, and no way for it to find out what nodes are receiving the events it generates (unless it is a *directOutput* **Script** that is directly sending events to nodes, of course). This was done to restrict the number of nodes to which a script potentially has access, allowing browsers more opportunities for optimization (refer back to Section 2.7.5, Scripts with Direct Outputs). Passing some sort of opaque node identifier with each event was also considered, and would have allowed scripts to do some interesting things with events that were fanned-in from several different nodes. However, that feature probably would not be used often enough to justify the cost of passing an extra parameter with every event.

2.7.9 Accessing Fields and Events

The fields, eventIns, and eventOuts of a **Script** node are accessible from scripting language functions. The **Script**'s eventIns can be routed to and its eventOuts can be routed from. Another **Script** node with a pointer to this node can access its eventIns and eventOuts just like any other node.

Accessing Fields and EventOuts of the Script

Fields defined in the **Script** node are available to the script through a language-specific mechanism (e.g., a member variable is automatically defined for each field and event of the **Script** node). The field values can be read or written and are persistent across function calls. EventOuts defined in the **Script** node can also be read—the value is the last value sent.

Accessing Fields and EventOuts of Other Nodes

The script can access any exposedField, eventIn, or eventOut of any node to which it has a pointer. The syntax of this mechanism is language dependent. The following example illustrates how a **Script** node accesses and modifies an exposedField of another node (i.e., sends a *set_translation* eventIn to the **Transform** node) using a fictitious scripting language:

```
DEF SomeNode Transform { }
Script {
  field    SFNode   tnode USE SomeNode
  eventIn SFVec3f pos
  directOutput TRUE
  url "javascript:
    function pos(value, timestamp) {
      tnode.set_translation = value;
    }"
}
```

DESIGN NOTE

If the **Script** accesses the eventIns or eventOuts of other nodes, then it must have its *directOutput* field set to TRUE, as previously described in Section 2.7.5, Scripts with Direct Outputs.

EventIns of other nodes are write-only; the only operation a *directOutput* **Script** may perform on such eventIns is sending them an event. Note that this is exactly the opposite of the **Script** node's own eventIns, which are read-only—the **Script** can just read the value and time stamp for events it receives.

EventOuts of other nodes are read-only; the only operation a *directOutput* **Script** may perform on them is reading the last value they generated (see Chapter 4, Fields and Events, for the definition of the initial value of eventOuts before they have generated any events). A **Script**'s own eventOuts, on the other hand, can be both read and written by the script.

Fields of other nodes are completely opaque and private to the node. A **Script** may read and write its own fields as it pleases, of course. If fields were not private to the nodes that owned them it would be quite difficult to write a robust **Script** node, since other nodes could possibly change the **Script**'s fields at any time.

ExposedFields of other nodes are just an eventIn, an eventOut, and a field. The eventIn may be written to by a *directOutput* **Script,** and the eventOut may be read, giving complete read/write access to the field.

Sending EventOuts

Each scripting language provides a mechanism for allowing scripts to send a value through an eventOut defined by the **Script** node. For example, one scripting language may define an explicit function for sending each eventOut, while another language may use assignment statements to automatically defined eventOut variables to send the eventOut implicitly. The results of sending multiple values through an eventOut during a single script execution are undefined; it may result in multiple eventOuts with the same time stamp or a single eventOut with the value of the last assigned value.

DESIGN NOTE

The specification should be more precise here. To avoid potential problems, you should not write scripts that generate events from the same eventOut that have the same time stamp. And browser implementors should create **Script** node implementations that send out only the "last" eventOut with a given time stamp, assuming that the scripting language being used has a well-defined execution order (which may not be true if languages that support implicit parallelism are ever used with VRML).

2.7.10 Browser Script Interface

The browser interface provides a mechanism for scripts contained by **Script** nodes to get and set browser state, such as the URL of the current world. This section describes the semantics of functions/methods that the browser interface supports. A C-like syntax is used to define the type of parameters and returned values, but is hypothetical. See the specific appendix for a language for the actual syntax required. In this hypothetical syntax, types are given as VRML field types. Mapping of these types into those of the underlying language (as well as any type conversion needed) is described in the appropriate language reference.

```
SFString getName( );
SFString getVersion( );
```

The `getName()` and `getVersion()` methods get the name and version of the browser currently in use. These values are defined by the browser writer and identify the browser in some unspecified way. They are not guaranteed to be unique or to adhere to any particular format, and are for information only. If the information is unavailable, these methods return empty strings.

```
SFFloat getCurrentSpeed( );
```

The `getCurrentSpeed()` method returns the speed, in meters per second, at which the currently bound viewpoint is moving relative to the viewpoint's coordinate system. If speed of motion is not meaningful in the current navigation type, or if the speed cannot be determined for some other reason, 0.0 is returned.

SFFloat getCurrentFrameRate( );

The getCurrentFrameRate() method returns the current frame rate in frames per second. The way in which this is measured and whether or not it is supported at all is browser dependent. If the frame rate is not supported, or can't be determined, 0.0 is returned.

SFString getWorldURL( );

The getWorldURL() method returns the URL for the root of the currently loaded world.

void replaceWorld(MFNode nodes);

The replaceWorld() method replaces the current world with the world represented by the passed nodes. This will usually not return, since the world containing the running script is being replaced.

void loadURL(MFString url, MFString parameter);

The loadURL() method loads the URL with the passed parameters. A parameter is as described in the **Anchor** node. This method returns immediately, but if the URL is loaded into this browser window (e.g., there is no target parameter to redirect it to another frame), the current world will be terminated and replaced with the data from the new URL at some time in the future.

void setDescription(SFString description);

The setDescription() method sets the passed string as the current description. This message is displayed in a browser-dependent manner. To clear the current description, send an empty string.

MFNode createVrmlFromString(SFString vrmlSyntax);

The createVrmlFromString() method takes a string consisting of a VRML world description, parses the nodes contained therein, and returns the root nodes of the corresponding world. The string must contain valid, complete, and self-contained VRML syntax (see Section 2.1, File Syntax and Structure), but it does not contain a VRML header.

void createVrmlFromURL(MFString url, SFNode node,
                        SFString event);

The createVrmlFromURL() instructs the browser to load a VRML scene description from the given URL or URLs. After the scene is loaded, event is sent to the passed node returning the root nodes of the corresponding world. The URL refers to a file that contains valid, complete, and self-contained VRML syntax (see Section 2.1, File Syntax and Structure).

```
void addRoute( SFNode fromNode, SFString fromEventOut,
            SFNode toNode, SFString toEventIn );
void deleteRoute( SFNode fromNode, SFString fromEventOut,
            SFNode toNode, SFString toEventIn );
```

These methods respectively add and delete a route between the given event names for the given nodes.

DESIGN NOTE

The composability and scalability design goals put severe restrictions on the **Script** node browser interface API. For example, a call that returned the root nodes of the world was considered and rejected because it would allow a script unrestricted access to almost all of the nodes in the world, severely limiting a browser's ability to reason about what might and might not be changing. Many features that were initially part of the API were moved into nodes in the scene, because doing so made the design much more composable and consistent.

The functions that are left are very general and quite powerful. Several of the standard nodes in the VRML specification could be implemented via prototypes that used these API calls. For example, the **Anchor** node could be implemented as a **Group,** a **Touch-Sensor,** and a **Script** that made `loadURL()` and `setDescription()` calls at the appropriate times, and an **Inline** could be implemented as a **Group** and a **Script** that called `createVrmlFromURL(url, group, "set_children")` in its `initialize()` method.

2.8 Browser Extensions

2.8.1 Creating Extensions

Browsers that wish to add functionality beyond the capabilities in the specification should do so by creating prototypes or external prototypes. If the new node cannot be expressed using the prototyping mechanism (i.e., it cannot be expressed as VRML scene graph), then it should be defined as an external prototype with a unique URN specification (see Section 2.1.7, Uniform Resource Names [URNs]). Authors who use the extended functionality may provide multiple, alternative URLs or URNs to represent the content to ensure that it is viewable on all browsers.

For example, suppose a browser wants to create a native **Torus** geometry node implementation:

```
EXTERNPROTO Torus [ field SFFloat bigR, field SFFloat smallR ]
[
   "urn:inet:foo.com:library:Torus",
   "http://.../proto_torus.wrl"
]
```

This browser will recognize the URN and use its own private implementation of the **Torus** node. Other browsers may not recognize the URN, and will skip to the next entry in the URL list and search for the specified prototype file. If no URLs or URNs are found, the **Torus** is assumed to be an empty node.

Note that the prototype name **Torus**, in this example, has no meaning whatsoever. The URL uniquely and precisely defines the name and location of the node implementation. The prototype name is strictly a convention chosen by the author and shall not be interpreted in any semantic manner. The following example uses both **Ring** and **Donut** to name the **Torus** node, but the following URL specifies the actual definition of the **Torus** node: `"urn:inet:foo.com:library:Torus, http://.../proto_torus.wrl"`

```
#VRML V2.0 utf8
EXTERNPROTO Ring [field SFFloat bigR, field SFFloat smallR ]
   ["urn:inet:foo.com:library:Torus", "http://.../proto_torus.wrl"]
EXTERNPROTO Donut [field SFFloat bigR, field SFFloat smallR ]
   ["urn:inet:foo.com:library:Torus", "http://.../proto_torus.wrl"]
Transform { ... children Shape { geometry Ring {} } }
Transform { ... children Shape { geometry Donut {} } }
```

2.8.2 Reading Extensions

VRML-compliant browsers must recognize and implement the PROTO and EXTERNPROTO specifications. Note that the prototype names (e.g., **Torus**) have no semantic meaning whatsoever. Rather, the URL uniquely determines the location and semantics of the node. Browsers shall not use the PROTO or EXTERNPROTO name to imply anything about the implementation of the node.

DESIGN NOTE

Implementing built-in extensions this way has several big advantages over just "magically" recognizing a prototype node type name:

1. The URN standard defines a global namespace, eliminating potential naming conflicts. Once the URN standard is widely adopted, there will be an infrastructure supporting the global namespace, and features such as transparent replication of commonly used objects and extensions across the Internet will be possible with no changes to the VRML file format.

2. The EXTERNPROTO mechanism allows a name remapping to occur, allowing the long, globally unique URN names to be given shorter names. Conflicts between the short names are easy to avoid, because the names are under the control of the VRML file creator.

2.9 Node Concepts

2.9.1 Bindable Children Nodes

The **Background, Fog, NavigationInfo,** and **Viewpoint** nodes have the unique behavior that only one of each type can be active (i.e., affecting the user's experience) at any point in time. The browser shall maintain a stack for each type of binding node. Each of these nodes includes a *set_bind* eventIn and an *isBound* eventOut. The *set_bind* eventIn is used to move a given node to and from its respective top of a stack. A TRUE value sent to the *set_bind* eventIn moves the node to the top of the stack and a FALSE value removes it from the stack. The *isBound* eventOut is output when a given node is moved to the top of the stack, removed from the stack, or is pushed down in the stack by another node being placed on top. That is, the *isBound* event is sent when a given node ceases to be the active node. The node at the top of stack (i.e., the most recently bound node) is the active node for its type and is used by the browser to set world state. If the stack is empty (i.e., either the file has no binding nodes for a given type or the stack has been popped until empty), then the default field values for that node type are used to set world state. The results are undefined if a multi-instanced (DEF/USE) binding node is bound.

Note that the binding state of a bindable node is not affected by the scene graph state. Therefore, binding nodes are not affected by the state of a **Switch** or **LOD** node.

TIP

In general, you should avoid creating multiple instances of bindable nodes (i.e., don't USE bindable nodes). Results are undefined for multi-instanced bindable nodes because the effects of binding a **Background, Fog,** or **Viewpoint** node depend on the coordinate space in which it is located. If it is multi-instanced, then it (probably) exists in multiple coordinate systems. For example, consider a **Viewpoint** node that is multi-instanced. The first instance (DEF VIEW) specifies it at the origin and the second instance (USE VIEW) translates it to (10,10,10):

```
# Create 1st instance
DEF VIEW Viewpoint { position 0 0 0 }
Transform {
  translation 10 10 10
  children USE VIEW  # creates 2nd instance
}
```

Binding to VIEW is ambiguous since it implies that the user should view the world from two places at once (0 0 0) and (10 10 10). Therefore the results are undefined and browsers are free to do nothing, pick the first instance, pick the closest instance, or even split the window in half and show the user both views. In any case, avoid USE-ing bindable nodes.

Since USE-ing any of a bindable node's parents will also result in the bindable node being in two places at once, you should avoid doing that also. For example:

```
Group { children [
  Transform {
    translation -5 -5 -5
    children DEF G Group {
      children [
        DEF VIEW Viewpoint { }
        Shape { geometry ... etc... }
      ]
    }
  }
  Transform { translation 3 4 0
    children USE G   # Bad, VIEW is now multiply instanced
  }
]}
```

This results in the VIEW **Viewpoint** being at two places at once ((-5,-5,-5) and (3,4,0)). If you send a *set_bind* event to VIEW, results are undefined. Nothing above a bindable node should be USE'd.

So, what if you do want to create a reusable piece of the scene with viewpoints inside it? Instead of using USE, you should use the PROTO mechanism, because a PROTO creates a copy of everything inside it:

```
PROTO G [ eventIn SFBool bind_to_viewpoint ]
{
  Group { children [
    DEF VIEW Viewpoint { set_bind IS bind_to_viewpoint }
    Shape { geometry ... etc ... }
  ]}
}
```

```
Group { children [
  Transform {
    translation -5 -5 -5
    children DEF G1 G { }
  }
  Transform { translation 3 4 0
    children DEF G2 G { }  # No problem, create 2nd Viewpoint
  }
]}
```

You can use either **Viewpoint** by sending either G1 or G2 a *bind_to_viewpoint* event. Smart browser implementations will notice that the geometry for both G1 and G2 is exactly the same and can never change, allowing them to share the same geometry between both G1 and G2, and making the PROTO version extremely efficient.

The bind stack behaves as follows:

1. During read

    - the first-encountered *<binding node>* is bound by pushing it to the top of the *<binding node>* stack

       - Nodes contained within **Inline** nodes are not candidates for the first-encountered *<binding node>*.

       - The first node within a prototype is valid as the first-encountered *<binding node>*.

    - the first-encountered node sends an *isBound* TRUE event

2. When a *set_bind* TRUE eventIn is received by a *<binding node>*

    - if it is not on the top of the stack

       - the existing top-of-stack node sends an *isBound* FALSE eventOut

       - the new node is moved to the top of the stack (i.e., there is only one entry in the stack for any node at any time) and becomes the currently bound *<binding node>*

       - the new top-of-stack node sends an *isBound* TRUE eventOut

    - else if the node is already at the top of the stack, then this event has no effect (and no *isBound* event is sent)

3. When a *set_bind* FALSE eventIn is received by a *<binding node>*

    - it is removed from the stack

- if it is on the top of the stack

    - it sends an *isBound* FALSE eventOut

    - the next node in the stack becomes the currently bound *<binding node>* (i.e., pop) and issues an *isBound* TRUE eventOut

4. If a *set_bind* FALSE eventIn is received by a node not in the stack, the event is ignored and *isBound* events are not sent.

5. When a node replaces another node at the top of the stack, the *isBound* TRUE and FALSE eventOuts from the two nodes are sent simultaneously (i.e., identical time stamps).

6. If a bound node is deleted, then it behaves as if it received a *set_bind* FALSE event (see #3).

TIP

The binding stack semantics were designed to make it easy to create composable worlds—worlds that can be included in larger *metaworlds*. As an example, imagine that you've created a model of a planet, complete with buildings, scenery, and a transportation system that uses **TouchSensors** and animated **Viewpoints** so that it is easy to get from place to place. Someone else might like to use your planet as part of a solar system he is building, animating the position and orientation of the planet to make it spin around the sun. To make it easy to go from a tour of the solar system to your planetary tour, they can place an entry viewpoint on the surface of your planet.

The binding stack becomes useful when the viewer travels to (binds to) the entry viewpoint and then travels around the planet binding and unbinding from your viewpoints. If there was no binding stack, then when the viewer was unbound from one of the planet's viewpoints they would no longer move with the planet around the sun, and would suddenly find themselves watching the planet travel off into space. Instead, the entry viewpoint will remain in the binding stack, keeping the user in the planet's coordinate system until he decides to continue the interplanetary tour.

The binding stacks keep track of where the user is in the scene graph hierarchy, making it easy to create worlds within worlds. If you have several bindable nodes that are at the same level in the scene hierarchy, you will probably want to manage them as a group, unbinding the previous node (if any) when another is bound. In the solar system example, the solar system creator might put a teleport station on the surface of each world, with a list of planetary destinations. The teleport station would consist of the entry viewpoint and a signpost that would trigger a script to unbind the user from this planet's viewpoint and bind him to the new planet's entry viewpoint (and, perhaps, start up teleportation animations or sounds). All of the entry viewpoints are siblings in the scene graph hierarchy and each should be unbound before binding to the next.

If you want your worlds to be usable as part of a larger metaworld, you should make sure each bindable node has a well-defined scope (in either space or time) during which it will be bound. For example, although you could create a **TimeSensor** that constantly sent *set_bind* TRUE events to a bindable node, doing so will result in a world that won't work well with other worlds.

2.9.2 Geometry

Geometry nodes must be contained by a **Shape** node in order to be visible to the user. The **Shape** node contains exactly one geometry node in its *geometry* field. This node must be one of the following node types:

- Box
- Cone
- Cylinder
- ElevationGrid
- Extrusion
- IndexedFaceSet
- IndexedLineSet
- PointSet
- Sphere
- Text

These property nodes are separated out as individual nodes so that instancing and sharing is possible between different geometry nodes. All geometry nodes are specified in a local coordinate system and are affected by parent transformations.

DESIGN NOTE

Putting the geometric properties in separate nodes, instead of just giving the geometry or **Shape** nodes more fields, will also make it easier to extend VRML in the future. For example, supporting new material properties such as index of refraction requires only the specification of a new type of **Material** node, instead of requiring the addition of a new field to every geometry node. The texture nodes that are part of the specification are another good example of why making properties separate nodes is a good idea. Any of the three texture node types (**ImageTexture, PixelTexture,** or **MovieTexture**) can be used with any of the geometry nodes.

Separating out the properties into different nodes makes VRML files a little bigger and makes them harder to create using a text editor. The prototyping mechanism can be used to create new node types that don't allow properties to be shared, but reduce file size. For example, if you want to make it easy to create cubes at different positions with different colors you might define

```
PROTO ColoredCube [ field SFVec3f position 0 0 0
                    field SFColor color 1 1 1 ]
{
  Transform { translation IS position
    children Shape {
      geometry Cube { }
      appearance Appearance {
        material Material { diffuseColor IS color }
      }
    }
  }
}
```

which might be used like this:

```
Group { children [
  ColoredCube { color 1 0 0  position 1.3  4.97 0 }
  ColoredCube { color 0 1 0  position 0 -6.8  3 }
]}
```

Using the PROTO mechanism to implement application-specific compression can result in very small VRML files, but does make it more difficult to edit in general-purpose, graphical VRML tools.

Application of Material, Texture, and Colors

See Section 2.9.6, Lighting Model, for details on how material, texture, and color specifications interact.

Shape Hints Fields

The **ElevationGrid, Extrusion,** and **IndexedFaceSet** nodes each have three SFBool fields that provide hints about the shape—whether it contains ordered vertices, whether the shape is solid, and whether it contains convex faces. These fields are *ccw, solid,* and *convex.*

The *ccw* field indicates the orientation of the default normals (used for backface culling and default normal calcuation). Each **Shape** node interprets this field uniquely. The *solid* field indicates whether the geometry represents a completely enclosed volume (TRUE), and can be used as a hint to perform backface culling: If the angle between a unit vector from the eye (transformed into the local coordinate system of the geometry) to the center of the polygon and a unit normal vector computed for the polygon (using the *ccw* field to determine direction) is less than

90 degrees, the polygon may be backface culled. If *solid* is FALSE (i.e., polygons are to be treated as two-sided surfaces), backface culling cannot be performed. The *convex* field indicates whether all faces in the shape are convex (TRUE). If *convex* is FALSE, browsers must assume that all faces of that geometry are concave.

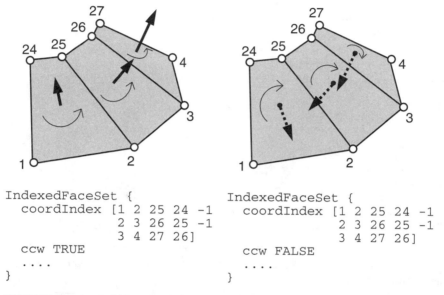

```
IndexedFaceSet {                    IndexedFaceSet {
    coordIndex [1 2 25 24 -1           coordIndex [1 2 25 24 -1
               2 3 26 25 -1                       2 3 26 25 -1
               3 4 27 26]                         3 4 27 26]
    ccw TRUE                            ccw FALSE
    ....                                ....
}                                   }
```

FIGURE 2-4 *ccw Field*

These hints allow VRML implementations to optimize certain rendering features. Optimizations that may be performed include enabling backface culling and disabling two-sided lighting. For example, if an object is solid and has ordered vertices, an implementation may turn on backface culling and turn off two-sided lighting. If the object is not solid but has ordered vertices, it may turn off backface culling and turn on two-sided lighting.

TIP

> It is recommended that you avoid creating nonplanar polygons, even though it is legal within VRML. Since the VRML specification does not specify a triangulation scheme, each browser may triangulate differently. This is especially important when creating objects with a low number of polygons; the triangulation is more apparent. One way to avoid this issue is to generate triangles rather than polygons.

TIP

> Default field values throughout VRML were chosen to optimize for rendering speed. You should try to create objects that adhere to the following defaults: *solid* TRUE, *convex* TRUE, and *ccw* TRUE. You should be especially careful if you provide normals for your objects that the orientation of the normals match the setting of the *ccw* field; getting this wrong can result in completely black surfaces in some renderers.

DESIGN NOTE

It might be simpler if VRML simply had *backface* and *twoSide* flags to control polygon backface removal and two-sided lighting (although another flag to indicate the orientation of polygons would still be needed). However, the hints chosen allow implementations to perform these common optimizations without tying the VRML specification to any particular rendering technique. Backface removal, for example, should not be done if using a renderer that can display reflections.

creaseAngle Field

The *creaseAngle* field, used by the **ElevationGrid**, **Extrusion**, and **IndexedFaceSet** nodes, affects how default normals are generated. For example, when an **IndexedFaceSet** has to generate default normals, it uses the *creaseAngle* field to determine which edges should be smoothly shaded and which ones should have a sharp crease. The crease angle is the positive angle between surface normals on adjacent polygons. For example, a crease angle of 0.5 radians means that an edge between two adjacent polygonal faces will be smoothly shaded if the normals to the two faces form an angle that is less than 0.5 radians (about 30 degrees). Otherwise, it will be faceted. Crease angles must be greater than or equal to 0.0.

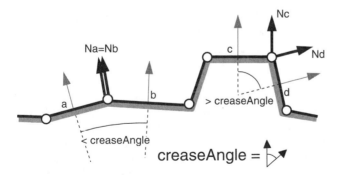

FIGURE 2-5 creaseAngle *Field*

DESIGN NOTE

Specifying a single crease angle for each of your shapes instead of specifying individual normals at each of its vertices is a great bandwidth-saving technique. For almost every shape there is an appropriate crease angle that will produce smooth surfaces and sharp creases in the appropriate places.

DESIGN NOTE

An almost infinite number of geometry nodes could have been added to VRML 2.0. It was not easy to decide what should be included and what should be excluded, and additions were kept to a minimum because an abundance of geometry types makes it more difficult to write tools that deal with VRML files. A new geometry was likely to be included if it

1. Is much smaller than the equivalent **IndexedFaceSet.** The Open Inventor **IndexedTriangleStripSet** primitive was considered and rejected, because it was only (on average) one and one-half to two times smaller than the equivalent **IndexedFaceSet. ElevationGrids** and **Extrusions** are typically more than four times smaller than the equivalent **IndexedFaceSet.**

2. Is reasonably easy to implement. Computational Solid Geometry (CSG) and trimmed Non-Uniform Rational B-Splines (NURBS) were often-requested features that pass the "much smaller" criteria, but are very difficult to implement robustly.

3. Is used in a large percentage of VRML worlds. Any number of additional primitive shapes—**Torus, TruncatedCylinder, Teapot**—could have been added as a VRML primitive, but none of them are used often enough (outside of computer graphics research literature) to justify their inclusion in the standard. In fact, the designers of VRML felt that the **Sphere, Cone, Cylinder** and **Box** primitives would not satisfy this criteria, either; they are part of VRML 2.0 only because they were part of VRML 1.0, and it is very difficult to remove any feature once a product or specification is widely used.

2.9.3 Interpolators

Interpolator nodes are designed for linear keyframe animation. That is, an interpolator node defines a piecewise linear function, $f(t)$, on the interval (*−infinity, infinity*). The piecewise linear function is defined by n values of t, called *key,* and the n corresponding values of $f(t)$, called *keyValue.* The keys must be monotonic nondecreasing and are not restricted to any interval. An interpolator node evaluates $f(t)$ given any value of t (via the *set_fraction* eventIn).

TIP

In other words, interpolators are used to perform keyframe animations. You specify a list of keyframe values and times, and the VRML browser will automatically interpolate the "in-betweens." VRML allows only linear interpolation; it does not support spline curve interpolation, which can be found in most commerical animation systems. This limitation was made in order to keep VRML implementations small, fast, and simple. Note that it is possible for authoring systems to use sophisticated spline curves during authoring, but publish the resulting VRML file using the linear interpolators (thus getting the best of both worlds). You may find that it is necessary to specify a lot of keyframes to produce smooth or complex animations.

Note that there are several different types of interpolators; each one animates a different field type. For example, the **PositionInterpolator** is used to animate an object's position (i.e., **Transform** node's *translation* field) along a motion path (defined by *keyValue*). To produce typical animated object motion, you can employ both a **PositionInterpolator** and an **OrientationInterpolator**. The **PositionInterpolator** moves the object along a motion path, while the **OrientationInterpolator** rotates the object as it moves.

TIP

Remember that **TimeSensor** outputs *fraction_changed* events in the 0.0 to 1.0 range, and that interpolator nodes routed *from* **TimeSensors** should restrict their *key* field values to the 0.0 to 1.0 range to match the **TimeSensor** output and thus produce a full interpolation sequence.

Let the n keys $k_0, k_1, k_2, \ldots, k_{n-1}$ partition the domain $(-\infty, \infty)$ into the $n + 1$ subintervals given by $(-\infty, k_0), [k_0, k_1), [k_1, k_2), \ldots, [k_{n-1}, \infty)$. Also, let the n values $v_0, v_1, v_2, \ldots, v_{n-1}$ be the values of an unknown function, $F(t)$, at the associated key values. That is, $v_j = F(k_j)$. The piecewise linear interpolating function, $f(t)$, is defined to be

$$f(t) = v_0, \qquad \qquad \text{if } t < k_0$$

$$= v_{n-1}, \qquad \qquad \text{if } t > k_{n-1}$$

$$= v_i, \qquad \qquad \text{if } t = k_i \text{ for some value of i, where } -1 < i < n$$

$$= \text{linterp}(t, v_j, v_{j+1}), \quad \text{if } k_j < t < k_{j+1}$$

where linterp (t, x, y) is the linear interpolant and $-1 < j < n - 1$.

The third conditional value of $f(t)$ allows the defining of multiple values for a single key; in other words, limits from both the left and right at a discontinuity in $f(t)$. The

first specified value will be used as the limit of *f(t)* from the left, and the last specified value will be used as the limit of *f(t)* from the right. The value of *f(t)* at a multi-
defined key is indeterminate, but should be one of the associated limit values.

There are six different types of interpolator nodes, each based on the type of value
that is interpolated:

- ColorInterpolator
- CoordinateInterpolator
- NormalInterpolator
- OrientationInterpolator
- PositionInterpolator
- ScalarInterpolator

All interpolator nodes share a common set of fields and semantics:

```
exposedField MFFloat        key          [...]
exposedField MF<type>       keyValue     [...]
eventIn       SFFloat        set_fraction
eventOut      [S|M]F<type>  value_changed
```

The type of the *keyValue* field is dependent on the type of the interpolator (e.g., the
ColorInterpolator's *keyValue* field is of type MFColor). Each value in the *keyValue*
field corresponds in order to a parameter value in the *key* field. Therefore, there
exists exactly the same number of values in the *keyValue* field as key values in the
key field.

DESIGN NOTE

Creating new field types that are more convenient for animation keyframes was considered. This led to thinking about a syntax to create arbitrary new field types. For example, the keyframes for a **PositionInterpolator** could be defined as M[SFFloat,SFVec3f]
(any number of pairs consisting of a float and a vec3f). An SFVec3f might be defined
as [SFFloat, SFFloat, SFFloat]. However, creating an entire data type description language to solve what is only a minor annoyance would have had major ramifications on
the rest of VRML and was judged to be gratuitous engineering.

The *set_fraction* eventIn receives a SFFloat event and causes the interpolator function to evaluate. The results of the linear interpolation are sent to the *value_changed*
eventOut.

DESIGN NOTE

Restricting interpolators to do linear interpolation was controversial, because using curves to do motion interpolation is common. However, there was no single, obvious choice for a curve representation and it seemed unlikely that a technical discussion would be able to resolve the inevitable debate over which curve representation is best. Because simple linear interpolation would be needed even if nonlinear interpolation was part of the specification, and because any nonlinear interpolation can be linearly approximated with arbitrary precision, only linear interpolators made it into the VRML 2.0 specification.

If you are faced with the task of translating an animation curve into VRML's linear interpolators, you have three choices. You can choose a temporal resolution and tessellate the curve into a linear approximation, balancing the quality of the approximation against the size of the resulting file. Better yet, give the user control over the quality versus size trade-off.

Or you can write a script that performs this tessellation when the VRML file is read, put it into an appropriate prototype (which will contain an empty interpolator and the script, with an `initialize()` method that fills in the fields of the interpolator based on the curve's parameters), and write out the curve representation directly into the VRML file (as fields of prototype instances). Bandwidth requirements will be much smaller since the PROTO definition only needs to be sent once and the untessellated curve parameters will be much smaller than the linear approximation. Animations implemented this way may still require significant memory resources, however, since the tessellation is performed at start-up and stored in memory.

You can also write a script that directly implements the mathematics of the curve interpolation, and put that into a prototype. In fact, all of the linear interpolators defined as part of the VRML standard can be implemented as prototyped **Script** nodes. The reason they are part of the standard is to allow implementations to create highly optimized interpolators, since they are very common. Therefore, if you want your animations to be executed as quickly as possible, you should tessellate the animation curve (preferably after it has been downloaded, as described in the previous paragraph) and put the result in an interpolator. However, if you want to minimize memory use or maximize the quality of the animation, you should write a script that takes in *set_fraction* events and computes appropriate *value_changed* events directly.

Four of the six interpolators output a single-value field to *value_changed*. The exceptions, **CoordinateInterpolator** and **NormalInterpolator,** send multivalue results to *value_changed*. In this case, the *keyValue* field is an $n \times m$ array of values, where n is the number of keys and m is the number of values per key. It is an error if m is not a positive integer value.

The following example illustrates a simple **ScalarInterpolator** that contains a list of float values (`11.0`, `99.0`, `33.0`) and the keyframe times (`0.0`, `5.0`, `10.0`), and outputs a single float value for any given time:

```
ScalarInterpolator {
  key [ 0.0,  5.0,  10.0]
  value [11.0, 99.0, 33.0]
}
```

For an input of `2.5` (via *set_fraction*), this **ScalarInterpolator** would send an output value of

```
eventOut SFFloat value_changed 55.0 # = 11. + ((99.-11)/(5.-0.)) x 2.5
```

whereas the following **CoordinateInterpolator** defines an array of coordinates for each keyframe value and sends an array of coordinates as output:

```
CoordinateInterpolator {
  key   [ 0.0,  0.5,  1.0]
  value [ 0  0  0, 10 10 30,  # 2 values @ key 0.0
         10 20 10, 40 50 50,  # key 0.5
         33 55 66, 44 55 65 ] # key 1.0
}
```

In this case, there are two coordinates for every keyframe. The first two coordinates (`0`, `0`, `0`) and (`10`, `10`, `30`) represent the value at keyframe 0.0, the second two coordinates (`10`, `20`, `10`) and (`40`, `50`, `50`) represent that value at keyframe 0.5, and so on. If a *set_fraction* value of 0.25 (meaning 25% of the animation) was sent to this **CoordinateInterpolator,** the resulting output value would be

```
eventOut MFVec3f value_changed [ 5 10 5, 25 30 40 ]
```

If an interpolator node's value eventOut is read (e.g., *get_value*) before it receives any inputs, then *keyValue*[0] is returned.

The location of an interpolator node in the scene graph has no affect on its operation. For example, if a parent of an interpolator node is a **Switch** node with *whichChoice* set to −1 (i.e., ignore its children), the interpolator continues to operate as specified (receives and sends events).

TIP

> The spatial hierarchy of grouping nodes in the scene graph has nothing to do with the logical hierarchy formed by ROUTE statements. Interpolator (and **Script**) nodes have no particular location in the virtual world, so their position in the spatial hierarchy is irrelevant. You can make them the child of whichever grouping node is convenient or put them all at the end of your VRML file just before all the ROUTE statements.

2.9.4 Light Sources

In general, **Shape** nodes are illuminated by the sum of all of the lights in the world that affect them. This includes the contribution of both direct and ambient illumination from light sources. Ambient illumination models the scattering and reflection of light originally emitted directly by light sources. The amount of ambient light is associated with the individual lights in the scene. This is a gross approximation as to how ambient reflection actually occurs in nature.

DESIGN NOTE

The VRML lighting model is a gross approximation of how lighting actually occurs in nature. It is a compromise between speed and accuracy, with more emphasis put on speed. A more physically accurate lighting model would require extra lighting calculations and result in slower rendering. VRML's lighting model is similar to those used by current computer graphics software and hardware.

There are three types of light source nodes:

- **DirectionalLight**
- **PointLight**
- **SpotLight**

All light source nodes contain an *intensity,* a *color,* and an *ambientIntensity* field. The *intensity* field specifies the brightness of the direct emission from the light; the *ambientIntensity* field specifies the intensity of the ambient emission from the light. Light intensity may range from 0.0 (no light emission) to 1.0 (full intensity). The *color* field specifies the spectral color properties of the light emission as an RGB value in the 0.0 to 1.0 range.

DESIGN NOTE

The *intensity* field is really a convenience; adjusting the RGB values in the *color* field appropriately is equivalent to changing the intensity of the light. Or, in other words, the light emitted by a light source is equal to *intensity* × *color.* Similarly, setting the *on* field to FALSE is equivalent to setting the *intensity* and *ambientIntensity* fields to zero.

Some photorealistic rendering systems allow *light sinks*—light sources with a negative intensity. They also sometimes support intensities of greater than 1.0. Interactive rendering libraries typically don't support those features, and since VRML is designed for interactive playback the specification only defines results for values in the 0.0 to 1.0 range.

PointLight and **SpotLight** illuminate all objects in the world that fall within their volume of lighting influence regardless of location within the file. **PointLight** defines this volume of influence as a sphere centered at the light (defined by a radius). **SpotLight** defines the volume of influence as a solid angle defined by a radius and a cutoff angle. **DirectionalLight** illuminates only the objects descended from the light's parent grouping node (including any descendant children of the parent group node).

DESIGN NOTE

A good light source specification is difficult to design. There are two primary problems: first, how to scope light sources so that the "infinitely scalable" property of VRML is maintained and second, how to specify both the light's coordinate system and the objects that it illuminates.

If light sources are not scoped in some way, then a VRML world that contains a lot of light sources requires that all of the light sources be taken into account when drawing any part of the world. By scoping light sources, only a subset of the lights in the world ever need to be considered, allowing worlds to grow arbitrarily large.

For **PointLight** and **SpotLight,** the scoping problem is addressed by giving them a radius of effect. Nothing outside of the radius is affected by the light. Implementors will be forced to approximate this ideal behavior, because current interactive rendering libraries typically only support light attenuation and do not support a fixed radius beyond which no light falls. Content creators should choose attenuation constants such that the intensity of a light source is very close to zero at the cutoff radius (or, alternatively, choose a cutoff radius based on the attenuation constants).

A directional light sends parallel rays of light from a particular direction. Attenuation makes no sense for a directional light, since the light is not emanating from any particular location. Therefore, it makes no sense to try to specify a cutoff radius or any other spatial scoping. Instead, **DirectionalLight** is scoped by its position in the scene hierarchy, illuminating only sibling geometry (geometry underneath the same **Group** or **Transform** as the **DirectionalLight**). Although unrealistic, defining **DirectionalLight** this way allows efficient implementations and allows content creators a reasonable amount of control over the lighting of their virtual worlds.

The second problem—defining the light's coordinate system separately from which objects the light illuminates—is addressed by the cutoff radius field of **PointLight** and **SpotLight.** Their position in the scene hierarchy determines only their location in space; they illuminate all objects that fall within the cutoff radius of that location. This makes implementing them more difficult, since the position of all point lights and spot lights must be known before anything is drawn. Current interactive rendering hardware and software make it even more difficult, since they support only a small number of light sources (e.g., eight) at once. Implementors can either turn light sources on and off as different pieces of geometry are drawn or can just use a few of the light sources and ignore the rest. The VRML 2.0 specification requires only that eight simultaneous light sources be supported (see Chapter 5, Conformance and Minimum Support Requirements). World creators should bear this in mind and minimize the number of light sources turned on at any given time.

DirectionalLight does not attempt to decouple its position in the scene hierarchy from the objects that it illuminates. That can result in unrealistic behavior. For example, a directional light that illuminates everything inside a room will not illuminate an object that travels into the room unless that object is in the room's part of the scene hierarchy, and an object that moves outside the room will continue to be lit by the directional light until it is moved outside of the room **Group**. A better solution for moving objects around the scene hierarchy as their position in the virtual world changes may eventually be needed, but until then content creators will have to use existing mechanisms to get their desired results (e.g., by knowing the **Group** for each room in their virtual world and using *addChildren/removeChildren* events to move objects from one **Group** to another as they travel around the virtual world).

2.9.5 Lighting Model

Lighting "Off"

A **Shape** node is unlit if any of the following are true:

- The shape's *appearance* field is NULL (default)
- The material field in the **Appearance** node is NULL (default)

DESIGN NOTE

A shape will be lit if you specify a material to be used for lighting. Shapes are unlit and bright white by default; you will almost always specify either colors (using a **Color** node) or a material (using a **Material** node). No lighting was chosen as the default because it is faster than lighting (wherever possible in VRML, default values were chosen to give maximum performance), and bright white was chosen so objects show up against the default black background.

If the shape is unlit, then the color (I_{rgb}) and alpha (A, 1-*transparency*) of the shape at each point on the shape's geometry is given as listed in Table 2-3:

TABLE 2-3 *Unlit geometry color application*

Unlit geometry	Color per vertex/per face	Color NULL
No texture	$I_{rgb} = I_{Crgb}$ $A = 1$	$I_{rgb} = (1, 1, 1)$ $A = 1$
Intensity texture (one component)	$I_{rgb} = I_T \times I_{Crgb}$ $A = 1$	$I_{rgb} = (I_T\ I_T\ I_T)$ $A = 1$
Intensity and alpha texture (two component)	$I_{rgb} = I_T \times I_{Crgb}$ $A = A_T$	$I_{rgb} = (I_T\ I_T\ I_T)$ $A = A_T$
RGB texture (three component)	$I_{rgb} = I_{Trgb}$ $A = 1$	$I_{rgb} = I_{Trgb}$ $A = 1$
RGBA texture (four component)	$I_{rgb} = I_{Trgb}$ $A = A_T$	$I_{rgb} = I_{Trgb}$ $A = A_T$

A = alpha
A_T = normalized (0–1) alpha value from two- or four-component texture image
I_{Crgb} = interpolated per-vertex color, or per-face color, from **Color** node
I_{rgb} = color
I_T = normalized (0–1) intensity from one- to two-component texture image
I_{Trgb} = color from three- to four-component texture image

DESIGN NOTE

If a full-color texture is given, it defines the colors on unlit geometry (if per-vertex or per-face colors are also given, they are ignored). If an intensity map (one- or two-component texture) is given, then it is either used as a gray-scale texture or, if colors are also specified, it is used to modulate the colors. If there is no texture, then either the per-vertex or per-face colors are used, if given, or white is used. Alpha values are always either 1.0 (fully opaque) or come from the texture image, if the texture image contains transparency.

If colors are specified per vertex, then they should be interpolated across each polygon (*polygon* and *face* mean the same thing—a series of vertices that lie in the same plane and define a closed 2D region). The method of interpolation is not defined. Current rendering libraries typically triangulate polygons with more than three vertices and interpolate in RGB space, but neither is required. Pretriangulate your shapes and limit the color differences across any given triangle (by splitting triangles into smaller triangles, if necessary) if you want to guarantee similar results in different implementations. Also note that some implementations may not support per-vertex coloring at all and may approximate it by averaging the vertex colors to produce one color per polygon.

Allowing the specification of transparency values per face or per vertex was considered. While that would have made the **Color** node more consistent with the **Material** and texture nodes (which allow both colors and transparencies to be specified), it would have added complexity to an already complex part of the specification for a feature that would be rarely used.

Lighting "On"

If the shape is lit (a **Material** and an **Appearance** node are specified for the shape), then the **Color** and texture nodes determine the diffuse color for the lighting equation, as specified in Table 2-4.

TABLE 2-4 *Lit geometry color application*

Lit geometry	Color per vertex/per face	Color NULL
No texture	$O_{Drgb} = I_{Crgb}$ $A = 1 - T_M$	$O_{Drgb} = I_{Mrgb}$ $A = 1 - T_M$
Intensity texture (one component)	$O_{Drgb} = I_T \times I_{Crgb}$ $A = 1 - T_M$	$O_{Drgb} = I_T \times I_{Mrgb}$ $A = 1 - T_M$
Intensity and alpha texture (two component)	$O_{Drgb} = I_T \times I_{Crgb}$ $A = A_T$	$O_{Drgb} = I_T \times I_{Mrgb}$ $A = A_T$
RGB texture (three component)	$O_{Drgb} = I_{Trgb}$ $A = 1 - T_M$	$O_{Drgb} = I_{Trgb}$ $A = 1 - T_M$
RGBA texture (four component)	$O_{Drgb} = I_{Trgb}$ $A = A_T$	$O_{Drgb} = I_{Trgb}$ $A = A_T$

A = alpha
A_T = normalized (0–1) alpha value from two- or four-component texture image
I_{Crgb} = interpolated per-vertex color, or per-face color, from **Color** node
I_{Mrgb} = **Material** *diffuseColor*
I_T = normalized (0–1) intensity from one- to two-component texture image
I_{Trgb} = color from three- to four-component texture image
O_{Drgb} = diffuse factor used in the lighting equations
T_M = **Material** *transparency*

DESIGN NOTE

The rules (expressed in Table 2-4) for combining texture, **Color,** and **Material** nodes are as follows:

Textures have the highest priority; texture colors will be used if a full-color texture is specified (and the colors in the **Color** node or *diffuseColor* of the **Material** node will be ignored). If an intensity texture is specified, it will be used to modulate the diffuse colors from either the **Color** or **Material** nodes. If the texture contains transparency information, it is always used instead of the **Material**'s *transparency* field.

Per-vertex or per-face colors specified in a **Color** node have the next highest priority and override the **Material** node's *diffuseColor* field unless a full-color texture is being used.

The *diffuseColor* specified in the **Material** node has lowest priority and will be used only if there is no full-color texture or **Color** node. The texture and **Color** nodes affect only the *diffuseColor* of the **Material**; the other **Material** parameters (*specularColor, emissiveColor,* etc.) are always used as is.

Lighting Equations

An ideal VRML 2.0 implementation will evaluate the following lighting equation at each point on a surface. RGB intensities at each point on a geometry (I_{rgb}) are given by

$$I_{rgb} = I_{Frgb} \times (1 - s_0) + s_0 \times (O_{Ergb} + SUM (on_i \times attenuation_i \times spot_i \times I_{Lrgb}$$

$$\times (ambient_i + diffuse_i + specular_i)))$$

where:

$ambient_i = I_{ia} \times O_{Drgb} \times O_a$
$diffuse_i = k_d \times O_{Drgb} \times (N \cdot L)$
$specular_i = k_s \times O_{Srgb} \times (N \cdot ((L + V) / |L + V|)^{shininess \times 128}$
SUM: sum over all light sources i
$\cdot$ = modified vector dot product; if dot product <0 then 0, else dot product
I_{Frgb} = currently bound **Fog**'s color
I_{Lrgb} = light i *color*
I_{ia} = light i *ambientIntensity*
L = (**Point/SpotLight**) normalized vector from point on geometry to light source i position
L = (**DirectionalLight**) negative direction of light source i
N = normalized normal vector at this point on geometry
O_a = **Material** *ambientIntensity*
O_{Drgb} = diffuse color, from **Material, Color,** and/or texture node
O_{Ergb} = **Material** *emissiveColor*
O_{Srgb} = **Material** *specularColor*

V = normalized vector from point on geometry to viewer's position

$attenuation_i = 1 / \max(c_1 + c_2 \times d_L + c_3 \times d_L^2, 1)$

c_1, c_2, c_3 = light i attenuation

d_V = distance from point on geometry to viewer's position, in currently bound
     Fog node's coordinate system

d_L = distance from light to point on geometry, in light's coordinate system

$k_d = k_s$ = light i intensity

$on_i = 1$ if light source i affects this point on the geometry

$on_i = 0$ if light source does not affect this geometry (if farther away than radius
     for **PointLight** or **SpotLight**, outside of enclosing **Group/Transform**
     for a **DirectionalLight**, or *on* field is FALSE)

shininess = **Material** *shininess*

$spot_i = 1$ for **DirectionalLight** and **PointLight** (see Table 2.5 for **SpotLight**)

$spotAngle_i$ = angle between $spotDir_i$ and $-L$

$spotBeam_i$ = **SpotLight** i *beamWidth* angle

$spotCutoff_i$ = **SpotLight** i *cutOffAngle*

$spotDir_i$ = normalized **SpotLight** i *direction*

visRange = Fog *visibilityRange*

TABLE 2-5 *Calculating $spot_i$ values for spotlights*

Spotlight conditions	*spot$_i$* value
$spotAngle_i > spotCutoff_i$	0
$spotAngle_i < spotBeam_i$	1
else	$1 - (\cos(spotBeam_i) - \cos(spotAngle_i))/$ $(\cos(spotBeam_i) - \cos(spotCutoff_i))$

TABLE 2-6 *Calculating s_0 (fog) values*

Fog conditions	s_0 value
no fog	1
fogType "LINEAR", $d_V < visRange$	$(visRange - d_V) / visRange$
fogType "LINEAR", $d_V > visRange$	0
fogType "EXPONENTIAL", $d_V < visRange$	$\exp(-d_V / (visRange - d_V))$
fogType "EXPONENTIAL", $d_V > visRange$	0

TIP

The following design note is useful to both authors and implementors.

DESIGN NOTE

These lighting equations are intended to make it easier for implementors to match the ideal VRML lighting model to the lighting equations used by their rendering library. However, understanding the lighting equations and understanding the approximations commonly made to map them to common rendering libraries can help you create content that looks good on all implementations of VRML.

Performing the lighting computation per pixel (Phong shading) is not feasible on current graphics software and hardware; the hardware and software just aren't fast enough. However, within the next couple of years per-pixel lighting will probably be a common feature of very high-performance graphics hardware, and it may be a common feature in inexpensive software and hardware in five years, so VRML specifies an ideal lighting model that can grow with hardware progress. Because 3D graphics technology is evolving so fast, it is better to anticipate future developments and allow current implementations to approximate an ideal specification, rather than choosing a least-common-denominator model that will limit future implementations.

Current implementations typically perform lighting calculations only for each vertex of each polygon. The resulting colors are then linearly interpolated across the polygon (Gouraud shading). The most noticeable effects of this approximation are fuzzy or inaccurate edges for specular highlights, spotlights, and point lights, since the tessellation of the geometry affects where lighting calculations are done. The approximation can be improved by subdividing the polygons of the geometry, creating more vertices (and therefore forcing implementations to do more lighting calculations). This will, of course, decrease performance.

Application of a texture map should ideally occur before lighting, replacing the diffuse term of the lighting equation at each pixel. However, since lighting computations are done per vertex and not per pixel, texture maps are combined with the interpolated color. That is, instead of performing the ideal lighting calculation

$$O_{Ergb} + SUM(on_i \times attenuation_i \times spot_i \times I_{Lrgb} \times (I_{ia} \times O_{Drgb} \times O_a + k_d \times O_{Drgb} \times (N \cdot L) + specular_i))$$

this approximation is computed when texturing

$$I_{Trgb} \times (O_{Ergb} + SUM(on_i \times attenuation_i \times spot_i \times I_{Lrgb} \times (I_{ia} \times O_a + k_d \times (N \cdot L) + specular_i)))$$

The terms inside the parentheses are computed per vertex and interpolated across the polygon, and a color is computed from the texture map and multiplied per pixel. Note that the approximation equals the ideal equation for purely diffuse objects (objects where $O_{Ergb} = specular_i = 0.0$), and since the diffuse term dominates for most objects, the approximation will closely match the ideal for most textured objects. Errors are caused by the texture affecting the specular and emissive colors of the object.

Finally, implementations will be forced to quantize the ideal 0.0 to 1.0 RGB colors of the VRML specification into the number of colors supported by your graphics hardware. This is becoming less of an issue each year as more and more hardware supports millions of colors (24 bits of color—16 million colors—is near the limit of human perception), but displayed colors can vary widely on displays that support only thousands or hundreds of colors. In addition, different computer monitors can display the same colors quite differently, resulting in different-looking worlds. The VRML file format does not attempt to address any of these issues; it is meant to be only an ideal description of a virtual world.

The VRML lighting equations in this section are based on the simple illumination equations given in *Computer Graphics: Principles and Practice* by Foley, van Dam, Feiner, and Hughes, Section 16.1, Illumination and Shading, and in the *OpenGL 1.1 Specification* (`http://www.sgi.com/Technology/openGL/spec.html`), Sections 2.13, Lighting, and 3.9, Fog.

2.9.6 Sensor Nodes

There are several different kinds of sensor nodes (**ProximitySensor, TimeSensor, VisibilitySensor**) and a variety of pointing device sensors (**Anchor, CylinderSensor, PlaneSensor, SphereSensor, TouchSensor**). Sensors are children nodes in the hierarchy and therefore may be parented by grouping nodes (see Section 2.3.1, Grouping and Children Nodes).

The **ProximitySensor** detects when the user navigates into a specified invisible region in the world. The **TimeSensor** is a clock that has no geometry or location associated with it—it is used to start and stop time-based nodes, such as interpolators. The **VisibilitySensor** detects when a specific part of the world becomes visible to the user. Pointing device sensors detect user pointing events, such as clicking over geometry (i.e., **TouchSensor**). Proximity, time, and visibility sensors are additive. Each type is processed independently, whether the other types exist or overlap.

Pointing Device Sensors

The following nodes are considered to be pointing device sensors:

- **Anchor**
- **CylinderSensor**
- **PlaneSensor**
- **SphereSensor**
- **TouchSensor**

Pointing device sensors are activated when the user points to geometry that is influenced by a specific pointing device sensor. These sensors have influence over all geometry that is descendant from the sensor's parent group. (In the case of the **Anchor** node, the **Anchor** itself is considered to be the parent group.) Typically, the pointing device sensor is a sibling to the geometry that it influences. In other cases, the sensor is a sibling to groups that contain geometry (which are influenced by the pointing device sensor).

DESIGN NOTE

It is a little bit strange that pointing device sensors sense hits on all of their sibling geometry. Geometry that occurs before the pointing device sensor in the children list is treated exactly the same as geometry that appears after the sensor in the children list. This is a consequence of the semantics of grouping nodes. The order of children in a grouping node is irrelevant, so the position of a pointing device sensor in the children list does not matter.

Adding a sensor MFNode field to the grouping nodes as a place for sensors (instead of just putting them in the *children* field) was considered, but rejected because it added complexity to the grouping nodes, was less extensible, and produced little benefit.

For a given user activation, the lowest, enabled pointing device sensor in the hierarchy is activated. All other pointing device sensors that are above it or disabled are ignored until deactivation. The hierarchy is defined by the geometry node, which is activated along with the entire hierarchy upward. If there are multiple pointing device sensors tied for lowest, then each of these is activated simultaneously and independently, possibly resulting in multiple sensors being activated and outputting simultaneously. This feature allows useful combinations of pointing device sensors (e.g., **TouchSensor** and **PlaneSensor**). If a pointing device sensor is instanced (DEF/USE), geometry associated with any of its parents must be tested for intersection and activation. Note that a sensor must be enabled before the pointing device is activated in order to be a candidate for activation. Pointing device sensors ignore *enable* events while the pointing device is activated. If a pointing device sensor is enabled when the pointing device is activated, it will be enabled after the pointing device is deactivated. If a sensor is not enabled when the pointing device is activated, it cannot be enabled for the duration of that activation.

DESIGN NOTE

There's an intentional inconsistency between the behavior of the pointing device sensors and the proximity, visibility, and time sensors. The pointing device sensors follow a "lowest-ones-activate" policy, but the others follow an "all-activate" policy. These different policies were chosen based on expected usage.

A **TouchSensor,** for example, is expected to be used for things like push-buttons in the virtual world. Hierarchical **TouchSensors** might be used for something like a TV set that had both buttons inside it to turn it on and off, change the channel, and so forth, but also had a **TouchSensor** on the entire TV that activated a hyperlink (perhaps bringing up the Web page for the product being advertised on the virtual TV). In this case, it would be inconvenient if the hyperlink was also activated when the channel-changing buttons were pressed.

On the other hand, for most expected uses of proximity and visibility sensors it is more convenient if they act completely independently of each other. In either case, the opposite behavior is always achievable by either rearranging the scene graph or enabling and disabling sensors at the right times.

More complicated policies for the pointing device sensors were considered, giving the world creator control over whether or not events were processed and/or propagated upward at each sensor. However, the simpler policy was chosen because it had worked well in the Open Inventor toolkit and because any desired effect can be achieved by rearranging the position of sensors in the scene graph and/or using a script to enable and disable sensors.

The **Anchor** node is considered to be a pointing device sensor when trying to determine which sensor (or **Anchor**) to activate. For example, in the following file a click on `Shape3` is handled by `SensorD`, a click on `Shape2` is handled by `SensorC` and the `AnchorA`, and a click on `Shape1` is handled by `SensorA` and `SensorB`:

```
Group { children [
   DEF Shape1   Shape       { ... }
   DEF SensorA TouchSensor { ... }
   DEF SensorB PlaneSensor { ... }
   DEF AnchorA Anchor {
      url "..."
      children [
         DEF Shape2   Shape { ... }
         DEF SensorC TouchSensor { ... }
         Group { children [
            DEF Shape3   Shape { ... }
            DEF SensorD TouchSensor { ... }
         ]}
      ]
   }
]}
```

Drag Sensors

Drag sensors are a subset of pointing device sensors. There are three drag sensors (**CylinderSensor, PlaneSensor, SphereSensor**) in which pointer motions cause events to be generated according to the "virtual shape" of the sensor. For instance, the output of the **SphereSensor** is an SFRotation, *rotation_changed,* which can be connected to a **Transform** node's *set_rotation* field to rotate an object. The effect is that the user grabs an object and spins it about the center point of the **SphereSensor**.

DESIGN NOTE

The **TouchSensor** and the drag sensors map a 2D pointing device in the 3D world, and are the basis for direct manipulation of the objects in the virtual world. **TouchSensor** samples the motion of the pointing device over the surface of an object, **PlaneSensor** projects the motion of the pointing device onto a 3D plane, and **SphereSensor** and **CylinderSensor** generate 3D rotations from the motion of the pointing device. Their functionality is limited to performing the mapping from 2D into 3D; they must be combined with geometry, transformations, or script logic to be useful. Breaking apart different pieces of functionality into separate nodes does make it more difficult to perform common tasks, but it creates a design that is much more flexible. Features may be combined in endless variations, resulting in a specification with a whole that is greater than the sum of its parts (and, of course, the prototyping mechanism can be used to make the common variations easy to reuse).

To simplify the application of these sensors, each node has an *offset* and an *autoOffset* exposedField. Whenever the sensor generates output as a response to pointer motion, the output value (e.g., **SphereSensor**'s *rotation_changed*) is added to the *offset*. If *autoOffset* is TRUE (default), *offset* is set to the last output value when the pointing device button is released (*isActive* FALSE). This allows subsequent grabbing operations to generate output relative to the last release point. A simple dragger can be constructed by sending the output of the sensor to a **Transform** with a child that is the object being grabbed. For example:

```
Group { children [
  DEF S SphereSensor { autoOffset TRUE }
  DEF T Transform {
    children Shape { geometry Box {} }
  }
]}
ROUTE S.rotation_changed TO T.set_rotation
```

The box will spin when it is grabbed and moved via the pointer.

When the pointing device button is released, *offset* is set to the last output value and an *offset_changed* event is sent out. This behavior can be disabled by setting the *autoOffset* field to FALSE.

DESIGN NOTE

The original Moving Worlds drag sensors did not have *offset* or *autoOffset* fields. This resulted in drag sensors that reset themselves back to zero at the beginning of each use and made it extremely difficult to create the typical case of an accumulating sensor. By adding the *offset* field, it enables drag sensors to accumulate their results (e.g., translation, rotation) by saving their last *<value>_changed* in the *offset* field.

2.9.7 Time-dependent Nodes

AudioClip, **MovieTexture**, and **TimeSensor** are time-dependent nodes that should activate and deactivate themselves at specified times. Each of these nodes contains the *startTime, stopTime,* and *loop* exposedFields, and the *isActive* eventOut. The exposedField values are used to determine when the container node becomes active or inactive. Also, under certain conditions, these nodes ignore events to some of their exposedFields. A node ignores an eventIn by not accepting the new value and not generating an *eventOut_changed* event.

DESIGN NOTE

AudioClip and **MovieTexture** could have been designed to be driven by a **TimeSensor** (like the interpolator nodes) instead of having the *startTime,* and so forth, controls. However, that would have caused several implementation difficulties. Playback of sound and movies is optimized for continuous, in-order play; multimedia systems often have specialized hardware to deal with sound and (for example) MPEG movies. Efficiently implementing the **AudioClip** and **MovieTexture** nodes is much harder if those nodes do not know the playback speed, whether or not the sound/movie should be repeated, and so on. In addition, sounds and movies may require "preroll" time to prepare to playback; this is possible only if the **AudioClip** or **MovieTexture** know their start time. In this case, separating out the time-generation functionality, although it would make a more flexible system (playing movies backward by inverting the *fraction_changed* events coming from the **TimeSensor** going to a **MovieTexture** would be possible, for example), it would make it unacceptably hard to implement efficiently (it is difficult to play an MPEG movie backward efficiently because of the frame-to-frame compression that is done, for example).

Time-dependent nodes can execute for zero or more cycles. A cycle is defined by field data within the node. If, at the end of a cycle, the value of *loop* is FALSE, then execution is terminated (discussed later). Conversely, if *loop* is TRUE at the end of a cycle, then a time dependent node continues execution into the next cycle. A time dependent node with *loop* TRUE at the end of every cycle continues cycling forever if *startTime* ≥ *stopTime*, or until *stopTime* if *stopTime* > *startTime*.

DESIGN NOTE

Unless you set the *stopTime* field, a time-dependent node either cycles once (if *loop* is FALSE) or plays over and over again (if *loop* is TRUE). For **MovieTexture,** one cycle corresponds to displaying the movie once; for **AudioClip,** playing the sound once; for **TimeSensor,** generating *fraction_changed* events that go from 0.0 to 1.0 once.

The *startTime, stopTime,* and *loop* fields are generally all you need to accomplish simple tasks. *StartTime* is simply the time at which the animation or sound or movie should start. *StopTime* was named *interruptTime* in a draft version of the VRML specification; it allows you to stop the animation/sound/movie while it is playing. And *loop* just controls whether or not the animation/sound/movie is repeated.

A time-dependent node will generate an *isActive* TRUE event when it becomes active and will generate an *isActive* FALSE event when it becomes inactive. These are the only times at which an *isActive* event is generated (i.e., they are not sent at each tick of a simulation).

A time-dependent node is inactive while the current time is less than *startTime*. When the current time exceeds *startTime,* an *isActive* TRUE event is generated and the time-dependent node becomes active. When a time-dependent node is read from a file, and the routes specified within the file have been established, the node should determine if it is active and, if so, generate an *isActive* TRUE event and begin generating any other necessary events. However, if a node becomes inactive at any time before the reading of the file, then no events are generated on the completion of the read.

An active time-dependent node deactivates when the current time exceeds *stopTime,* if *stopTime > startTime*. The value of *stopTime* is ignored if *stopTime ≤ startTime*. Also, an active time-dependent node will become inactive at the end of the current cycle if *loop* = FALSE. If an active time-dependent node receives a *set_loop* FALSE event, then execution continues until the end of the current cycle or until *stopTime* (if *stopTime > startTime*), whichever occurs first. The termination at the end of cycle can be overridden by a subsequent *set_loop* TRUE event.

Set_startTime events to an active time-dependent node are ignored. *Set_stopTime* events, where *set_stopTime ≤ startTime,* to an active time-dependent node are also ignored. A *set_stopTime* event to an active time-dependent node, where *startTime < set_stopTime ≤ now,* results in events being generated as if *stopTime = now*. That is, final events, including an *isActive* FALSE, are generated and the node becomes inactive. The *stopTime_changed* event will have the *set_stopTime* value. Other final events are node dependent (compare with **TimeSensor**).

DESIGN NOTE

To get precise, reproducible behavior, there are a lot of edge conditions that must be handled the same way in all implementations. Creating a concise, precise specification that defined the edge cases was one of the most difficult of the VRML 2.0 design tasks.

One problem was determining how to handle *set_stopTime* events with values that are in the past. In theory, if the world creator sends a **TimeSensor** a *set_stopTime* "yesterday" event, they are asking to see the state of the world as if the time sensor had stopped yesterday. And, theoretically, a browser could resimulate the world from yesterday until today, replaying any events and taking into account the stopped time sensor. However, requiring browsers to interpret events that occurred in the past is unreasonable; so, instead, *set_stopTime* events in the past are either ignored (if *stopTime < startTime*) or are reinterpreted to mean "now."

A time-dependent node may be restarted while it is active by sending it a *set_stopTime = now* event (which will cause the node to become inactive) and a *set_startTime* event (setting it to *now* or any time in the future). Browser authors should note that these events will have the same time stamp and should be processed as *set_stopTime*, then *set_startTime* to produce the correct behavior.

TIP

To pause and then restart an animation, do the following in a script: Set the *stopTime* to *now* to pause the animation. To restart, you must adjust both the *startTime* and the *stopTime* of the animation. Advance the *startTime* by the amount of time that the animation has been paused so that it will continue where it left off. This is easily calculated as *startTime = startTime + now − stopTime* (where *now* is the time stamp of the event that causes the animation to be restarted). Set the *stopTime* to zero or any other value less than or equal to *startTime*, so that it is ignored and the animation restarts.

DESIGN NOTE

There are implicit dependencies between the fields of time-dependent nodes. If a time-dependent node receives several events with exactly the same time stamp, these dependencies force the events to be processed in a particular order. For example, if, at time T, a **TimeSensor** node receives both a *set_active* FALSE and a *set_startTimeT* event (both with time stamp T), the node must behave as if the *set_active* event is processed first and must not start playing. Similarly, *set_stopTime* events must be processed before *set_startTime* events with the same time stamp.

Set_startTime events are ignored if a time-dependent node is active, because doing so makes writing robust animations much easier. For example, if you have a button (a touch sensor and some geometry) that starts an animation, you usually want the animation to finish playing, even if the user presses the button again while the animation is playing. You can easily get the other behavior by setting both *stopTime* and *startTime* when the button is pressed. If *set_startTime* events were not ignored when the node was active, then achieving "play-to-completion" behavior would require use of a **Script** to manage *set_startTime* events.

The default values for each of the time-dependent nodes have been specified such that a node with default values became inactive in the past (and, therefore, will generate no events on reading). A time-dependent node can be made active upon reading by specifying *loop* TRUE. This use of a nonterminating time-dependent node should be used with caution since it incurs continuous overhead on the simulation.

DESIGN NOTE

If you want your worlds to be scalable, everything in them should have a well-defined scope in space or time. Spatial scoping means specifying bounding boxes that represent the maximum range of an object's motion whenever possible, and arranging objects in spatial hierarchies. Temporal scoping means giving any animations well-defined starting and ending times. If you create an animation that is infinitely long—a windmill turning in the breeze, perhaps—you should try to specify its spatial scope, so that the browser can avoid performing the animation if that part of space cannot be seen.

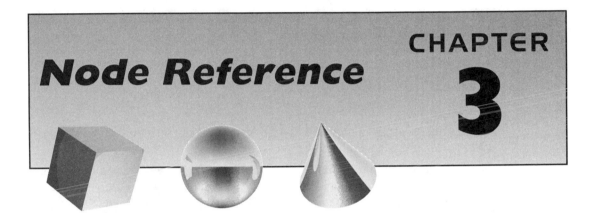

CHAPTER 3

Node Reference

This chapter provides a detailed definition of the syntax and semantics of each node in the VRML specification. The nodes are listed in alphabetical order.

Anchor

```
Anchor {
  eventIn      MFNode    addChildren
  eventIn      MFNode    removeChildren
  exposedField MFNode    children        []
  exposedField SFString  description     ""
  exposedField MFString  parameter       []
  exposedField MFString  url             []
  field        SFVec3f   bboxCenter      0 0 0
  field        SFVec3f   bboxSize        -1 -1 -1
}
```

The **Anchor** grouping node causes a URL to be fetched over the network when the viewer activates (e.g., clicks) some geometry contained within the **Anchor**'s children. If the URL pointed to is a legal VRML world, then that world replaces the world of which the **Anchor** is a part. If a non-VRML data type is fetched, it is up to the browser to determine how to handle that data; typically, it will be passed to an appropriate general viewer.

DESIGN NOTE

The name *Anchor* comes from the HTML Anchor tag (<A HREF=...>), which is used to create hyperlinked text in HTML. It was called *WWWAnchor* in VRML 1.0, but the *WWW* was dropped.

Exactly how a user activates a child of the **Anchor** depends on the pointing device and is determined by the VRML browser. Typically, clicking with the pointing device will result in the new scene replacing the current scene. An **Anchor** with an empty ("") *url* does nothing when its children are chosen. See Section 2.9.6, Sensor Nodes, for a description of how multiple **Anchors** and pointing device sensors are resolved on activation.

See Section 2.1.3, Grouping and Children Nodes, for a description of *children*, *addChildren*, and *removeChildren* fields and eventIns.

The *description* field in the **Anchor** allows for a prompt to be displayed as an alternative to the URL in the *url* field. Ideally, browsers will allow the user to choose the *description*, the URL, or both to be displayed for a candidate **Anchor**.

DESIGN NOTE

The candidate **Anchor** is the **Anchor** with geometry that is underneath the pointing device. The pointing device is usually a mouse (or a mouse substitute like a trackball or touchpad).

The *parameter* exposedField may be used to supply any additional information to be interpreted by the VRML or HTML browser. Each string should consist of "keyword=value" pairs. For example, some browsers allow the specification of a target for a link to display a link in another part of the HTML document. The *parameter* field is then

```
Anchor {
  parameter [ "target=name_of_frame" ]
  ...
}
```

DESIGN NOTE

The *parameter* field was added to allow **Anchors** to bring up hyperlinks in other HTML frames on the same Web page. When VRML 2.0 was originally being designed, Netscape Navigator was the only HTML browser that supported multiple frames, so instead of adding a *frame* or *target* field just to support that feature, the more general *parameter* field was added to **Anchor**. That avoided adding any Netscape-specific features to VRML and allows for future additions.

An **Anchor** may be used to bind the initial **Viewpoint** in a world by specifying a URL ending with "#ViewpointName", where "ViewpointName" is the name of a viewpoint defined in the file. For example

```
Anchor {
  url "http://www.school.edu/vrml/someScene.wrl#OverView"
  children  Shape { geometry Box {} }
}
```

specifies an anchor that loads the file `someScene.wrl`, and binds the initial user view to the **Viewpoint** named `OverView` (when the **Box** is activated). If the named **Viewpoint** is not found in the file, then it is ignored and the default **Viewpoint** is used. If no world is specified, then this means that the **Viewpoint** specified should be bound (*set_bind* TRUE). For example

```
Anchor {
  url "#Doorway"
  children Shape { geometry Sphere {} }
}
```

binds the viewer to the viewpoint defined by the `Doorway` **Viewpoint** in the current world when the sphere is activated. In this case, if the **Viewpoint** is not found, then nothing is done on activation.

See Section 2.1.3, URLs, for more details on the *url* field.

TIP

Since navigating around 3D worlds can be difficult, it is recommended that authors provide navigation assists whenever possible. The **Anchor** node serves as an excellent tool for creating simple guided tours or navigation aids in a 3D world. Place signposts or other recognizable objects (e.g., labeled buttons) throughout the world with **Anchor** nodes as parents, and define each **Anchor** to refer to a **Viewpoint** defined in the world (e.g., Anchor { url "#someViewpoint" ... }. Typically, there should be at least one visible signpost from every **Viewpoint**. This ensures that the user knows where to go after visiting each stop. When creating guided tours, authors should include backward and forward links at each signpost. Remember that VRML does not specify what happens during the transition to a **Viewpoint** and thus could perform a jump cut, an animated movement, or some other transitional effect. If an author wishes to control the transition precisely, then the only option is to use **TouchSensors** with **Scripts** programmed to bind and unbind **Viewpoints**, which are animated by **PositionInterpolators** and **OrientationInterpolators**. This is a much more complicated task than using the simple **Anchor** node.

The *bboxCenter* and *bboxSize* fields specify a bounding box that encloses the **Anchor**'s children. This is a hint that may be used for optimization purposes. If the specified bounding box is smaller than the actual bounding box of the children at any time, then the results are undefined. A default *bboxSize* value, $(-1, -1, -1)$, implies that the bounding box is not specified and if needed must be calculated by the browser. See Section 4.3.6, Bounding Boxes, for a description of *bboxCenter* and *bboxSize* fields.

DESIGN NOTE

Anchor is equivalent to a prototype containing a couple of **Group** nodes, a **TouchSensor,** and a **Script.** It is a standard node partly because it makes it easier to convert VRML 1.0 files (which use **WWWAnchor**) to VRML 2.0, and partly because it is convenient to have simple hyperlinking support prepackaged in a convenient form.

There are many hyperlinking tasks for which **Anchor** is inadequate. For example, if you want a hyperlink to occur after the user has accomplished some task, then you must use a **Script** node that calls `loadURL()`. If you want to load several different pieces of information into several other frames you will also have to use a **Script** that makes several calls to `loadURL()`. The basic building blocks of **Scripts** and sensors allow you to do almost anything; the **Anchor** node is only meant to address the most basic hyperlinking tasks.

EXAMPLE

The following example illustrates typical use of the **Anchor** node. The first **Anchor** links the **Box** geometry to another VRML world that replaces this one after the **Anchor** is activated. The second **Anchor** links the **Sphere** to a **Viewpoint** in this world. When the user clicks on the **Sphere**, the browser's view is transported to the **Viewpoint**. The third **Anchor** links a **Cone** to a frame on an HTML page. When the user clicks on the **Cone**, the frame is activated:

```
#VRML V2.0 utf8
Group {
  children [
    Transform {
      translation -5 0 0
      children Anchor {
        url "http://www.barbie.web/~barbie/dollhouse.wrl"
        description "Link to Barbie's home world"
        children Shape {
          geometry Box {}
          DEF A1 Appearance { material Material {
            diffuseColor 1 1 1  ambientIntensity 0.33
            specularColor 1 1 1  shininess 0.5
          }}
        }
      }
    }
    Transform {
      children Anchor {
        url "#NiceView"
        description "Link to a nice view in this scene"
        children Shape { geometry Sphere {} appearance USE A1 }
      }
    }
    Transform {
      translation 5 0 0
      children Anchor {
        url "http://www.barbie.web/~barbie/index.html"
        description "Link to frame in Barbie's home page"
        parameter "target=name_of_frame"
        children Shape { geometry Cone {} appearance USE A1 }
      }
    }
    DEF NiceView Viewpoint {
      position 0 0 -20
      description "A Nice View"
    }
  ]
}
```

Appearance

```
Appearance {
  exposedField SFNode material          NULL
  exposedField SFNode texture           NULL
  exposedField SFNode textureTransform  NULL
}
```

The **Appearance** node specifies the visual properties of geometry by defining the **Material** and texture nodes. The value for each of the fields in this node can be NULL. However, if the field is non-NULL, it must contain one node of the appropriate type.

The *material* field, if specified, must contain a **Material** node. If the *material* field is NULL or unspecified, lighting is off (all lights are ignored during rendering of the object that references this **Appearance**) and the unlit object color is (0, 0, 0) (see Section 2.9.5, Lighting Model, for details of the VRML lighting model).

The *texture* field, if specified, must contain one of the various types of texture nodes (**ImageTexture**, **MovieTexture**, or **PixelTexture**). If the *texture* field is NULL or unspecified, the object that references this **Appearance** is not textured.

The *textureTransform* field, if specified, must contain a **TextureTransform** node. If the *texture* field is NULL or unspecified, or if the *textureTransform* field is NULL or unspecified, the *textureTransform* field has no effect.

TIP

Appearance nodes should be shared whenever possible. DEF the first use of an **Appearance** node in the file and USE it for all subsequent **Shapes** with identical appearance values. This can result in memory savings and performance gains (depending on the browser implementation).

If the world is large and **Appearance** nodes are frequently shared, it may be handy to create a separate VRML file that contains all of the **Appearance nodes,** each with a PROTO name (e.g., A1, A2, GOLD, Shiny_Red). In the world file that contains the **Shape** nodes, insert one EXTERNPROTO at the top of the file for each **Appearance** to be used and then use the EXTERNPROTO name in the **Shape** definition. For example, the following file is the **Appearance** library (AppearanceLibrary.wrl) defining the **Appearances** to be used by another VRML file:

```
#VRML V2.0 utf8
PROTO A1[]{ Appearance { ... } }
PROTO A2[]{ Appearance { ... } }
...
```

And here's how the **Appearance** library would be used:

```
#VRML V2.0 utf8
EXTERNPROTO A1[] "AppearanceLibrary.wrl#A1" # List each one...
EXTERNPROTO A2[] "AppearanceLibrary.wrl#A2"
...
Shape {
  appearance A1 { }
  ...
}
```

Note that this scheme can be used for a variety of different node types (e.g., **Material**).

FIGURE 3-1 *Appearance Node Example*

EXAMPLE

The following example illustrates typical use of the **Appearance** node:

```
#VRML V2.0 utf8
Shape {
  appearance Appearance {
    material Material {
      specularColor 1 1 1
      shininess 0.2
    }
    texture ImageTexture { url "marble.gif" }
  }
  geometry Sphere { radius 1.3 }
}
```

```
Shape {
  appearance Appearance {
    material Material { diffuseColor 0.9 0.9 0.9 }
  }
  geometry Box {}
}
Background { skyColor 1 1 1 }
```

AudioClip

```
AudioClip {
    exposedField    SFString    description         ""
    exposedField    SFBool      loop                FALSE
    exposedField    SFFloat     pitch               1.0
    exposedField    SFTime      startTime           0
    exposedField    SFTime      stopTime            0
    exposedField    MFString    url                 []
    eventOut        SFTime      duration_changed
    eventOut        SFBool      isActive
}
```

An **AudioClip** node specifies audio data that can be referenced by other nodes that require an audio source.

TIP

The **Sound** node is the only node in VRML 2.0 that uses an audio source, and the **Audio-Clip** node is specified in the **Sound**'s *source* field.

The *description* field is a textual description of the audio source. A browser is not required to display the *description* field but may choose to do so in addition to or in place of playing the sound.

The *url* field specifies the URL from which the sound is loaded. Browsers shall support at least the wavefile format in uncompressed PCM format (*Waveform Audio File Format—Multimedia Programming Interface and Data Specification v.1.0* by IBM and Microsoft Corporation, 1991, `ftp://ftp.cwi.nl/pub/audio/RIFF-format`). It is recommended that browsers also support the MIDI file type 1 sound format ("Musical Instrument Digital Interface," International MIDI Association, `ftp:// rtfm.mit.edu/pub/usenet/news.answers/music/midi/bibliography`). MIDI files are presumed to use the General MIDI patch set. See Section 2.1.3, URLs, for details on the *url* field. Results are not defined when the URL references unsupported data types.

DESIGN NOTE

A very small number of formats are required or recommended by the VRML specification so that content creators can create worlds that should work with any VRML implementation. Several criteria are used to decide which audio (and movie and texture) formats VRML implementations should be required to support:

1. The format must be free of legal restrictions on its use (either creation or playback).

2. It must be well documented, preferably by a standards group independent of any one company.

3. There must be implementations available on multiple platforms and there must be implementations available on the most popular platforms (Mac, PC, and UNIX).

4. It should already be widely used on the Web and widely supported by content creation tools. In addition, if there are multiple formats that meet all of the requirements but have very similar functionality, only one is required. Deciding which is "best" is often very difficult, but fortunately VRML implementors are motivated to listen to their customers and are free to support any format they wish.

In the particular case of audio, uncompressed .wav files were chosen because they met all of these criteria. Several different forms of compression for .wav files are available, but at the time VRML 2.0 was being designed, none were available nor widely used on all platforms. MIDI is recommended as a very bandwidth-efficient way of transmitting musical information and complements the more general (but much larger) .wav format nicely.

The *loop*, *startTime*, and *stopTime* exposedFields and the *isActive* eventOut, and their effects on the **AudioClip** node, are discussed in detail in Section 2.9.7, Time Dependent Nodes. The "cycle" of an audio clip is the length of time in seconds for one playing of the audio at the specified pitch.

The *pitch* field specifies a multiplier for the rate at which sampled sound is played. Only positive values are valid for *pitch* (a value of 0 or less will produce undefined results). Changing the *pitch* field affects both the pitch and playback speed of a sound. A *set_pitch* event to an active **AudioClip** is ignored (and no *pitch_changed* eventOut is generated). If *pitch* is set to 2.0, the sound should be played one octave higher than normal and played twice as fast. For a sampled sound, the *pitch* field alters the sampling rate at which the sound is played. The proper implementation of the pitch control for MIDI (or other note sequence sound clip) is to multiply the tempo of the playback by the *pitch* value and adjust the MIDI Coarse Tune and Fine Tune controls to achieve the proper pitch change.

DESIGN NOTE

There are a large number of parameters that can be used to alter an audio sound track. VRML 2.0 allows only the pitch and volume (which is specified in the *intensity* field of the **Sound** node) to be modified. This gives the world creator a lot of flexibility with a minimal number of "knobs" to tweak, making implementation reasonably easy.

A *duration_changed* event is sent whenever there is a new value for the "normal" duration of the clip. Typically this will only occur when the current *url* in use changes and the sound data has been loaded, indicating that the clip is playing a different sound source. The duration is the length of time in seconds for one cycle of the audio for a pitch set to 1.0. Changing the *pitch* field will not trigger a *duration_changed* event. A *duration* value of −1 implies the sound data has not yet been loaded or the value is unavailable for some reason.

The *isActive* eventOut can be used by other nodes to determine if the clip is currently active. If an **AudioClip** is active, then it should be playing the sound corresponding to the sound time (i.e., in the sound's local time system with sample 0 at time 0): fmod (now—*startTime*, *duration / pitch*).

DESIGN NOTE

You can think of **AudioClip** as the sound-generation equipment, while the **Sound** node functions as the sound-emitting equipment. **AudioClip** has all of the controls for starting and stopping the sound, looping it, and so forth. The **Sound** node controls how the sound is emitted—what volume, where in space, and so on. A single **AudioClip** can be used with several different **Sound** nodes, just like a single tape player might be connected to several sets of speakers.

TIP

Be careful with how many audio tracks are playing simultaneously. Read the browser release notes carefully to discover how many tracks are supported simultaneously. It is generally safe to limit the number of audio tracks to two or three at one time. Use **ProximitySensors** and the *min/maxFront* and *min/maxBack* fields of the **Sound** node to localize sounds to nonoverlapping regions.

EXAMPLE

The following example creates two **Sound** nodes that employ **AudioClip** nodes. The first **Audio-Clip** is used for a repeating (*loop* TRUE) sound that emits from the center of the world. This example illustrates the case of a sound that is looping forever, starting when the user first enters the world. This is done by setting the *loop* field to TRUE and leaving the *stopTime* equal to the *startTime* (default for both is zero). The second **AudioClip** is issued whenever the user enters or exits the box defined by the **ProximitySensor**:

```
#VRML V2.0 utf8
Group { children [
  Sound {           # Looped midi soundtrack
    source DEF AC1 AudioClip {
      loop TRUE   # Loop forever
      url "loopy.mid"
    }
    spatialize TRUE
    minFront 0 maxFront 20
    minBack 0  maxBack 20
  }
  Sound {          # Chimes when user goes through space near origin
    source DEF AC2 AudioClip { url "Bell.wav" }
    minFront 20 maxFront 100
    minBack 20 maxBack 100
  }
  DEF PS ProximitySensor { center 0 5 0  size 10 10 10 }
  Shape {
    geometry Box { size 5 0.05 5 }
    appearance Appearance { material Material {} }
  }
  Shape {          # Floor
    geometry IndexedFaceSet {
      coord Coordinate { point [ -50 0 -50, -50 0 50,
                                  50 0 50,   50 0 -50 ] }
      coordIndex [ 0 1 2 3 ]
    }
  }
  Viewpoint { position 0 1 25 description "Outside sound ranges" }
  Viewpoint { position 0 1 2 description "Inside sound ranges" }
]}
# Sound bell when user enters/exits 10x10x10 space around origin
ROUTE PS.enterTime TO AC2.set_startTime
ROUTE PS.exitTime TO AC2.set_startTime
```

Background

```
Background {
  eventIn       SFBool    set_bind
  exposedField  MFFloat   groundAngle   []
  exposedField  MFColor   groundColor   []
  exposedField  MFString  backUrl       []
  exposedField  MFString  bottomUrl     []
  exposedField  MFString  frontUrl      []
  exposedField  MFString  leftUrl       []
  exposedField  MFString  rightUrl      []
  exposedField  MFString  topUrl        []
  exposedField  MFFloat   skyAngle      []
  exposedField  MFColor   skyColor      [ 0 0 0 ]
  eventOut      SFBool    isBound
}
```

The **Background** node is used to specify a color backdrop that simulates ground and sky, as well as a background texture, or panorama, that is placed behind all geometry in the scene and in front of the ground and sky. **Background** nodes are specified in the local coordinate system and are affected by the accumulated rotation of their parents (see the following discussion).

Background nodes are *bindable nodes* (see Section 2.9.1, Bindable Children Nodes). There exists a **Background** stack, in which the topmost **Background** on the stack is the currently active **Background** and is thus applied to the view. To move a **Background** to the top of the stack, a TRUE value is sent to the *set_bind* eventIn. Once active, the **Background** is then bound to the browsers view. A FALSE value of *set_bind* removes the **Background** from the stack and unbinds it from the browser viewer. (See Section 2.9.1, Bindable Children Nodes, for more details on the bind stack.)

The ground and sky backdrop is conceptually a partial sphere (i.e., ground) enclosed inside of a full sphere (i.e., sky) in the local coordinate system, with the viewer placed at the center of the spheres. Both spheres have an infinite radius (epsilon apart) and each is painted with concentric circles of interpolated color perpendicular to the local *y*-axis of the sphere. The **Background** node is subject to the accumulated rotations of its parent transformations—scaling and translation transformations are ignored. The sky sphere is always slightly farther away from the viewer than the ground sphere—the ground appears in front of the sky in cases where they overlap.

The *skyColor* field specifies the color of the sky at the various angles on the sky sphere. The first value of the *skyColor* field specifies the color of the sky at 0.0 radians, the north pole (i.e., straight up from the viewer). The *skyAngle* field specifies the angles from the north pole in which concentric circles of color appear. The north pole of the sphere is implicitly defined to be 0.0 radians, the natural horizon at $\pi/2$ radians, and the south pole is π radians. The *skyAngle* is restricted to increasing values in the range 0.0 to π. There must be one more *skyColor* value than there are *skyAngle* values. The first color value is the color at the north pole, which is not specified in the *skyAngle* field. If the last *skyAngle* is less than π, then the color band between the last *skyAngle* and the south pole is clamped to the last *skyColor*. The sky color is linearly interpolated between the specified *skyColor* values.

The *groundColor* field specifies the color of the ground at the various angles on the ground sphere. The first value of the *groundColor* field specifies the color of the ground at 0.0 radians, the south pole (i.e., straight down). The *groundAngle* field specifies the angles from the south pole that the concentric circles of color appear. The south pole of the sphere is implicitly defined at 0.0 radians. The *groundAngle* is restricted to increasing values in the range 0.0 to $\pi/2$. There must be one more *groundColor* value than there are *groundAngle* values. The first color value is for the south pole, which is not specified in the *groundAngle* field. If the last *groundAngle* is less than $\pi/2$ (it usually is), then the region between the last *groundAngle* and the equator is invisible. The ground color is linearly interpolated between the specified *groundColor* values.

The *backUrl*, *bottomUrl*, *frontUrl*, *leftUrl*, *rightUrl*, and *topUrl* fields specify a set of images that define a background panorama between the ground/sky backdrop and the world's geometry. The panorama consists of six images, each of which is

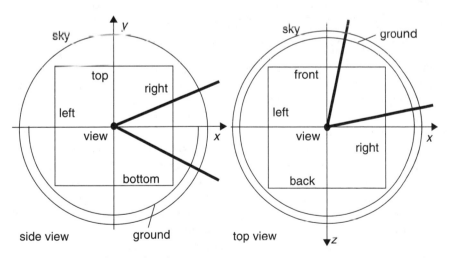

FIGURE 3-2 *Background* Node

mapped onto the faces of an infinitely large cube centered in the local coordinate system. The images are applied individually to each face of the cube; the entire image goes on each face. On the front, back, right, and left faces of the cube, when viewed from the inside with the *y*-axis up, the texture is mapped onto each face with the same orientation as the if image was displayed normally in two dimensions. On the top face of the cube, when viewed from the inside looking up along the +*y*-axis, with the +*z*-axis as the view-up direction, the texture is mapped onto the face with the same orientation as the if image was displayed normally in two dimensions. On the bottom face of the box, when viewed from the inside, down the −*y*-axis with the −*z*-axis as the view-up direction, the texture is mapped onto the face with the same orientation as if the image was displayed normally in two dimensions.

DESIGN NOTE

The panorama URLs behave like **ImageTexture** nodes. It might have been nice to specify each as textures, instead of as URLs. That is, instead of MFString *backURL*, the **Background** node could have had an SFNode *backTexture* field that pointed to an **ImageTexture, PixelTexture,** or **MovieTexture.** This would have allowed animated backgrounds. However, this generalization was noticed too late in the VRML 2.0 definition process and only static backgrounds are supported (which is probably a good thing, since implementations might have trouble supporting animated backgrounds).

Panoramic images may be one component (gray scale), two component (gray scale plus alpha), three component (full RGB color), or four component (full RGB color plus alpha). Alpha values in the panoramic images (i.e., two- or four-component images) specify that the panorama is semitransparent or transparent in regions, allowing the ground color and sky color to be visible. Often, the *bottomUrl* and *topUrl* images will not be specified, to allow sky and ground to show. The other four images may depict surrounding mountains or other distant scenery. Browsers are required to support the JPEG *Digital Compression and Coding of Continuous-tone Still Images, Part 1: Requirements and Guidelines* (ISO/IEC IS 10918-1, Joint Photographic Experts Group, International Organization for Standardization, 1991) and PNG image file formats (*Portable Networked Graphics Specification, version 0.96,* W3C Working Draft 11-Mar-1996, `http://www.w3.org/pub/WWW/TR/WD-png` and `http://www.boutell.com/boutell/png/`) and, in addition, may support any other image format. Support for the GIF format (*Graphics Interchange Format,* version 89a, `http://www.radzone.org/tutorials/gif89a.txt` and `http://www.w3.org/pub/WWW/Graphics/GIF/specgif87.txt`), including transparent backgrounds, is recommended. See Section 2.1.3, URLs, for details on the URL fields.

Ground colors, sky colors, and panoramic images do not translate with respect to the viewer, though they do *rotate* with respect to the viewer. That is, the viewer can never get any closer to the background, but can turn to examine all sides of the panoramic cube, and can look up and down to see the concentric rings of ground and sky (if visible).

TIP

Remember that the panorama is rendered in front of the ground and sky. When using a panorama, the ground and sky should not be specified unless it is partially transparent, as a result of using two- or four-component images with transparency.

Background is not affected by **Fog**. Therefore, if a **Background** is active (i.e., bound) while a **Fog** is active, then the background will be displayed with no fogging effects. It is the author's responsibility to set the **Background** values to match the **Fog** (e.g., ground colors fade to fog color with distance, and panoramic images are tinted with fog color).

The first **Background** node found during reading of the world is automatically bound (receives *set_bind* TRUE) and is used as the initial background when the world is loaded.

TIP

The default **Background** node is entirely black. If you just want simply to set a single color to be used for the background, insert a **Background** node into your scene with a single sky color that is the right color. Implementations should optimize for this case and clear the window to that color before drawing the scene.

TIP

The **Background** node provides functionality similar to Apple's QuickTimeVR with its panoramic images. The user can be restricted to one spot using a **NavigationInfo** that specifies a speed of navigation of 0.0, and can only turn to look at the background images that can give the illusion of a full 3D environment. By binding and unbinding **Background** nodes as the user clicks on **TouchSensors** or as **Script** nodes execute, the user can be given the illusion of moving through 3D space when it is, in reality, a set of prerendered views.

EXAMPLE

The following file illustrates two typical examples of the **Background** node. The first **Background** node specifies the sky and ground colors, but does not specify panoramic images. This typically results in faster rendering. A **TouchSensor** was added to the scene that is used to bind the second **Background** node when the user clicks and holds over the flagpole. The second **Background** node defines a panoramic image of the night sky. Note that since the panorama is completely opaque and is rendered in front of the ground and sky, there is no point in specifying ground or sky values. Since there is no ground plane geometry defined in the scene, binding the second **Background** creates an illusion of floating in space:

```
#VRML V2.0 utf8
Transform { children [
  DEF B1 Background {       # Gray ramped sky
    skyColor [ 0 0 0, 1.0 1.0 1.0 ]
    skyAngle 1.6
    groundColor [ 1 1 1, 0.8 0.8 0.8, 0.2 0.2 0.2 ]
    groundAngle [ 1.2, 1.57 ]
  }
  DEF B2 Background {       # Night sky
    backUrl "Bg.gif"
    leftUrl "Bg.gif"
    bottomUrl "Bg.gif"
    frontUrl "Bg.gif"
    rightUrl "Bg.gif"
    topUrl "Bg.gif"
  }
  Transform { children [    # Click flag and hold to see Night sky
    DEF TS TouchSensor {}
    Shape {                 # Flag and flag-pole at origin
      appearance DEF A Appearance { material Material {} }
      geometry IndexedFaceSet {
        coord Coordinate {
          point [ -.1 0 -.1, 0 0 .1, .1 0 -.1,
                  -.1 3 -.1, 0 3 .1, .1 3 -.1,
                   .1 2.4 0, .1 2.9 0, -1.4 2.65 -.8 ]
        }
        coordIndex [ 0 1 4 3 -1  1 2 5 4 -1  2 0 3 5 -1  3 4 5 -1 6 7 8 ]
      }
    }
    Shape {                 # Floor
      appearance USE A
      geometry IndexedFaceSet {
        coord Coordinate { point [ -2 0 -2, -2 0 2, 2 0 2, 2 0 -2 ] }
        coordIndex [ 0 1 2 3 ]
      }
    }
```

```
      DirectionalLight { direction -0.707 -.707 0  intensity 1 }
    ]}
    Viewpoint { position 0 1.5 10 }
  ]}
  ROUTE TS.isActive TO B2.set_bind
```

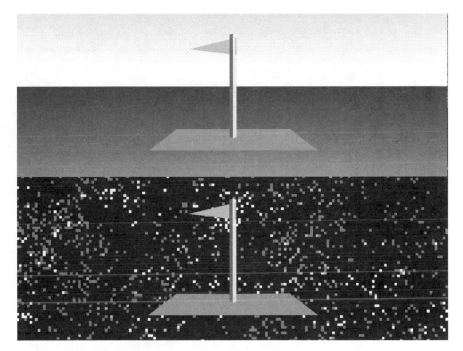

FIGURE 3-3 *Background Example, Before and After Clicking the Flag*

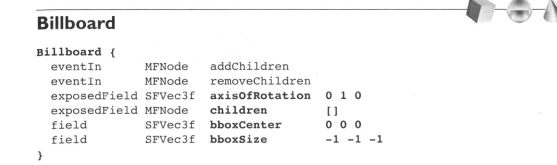

Billboard

```
Billboard {
  eventIn      MFNode    addChildren
  eventIn      MFNode    removeChildren
  exposedField SFVec3f   axisOfRotation   0 1 0
  exposedField MFNode    children         []
  field        SFVec3f   bboxCenter       0 0 0
  field        SFVec3f   bboxSize         -1 -1 -1
}
```

The **Billboard** node is a grouping node that modifies its coordinate system so that the **Billboard** node's local *z*-axis turns to point at the viewer. The **Billboard** node has children that may be other grouping or leaf nodes.

The *axisOfRotation* field specifies which axis to use to perform the rotation. This axis is defined in the local coordinates of the **Billboard** node. The default (0,1,0) is useful for objects such as images of trees and lamps positioned on a ground plane. But when an object is oriented at an angle, for example on the incline of a mountain, then the axis of rotation may also need to be oriented at a similar angle.

A special case of billboarding is screen alignment in which the object always rotates to stay aligned with the viewer, even when the viewer elevates, pitches, and rolls. This special case is distinguished by setting *axisOfRotation* to (0,0,0).

TIP

> Screen-aligned billboards are especially useful for labels that follow the viewer and are always readable. Typically, a **Text** node or **Image Texture** would be parented by a **Billboard** node with *axisOfRotation* set to (0,0,0). See the following example.

To rotate the billboard to face the viewer, determine the line between the billboard's origin and the viewer's position; call this the *billboard-to-viewer* line. The axis of rotation and the billboard-to-viewer line define a plane. The local *z*-axis of the billboard is then rotated into that plane, pivoting around the axis of Rotation.

If the axis of rotation and the billboard-to-viewer line are coincident (the same line), then the plane cannot be established and the rotation results of the billboard are undefined. For example, if *axisOfRotation* is set to (0,1,0) (*y*-axis) and the viewer flies over the billboard and peers directly down the *y*-axis, the results are undefined.

Multiple instances of **Billboards** (DEF/USE) operate as expected—each instance rotates in its unique coordinate system to face the viewer.

See Section 2.3.1, Grouping and Children Nodes, for a description of the *children*, *addChildren*, and *removeChildren* fields and eventIns.

The *bboxCenter* and *bboxSize* fields specify a bounding box that encloses the **Billboard**'s children. This is a hint that may be used for optimization purposes. If the specified bounding box is smaller than the actual bounding box of the children at any time, then the results are undefined. A default *bboxSize* value, (−1,−1,−1), implies that the bounding box is not specified and if needed must be calculated by the browser. See Section 2.3.6, Bounding Boxes, for a description of *bboxCenter* and *bboxSize* fields.

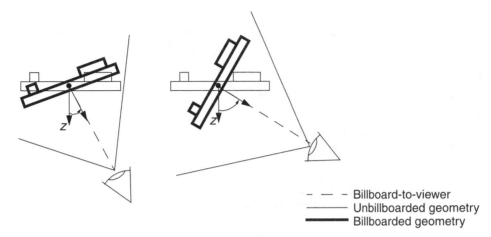

FIGURE 3-4 *Billboard* Node

- – – – Billboard-to-viewer
——— Unbillboarded geometry
▬▬▬ Billboarded geometry

DESIGN NOTE

The **Billboard** node is really just a very fancy **Transform** node that modifies its own rotation based on the relationship between the **Transform** node and the user's view. In fact, a **Billboard** could be prototyped that way by combining a **Transform** node, a **ProximitySensor** to detect the user's view, and a **Script** to perform the necessary computations. However, **Billboard** transformations must be updated whenever the viewer moves, and it is much more efficient for the **Billboard** functionality to be built in to VRML implementations rather than left to **Script** nodes.

Billboards are often used with transparent textured rectangles to approximate 3D geometry with a 2D "cutout," also known as a *sprite.* If you have images of trees (with appropriate transparency values with the image), you might define a sprite prototype as

```
PROTO Sprite [ field MFString texture [ ] ]
{
  Billboard {
    axisOfRotation 0 1 0  # Rotate about Y (up) axis
    children Shape {
      appearance Appearance {
        texture ImageTexture { url IS texture }
      }
      geometry IndexedFaceSet {
        coord Coordinate {
          point [ 0 0 0  1 0 0  1 1 0  0 1 0 ]
        }
        texCoord TextureCoordinate {
          point [ 0 0  1 0  1 1  0 1 ]
        }
```

```
        coordIndex [ 0 1 2 3 -1 ]
      }
    }
  }
}
```

then place several tree cutouts in your scene, like this:

```
Transform {
  translation 13.4   0   55.0
  children Sprite { texture "Oak.png" }
}
Transform {
  translation -14.92   0   23
  children Sprite { texture "Maple.png" }
}
```

Objects defined like this may be much faster both to create and to display than objects defined using a lot of polygons.

EXAMPLE

The following example illustrates typical use of the **Billboard** node. The first **Billboard** defines a tree by specifying a four-component image texture that billboards about its *y*-axis. This is one of the most typical uses of **Billboard**. The second **Billboard** node is almost identical to the first, but billboards around its *x*-axis. The third **Billboard** node illustrates the use of the screen-aligned billboard by setting the *axisOfRotation* field to (0,0,0):

```
#VRML V2.0 utf8
Transform { children [
  Transform {
    translation 5 0 0
    children DEF TREE Billboard { # Billboard about Y-axis
      children DEF S Shape {
        geometry IndexedFaceSet {
          coord Coordinate { point [ -2 0 0, 2 0 0, 2 5 0, -2 5 0 ] }
          texCoord TextureCoordinate { point [ 0 0, 1 0, 1 1, 0 1 ] }
          coordIndex [ 0 1 2 3 ]
        }
        appearance Appearance {
          texture ImageTexture { url "Tree.gif" }
        }
      }
    }
  }
  Transform {
    translation -6 0 -1
```

```
      children Billboard { # Billboard about X-axis
        axisOfRotation 1 0 0
        children USE S
    }
  }
  Transform { # Screen-aligned label for flag-pole
    translation 0 3.3 0
    children Billboard {
      axisOfRotation 0 0 0
      children Shape {
        geometry Text {
          string "Top of flag pole"
          fontStyle FontStyle { size 0.5 }
        }
        appearance Appearance {
          material Material { diffuseColor 0 0 0 }
        }
      }
    }
  }
  Billboard { # Flagpole at origin
    axisOfRotation 0 1 0
    children Shape {
      appearance DEF A Appearance { material Material {} }
      geometry IndexedFaceSet {
        coord Coordinate {
          point [ -.1 0 -.1, 0 0 .1, .1 0 -.1,
                  -.1 3 -.1, 0 3 .1, .1 3 -.1,
                   .1 2.4 0, .1 2.9 0, -1.4 2.65 -.8 ]
        }
        coordIndex [ 0 1 4 3 -1 1 2 5 4 -1 2 0 3 5 -1 3 4 5 -1 6 7 8 ]
      }
    }
  }
  Shape { # Floor
    appearance Appearance {
      texture ImageTexture { url "marble.gif" }
    }
    geometry IndexedFaceSet {
      coord Coordinate {
        point [ -50 0 -50, -50 0 50, 50 0 50, 50 0 -50 ]
      }
      coordIndex [ 0 1 2 3 ]
    }
  }
  DirectionalLight { direction 0 1 0 }
  Viewpoint { position 0 1.5 10 }
  Background { skyColor 1 1 1 }
]}
```

FIGURE 3-5 *A Few Frames From the **Billboard** Example*

Box

```
Box {
  field     SFVec3f size  2 2 2
}
```

The **Box** node specifies a rectangular parallelepiped box in the local coordinate system centered at (0,0,0) in the local coordinate system and aligned with the coordinate axes. By default, the box measures two units in each dimension, from −1 to +1. The **Box**'s *size* field specifies the extent of the box along the *x*-, *y*-, and *z*-axes and must be greater than 0.0.

Textures are applied individually to each face of the box; the entire untransformed texture goes on each face. On the front, back, right, and left faces of the box, when viewed from the outside with the *y*-axis up, the texture is mapped onto each face with the same orientation as if the image were displayed normally in two dimensions. On the top face of the box, when viewed from the outside down the +*y*-axis toward the origin with the −*z*-axis as the view-up direction, the texture is mapped onto the face with the same orientation as if the image were displayed normally in two dimensions. On the bottom face of the box, when viewed from the outside up the −*y*-axis toward the origin with the +*z*-axis as the view-up direction, the texture is mapped onto the face with the same orientation as if the image were displayed normally in two dimensions. **TextureTransform** affects the texture coordinates of the **Box**.

Box **127**

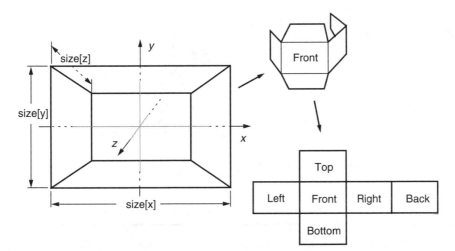

FIGURE 3-6 *Box Node*

The **Box** geometry is considered to be solid and thus requires outside faces only. When viewed from the inside, the results are undefined.

TIP

Box nodes are specified in the *geometry* field of a **Shape** node; they may not be children of a **Transform** or **Group** node.

Box was called **Cube** in VRML 1.0 (which was a misnomer because its *width, height,* and *depth* could be varied). Implementations usually draw boxes as 12 triangles (you should keep this in mind if you are tempted to create a scene that contains 1,000 boxes). If you can, instead, create the same scene using fewer than 12,000 triangles in an **IndexedFaceSet**, you should use the **IndexedFaceSet**.

DESIGN NOTE

The *size* field of **Box** is not exposed and so cannot change once the **Box** has been created. This was done to make very efficient, lightweight implementations possible.

TIP

To change the size of a **Box** node after it is created, use a **Script** node that sends changes to the **Transform** node that parents the **Shape** containing the **Box**:

```
DEF BoxTransform Transform {
   children Shape { geometry Box { size 3 4 2 } } # initial box size
}
...
DEF BoxScaler Script {
    eventIn ...                # some event triggers the change
    eventOut SFVec3f scale     # output that changes the Box's size
    url "..."                  # script that computes scale values
}
ROUTE BoxScaler.scale TO BoxTransform.scale
```

EXAMPLE

The following example illustrates the use of the **Box** node. Note the default mapping of the texture on the faces of the box:

```
#VRML V2.0 utf8
Transform { children [
  Shape {
    geometry Box { }
    appearance Appearance {
      material Material { diffuseColor 1 1 1 }
      texture ImageTexture { url "marble2.gif" }
    }
  }
  Shape {
    geometry Box { size 1 1 3 }
    appearance Appearance {
      material Material { diffuseColor 0.8 0.8 0.8 }
    }
  }
  Shape {
    geometry Box { size 3 1 1 }
    appearance Appearance {
      material Material { diffuseColor 0.6 0.6 0.6 }
    }
  }
  Shape {
    geometry Box { size 1 3 1 }
    appearance Appearance {
      material Material { diffuseColor 1 1 1 }
    }
  }
  NavigationInfo { type "EXAMINE" }
  Background { skyColor 1 1 1 }
]}
```

FIGURE 3-7 *Example* **Box** *Nodes with Texture Image*

Collision

```
Collision {
  eventIn      MFNode    addChildren
  eventIn      MFNode    removeChildren
  exposedField MFNode    children         []
  exposedField SFBool    collide          TRUE
  field        SFVec3f   bboxCenter       0 0 0
  field        SFVec3f   bboxSize         -1 -1 -1
  field        SFNode    proxy            NULL
  eventOut     SFTime    collideTime
}
```

Browser shall detect geometric collisions between the user's avatar (see **Navigation-Info**) and the scene's geometry during navigation to prevent the avatar from penetrating geometry. If there are no **Collision** nodes specified in a scene, browsers shall detect collision with all "collidable" objects during navigation. Note that some geometry nodes are ignored during collision detection; see each geometry node's section for details.

The **Collision** node is a grouping node that may turn off collision detection for its descendants, specify alternative objects to use for collision detection, and send events signaling that a collision has occurred between the user's avatar and the **Collision** group's geometry or alternate.

See Section 2.3.1, Grouping and Children Nodes, for a description of the *children*, *addChildren*, and *removeChildren* fields and eventIns.

The **Collision** node's *collide* field enables and disables collision detection. If *collide* is set to FALSE, the children and all descendants of the **Collision** node will not be checked for collision, even though they are drawn. This includes any descendant **Collision** nodes that have *collide* set to TRUE (i.e., setting *collide* to FALSE turns it off for every node below it).

Collision nodes with the *collide* field set to TRUE detect the nearest collision with their descendant geometry (or proxies). Note that not all geometry is capable of colliding (see each geometry node's section for details). When the nearest collision is detected, the collided **Collision** node sends the time of the collision through its *collideTime* eventOut. This behavior is recursive. If a **Collision** node contains a child, descendant, or proxy (discussed later) that is a **Collision** node, and both **Collisions** detect that a collision has occurred, then both send a *collideTime* event out at the same time, and so on.

TIP

The geometries that are not capable of colliding are **IndexedLineSet, PointSet,** and **Text.** Detecting collisions between 2D or 1D geometries and the 3D viewer is difficult, so they are defined to be transparent to collisions. If this is a problem, a proxy geometry (discussed later) can be specified for each **IndexedLineSet, PointSet,** and **Text.**

Surface properties (e.g., transparent textures or materials) have no affect on collisions. This isn't very realistic, but it can be very useful and makes implementation of **Collision** much easier. Again, **Collision** proxy geometry may be used if you want collision testing to match a partially transparent geometry.

The *bboxCenter* and *bboxSize* fields specify a bounding box that encloses the **Collision**'s children. This is a hint that may be used for optimization purposes. If the specified bounding box is smaller than the actual bounding box of the children at any time, then the results are undefined. A default *bboxSize* value, (−1,−1,−1), implies that the bounding box is not specified and if needed must be calculated by the browser. See Section 2.3.6, Bounding Boxes, for a description of the *bboxCenter* and *bboxSize* fields.

The collision proxy, defined in the *proxy* field, is a legal child node (see Section 2.3.1, Grouping and Children Nodes) that is used as a substitute for the **Collision**'s children during collision detection. The proxy is used strictly for collision detection—it is not drawn.

If the value of the *collide* field is FALSE, then collision detection is not performed with the children or proxy descendant nodes. If the root node of a scene is a **Collision** node with the *collide* field set to FALSE, then collision detection is disabled for the entire scene, regardless of whether descendent **Collision** nodes have set *collide* TRUE.

If the value of the *collide* field is TRUE and the *proxy* field is non-NULL, then the *proxy* field defines the scene in which collision detection is performed. If the *proxy* value is NULL, the children of the **Collision** node are collided against.

If *proxy* is specified, then any descendant children of the **Collision** node are ignored during collision detection. If *children* is empty, *collide* is TRUE, and *proxy* is specified, then collision detection is done against the proxy but nothing is displayed (i.e., invisible collision objects).

TIP

> Navigating in 3D worlds can often be difficult. Whenever possible, use the **Collision** node with a simple, invisible proxy geometry (e.g., a force field) to constrain the avatar navigation to the regions of the world that are intended to be navigated (and to increase performance of collision detection). This technique avoids avatars from getting "stuck" in tight spots, wandering around aimlessly, or investigating portions of the scene that are not intended to be seen. Combining this with **Anchors** for guided tours or reference points can greatly improve world usability. When using invisible **Collision** objects to constrain avatars, it is recommended that a sound effect be issued on collision with the invisible geometry so that the user receives some extra feedback that the "force field" exists (route the *collideTime* eventOut from the **Collision** node to a **Sound** node's **AudioClip** *startTime*).

The *collideTime* eventOut generates an event specifying the time when the user's avatar (see **NavigationInfo**) intersects the collidable children or proxy of the **Collision** node. An ideal implementation computes the exact time of intersection. Implementations may approximate the ideal by sampling the positions of collidable objects and the user. Refer to the **NavigationInfo** node section in this section for parameters that control the user's size.

Browsers are responsible for defining the navigation behavior when collisions occur. For example, when the user comes sufficiently close to an object to trigger a collision, the browser may have the user bounce off the object, come to a stop, or glide along the surface.

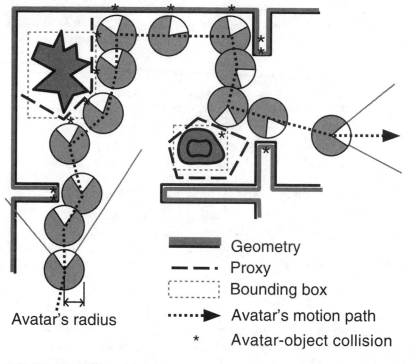

Geometry

Proxy

Bounding box

Avatar's motion path

*   Avatar-object collision

Avatar's radius

FIGURE 3-8 *Collision Node*

DESIGN NOTE

A navigation type of NONE (see the **NavigationInfo** node) implies that the world creator is controlling all navigation, in which case the world creator can use a **Collision** node to detect and respond to collisions.

Note that the **Collision** node only handles collisions between the user and the world, it does *not* detect collisions between arbitrary objects in the world. General, object-to-object collision detection is not specified in VRML 2.0.

Collision detection and *terrain following* are often confused. Terrain following means keeping the viewer's feet on the ground and is a function of the VRML browser's user interface. The *avatarSize* field of the **NavigationInfo** node can be used to control the viewer's height above the terrain, and browsers may decide to treat objects that are invisible to collisions as also being invisible to terrain-following calculations.

EXAMPLE

The following example illustrates several uses of the **Collision** node. Note the use of the invisible proxy to restrict avatar navigation in the second room:

```
#VRML V2.0 utf8
Group { children [
  # 1st room - walls and objects are collidable
  Collision { children [
    Shape {
      appearance DEF WHITE Appearance {
        material DEF M Material {
          diffuseColor 1 1 1
          ambientIntensity .33
        }
      }
      geometry Extrusion {
        crossSection [ 23 -17, 20 -17, 20 -30,
                       0 -30, 0 0, 20 0, 20 -13,
                       23 -13 ]
        spine [ 0 0 0, 0 3 0 ]
        ccw FALSE
      }
    }
    # Cone in the 1st room
    Transform { translation 5 1 -24
      children Collision {
        proxy DEF BBOX Shape { geometry Box{} }
        children DEF CONE Shape { geometry Cone {} }
    }}
    # Sphere in 1st room
    Transform { translation 15 0.3 -26
      children Collision {
        proxy USE BBOX
        children DEF SPHERE Shape {
          geometry Sphere {}
    }}}
    # Box in the 1st room
    Transform { translation 15 0.3 -5
      children Collision {
        proxy USE BBOX
        children DEF BOX Shape { geometry Box {} }
    }}
  ]} # end of first room
  # Second room - uses proxy to constrain user
  Collision {
    proxy Shape {
      geometry Extrusion {
```

```
      crossSection [ 23 -17, 40 -25, 40 -5, 23 -13 ]
      spine [ 0 0 0, 0 3 0 ]
    }
  }
  # These children cannot be collided with
  children [
    Shape {          # 2nd room
      appearance USE WHITE
      geometry Extrusion {
        crossSection [ 23 -17, 23 -30, 43 -30,
                       43 0, 23 0, 23 -13 ]
        spine [ 0 0 0, 0 3 0 ]
      }
    }
    Transform {
      translation 25 1 -24
      children USE CONE
    }
    Transform {
      translation 40 0.3 -2
      children USE SPHERE
    }
    Transform {
      translation 40 0.3 -28
      children USE BOX
    }
  ]}

  # Translucent force field - no collision
  Collision {
    collide FALSE
    children Shape {
      geometry Extrusion {
        crossSection [ 21.5 -17, 21.5 -13 ]
        spine [ 0 0.2 0, 0 2.5 0 ]
        solid FALSE
  }}}
  Viewpoint { position 3.0 1.6 -2 }
  PointLight { location 22 20 -15 radius 20 }
]}
```

Color

```
Color {
  exposedField MFColor color   []
}
```

This node defines a set of RGB colors to be used in the fields of another node.

Color nodes are only used to specify multiple colors for a single piece of geometry, such as a different color for each face or vertex of an **IndexedFaceSet**. A **Material** node is used to specify the overall material parameters of a lighted geometry. If both a **Material** and a **Color** node are specified for a geometry, the colors should ideally replace the diffuse component of the material.

TIP

> Using the **Color** node to specify colors per vertex of **IndexedFaceSet** nodes is a very efficient and effective alternative to texture mapping. If designed properly, color per vertex can produce rich lighting and color effects. Typically, color-per-vertex rendering is much faster than texture mapping and is thus worth the effort. Note, however, that some browsers do not support color-per-vertex rendering; verify that it is supported before using this feature.

Textures that specify RGB triplets (three- and four-component textures) take precedence over colors. Specifying both a texture and a **Color** node for a geometry will result in the **Color** node being ignored. Monochrome textures (one- and two-component textures) modulate the brightness of the color. See Section 2.9.5, Lighting Model, for details on lighting equations.

TIP

> **Color** nodes belong in the *color* field of **ElevationGrid, IndexedFaceSet, Indexed-LineSet,** or **PointSet** nodes.
>
> A **Color** node can function as a general color map for **IndexedFaceSet** and **Indexed-LineSet** nodes. You simply DEF the **Color** node and USE it repeatedly, using the indexing feature of **IndexedFaceSet** or **IndexedLineSet** to refer to colors by index rather than by absolute RGB value. If you are translating from an application that only supports a limited (e.g., 256-color) color palette, then this technique can make the resulting VRML files much smaller than respecifying the RGB colors over and over.

EXAMPLE

> The following example illustrates the use of the **Color** node in conjunction with the **Indexed-FaceSet** node. The first **IndexedFaceSet** uses a **Color** node that specifies two colors: black (0,0,0) and white (1,1,1). Each vertex of each face of the **IndexedFaceSet** is assigned one of these two colors by the *colorIndex* field of the **IndexedFaceSet**. The second **IndexedFaceSet/Color** is almost identical, but does not specify a *colorIndex* field in the **IndexedFaceSet** and thus relies on the *coordIndex* field to assign colors (see **IndexedFaceSet**). The third **IndexedFaceSet/Color** applies color to each face of the **IndexedFaceSet** by setting *colorPerVertex* FALSE and specifying *colorIndex* for each face.

```
#VRML V2.0 utf8
Group { children [
  Transform {
    translation -3 0 0
    children Shape {
      appearance DEF A1 Appearance { material Material {} }
      geometry IndexedFaceSet {
        coord DEF C1 Coordinate {
          point [ 1 0 1, 1 0 -1, -1 0 -1, -1 0 1, 0 3 0 ]
        }
        coordIndex [ 0 1 4 -1  1 2 4 -1  2 3 4 -1  3 0 4 ]
        color Color { color [ 0 0 0, 1 1 1 ] }
        colorIndex [ 0 0 1 -1  0 0 1 -1  0 0 1 -1  0 0 1 ]
      }
    }
  }
  Transform {
    children Shape {
      appearance USE A1
      geometry IndexedFaceSet {  # uses coordIndex for colorIndex
        coord USE C1
        coordIndex [ 0 1 4 -1  1 2 4 -1  2 3 4 -1  3 0 4 ]
        color Color { color [ 1 1 1, 1 1 1, 1 1 1, 1 1 1, 0 0 0 ]}
      }
    }
  }
  Transform {
    translation 3 0 0
    children Shape {
      appearance USE A1
      geometry IndexedFaceSet {
        coord USE C1
        coordIndex [ 0 1 4 -1  1 2 4 -1  2 3 4 -1  3 0 4 ]
        color Color { color [ 0 0 0, 1 1 1 ] }
        colorIndex [ 0, 1, 0, 1 ] # alternate every other face
        colorPerVertex FALSE
      }
    }
  }
  Background { skyColor 1 1 1 }
]}
```

FIGURE 3-9 *Color Node Example*

ColorInterpolator

```
ColorInterpolator {
  eventIn       3FFloat set_fraction
  exposedField MFFloat  key          []
  exposedField MFColor  keyValue     []
  eventOut      SFColor value_changed
}
```

This node interpolates among a set of MFColor key values to produce an SFColor (RGB) *value_changed* event. The number of colors in the *keyValue* field must be equal to the number of keyframes in the *key* field. The *keyValue* field and *value_changed* events are defined in RGB color space. A linear interpolation, using the value of *set_fraction* as input, is performed in HSV color space.

(Refer to Section 2.9.3, Interpolators, for a more detailed discussion of interpolators.)

TIP

The **ColorInterpolator** outputs an SFColor, suitable for use in any of the color fields of a **Material** node (*diffuseColor, specularColor, emissiveColor*). Unfortunately, a **Color-Interpolator** cannot be used to interpolate multiple colors (it does not generate an MFColor output) and so cannot be used with a **Color** node. If you do need to change the colors in a **Color** node, you will have to write a **Script** that does the appropriate calculations.

DESIGN NOTE

Defining the keys in RGB space but doing the interpolation in HSV space may seem somewhat strange. If the *key* values are very close together, then the differences between the two spaces are minimal. However, if there are large differences between the *keys*, then doing the interpolation in HSV space gives better perceptual results, since interpolating between two *keys* with the same intensity will not result in any intensity changes. That isn't true of RGB space: Interpolate from full-intensity red (1,0,0) to full-intensity green (0,1,0) and halfway you'll get half-intensity yellow (0.5,0.5,0).

EXAMPLE

The following example illustrates the use of the **ColorInterpolator** node. An infinitely looping **TimeSensor** is routed to a **ColorInterpolator** that is routed to the *diffuseColor* of a **Material** that is coloring the **Box, Sphere,** and **Cone:**

```
#VRML V2.0 utf8
Transform { children [
  Transform {
    translation -4 0 0
    children Shape {
      geometry Box {}
      appearance DEF A Appearance {
        material DEF M Material { diffuseColor .8 .2 .2 }
      }
    }
  }
  Transform {
    translation 0 0 0
    children Shape { geometry Sphere {}  appearance USE A }
  }
  Transform {
    translation 4 0 0
    children Shape { geometry Cone {}  appearance USE A }
  }
  NavigationInfo { type "EXAMINE" }
]}
```

```
DEF CI ColorInterpolator {
   key [ 0 .2 .4 .6 .8 1 ]
   keyValue [ .8 .2 .2  .2 .8 .2  .2 .2 .8  .8 .8 .8  1 0 1 .8 .2 .2 ]
}
DEF TS TimeSensor { loop TRUE  cycleInterval 5 }
ROUTE TS.fraction_changed TO CI.set_fraction
ROUTE CI.value_changed TO M.set_diffuseColor
```

Cone

```
Cone {
    field    SFBool     bottom        TRUE
    field    SFFloat    bottomRadius  1
    field    SFFloat    height        2
    field    SFBool     side          TRUE
}
```

The **Cone** node specifies a cone that is centered in the local coordinate system and that has a central axis that is aligned with the local *y*-axis. The *bottomRadius* field specifies the radius of the cone's base, and the *height* field specifies the height of the cone from the center of the base to the apex. By default, the cone has a radius of 1.0 at the bottom and a height of 2.0, with its apex at $y = 1$ and its bottom at $y = -1$. Both *bottomRadius* and *height* must be greater than 0.0.

The *side* field specifies whether sides of the cone are created and the *bottom* field specifies whether the bottom cap of the cone is created. A value of TRUE specifies that this part of the cone exists, while a value of FALSE specifies that this part does not exist (not rendered). Parts with field values of FALSE are not collided with during collision detection.

When a texture is applied to the sides of the cone, the texture wraps counterclockwise (from above) starting at the back of the cone. The texture has a vertical seam at the back in the *yz* plane, from the apex (0,height/2,0) to the point (0,0,–r). For the bottom cap, a circle is cut out of the unit texture square centered at (0,–height/2,0) with dimensions (2 × bottom radius) by (2 × bottom radius). The bottom cap texture appears right side up when the top of the cone is rotated toward the –z-axis. **TextureTransform** affects the texture coordinates of the cone.

The cone geometry is considered to be solid and thus requires outside faces only. When viewed from the inside the results are undefined.

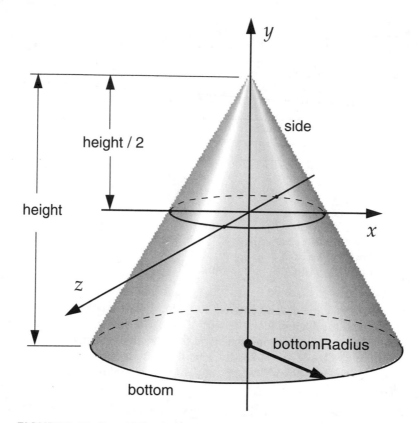

FIGURE 3-10 *Cone Node*

TIP

> **Cone** nodes are specified in the *geometry* field of a **Shape** node; they may not be children of a **Transform** or **Group** node.

DESIGN NOTE

The VRML 1.0 version of the **Cone** was almost exactly the same. The only difference is the specification of the cone parts. VRML 1.0 has a special SFBitmask field for specifying a set of bits. One of the simplifications done in VRML 2.0 was removing that field type, since the same results can be achieved using multiple SFBool fields. So, the VRML 1.0 **Cone**'s *parts* SFEnum field becomes the *side* and *bottom* SFBool fields.

Like the rest of the geometry primitives (**Box, Sphere,** and **Cylinder**), none of the fields of **Cone** are exposed, allowing very lightweight, efficient implementations. If you need to change the size of a cone, you must modify a parent **Transform** node's *scale* field. If you want to turn the parts of a **Cone** on and off, you must either simulate that by using a **Switch** node containing several **Cone Shapes,** or you must remove the **Cone** from its **Shape** (effectively deleting it) and replace it with a newly created **Cone.**

EXAMPLE

The following example illustrates the use of the **Cone** node. The first cone sits on top of the second cone. Note the default texture map orientation as seen in the second **Cone:**

```
#VRML V2.0 utf8
Transform { children [
  Transform {
    translation 0 2.0 0         # sit on top of other Cone
    children Transform {
      translation 0 -1 0
      children Shape {
        geometry Cone { bottomRadius 2 height 1 }
        appearance Appearance {
          material Material { diffuseColor 1 1 1 }
        }
      }
    }
  }
  Transform {
    translation 0 1 0           # sit on y=0
    children Transform {
      translation 0 -1 0
      children Shape {
        geometry Cone { bottomRadius 2 height 4 bottom FALSE }
        appearance Appearance {
          material Material { diffuseColor 1.0 1.0 1.0 }
          texture ImageTexture { url "marble2.gif" }
        }
      }
    }
  }
  DirectionalLight { direction -.5 -0.5 .6 }
  Background { skyColor 1 1 1 }
  NavigationInfo { type "EXAMINE" }
]}
```

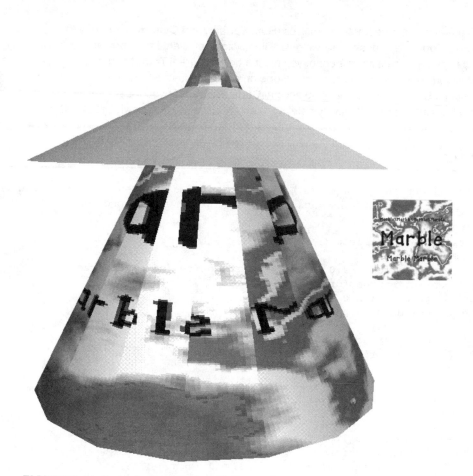

FIGURE 3-11 *Example Cone Nodes with Texture Image*

Coordinate

```
Coordinate {
  exposedField MFVec3f point   []
}
```

This node defines a set of 3D coordinates to be used in the *coord* field of vertex-based geometry nodes (such as **IndexedFaceSet, IndexedLineSet,** and **PointSet**).

EXAMPLE

See **IndexedFaceSet**, **IndexedLineSet**, and **PointSet** for examples of the **Coordinate** node.

DESIGN NOTE

The VRML 1.0 term for the **Coordinate** node is **Coordinate3**. The "3" was originally added in case support for 2D coordinates was added. It was dropped because the VRML 2.0 naming philosophy is to give each node the most obvious name and not try to predict how the specification will change in the future. If carried out to its logical extreme, then a philosophy of planning for future extensions might give **Coordinate** the name **CartesianCoordinate3Float,** since support for polar or spherical coordinates might possibly be added in the future, as might double-precision or integer coordinates.

CoordinateInterpolator

```
CoordinateInterpolator {
    eventIn       SFFloat  set_fraction
    exposedField  MFFloat  key            []
    exposedField  MFVec3f  keyValue       []
    eventOut      MFVec3f  value_changed
}
```

This node linearly interpolates among a set of MFVec3f values. This would be appropriate for interpolating **Coordinate** positions for a geometric morph.

The number of coordinates in the *keyValue* field must be an integer multiple of the number of keyframes in the *key* field. That integer multiple defines how many coordinates will be contained in the *value_changed* events.

TIP

Remember that **TimeSensor** outputs *fraction_changed* events in the 0.0 to 1.0 range, and that interpolator nodes routed *from* **TimeSensors** should restrict their *key* field values to the 0.0 to 1.0 range to match the **TimeSensor** output and thus produce a full interpolation sequence.

Refer to Section 2.9.4, Interpolators, for a more detailed discussion of interpolators.

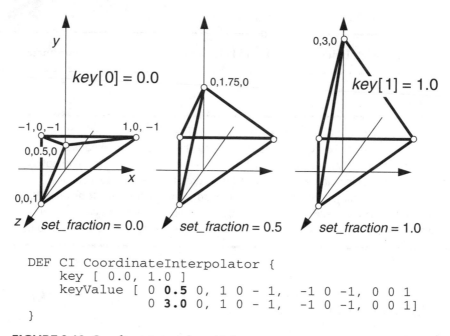

```
DEF CI CoordinateInterpolator {
     key [ 0.0, 1.0 ]
     keyValue [ 0 0.5 0, 1 0 - 1,   -1 0 -1, 0 0 1
                0 3.0 0, 1 0 - 1,   -1 0 -1, 0 0 1]
}
```

FIGURE 3-12 *CoordinateInterpolator Node*

DESIGN NOTE

The **CoordinateInterpolator** was near the edge of the "cut line" for what features should be included in VRML 2.0 and what features should be left out. The following pros and cons influenced the decision and should give you an idea of how decisions were made on which features should be part of the specification.

Con: There is a strong desire to keep the VRML specification as small as possible. A big, bloated specification is hard to implement, hard for which to write conformance tests, takes a very long time to create, and encourages incompatible, partial implementations.

Pro: Coordinate morphing is a feature that many people requested. VRML 2.0 was designed "in the open." Drafts of the specification were constantly made available on the WWW; polls were taken on general, high-level design issues; and there were constant discussions and debates on the *www-vrml* mailing list. This provided invaluable information that helped prioritize decisions about what should be included and excluded, and provided time for unpopular decisions to be either justified or reversed.

Con: CoordinateInterpolator functionality can be accomplished with a **Script** node. Features that are not "fundamental" (that can be implemented using other features of the specification) were likely to be cut.

Pro: CoordinateInterpolator calculations can require a lot of computing power. Interpolating hundreds or thousands of coordinates is computationally expensive compared to interpolating a single translation or rotation. Making **CoordinateInterpolator** a standard node encourages highly optimized implementations, which will be much faster than a **Script** node equivalent.

Con: Implementing shapes with coordinates that may change over time can be difficult. Many interactive rendering libraries are optimized for the display of scenes made up of rigid-body objects, assuming that not many objects will change shape. Changing coordinates also requires that normals be regenerated (if explicit normals are not specified), which is also a fairly expensive operation. Adding **CoordinateInterpolator** to the specification encourages world creators to use a feature that might result in poor performance on many machines.

In the end, the positives outweighed the negatives, but it was not an easy decision and several other possible interpolators did not make the cut (there is no **TextureCoordinateInterpolator** because there isn't a strong enough demand for it, for example).

EXAMPLE

The following example illustrates a typical use of the **CoordinateInterpolator** node (see Figure 3-12). A **TouchSensor** is routed to a **TimeSensor** that fires the **CoordinateInterpolator**:

```
#VRML V2.0 utf8
Group {
  children [
    DEF CI CoordinateInterpolator {
      key [ 0.0, 1.0 ]
      keyValue [ 1 0 -1, -1 0 -1, 0 0 1, 0 0.5 0,
                 1 0 -1, -1 0 -1, 0 0 1, 0 3.0 0 ]
    }
    Shape {
      geometry IndexedFaceSet {
        coord DEF C Coordinate {
          point [ 1 0 -1, -1 0 -1, 0 0 1, 0 0.5 0 ]
        }
        coordIndex [ 0 1 3 -1  1 2 3 -1  2 0 3 ]
      }
      appearance Appearance { material Material {} }
    }
    DEF T TouchSensor {}  # Click to start the morph
    DEF TS TimeSensor {   # Drives the interpolator
      cycleInterval 3.0 # 3 second morph
      loop TRUE
    }
    Background { skyColor 1 1 1 }
  ]
}
```

```
ROUTE CI.value_changed TO C.point
ROUTE T.touchTime TO TS.startTime
ROUTE TS.fraction_changed TO CI.set_fraction
```

Cylinder

```
Cylinder {
    field    SFBool     bottom   TRUE
    field    SFFloat    height   2
    field    SFFloat    radius   1
    field    SFBool     side     TRUE
    field    SFBool     top      TRUE
}
```

The **Cylinder** node specifies a capped cylinder centered at (0,0,0) in the local coordinate system and with a central axis oriented along the local y-axis. By default, the cylinder is sized at −1 to +1 in all three dimensions. The *radius* field specifies the cylinder's radius and the *height* field specifies the cylinder's height along the central axis. Both *radius* and *height* must be greater than 0.0.

The cylinder has three parts: the *side*, the *top* (y = +height/2) and the *bottom* (y = −height/2). Each part has an associated SFBool field that indicates whether the part exists (TRUE) or does not exist (FALSE). If the parts do not exist they are not considered during collision detection.

When a texture is applied to a cylinder, it is applied differently to the sides, top, and bottom. On the sides, the texture wraps counterclockwise (from above) starting at the back of the cylinder. The texture has a vertical seam at the back, lying in the *yz* plane. For the top and bottom caps, a circle is cut out of the unit texture square centered at (0,+/− height,0) with dimensions 2 × radius by 2 × radius. The top texture appears right side up when the top of the cylinder is tilted toward the +z-axis, and the bottom texture appears right side up when the top of the cylinder is tilted toward the −z-axis. **TextureTransform** affects the texture coordinates of the **Cylinder**.

The cylinder geometry is considered to be solid and thus requires outside faces only. When viewed from the inside, the results are undefined.

TIP

Cylinder nodes belong in the *geometry* field of a **Shape** node; they may not be children of a **Transform** or **Group** node.

VRML 1.0 allowed the application of separate materials to each of the parts of the cylinder. That feature was removed because it was rarely used and because removing it simplified both the **Cylinder** node and the **Material** node (which was constrained to containing only one material definition). To accomplish the equivalent functionality with VRML 2.0, you must define three separate cylinder shapes, each with a different part and a different material. This is a more general mechanism, allowing each part to have a different texture or material.

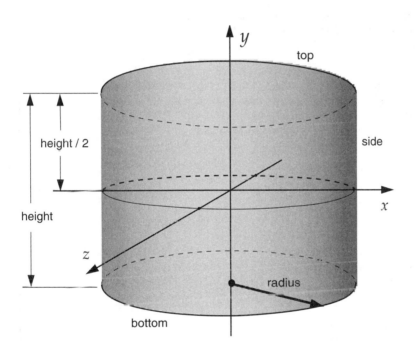

FIGURE 3-13 *Cylinder Node*

EXAMPLE

The following example illustrates use of the **Cylinder** node. Note the default orientation of the texture map on the cylinder sides and caps:

```
#VRML V2.0 utf8
Group { children [
  DEF C1 Shape {
    appearance Appearance {
      material DEF M1 Material {
        diffuseColor 1 1 1
        specularColor 1 1 1
```

```
              shininess .9
          }
          texture ImageTexture { url "marble2.gif" }
      }
      geometry Cylinder { radius 1  height 5.0 }
  }
  Transform {
    translation 0 1 0
    rotation 0 0 1 1.571
    children Shape {
      appearance DEF A1 Appearance { material USE M1 }
      geometry Cylinder { radius 0.5 height 4.0 }
    }
  }
  Transform {
    translation 0 -2.5 0
    children DEF C2 Shape {
      appearance USE A1
      geometry Cylinder { radius 1.5 height 0.5 }
    }
  }
  Transform {
    translation 0 1 0
    rotation 0 0 1 1.571
    scale 0.25 1.5 1
    children USE C1
  }
  Transform {
    translation 0 2.5 0
    scale 0.75 0.5 0.75
    children USE C2
  }
  Background { skyColor 1 1 1 }
  NavigationInfo { type "EXAMINE" }
]}
```

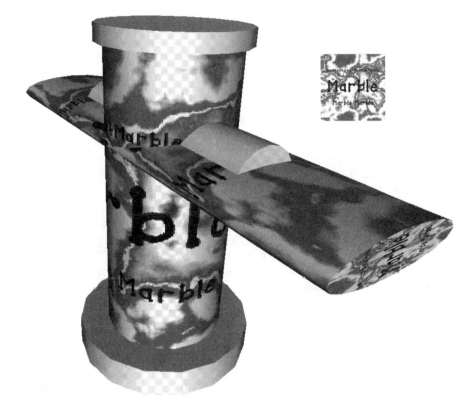

FIGURE 3-14 *Cylinder Node Example with Texture Image*

CylinderSensor

```
CylinderSensor {
  exposedField SFBool      autoOffset TRUE
  exposedField SFFloat     diskAngle  0.262
  exposedField SFBool      enabled    TRUE
  exposedField SFFloat     maxAngle   -1
  exposedField SFFloat     minAngle   0
  exposedField SFFloat     offset     0
  eventOut     SFBool      isActive
  eventOut     SFRotation  rotation_changed
  eventOut     SFVec3f     trackPoint_changed
}
```

The **CylinderSensor** maps pointing device (e.g., mouse or wand) motion into a rotation on an invisible cylinder that is aligned with the *y*-axis of its local space.

The *enabled* exposedField enables and disables the **CylinderSensor.** If TRUE, the sensor reacts appropriately to user events; if FALSE, the sensor does not track user input or send output events. If *enabled* receives a FALSE event and *isActive* is TRUE, the sensor becomes disabled and deactivated, and outputs an *isActive* FALSE event. If *enabled* receives a TRUE event, the sensor is enabled and ready for user activation.

The **CylinderSensor** generates events if the pointing device is activated while over any descendant geometry nodes of its parent group and then moved while activated. Typically, the pointing device is a 2D device such as a mouse. The pointing device is considered to be moving within a plane at a fixed distance from the viewer and perpendicular to the line of sight; this establishes a set of 3D coordinates for the pointer. If a 3D pointer is in use, then the sensor generates events only when the pointer is within the user's field of view. In either case, the pointing device is considered to "pass over" geometry when that geometry is intersected by a line extending from the viewer and passing through the pointer's 3D coordinates. If multiple sensors' geometries intersect this line (hereafter called the *bearing*), only the nearest will be eligible to generate events.

On activation of the pointing device (e.g., mouse button down) over the sensor's geometry, an *isActive* TRUE event is sent. The angle between the bearing vector and the local *y*-axis of the **CylinderSensor** determines whether the sides of the invisible cylinder or the caps (disks) are used for manipulation. If the angle is less than the disk angle, then the geometry is treated as an infinitely large disk and dragging motion is mapped into a rotation around the local *y*-axis of the sensor's coordinate system. The feel of the rotation is as if you were rotating a dial or crank. For each subsequent position of the bearing, a *rotation_changed* event is output that corresponds to a relative rotation from the original intersection, plus the *offset* value. *TrackPoint_changed* events reflect the unclamped drag position on the surface of this disk. When the pointing device is deactivated and *autoOffset* is TRUE, *offset* is set to the last rotation angle and an *offset_changed* event is generated. See Section 2.9.6, Sensor Nodes, for more details on *autoOffset* and *offset_changed*.

If the angle between the bearing vector and the local *y*-axis of the **CylinderSensor** is greater than or equal to *diskAngle*, then the sensor behaves like a cylinder or rolling pin. The shortest distance between the point of intersection (between the bearing and the sensor's geometry) and the *y*-axis of the parent group's local coordinate system determines the radius of an invisible cylinder used to map pointing device motion and mark the zero-rotation value. For each subsequent position of the bearing, a *rotation_changed* event is output that corresponds to a relative rotation from the original intersection, plus the *offset* value. *TrackPoint_changed* events reflect the unclamped drag position on the surface of this cylinder. When the pointing device is deactivated and *autoOffset* is TRUE, *offset* is set to the last rotation angle and an *offset_changed* event is generated. See Section 2.9.6, Sensor Nodes, for more details.

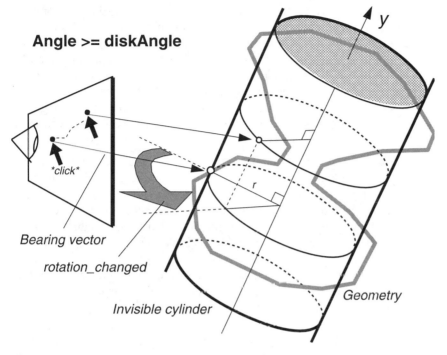

Angle >= diskAngle

Bearing vector

rotation_changed

Invisible cylinder

Geometry

click

FIGURE 3-15 *CylinderSensor Node: Bearing Angle ≥ Disk Angle*

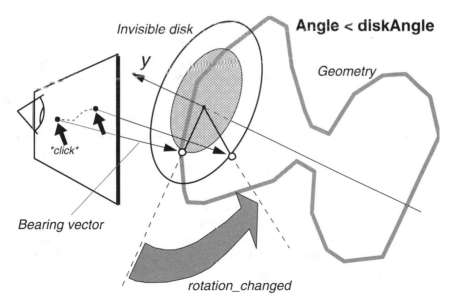

Invisible disk

Angle < diskAngle

Geometry

click

Bearing vector

rotation_changed

FIGURE 3-16 *CylinderSensor Node: Bearing Angle < Disk Angle*

When the sensor generates an *isActive* TRUE event, it grabs all further motion events from the pointing device until it is released and an *isActive* FALSE event is generated. Other pointing device sensors cannot generate events during this time. Motion of the pointing device while *isActive* is TRUE is referred to as *drag*. If a 2D pointing device is in use, *isActive* events will typically reflect the state of the primary button associated with the device (i.e., *isActive* is TRUE when the primary button is pressed and FALSE when it is released). If a 3D pointing device (e.g., wand) is in use, *isActive* events will typically reflect whether the pointer is within or in contact with the sensor's geometry.

While the pointing device is activated, *trackPoint_changed* and *rotation_changed* events are output and are interpreted from pointing device motion based on the sensor's local coordinate system at the time of activation. *TrackPoint_changed* events represent the unclamped intersection points on the surface of the invisible cylinder or disk. If the initial angle results in cylinder rotation (as opposed to disk behavior), and if the pointing device is dragged off the cylinder while activated, browsers may interpret this in several ways (e.g., clamp all values to the cylinder, continue to rotate as the point is dragged away from the cylinder, etc.). Each movement of the pointing device, while *isActive* is TRUE, generates *trackPoint_changed* and *rotation_changed* events.

MinAngle and *maxAngle* may be set to clamp *rotation_changed* events to a range of values (measured in radians about the local *z*- and *y*-axes as appropriate). If *minAngle* is greater than *maxAngle*, *rotation_changed* events are not clamped. See Section 2.9.6, Sensor Nodes, for more details.

TIP

> It is usually a bad idea to route a drag sensor to its own parent. Typically, the drag sensor will route to a **Transform,** which does not affect the sensor. See the following examples.

DESIGN NOTE

SphereSensor and **CylinderSensor** map the 2D motions of a mouse (or other pointing device) into 3D rotations. **CylinderSensor** constrains the rotation to a single axis, while **SphereSensor** allows arbitrary rotation.

A **CylinderSensor** is not useful by itself; you must also specify some geometry to act as the "knob" and must do something with the *rotation_changed* events. Usually, the geometry will be put into a **Transform** node and the *rotation_changed* events will be sent to the **Transform**'s *set_rotation* eventIn, so that the geometry rotates as the user manipulates the **CylinderSensor.** For example:

```
#VRML V2.0 utf8
Group { children [
```

```
DEF CS CylinderSensor { }
DEF T Transform {
  children Shape {
    appearance Appearance { material Material { } }
    geometry Cylinder { }
  }
}
]}
ROUTE CS.rotation_changed TO T.set_rotation
```

Typically the *rotation_changed* will also be routed to a **Script** that extracts the rotation angle, scales it appropriately, and uses it to control something else (the intensity of a **Sound** node in a virtual radio, perhaps). Adding an *angle_changed* SFFloat eventOut to give just the angle was considered, but extracting the angle from a rotation in a **Script** is easy, and a **Script** is necessary in most cases to perform the appropriate offset and scaling anyway.

An earlier design made **CylinderSensor** a grouping node that acted as a "smart **Transform**" that modified itself when the user interacted with it. That design was dropped because it was less flexible. Separating what causes the sensor to activate (its sibling geometry) from its effects on the scene (to what it is routed) adds capabilities without adding complexity to the VRML specification. For example, if you want to quantize a **CylinderSensor** so that it only rotates in five-degree increments, you can ROUTE the *rotation_changed* events to a **Script** that quantizes them and ROUTE the results to the **Transform**'s *set_rotation* (and to anything else that would otherwise be routed from *rotation_changed*).

Originally, **CylinderSensor** was two nodes: **CylinderSensor** and **DiskSensor.** They were combined by introducing the *diskAngle* field. The problem with the original design was a singularity caused by the 2D-to-3D mapping. If the user was viewing the sensors nearly edge on, the rotation calculations became inaccurate and interaction suffered. By combining the two sensors into one and switching from one behavior to another, good interaction is maintained no matter what the relationship between the viewer and the sensor.

Setting *diskAngle* to extreme values results in purely cylindrical or disk behavior, identical to the original nodes. A disk angle of 0 degrees will result in disk interaction behavior no matter what the angle between the viewer and the axis of rotation. A disk angle of 90 degrees or greater ($\pi/2$ radians or greater) will force cylindrical behavior. The default was determined by trial and error to be a reasonable value. It corresponds to 15 degrees, resulting in cylindrical interaction when viewed from the sides and disk interaction when viewed from the top or bottom.

EXAMPLE

The following example illustrates the use of the **CylinderSensor** node.

```
#VRML V2.0 utf8
Group { children [
  # The target object to be rotated needs four Transforms.
  # Two are used to orient the local coordinate system, and
  # two are used as the targets for the sensors (T1 and T2).
  DEF T1 Transform { children
    Transform { rotation 0 0 1 -1.57 children
      DEF T2 Transform { children
        Transform { rotation 0 0 1 1.57 children
          Shape {
            appearance DEF A1 Appearance {
              material Material { diffuseColor 1 1 1 }
            }
            geometry Cone { bottomRadius 2 height 4 }
  }}}}}
  Transform {        # Left crank geometry
    translation -1 0 3
    rotation 0 0 1 -1.57
    children [
      DEF T3 Transform { children
        DEF G1 Group { children [
          Transform {
            rotation 0 0 1 1.57
            translation -.5 0 0
            children Shape {
              appearance USE A1
              geometry Cylinder { radius .1 height 1 }
            }
          }
          Transform {
            rotation 0 0 1 1.57
            translation -1 0 0
            children Shape {
              geometry Sphere { radius .2 }
              appearance USE A1
            }
          }
        ]} # end Group
      }
      DEF CS1 CylinderSensor {    # Sensor for Left crank
        maxAngle 1.57             #      rotates Y axis => T1
        minAngle 0
      }
    ]
  }
```

```
  Transform {       # Right crank geometry
    translation 1 0 3
    rotation 0 0 1 -1.57
    children [
      DEF T4 Transform { children USE G1 }
      DEF CS2 CylinderSensor {     # Sensor for Right crank2
        maxAngle 1.57             #    rotates X-axis => T
        minAngle 0
      }
    ]
  }
  Transform {                      # Housing to hold cranks
    translation 0 0 3
    children Shape {
      geometry Box { size 3 0.5 0.5 }
      appearance USE A1
    }
  }
  Background { skyColor 1 1 1 }
]}
ROUTE CS1.rotation_changed TO T1.rotation  # rotates Y-axis
ROUTE CS1.rotation_changed TO T3.rotation  # rotates the L crank
ROUTE CS2.rotation_changed TO T2.rotation  # rotates X-axis
ROUTE CS2.rotation_changed TO T4.rotation  # rotates the R crank
```

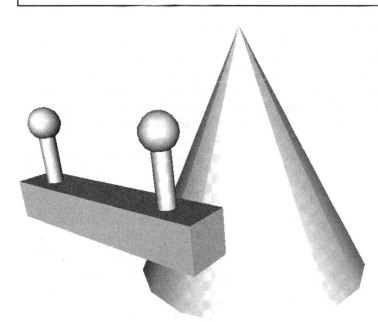

FIGURE 3-17 *CylinderSensor Node Example*

DirectionalLight

```
DirectionalLight {
  exposedField SFFloat  ambientIntensity  0
  exposedField SFColor  color             1 1 1
  exposedField SFVec3f  direction         0 0 -1
  exposedField SFFloat  intensity         1
  exposedField SFBool   on                TRUE
}
```

The **DirectionalLight** node defines a directional light source that illuminates along rays parallel to a given 3D vector. See Section 2.9.4, Light Sources, for a definition of the *ambientIntensity, color, intensity,* and *on* fields.

The *direction* field specifies the direction vector within the local coordinate system in which the light illuminates. Light is emitted along parallel rays from an infinite distance away. A directional light source illuminates only the objects in its enclosing parent group. The light may illuminate everything within this coordinate system, including all children and descendants of its parent group. The accumulated transformations of the parent nodes affect the light.

DESIGN NOTE

VRML 1.0 assumed a default global (i.e., affects all objects) ambient light source of intensity 1.0. VRML 2.0 does not define a global ambient light source. Instead, each light source node (**DirectionalLight, PointLight,** and **SpotLight**) have an *ambient-Intensity* field that represents that individual light's contribution to the overall ambient illumination. This has the nice result of increasing the overall ambient illumination as the number of lights in the scene increases. This is a gross, yet reasonable, approximation to the physical world. Note that the default value for *ambientIntensity* of light sources is 0.0 and thus default scenes will have zero ambient illumination.

TIP

The **DirectionalLight** node is similar to a floodlight in stage or film lighting. It is an excellent choice for simple scene lighting since directional lights are relatively easy to set up; typically result in bright, fully lit scenes; and render faster than the other light types.

Since directional lights do not have a *radius* field to limit the illumination effects, it is very important to parent **DirectionalLights** under the **Transform** node of the shapes that you want to illuminate. If you find that your scene is too bright or that objects are being illuminated by unknown lights, you may want to check for **DirectionalLights** under the wrong **Transform** node. Also, note that since some rendering libraries do not support scoped lights and thus illuminate all objects in the scene, this may have no effect.

Also note that lights in VRML are not occluded by geometry in the scene. This means that geometry nodes are illuminated by light sources regardless of whether other geometry *blocks* the light emanating from a light source. This can produce unrealistic lighting effects and takes getting used to. Note that it is possible to create shadow effects by creating transparent geometry (e.g., **IndexedFaceSet**) that creates the illusion of shadows.

See Section 2.9.5, Lighting Model, for a precise description of VRML's lighting equations.

TIP

Remember that VRML 2.0 does not define a default ambient light source. This means that the dark side of all objects in the scene will be very, very dark if you do not set the *ambientIntensity* field of one or more of the light sources. Typically, each light source node in the scene will contribute to the overall ambient illumination, and thus it is recommended to set the *ambientIntensity* to 1.0 for each light source. Remember that the default ambient field of the **Material** node (unfortunately also named *ambientIntensity*) is set to 0.2 and will ensure that the dark sides of the your objects are not too bright.

TIP

Use the light source nodes to control the overall contrast and brightness of your scene. To raise the dark areas (i.e., shadows) of the scene, increase all of the *ambientIntensity* field of the light sources. To reduce the hot spots, lower the *intensity* field of the light sources that are affecting the hot spot. By adjusting these two fields, you can control the

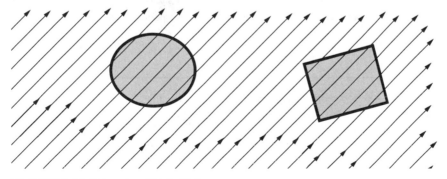

FIGURE 3-18 *DirectionalLight Node*

contrast and brightness of your scene. Also, remember that most rendering libraries do not provide control over the dynamic range of the image (e.g., a camera's f-stop), and thus if you find that your entire scene is too hot, lower the intensities of *all* of the light sources proportionally until the scene is within a normal luminance range (i.e., no hot spots). You might need to raise all of the *ambientIntensity* fields as well (described earlier) to compensate.

Some low-end renderers do not support the concept of per-object lighting. This means that placing **DirectionalLights** inside local coordinate systems, which implies lighting only the objects beneath the **Transform** with that light, is not supported in all systems. For the broadest compatibility, lights should be placed at the outermost scope.

TIP

Remember that the default **NavigationInfo** automatically adds an extra light source to your scene (mounted on the user's head). This needs to be considered when designing your scene lighting and must be anticipated or turned off (`NavigationInfo { headlight FALSE ... }`).

TIP

Most rendering libraries perform lighting calculations only at the vertices of the polygons and then interpolate the computed colors across the polygonal surface rather than compute the lighting at each point of the surface. This technique is known as *Gouraud shading* (named after Henri Gouraud) and is used to increase rendering performance (lighting calculations can be very expensive!). Gouraud shading can often produce undesirable aliasing artifacts when the number of vertices is too low and does not represent a reasonable sampling of the surface. Adding extra intermediate vertices to the geometry will typically improve the lighting, but can penalize rendering and download performance.

EXAMPLE

The following example illustrates use of the **DirectionalLight** node. The first **DirectionalLight** is contained by the root **Group** of the scene and thus illuminates all geometry in the scene. Each of the three subsequent **DirectionalLights** illuminate only the single **Shape** node that is contained by the light's parent **Transform** node. Also, note the use of the **NavigationInfo** node to turn off the browser's headlight:

```
#VRML V2.0 utf8
Group {
  children [
    DEF DL1 DirectionalLight {  # One light to shine on all objects
      ambientIntensity 0.39
      direction 0.24 -0.85 -0.46
    }
    Transform {       # One light to shine on the Box
      children [
        DEF DL2 DirectionalLight { direction -0.56 0.34 -0.75 }
        Transform {
          translation -3 0.77 -4.57
          rotation 0.30 0.94 -0.14 0.93
          scale 0.85 0.85 0.85
          scaleOrientation -0.36 -0.89 -0.29  0.18
          children Shape {
            appearance DEF A1 Appearance {
              material Material {
                ambientIntensity 0.34  diffuseColor .85 .85 .85
                specularColor 1 1 1  shininess .56
              }
            }
            geometry Box {}
    }}]}
    Transform {       # One light to shine on the Sphere
      children [
        DEF DL3 DirectionalLight { direction 0.50 0.84 0.21 }
        Transform {
          translation 0 0.7 -4.5
          children Shape { appearance USE A1 geometry Sphere {} }
    }]}
    Transform {       # One light to shine on the Cone
      children [
        DEF DL4 DirectionalLight { direction 0.81 -0.06 0.58 }
        Transform {
          translation 3 1.05 -4.45
          rotation 0 0 1  0.6
          children Shape { appearance USE A1 geometry Cone {} }
    }]}
    Transform {
      translation 0 -1.1 -4.33
      scale 5 0.15 3
      children Shape { appearance USE A1 geometry Box {} }
    }
    Background { skyColor 1 1 1 }
    NavigationInfo { type "EXAMINE" headlight FALSE }
  ]
}
```

FIGURE 3-19 *DirectionalLight Node Example*

ElevationGrid

```
ElevationGrid {
    eventIn        MFFloat    set_height
    exposedField   SFNode     color             NULL
    exposedField   SFNode     normal            NULL
    exposedField   SFNode     texCoord          NULL
    field          MFFloat    height            []
    field          SFBool     ccw               TRUE
    field          SFBool     colorPerVertex    TRUE
    field          SFFloat    creaseAngle       0
    field          SFBool     normalPerVertex   TRUE
    field          SFBool     solid             TRUE
    field          SFInt32    xDimension        0
    field          SFFloat    xSpacing          0.0
    field          SFInt32    zDimension        0
    field          SFFloat    zSpacing          0.0
}
```

The **ElevationGrid** node specifies a uniform rectangular grid of varying height in the *xz* plane of the local coordinate system. The geometry is described by a scalar array of height values that specify the height of a rectangular surface above each point of the grid.

The *xDimension* and *zDimension* fields indicate the number of dimensions of the grid height array in the *x* and *z* directions. Both *xDimension* and *zDimension* must be >1. The vertex locations for the rectangles are defined by the *height* field and the *xSpacing* and *zSpacing* fields:

- The *height* field is an *xDimension*-by-*zDimension* array of scalar values representing the height above the grid for each vertex.

- The *xSpacing* and *zSpacing* fields indicate the distance between vertices in the *x* and *z* directions respectively, and must be ≥ 0.

Thus, the vertex corresponding to the point P[i, j] on the grid is placed at

P[i, j].x = *xSpacing* * i

P[i, j].y = height[i + j * *xDimension*]

P[i, j].z = *zSpacing* * j

where $0 \leq i < xDimension$ and $0 \leq j < zDimension$

The *set_height* eventIn allows the height MFFloat field to be changed to allow animated **ElevationGrids.**

The default texture coordinates (*texCoord* NULL) range from (0,0) at the first vertex to (1,1) at the last vertex. The s texture coordinate will be aligned with *x*, and the *t* texture coordinate with *z*. Texture coordinates are explicitly specified by setting

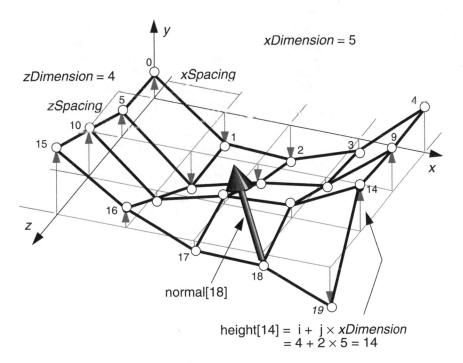

height[14] = i + j × *xDimension*
= 4 + 2 × 5 = 14

FIGURE 3-20 *ElevationGrid Node*

texCoord to a **TextureCoordinate** node containing the *xDimension* * *zDimension* texture coordinate:

P[i, j].texCoord = TextureCoordinate[i + j * *xDimension*]

The *colorPerVertex* field determines whether colors (if specified in the *color* field) should be applied to each vertex or each quadrilateral of the **ElevationGrid**. If *colorPerVertex* is FALSE and the *color* field is not NULL, then the *color* field must contain a **Color** node containing at least (*xDimension* − 1) × (*zDimension* − 1) colors. If *colorPerVertex* is TRUE and the *color* field is not NULL, then the *color* field must contain a **Color** node containing at least *xDimension* × *zDimension* colors. The *normalPerVertex* and *normal* fields behave similiar to the *colorPerVertex* and *color* fields, but specify normal vectors. If the *normal* field is specified it must contain a **Normal** node.

TIP

> The **ElevationGrid** node is a good candidate for the floor or terrain of the scene since it provides better compression than an **IndexedFaceSet** and thus shorter download time. It is best to divide the scene into regions to allow the browser to perform rendering optimizations. Thus, rather than creating a single **ElevationGrid** that spans the entire floor or terrain of the world, it is better to create a series of **ElevationGrids** that grid together to form the entire floor or terrain of the world. Choose a size that also lends itself to effective level of detail. Then, create an **LOD** for each **Elevation-Grid** node to increase rendering performance for sections that are a reasonable distance away. Experiment with different sizes by conducting performance tests in the browser. Be careful to match the seams between the various levels of adjacent **ElevationGrids**.

If the *ccw* field is TRUE, the default-generated normals shall have a positive *y* component (face upward). If *ccw* is FALSE, the normals shall have a negative *y* component (face downward). If the normals are explicitly specified, they should match the orientation defined by *ccw*, but are not required to do so. If the *solid* field is TRUE (the default), the side surface defined by the *ccw* field is drawn and the other side may be culled. For example, if *ccw* is TRUE, the top (face up) is drawn and the bottom side may be culled. See Section 2.9.2, Geometry, for a general description of the *ccw*, *solid*, and *creaseAngle* fields.

TIP

> Note that the default texture mapping produces a texture that is upside down when viewed from the positive z-axis. To orient the texture to a more intuitive mapping, use a **TextureTransform** node to reverse the *t* texture coordinate, like this:
>
> ```
> Shape {
>   appearance Appearance {
>     textureTransform TextureTransform { scale 1 -1 }
>   }
>   geometry ElevationGrid { ... }
> }
> ```
>
> This will produce a compact **ElevationGrid** with texture mapping that aligns to the natural orientation of the image. Note that this only works if the texture is repeated (default). If the texture is not repeated, you need to set the *translation* field of **Texture-Transform** to `translation 0 1`. Alternatively, you can specify texture coordinates in the *texCoord* field that map the first height coordinate to an *s* and *t* of (0,1), the last height to (1,0) and so on; this will produce larger files, though.

DESIGN NOTE

ElevationGrid is specified in the *geometry* field of a **Shape** node. Like all other geometry nodes, it may not be directly used as the child of a grouping node.

ElevationGrid was added to VRML 2.0 as a compact way of representing terrain. It is not a fundamental node; its functionality is a subset of what can be accomplished with the more general **IndexedFaceSet** node. Because terrain is common in virtual worlds (and because 2D grids with a value at each grid point are a very common data type used in many different applications) and because **ElevationGrid** is so much smaller than the equivalent **IndexedFaceSet,** it was added to the specification. For example, a 10×10 **ElevationGrid** requires a specification of $10 \times 10 = 100$ heights, plus two integers and two floats for the dimensions and spacing, or 102 floating point and two integer values. Accomplishing the equivalent using an **IndexedFaceSet** requires $10 \times 10 = 100$ 3D vertices, plus $81 \times 5 = 405$ integer indices (81 quadrilaterals plus end-of-face markers), or 300 floating point and 405 integer values. Even assuming that compression will make integer indices one-fourth as big as floating point coordinates, the **ElevationGrid** is still about four times smaller.

The *height* field of **ElevationGrid** is not completely exposed; you can set it using *set_height*, but there is no *height_changed* eventOut that you can route from or read from a **Script.** This was done to allow efficient implementations that convert **Elevation-Grids** into the equivalent **IndexedFaceSet** (or whatever representation is best for the underlying rendering library). If *height* were exposed, then such implementations would be forced to maintain the height array. Since it isn't, implementations can free that storage after the conversion is done.

TIP

Most interactive renderers do not draw quadrilaterals directly, but instead split them into triangles before rendering. The VRML specification does not specify how this should be done for **ElevationGrid.** Implementations are free to do whatever their underlying rendering libraries do. If your **ElevationGrids** are highly irregular, forming highly non-planar quadrilaterals, then results may vary between implementations.

EXAMPLE

The following example illustrates use of the **ElevationGrid** node. Note the default texture map orientation on the first **ElevationGrid** and how **TextureTransform** is used on the second **ElevationGrid** to orient the texture more naturally:

```
#VRML V2.0 utf8
Transform { children [
  Shape {
    geometry DEF EG ElevationGrid {
      xDimension 5
      xSpacing 1
      zDimension 4
      zSpacing 1
      height [            # 5x4 array of heights
        0 .707 1 .707 0
        0 .47 .667 .47 0
        0 .236 .33 .236 0
        0 0 0 0 0
      ]
      creaseAngle 0.8
    }
    appearance Appearance {
      material DEF M Material { diffuseColor 1 1 1 }
      texture DEF IT ImageTexture { url "marble2.gif" }
    }
  }
  Transform {
    translation 4.3 0 0
    children Shape {
      geometry ElevationGrid {
        xDimension 5
        xSpacing 1
        zDimension 4
        zSpacing 1
        height [            # 5x4 array of heights
          0 .707 1 .707 0
          0 .47 .667 .47 0
          0 .236 .33 .236 0
          0 0 0 0 0
        ]
```

```
            creaseAngle 0.8
        }
        appearance Appearance {
          material USE M
          texture USE IT
          textureTransform TextureTransform { scale 1 -1 }
        }
      }
    }
  DirectionalLight { direction -0.80 -0.6 0 }
  Viewpoint { position 3 2 8 }
  Background { skyColor 1 1 1 }
]}
```

Extrusion

```
Extrusion {
  eventIn MFVec2f      set_crossSection
  eventIn MFRotation   set_orientation
  eventIn MFVec2f      set_scale
  eventIn MFVec3f      set_spine
  field   SFBool       beginCap       TRUE
  field   SFBool       ccw            TRUE
  field   SFBool       convex         TRUE
  field   SFFloat      creaseAngle    0
  field   MFVec2f      crossSection   [ 1 1, 1 -1,  1 -1, -1 1, 1 1 ]
  field   SFBool       endCap         TRUE
  field   MFRotation   orientation    0 0 1 0
  field   MFVec2f      scale          1 1
  field   SFBool       solid          TRUE
  field   MFVec3f      spine          [ 0 0 0, 0 1 0 ]
}
```

The **Extrusion** node specifies geometric shapes based on a 2D cross section extruded along a 3D spine. The cross section can be scaled and rotated at each spine point to produce a wide variety of shapes.

An **Extrusion** is defined by a 2D cross section piecewise linear curve (described as a series of connected vertices), a 3D spine piecewise linear curve (also described as a series of connected vertices), a list of 2D scale parameters, and a list of 3D orientation parameters. Shapes are constructed as follows:

1. The cross-section curve, which starts as a curve in the xz plane, is first scaled about the origin by the first *scale* parameter (first value scales in x, second value scales in z).

2. It is then rotated about the origin by the first *orientation* parameter and translated by the vector given as the first vertex of the *spine* curve.

3. It is then extruded through space along the first segment of the *spine* curve.

4. Next, it is scaled and rotated by the second *scale* and *orientation* parameters, and extruded by the second segment of the *spine*, and so on.

The number of *scale* and *orientation* values shall equal the number of *spine* points, or contain one value that is applied to all points. The *scale* values must be >0.

A transformed cross section is found for each joint (i.e., at each vertex of the *spine* curve, where segments of the extrusion connect), and the joints and segments are connected to form the surface. No check is made for self-penetration. Each transformed cross section is determined as follows:

1. Start with the cross section as specified, in the *xz* plane.

2. Scale it about (0,0,0) by the value for *scale* given for the current joint.

3. Apply a rotation so that when the cross section is placed at its location on the *spine* it will be oriented properly. Essentially, this means that the cross section's *y*-axis (up vector coming out of the cross section) is rotated to align with an approximate tangent to the spine curve. *For all points other than the first or last*, the tangent for *spine*[i] is found by normalizing the vector defined by (*spine*[i + 1] − *spine*[i − 1]). *If the spine curve is closed*, the first and last points need to have the same tangent. This tangent is found as just stated, but using the points *spine*[0] for *spine*[i], *spine*[1] for *spine*[i + 1] and *spine*[n − 2] for *spine*[i − 1], where *spine*[n − 2] is the next-to-last point on the curve. The last point in the curve, *spine*[n − 1], is the same as the first, *spine*[0]. *If the spine curve is not closed*, the tangent used for the first point is just the direction from *spine*[0] to *spine*[1], and the tangent used for the last is the direction from *spine*[n − 2] to *spine*[n − 1]. *In the simple case where the spine curve is flat in the xy plane*, these rotations are all just rotations about the *z*-axis. In the more general case where the *spine* curve is any 3D curve, you need to find the destinations for all three of the local *x*-, *y*-, and *z*-axes so you can completely specify the rotation. The *z*-axis is found by taking the cross product of

$$S0 \times S1$$

where $S0 = spine[i + 1] - spine[i]$

$S1 = spine[i - 1] - spine[i]$

If the three points are colinear then this value is 0, so take the value from the previous point. Once you have the *z*-axis (from the cross product) and the y-axis (from the approximate tangent), calculate the x-axis as the cross product of the y- and z-axes.

4. Given the plane computed in step 3, apply the orientation to the cross section relative to this new plane. Rotate it counterclockwise about the axis and by the angle specified in the orientation field at that joint.

5. Finally, the cross section is translated to the location of the spine point.

Surfaces of revolution: If the cross section is an approximation of a circle and the spine is straight, then the **Extrusion** is equivalent to a surface of revolution where the *scale* parameters define the size of the cross section along the spine.

Cookie cutter extrusions: If the *scale* is (1,1) and the spine is straight, then the cross section acts like a cookie cutter, with the thickness of the cookie equal to the length of the spine.

Bend/twist/taper objects: These shapes are the result of using all fields. The spine curve bends the extruded shape defined by the cross section, the *orientation* parameters twist it around the spine, and the *scale* parameters taper it (by scaling about the spine).

Extrusion has three parts: the sides, the *beginCap* (the surface at the initial end of the spine) and the *endCap* (the surface at the final end of the spine). The caps have an associated SFBool field that indicates whether it exists (TRUE) or doesn't exist (FALSE).

When the *beginCap* or *endCap* fields are specified as TRUE, planar cap surfaces will be generated regardless of whether the cross section is a closed curve. (If the cross section isn't a closed curve, the caps are generated as if it were—equivalent to adding a final point to *crossSection* that's equal to the initial point. Note that an open surface can still have a cap, resulting (for a simple case) in a shape something like a soda can sliced in half vertically.) These surfaces are generated even if *spine* is also a closed curve. If a field value is FALSE, the corresponding cap is not generated.

Extrusion automatically generates its own normals. Orientation of the normals is determined by the vertex ordering of the triangles generated by **Extrusion**. The vertex ordering is in turn determined by the cross section curve. If the cross section is counterclockwise when viewed from the +y-axis, then the polygons will have counterclockwise ordering when viewed from "outside" the shape (and vice versa for clockwise-ordered cross sectional curves).

Texture coordinates are automatically generated by **Extrusions**. Textures are mapped so that the coordinates range in the *u* direction from 0 to 1 along the *crossSection* curve (with 0 corresponding to the first point in *crossSection* and 1 to the last) and in the *v* direction from 0 to 1 along the *spine* curve (again with 0 corresponding to the first listed spine point and 1 to the last). When *crossSection* is closed, the texture has a seam that follows the line traced by the *crossSection*'s start/end point as it travels along the spine. If *endCap* and/or *beginCap* exist, the *crossSection* curve is uniformly scaled and translated so that the largest dimension of the cross section (*x* or *z*) produces texture coordinates that range from 0.0 to 1.0. The *beginCap* and *endCap* textures' *s* and *t* directions correspond to the *x* and *z* directions in which the *crossSection* coordinates are defined.

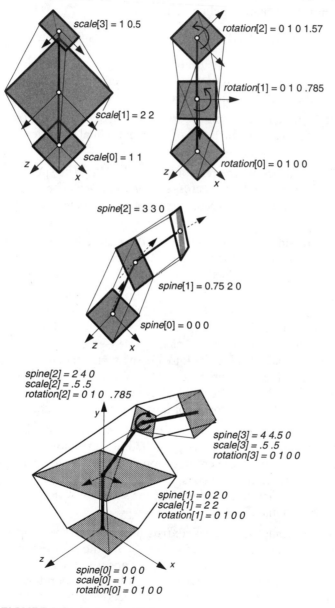

FIGURE 3-21 *Extrusion Node*

See Section 2.9.2, Geometry Nodes, for a description of the *ccw, solid, convex,* and *creaseAngle* fields.

DESIGN NOTE

Extrusion and **ElevationGrid** are the only new geometry types added to VRML 2.0; all the rest were part of VRML 1.0. Like **ElevationGrid**, **Extrusion** was added because it is commonly used (many shapes can be created with **Extrusion**) and because the equivalent **IndexedFaceSet** is much larger.

Extrusions are also much more convenient than **IndexedFaceSet.** Because implementations know the topology of an extrusion, normals are more easily generated. Texture coordinates are also easily generated and cannot be specified. You can use a **TextureTransform** node to modify the generated coordinates, but must use an **IndexedFaceSet** if you want complete control over texture map application.

Like **ElevationGrid,** several of **Extrusion**'s fields are only partially exposed to make it easier to create optimized implementations—you can set them, but you cannot read their value.

EXAMPLE

The following example illustrates the three typical uses of the **Extrusion** node. The first **Extrusion** node defines a surface-of-revolution object. The second **Extrusion** node defines a beveled, cookie cutter object. The third **Extrusion** node defines a bent-twisted-tapered object:

```
#VRML V2.0 utf8
Group { children [
  Transform {      # Surface of Revolution object
    translation -4 0 0
    children Shape {
      appearance DEF A Appearance {
        material Material {
          ambientIntensity 0.33
          diffuseColor 1 1 1
        }
        texture ImageTexture { url "marble2.gif" }
      }
      geometry DEF SOR Extrusion {
        crossSection [  1  0,  .866 -.5,     .5    -.866,
                        0 -1, -.5   -.866, -.866 -.5,
                       -1  0, -.866  .5,    -.5    .866,
                        0  1,  .5    .866,   .866  .5, 1 0 ]
        spine [ 0 0 0, 0 0.5 0, 0 1.5 0, 0 2 0, 0 2.5 0, 0 3 0,
                0 4 0, 0 4.5 0 ]
```

```
          scale [ 0.4 0.4, 1.2 1.2, 1.6 1.6, 1.5 1.5, 1.0 1.0,
                  0.4 0.4, 0.4 0.4, 0.7 0.7 ]
        }
      }
    }
    Transform {    # Beveled cookie-cutter object
      children Shape {
        appearance USE A
        geometry DEF COOKIE Extrusion {
          crossSection [ 1 0, 0.25 -0.25, 0 -1, -0.25 -0.25, -1 0,
                         -0.25 0.25, 0 1, 0.25 0.25, 1 0 ]
          spine [ 0 0 0, 0 0.2 0, 0 1 0, 0 1.2 0 ]
          scale [ 1 1, 1.3 1.3, 1.3 1.3, 1 1 ]
        }
      }
    }
    Transform {    # Bend/twist/taper object
      translation 3 0 0
      children Shape {
        appearance USE A
        geometry DEF BENDY Extrusion {
          crossSection [ 1 0, 0 -1, -1 0, 0 1, 1 0 ]
          spine [ 0 0 0, 0.5 0.5 0, 0.5 1 0, 0 1.5 0, 0 2 0,
                  -0.5 2.5 0, -0.5 3 0, 0 3.5 0 ]
          scale [ .3 .3, .2 .2, .1 .1, .1 .1, .1 .1, .1 .1, .1 .1,
                  .3 .3 ]
          orientation [ 0 1 0 0.0, 0 1 0 -.3, 0 1 0 -.6, 0 1 0 -.9,
                        0 1 0 -1.2, 0 1 0 -1.5, 0 1 0 -1.8, 0 1 0 -2.1 ]
          creaseAngle 0.9
        }
      }
    }
    Background { skyColor 1 1 1 }
    DirectionalLight { direction 0 0 1 }
    NavigationInfo { type "EXAMINE" }
  ]}
```

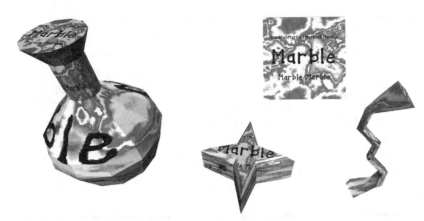

FIGURE 3-22 *Extrusion Node Example with Image Texture*

Fog

```
Fog {
    exposedField SFColor   color            1 1 1
    exposedField SFString  fogType          "LINEAR"
    exposedField SFFloat   visibilityRange  0
    eventIn      SFBool    set_bind
    eventOut     SFBool    isBound
}
```

The **Fog** node provides a way to simulate atmospheric effects by blending objects with the color specified by the *color* field based on the objects' distance from the viewer. The distances are calculated in the coordinate space of the **Fog** node. The *visibilityRange* specifies the distance (in the **Fog** node's coordinate space) at which objects are totally obscured by the fog. Objects located *visibilityRange* meters or more away from the viewer are drawn with a constant color of *color*. Objects very close to the viewer are blended very little with the fog color. A *visibilityRange* of 0.0 or less disables the **Fog** node. Note that *visibilityRange* is affected by the scaling transformations of the **Fog** node's parents—translations and rotations have no effect on *visibilityRange*.

DESIGN NOTE

Controlling the fog color allows many interesting effects. A foggy day calls for a fog color of light gray; a foggy night calls for a dark gray fog color. You can get a depth-cuing effect in which objects get darker the farther they are from the viewer by using a black fog color, and can get smoke and/or fire by making the fog blue or red. Use *visibilityRange* to control the density of the fog, smoke, or haze.

Fog nodes are bindable children nodes (see Section 2.9.1, Bindable Children Nodes) and thus there exists a **Fog** stack, in which the topmost **Fog** node on the stack is currently active. To push a **Fog** node to the top of the stack, a TRUE value is sent to the *set_bind* eventIn. Once active, the **Fog** is then bound to the browser's view. A FALSE value of *set_bind*, pops the **Fog** from the stack and unbinds it from the browser viewer. (See Section 2.9.1, Bindable Children Nodes, for more details on the **Fog** stack.)

DESIGN NOTE

You can use the **Fog** stack to create effects like the inside of a house that is free of fog located in a very foggy town. When the user enters the house, a **ProximitySensor** can be used to bind a **Fog** node that turns off **Fog.** When the user leaves the house, the **Fog** node is unbound and the user sees the foggy street. The transition from outdoors to indoors might also involve binding a **Background** node with prerendered foggy street scenes that will be seen out of the windows of the house and binding a **NavigationInfo** node to let the VRML browser know that the user can't see very far when they are inside the house.

The *fogType* field controls how much of the fog color is blended with the object as a function of distance. If *fogType* is **LINEAR** (the default), then the amount of blending is a linear function of the distance, resulting in a depth-cuing effect. If *fogType* is **EXPONENTIAL** then an exponential increase in blending should be used, resulting in a more natural fog appearance.

TIP

If the background color or image doesn't match the fog color, then you will see fog-colored silhouettes of faraway objects against the background. There are cases when it is useful to have only part of the background match the fog color, which is why the background is not forced to match the fog color when fogging is being done. For example, to simulate ground fog at night you might have a background that is fog colored close to the horizon, but has an image of slightly foggy stars straight overhead. As long as there were no objects floating in the sky overhead (which would appear foggy and spoil the effect), as viewers looked out over the city they would see the buildings fading into the fog while still seeing stars overhead.

See Section 2.9.5, Lighting Model, for details on lighting calculations.

DESIGN NOTE

Fog can be very useful as a technique to limit how much of the world the user can see at any one time, giving better rendering performance. It can also give users valuable depth cues that enhance the feeling of being in a 3D space. However, fog is a fairly advanced rendering feature that implementations may be forced to approximate by performing fogging calculations only once per vertex or even once per **Shape** node instead of the ideal, which is to fog each pixel rendered.

TIP

Use the **Fog** node in combination with **LOD** to reduce the visual complexity of the scene and thus increase rendering performance. Tune *visibiltyRange* to match the maximum range in the **LOD** nodes and set the last child of the **LOD** to a **WorldInfo** node. This has the effect of not rendering any objects outside the **Fog** range! Since the **Fog** creates a natural fade to the *visiblityRange*, users will not notice objects popping in and out as the **LOD** goes to maximum range. This can be a very effective technique for producing interactive frame rates. Experiment and tune the ranges for each particular scene. Also note that the *visiblityLimit* field of the **NavigationInfo** node can produce a similar result and should be considered as well (verify that the browser supports the *visibilityLimit* feature).

Also, use **ProximitySensors** to bind and unbind **Fog** nodes as the user enters and exits regions of the world with differing **Fog** values. In regions where there is no fog, set *visibilityRange* to 0 to disable **Fog**.

As stated, **Fog** nodes are typically used in conjunction with a **Background** node by setting the **Background**'s *skyColor* equal or similar to the **Fog**'s color.

EXAMPLE

The following example illustrates typical use of the **Fog** node. Notice how a **Background** node is created to correspond to each **Fog** node. **ProximitySensors** are used to bind and unbind the two **Fog** nodes:

```
#VRML V2.0 utf8
Group {
  children [
    DEF F1 Fog { color 1 1 1 visibilityRange 10 }          # Room fog
    DEF F2 Fog { color 0.5 0.5 0.5 visibilityRange 85 }    # Out fog
    DEF B1 Background { skyColor 1 1 1 }                    # Room bkg
    DEF B2 Background { skyColor 0.5 0.5 0.5 }              # Out bkg
    Transform {
      translation 0 1.5 0
      children DEF P1 ProximitySensor { size 4 3 4 }
    }
```

```
    Transform {
      translation 0 25 -52
      children DEF P2 ProximitySensor { size 100 50 100 }
    }
    Transform { children [              # A room with a cone inside
      Shape {                           # The room
        appearance DEF A Appearance {
          material DEF M Material {
            diffuseColor 1 1 1 ambientIntensity .33
          }
        }
        geometry IndexedFaceSet {
          coord Coordinate {
            point [ 2 0 -2, 2 0 2, -2 0 2, -2 0 -2,
                    2 2 -2, 2 2 2, -2 2 2, -2 2 -2 ]
          }
          coordIndex [ 0 1 5 4 -1, 1 2 6 5 -1, 2 3 7 6 -1, 4 5 6 7 ]
          solid FALSE
        }
      }
      Transform {                       # Cone in the room
        translation -1 0.5 -1.7
        children DEF S Shape {
          geometry Cone { bottomRadius 0.2 height 1.0 }
          appearance USE A
        }
      }
    ]}
    Transform { children [              # Outside the room
      Shape {                           # Textured ground plane
        appearance Appearance {
          material USE M
          texture ImageTexture { url "marble.gif" }
        }
        geometry IndexedFaceSet {
          coord Coordinate {
            point [ 50 0 -100, -50 0 -100, -50 0 2, 50 0 2 ]
          }
          coordIndex [ 0 1 2 3 ]
        }
      }
      Transform {                       # Object outside
        scale 20 20 20
        translation 0 10 -25
        children USE S
      }
    ]}
    Viewpoint { position 1.5 1.0 1.8 orientation 0 0 1 0 }
```

```
      DirectionalLight { direction 0 -1 0 }
  ]
}
ROUTE P1.isActive TO F1.set_bind # These routes bind and unbind the
ROUTE P1.isActive TO B1.set_bind #  room fog/bkg & outdoors fog/bkg
ROUTE P2.isActive TO F2.set_bind #  as the avatar enters/exits the
ROUTE P2.isActive TO B2.set_bind #  the ProximitySensors.
```

FIGURE 3-23 *Two Frames from a Fog Node Example*

FontStyle

```
FontStyle {
  field MFString  family       "SERIF"
  field SFBool    horizontal   TRUE
  field MFString  justify      "BEGIN"
  field SFString  language     " "
  field SFBool    leftToRight  TRUE
  field SFFloat   size         1.0
  field SFFloat   spacing      1.0
  field SFString  style        "PLAIN"
  field SFBool    topToBottom  TRUE
}
```

The **FontStyle** node defines the size, font family, and style of the text's font, as well as the direction of the text strings and any language-specific rendering techniques that must be used for non-English text. See the description of the **Text** node for details on the application of **FontStyle**.

The *size* field specifies the height (in object space units) of glyphs rendered and determines the spacing of adjacent lines of text. All subsequent strings advance in either *x* or *y* by −(*size* × *spacing*).

Font Family and Style

Font attributes are defined by the *family* and *style* fields. It is up to the browser to assign specific fonts to the various attribute combinations.

The *family* field specifies a case-sensitive MFString value that is a preference-ordered list of family font names. Browsers must support the following family names:

- `"SERIF"`, for a serif font such as Times Roman (the default),
- `"SANS"`, for a sans serif font such as Helvetica
- `"TYPEWRITER"`, for a fixed-pitch font such as Courier

Browsers may also support extended, browser-dependent family names. Browsers shall search the list, front to back, for the first supported or required family name in the list. A *family* value of empty quotes, `""`, is identical to `"SERIF"`.

TIP

If you use browser-dependent fonts (e.g., Serenity), make sure also to specify one of the three font families that are guaranteed to be supported. Typically, you will order the custom font families first, followed by a required family. For example:

```
FontStyle {
   family [ "Serenity", "OtherFamily", "SERIF" ]
}
```

DESIGN NOTE

The *family* field was originally an SFString field. However, a request was made to change the type to MFString to support the concept of extended font family names. This change was made after the August 1996 VRML draft and is backward compatible with files conforming to the August draft.

The *style* field specifies a case-sensitive SFString value that may be **PLAIN** (the default) for default plain type, **BOLD** for boldface type; **ITALIC** for italic type; or **BOLDITALIC** for bold and italic type. A style value of empty quotes, `""`, is identical to `"PLAIN"`.

DESIGN NOTE

The difficulty with fonts is that there are so many of them. Worse, fonts that look pretty much the same are given different names, because font names may be copyrighted while the "look" of a font may not. So, to get a sans serif font on a MacOS system, you might use Helvetica. On a Windows system, a very similar-looking font is called Arial.

This is all a big problem for VRML, which is striving to be a platform-independent international standard that requires no licensing to implement. So, the entire issue was sidestepped by allowing only the most basic attributes of a font to be specified and not allowing specification of any particular font.

Direction, Justification, and Spacing

The *horizontal*, *leftToRight*, and *topToBottom* fields indicate the direction of the text. The *horizontal* field indicates whether the text advances horizontally in its major direction (*horizontal* = TRUE, the default) or vertically in its major direction (*horizontal* = FALSE). The *leftToRight* and *topToBottom* fields indicate direction of text advance in the major (characters within a single string) and minor (successive strings) axes of a layout. Which field is used for the major direction and which is used for the minor direction is determined by the *horizontal* field.

For horizontal text (*horizontal* = TRUE), characters on each line of text advance in the positive *x* direction if *leftToRight* is TRUE or in the negative *x* direction if *leftToRight* is FALSE. Characters are advanced according to their natural advance width. Then, each line of characters is advanced in the negative *y* direction if *topToBottom* is TRUE or in the positive *y* direction if *topToBottom* is FALSE. Lines are advanced by the amount of *size* × *spacing*.

For vertical text (*horizontal* = FALSE), characters on each line of text advance in the negative *y* direction if *topToBottom* is TRUE or in the positive *y* direction if *topToBottom* is FALSE. Characters are advanced according to their natural advance height. Then, each line of characters is advanced in the positive *x* direction if *leftToRight* is TRUE or in the negative *x* direction if *leftToRight* is FALSE. Lines are advanced by the amount of *size* × *spacing*.

The *justify* field determines alignment of the text layout relative to the origin of the object coordinate system. It is an MFString that can contain two values. The first value specifies alignment along the major axis and the second value specifies alignment along the minor axis, as determined by the *horizontal* field. A *justify* value of " " is equivalent to the default value. If the second string (minor alignment) is not specified, then it defaults to the value **FIRST**. Thus, *justify* values of " ", **"BEGIN"**, and **["BEGIN" "FIRST"]** are equivalent.

The major alignment is along the *x*-axis when *horizontal* is TRUE and along the *y*-axis when *horizontal* is FALSE. The minor alignment is along the *y*-axis when *horizontal* is

TRUE and along the *x*-axis when *horizontal* is FALSE. The possible values for each enumerant of the *justify* field are `FIRST`, `BEGIN`, `MIDDLE`, and `END`. For major alignment, each line of text is positioned individually according to the major alignment enumerant. For minor alignment, the block of text representing all lines together is positioned according to the minor alignment enumerant. Tables 3-1 through 3-4 describe the behavior in terms of which portion of the text is at the origin.

TABLE 3-1 *Major alignment,* horizontal = *TRUE*

Enumerant	*leftToRight* = TRUE	*leftToRight* = FALSE
FIRST	Left edge of each line	Right edge of each line
BEGIN	Left edge of each line	Right edge of each line
MIDDLE	Centered about *x*-axis	Centered about *x*-axis
END	Right edge of each line	Left edge of each line

TABLE 3-2 *Major alignment,* horizontal = *FALSE*

Enumerant	*topToBottom* = TRUE	*topToBottom* = FALSE
FIRST	Top edge of each line	Bottom edge of each line
BEGIN	Top edge of each line	Bottom edge of each line
MIDDLE	Centered about *y*-axis	Centered about *y*-axis
END	Bottom edge of each line	Top edge of each line

TABLE 3-3 *Minor alignment,* horizontal = *TRUE*

Enumerant	*topToBottom* = TRUE	*topToBottom* = FALSE
FIRST	Baseline of first line	Baseline of first line
BEGIN	Top edge of first line	Bottom edge of first line
MIDDLE	Centered about *y*-axis	Centered about *y*-axis
END	Bottom edge of last line	Top edge of last line

TABLE 3-4 *Minor alignment,* horizontal = *FALSE*

Enumerant	*leftToRight* = TRUE	*leftToRight* = FALSE
FIRST	Left edge of first line	Right edge of first line
BEGIN	Left edge of first line	Right edge of first line
MIDDLE	Centered about *x*-axis	Centered about *x*-axis
END	Right edge of last line	Left edge of last line

The default minor alignment is **FIRST**. This is a special case of minor alignment when *horizontal* is TRUE. Text starts at the baseline at the *y*-axis. In all other cases, **FIRST** is identical to **BEGIN**. In Figures 3-24 and 3-25, each cross hair indicates where the *x*- and *y*-axes should be in relation to the text.

minor = ÷ "BEGIN" + "MIDDLE" + "FIRST" ÷ "END"			*top IoBottom*	
			TRUE	**FALSE**
major = "BEGIN" or "FIRST"	*leftToRight*	T R U E	This is a test of text.	of text. a test This is
		F A L S E	si sihT tset a .txet fo	.txet of tset a si sihT
major = "MIDDLE"	*leftToRight*	T R U E	This is a test of text.	of text. a test This is
		F A L S E	si sihT tset a .txet fo	.txet of tset a si sihT
major = "END"	*leftToRight*	T R U E	This is a test of text.	of text. a test This is
		F A L S E	si sihT tset a .txet fo	.txet of tset a si sihT

FIGURE 3-24 Horizontal = *TRUE*

minor = + "FIRST"/"BEGIN" + "MIDDLE" + "END"			topToBottom	
			TRUE	**FALSE**
major = "BEGIN" or "FIRST"	leftToRight	T R U E	This is a test of text	si si sihT test of a text
		F A L S E	of text. a test This is	text. test sihT of a
major = "MIDDLE"	leftToRight	T R U E	This is a test of text.	si sihT test a T text of
		F A L S E	of text a test This is	text. test sihT of a
major = "END"	leftToRight	T R U E	This is a test of text.	si sihT test a T text of
		F A L S E	of text a test This is	text. test sihT of a si

FIGURE 3-25 Horizontal = *FALSE*

DESIGN NOTE

All of these various combinations of *direction*, *justify*, and *spacing* can be useful. However, **FontStyle** is not one of the more commonly used nodes, yet its specification is as long as any other node—a good indication that it is probably overengineered. It is not expected that VRML worlds will contain pages and pages of text expressed as 3D **Text** nodes. 3D rendering libraries are not typically optimized for display of text, and trying to use a lot of text in a 3D world usually results in unreadable results. It is much better to combine the 3D world with explanatory text on the same Web page, with the 3D scene described using VRML and the 2D text described using HTML or another text formatting langauge.

The *language* field specifies the context of the language for the text string. Due to the multilingual nature of ISO 10646-1:1993, the *language* field is needed to provide a proper language attribute of the text string. The format is based on RFC 1766: language[_territory]. The value for the language tag is based on ISO 639 (i.e., zh for Chinese, jp for Japanese, sc for Swedish). The territory tag is based on the ISO 3166 country code (i.e., TW for Taiwan and CN for China for the zh Chinese language tag). If the *language* field is set to empty " ", then local language bindings are used. Please refer to these sites for more details:

- `http://www.chemie.fu-berlin.de/diverse/doc/ISO_639.html`
- `http://www.chemie.fu-berlin.de/diverse/doc/ISO_3166.html`

TIP

FontStyle nodes belong in the *fontStyle* field of **Text** nodes. If you want to use a single **FontStyle** for all of your text, you must DEF it and then repeatedly USE it for the second and subsequent **Text** nodes.

EXAMPLE

The following example illustrates a simple case of the **FontStyle** node.

```
#VRML V2.0 utf8
Group { children [
  Transform {
    translation 0 4 0
    children Shape {
      geometry Text {
        string "PLAIN FontStyle example."
        fontStyle FontStyle {}
    }
```

```
      appearance DEF A1 Appearance {
      material Material { diffuseColor 0 0 0 }
      }
    }
  }
  Transform {
    translation 0 2 0
    children Shape {
      geometry Text {
        string "BOLD FontStyle example."
        fontStyle FontStyle { style "BOLD" }
      }
      appearance USE A1
    }
  }
  Transform {
    translation 0 0 0
    children Shape {
      geometry Text {
        string "ITALIC FontStyle example."
        fontStyle FontStyle { style "ITALIC" }
      }
      appearance USE A1
    }
  }
  Transform {
    translation 0 -2 0
    children Shape {
      geometry Text {
        string "BOLDITALIC FontStyle example."
        fontStyle FontStyle { style "BOLDITALIC" }
      }
      appearance USE A1
    }
  }
  Background { skyColor 1 1 1 }
]}
```

PLAIN FontStyle example.

BOLD FontStyle example.

ITALIC FontStyle example.

BOLDITALIC FontStyle example.

FIGURE 3-26 *FontStyle Node Example*

Group

```
Group {
    eventIn        MFNode  addChildren
    eventIn        MFNode  removeChildren
    exposedField MFNode  children       []
    field          SFVec3f bboxCenter     0 0 0
    field          SFVec3f bboxSize       -1 -1 -1
}
```

A **Group** node is equivalent to a **Transform** node, without the transformation fields. (See Section 2.3.1, Grouping and Children Nodes, for a description of the *children*, *addChildren*, and *removeChildren* fields and eventIns.)

The *bboxCenter* and *bboxSize* fields specify a bounding box that encloses the **Group**'s children. This is a hint that may be used for optimization purposes. If the specified bounding box is smaller than the actual bounding box of the children at any time, then the results are undefined. A default *bboxSize* value, (−1,−1,−1), implies that the bounding box is not specified and if needed must be calculated by the browser. See Section 2.3.6, Bounding Boxes, for a description of the *bboxCenter* and *bboxSize* fields.

DESIGN NOTE

Group is equivalent to a simplified **Transform** node; it could be prototyped as

```
PROTO Group [
    eventIn MFNode addChildren
    eventIn MFNode removeChildren
    exposedField MFNode children  [ ]
    field SFVec3f bboxCenter 0 0 0
    field SFVec3f bboxSize  -1 -1 -1 ]
{
    Transform {
        addChildren IS addChildren
        removeChildren IS removeChildren
        children IS children
        bboxCenter IS bboxCenter
        bboxSize IS bboxSize
    }
}
```

Group is a standard node in the VRML specification because implementations can represent a **Group** more efficiently than the more general **Transform,** saving memory and slightly increasing rendering performance when the user wants only grouping and not transformation functionality.

The most difficult design decision for **Group** was what it should be named. VRML 1.0 also has a **Group** node, with similar but not identical functionality. It was feared that having a VRML 2.0 node with the same name but slightly different semantics might be confusing; the VRML 2.0 **Group** is semantically more like the VRML 1.0 **Separator** node. After a long debate, it was decided that naming decisions should not be influenced by the VRML 1.0 node names. It is expected that the number of people using VRML 2.0 will be much greater than the number of people who ever used VRML 1.0. Therefore, easy-to-learn and easy-to-understand names were chosen in favor of easing the transition from 1.0 to 2.0.

TIP

> **Group** nodes are a good choice as the root (first) node of the VRML file.

EXAMPLE

The following example illustrates use of the **Group** node. The first **Group** node contains two children and shows typical use of the root **Group** as a container for the entire scene. The second **Group** node contains three **Shapes** and is instanced later as the second child of the root **Group** node:

```
#VRML V2.0 utf8
Group {               # Root Group node
  children [
    DEF G1 Group { # Group containing box, sphere, and cone
      children [
        Transform {
          translation -3 0 0
          children Shape { geometry Box {} }
        }
        Transform {
          children Shape { geometry Sphere {} }
        }
        Transform {
          translation 3 0 0
          children Shape { geometry Cone {} }
        }
      ]
    }
    Transform {
      translation 0 -3 0
      children USE G1     # Instance of G1 group
    }
  ]
}
```

ImageTexture

```
ImageTexture {
  exposedField MFString url       []
  field        SFBool   repeatS TRUE
  field        SFBool   repeatT TRUE
}
```

The **ImageTexture** node defines a texture map by specifying an image file and general parameters for mapping to geometry. Texture maps are defined in a 2D coordinate system, (s, t), that ranges from 0.0 to 1.0 in both directions. The bottom edge of the image corresponds to the s-axis of the texture map, and left edge of the image corresponds to the t-axis of the texture map. The lower left pixel of the image corresponds to $s = 0$, $t = 0$, and the top-right pixel of the image corresponds to $s = 1$, $t = 1$.

TIP

> Figure 3-27 illustrates the image space of a texture map image (specified in the *url* field). Notice how the image defines the 0.0 to 1.0 *s* and *t* boundaries. Regardless of the size and aspect ratio of the texture map image, the left edge of the image always represents *s* = 0, the right edge, *s* = 1.0, the bottom edge, *t* = 0.0, and the top edge, *t* = 1.0. Also, notice how we have illustrated the texture map infinitely repeating in all directions. This shows what happens conceptually when *s* and *t* values, specified by the **TextureCoordinate** node, are outside of the 0.0 to 1.0 range.

The texture is read from the URL specified by the *url* field. To turn off texturing, set the *url* field to have no values (**[ ]**). Browsers are required to support the JPEG format (*Digital Compression and Coding of Continuous-tone Still Images, Part 1: Requirements and Guidelines,* ISO/IEC IS 10918-1, Joint Photographic Experts Group, International Organization for Standardization, 1991) and PNG (*Portable Networked Graphics Specification, version 0.96*, W3C Working Draft 11-Mar-1996, `http://www.w3.org/pub/WWW/TR/WD-png` and `http://www.boutell.com/boutell/png/`) image file formats, and, in addition, may support any other image formats. Support for the GIF format (*Graphics Interchange Format,* Version 89a, `http://www.radzone.org/tutorials/gif89a.txt` and `http:www.w3.org/pub/WWW/Graphics/GIF/spec-gif87.txt`), including transparent backgrounds, is also recommended. See Section 2.1.3, URLs, for details on the *url* field.

TIP

> **ImageTexture** nodes belong in the *texture* field of **Appearance** nodes.

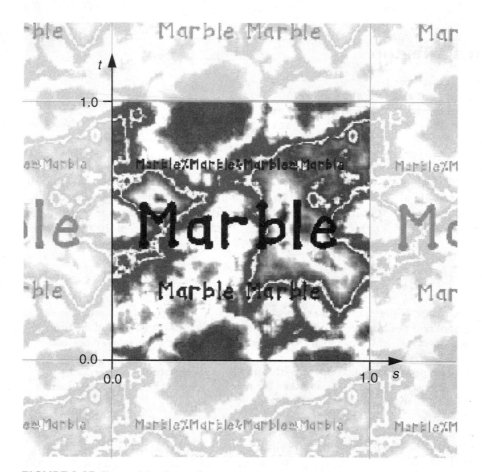

FIGURE 3-27 *Texture Map Image Space*

DESIGN NOTE

GIF is a very popular file format on the WWW and support for GIF-format textures would undoubtedly be required by the VRML specification if it was free of licensing restrictions. Browser implementors typically support displaying GIF-format textures, since they are so popular, and decompressing GIF images is allowed by Unisys with no licensing requirement. However, content-creation tools should migrate to the PNG image format, which is superior to GIF and is free of patents. Browsers that support GIF images should also support the GIF "transparency color" feature, which maps one color in the image as fully transparent (alpha = 0). Furthermore, if the color map of the GIF image is composed of only gray hues, the texture should be interpreted as a one-channel image (if there's no transparency color) or two-channel image (if there is a transparency color), and is modulated by **Material** *diffuseColor*.

Both PNG and JPEG (JFIF is actually the proper name for the popular file format that uses the JPEG compression algorithm, but only image-file-format techies care about the distinction) are required, rather than just one or the other, for a few reasons:

1. JPEG is a lossy compression algorithm, most appropriate for natural images; its compression adds noticeable artifacts to diagrams, text, and other man-made images. PNG uses a lossless compression algorithm that is more appropriate for these kinds of images.

2. JPEG allows only the specification of full-color (RGB) images. It does not include any transparency information nor does it support luminance images (except as full-color images that just happen to contain only shades of gray). PNG supports one- two- three-, and four-component images.

3. PNG is new and, as of early 1997, is not yet widely supported. JPEG is much more common.

Browsers should interpret PNG's transparency color and gray-scale color maps as just descibed for GIF images.

Texture images may be one component (luminance), two component (luminance plus transparency), three component (full RGB color), or four component (full RGB color plus transparency). An ideal VRML implementation will use the texture image to modify the diffuse color and transparency of an object's material (specified in a **Material** node), then perform any lighting calculations using the rest of the object's material properties with the modified diffuse color to produce the final image. The texture image modifies the diffuse color and transparency depending on how many components are in the image, as follows:

1. Diffuse color is multiplied by the luminance values in the texture image.

2. Diffuse color is multiplied by the luminance values in the texture image; material transparency is multiplied by transparency values in the texture image.

3. RGB colors in the texture image replace the material's diffuse color.

4. RGB colors in the texture image replace the material's diffuse color; transparency values in the texture image replace the material's transparency.

See Section 2.9.5, Lighting Model, for details on lighting equations and the interaction between textures, materials, and geometries.

Browsers may approximate this ideal behavior to increase performance. One common optimization is to calculate lighting only at each vertex and combine the texture image with the color computed from lighting (performing the texturing after lighting). Another common optimization is to perform no lighting calculations at all when texturing is enabled, displaying only the colors of the texture image.

TIP

DEF/USE textures: **ImageTextures** and **MovieTextures** should be instanced using DEF/USE whenever possible. Remember that **ImageTextures** often represent the largest percentage of a scene's file size and should be kept as small as possible without hurting image quality. Instanced **ImageTextures** can reduce download time and increase rendering speed.

TIP

Turn off lighting when using textures: To increase texture performance in cases when the lighting is not important or required, do *not* specify a **Material** node. This will instruct the browser to turn off the lighting calculations and render the geometry with the exact colors found in the texture map (and ignore the light sources in the scene and thus speed up rendering). This is especially useful for light-emitting surfaces, such as a television or movie screen, and for prelit surfaces, such as a wall with the lighting effects painted into the texture map, rather than computed by the browser (this effect is common in most 3D games). Here's a simple example of an object with no **Material** and thus no lighting computations:

```
#VRML V2.0 utf8
Shape {    # no Material --> turns off lighting
  appearance Appearance {
    texture ImageTexture { url "test.mpeg" }
  }
  geometry Box {}
}
```

TIP

Limit texture map size whenever possible: Texture maps often represent the largest aspect of your VRML file size. Therefore, to reduce download time it is critical to find ways to reduce texture map size. The obvious first step is to restrict your texture maps to the smallest resolution that still renders adequately. Another factor is to use one-component (gray-scale) textures whenever possible. Remember that the **Material** node's *diffuseColor* and the **Color** node tints one-component textures. For example, to create a green grass texture, create a small, repeatable (left-right and top-bottom edges match) gray-scale texture and apply a **Material** node or **Color** node with greenish color:

```
Shape {
  texture ImageTexture { url "grass.png" }
  material Material { diffuseColor 0.1 0.8 0.2 }
  geometry ...
}
```

Note that in order to use one-component textures *and* to turn lighting off, you can use an **IndexedFaceSet** with *colorPerVertex* FALSE (i.e., colors applied per face) and a **Color** node to tint the texture:

```
Shape {
  texture ImageTexture { url "grass.png" }
  # no material specified --> turns off lighting calculations
  geometry IndexedFaceSet {
    coord Coordinate { point [ ... ] }
    coordIndex [ ... ]
    texcoord TextureCoordinate { point [ ... ] }
    colorPerVertex FALSE                # color per face
    color Color { color 0.1 0.8 0.2 }  # green-ish color
    colorIndex [ 0 0 0 ... ]  # use same Color value for faces
  }
}
```

If you want to vary the color at each vertex or face (e.g., to add hue randomness), specify a list of different colors and apply to each vertex.

TIP

Beware of texture size limitations: It is critical to be aware of the specific texture mapping restrictions imposed by the rendering library of the each browser that you intend to use. For example, some rendering libraries require that all texture maps fit into a 128 x 128 resolution. Browsers will automatically filter all texture maps to this size, but produce blurry textures and waste valuable download time. Some rendering libraries require that the texture map's resolution be a power of two (e.g., 32, 64, 128). A conservative approach is to design your texture maps in the 128 x 128 or 256 x 256 resolution. Care-fully read the release notes of the browsers that you intend to use before wasting your time on high-resolution textures.

Keep in mind that if the browser (i.e., the underlying rendering library) requires texture maps at a specific resolution (e.g., 128 x 128) and you provide a texture map at 64 x 128, you will have wasted half of the texture memory. Therefore, to maximize performance, use as much of the required texture resolution for the actual texture maps by combin-ing smaller textures into a single texture map and use **TextureCoordinates** to map the individual objects to their appropriate subtextures. For example, imagine that you have one medium-size texture that represents a corporate sign, and smaller size tex-tures that represent small signs or repeating textures in the scene, such as stone, grass, bricks, and so forth. You can combine many textures into a single texture map and allo-cate proportional amounts as you see fit (Figure 3-28). Note, however, that combining multiple textures into one image interacts badly with a rendering technique called mip-mapping. Mip-mapping relies on the creation of low-resolution versions of the texture image; these low-resolution versions are displayed when the texture is far away. If there are multiple texture maps in the original image, the automatically created low-resolution images will not be correct—colors from different maps will be averaged together. A similar problem can occur if you use JPEG compression, which works on blocks of pixels. Pixels from the different maps in the image may be compressed together, resulting in errors along the edges of the individual texture maps.

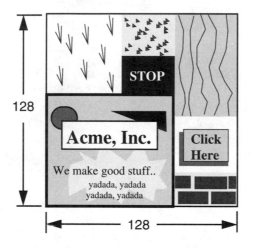

FIGURE 3-28 *Combining Subtextures into a Single Texture Map*

TIP

Use repeating textures to reduce file size: When building textures that are repeatable (e.g., grass, stone, bricks), create the smallest possible pattern that is repeatable without being obvious and ensure that the edges of the texture blend properly since the right edge of the texture will abut with the left edge and the top edge will abut with the bottom edge when repeated. Most paint and image-processing tools support this feature.

The *repeatS* and *repeatT* fields specify how the texture wraps in the s and t directions. If *repeatS* is TRUE (the default), the texture map is repeated outside the 0 to 1 texture coordinate range in the s direction so that it fills the shape. If *repeatS* is FALSE, the texture coordinates are clamped in the s direction to lie within the 0 to 1 range. The *repeatT* field is analogous to the *repeatS* field.

TIP

The term *clamping* means that the border pixels are used everywhere outside the range 0 to 1 and create a "frame" effect around the texture.

TIP

In general, if you are applying a nonrepeating texture to a polygon, the texture should have at least a one-pixel-wide constant-color border. That border pixel will be smeared across the polygon wherever the texture coordinates fall out of the 0 to 1 range.

Transparent textures in VRML act as "cookie cutters"—wherever the texture is fully transparent, you will be able to see through the object. An alternative is *decal* textures, with the underlying object material (or color) showing wherever the texture is fully transparent. Decal textures are not directly supported, but can be created using two different textures as follows: A mask must made from the full-color, four-component texture. The mask must be opaque wherever the full-color texture is transparent, and transparent wherever the full-color texture is opaque, with a constant intensity of 1.0. The full-color texture is applied to the geometry to draw the textured parts of the object. The mask is also applied to the geometry, effectively drawing the nontextured parts of the object. A two-component texture with a constant intensity of 1.0 is equivalent to a transparency-only texture map—the diffuse colors used for lighting are multiplied by 1.0, so the texture's intensity has no effect. This might be prototyped as follows:

```
PROTO DecalShape [
  exposedField MFString texture [ ]
  exposedField MFString mask [ ]
  exposedField SFNode geometry NULL
  exposedField SFNode material NULL  ]
{
  Group { children [
    Shape {
      appearance Appearance {
        texture ImageTexture { url IS texture }
        material IS material
      }
      geometry IS geometry
    }
    Shape {
      appearance Appearance {
        texture ImageTexture { url IS mask }
        material IS material
      }
      geometry IS geometry
    }
  }
}
```

The cookie cutter texturing behavior was chosen because it is more common than decaling and because decaling can be done using two cookie cutter textures, while the opposite is not true.

EXAMPLE

The following example illustrates the **ImageTexture** node. The first **ImageTexture** is a one-component (gray-scale) image that shows how *diffuseColor* of the **Material** and one-component textures multiply. The second **ImageTexture** shows a three-component image and illustrates how the *diffuseColor* is ignored in this case. The third **ImageTexture** shows how a four-component image (or an image with transparency) can be used to create semitransparent texturing. The fourth **ImageTexture** shows the effect of the *repeatS* and *repeatT* fields:

```
#VRML V2.0 utf8
Group { children [
  Transform {
    translation -2.5 0 0.5
    rotation 0 1 0 0.5
    children Shape {
      appearance Appearance { # 1-comp image(grayscale)
        texture ImageTexture { url "marble.gif" }
        material DEF M Material {
          # Diffuse multiplies image values resulting
          # in a dark texture
          diffuseColor .7 .7 .7
        }
      }
      geometry DEF IFS IndexedFaceSet {
        coord Coordinate {
          point [ -1.1 -1 0, 1 -1 0, 1 1 0, -1.1 1 0 ]
        }
        coordIndex [ 0 1 2 3 ]
      }
    }
  }
  Transform {
    translation 0 0 0
    children Shape {
      appearance Appearance { # image RGBs REPLACE diffuse
        texture ImageTexture {
          url "marbleRGB.gif"
        }
        material DEF M Material {
          diffuseColor 0 0 1 # Diffuse - no affect!
          shininess  0.5     # Other fields work
```

```
            ambientIntensity 0.0
          }
        }
        geometry USE IFS
    }
  }
Transform {
  translation 2.5 0 0
  children Shape {
    appearance Appearance {
      # RGBA values REPLACE diffuse/transp
      texture ImageTexture { url "marbleRGBA.gif" }
      material DEF M Material {
        # Diffuse and transp have no effect;
        # replaced by image values.
        # All other fields work fine.
        diffuseColor 0 0 0
        transparency 1.0
        shininess  0.5
        ambientIntensity 0.0
      }
    }
    geometry USE IFS
  }
}
Transform {
  translation 5 0 0.5
  rotation 0 1 0 -0.5
  children Shape {
    appearance Appearance {
      # Illustrates effect of repeat fields
      texture ImageTexture {
        url "marble.gif"
        repeatS FALSE
        repeatT FALSE
      }
      material DEF M Material { diffuseColor 1 1 1 }
    }
    geometry IndexedFaceSet {
      coord Coordinate {
        point [ -1 -1 0, 1 -1 0, 1 1 0, -1 1 0 ]
      }
      coordIndex [ 0 1 2 3 ]
      texCoord TextureCoordinate {
          point [ -0.25 -0.5, 1.25 -0.5, 1.25 1.5, -0.25 1.5 ]
      }
    }
  }
}
```

```
    Background {
      skyColor [ 1 1 1, 1 1 1, .5 .5 .5, 1 1 1, .2 .2 .2, 1 1 1 ]
      skyAngle [ 1.35, 1.4, 1.45, 1.5, 1.55 ]
      groundColor [ 1 1 1, 1 1 1, 0.4 0.4 0.4 ]
      groundAngle [ 1.3, 1.57 ]
    }
  ]}
```

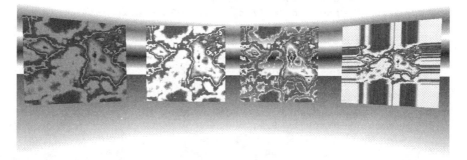

FIGURE 3-29 *Examples of **ImageTexture** Node*

IndexedFaceSet

```
IndexedFaceSet {
    eventIn        MFInt32  set_colorIndex
    eventIn        MFInt32  set_coordIndex
    eventIn        MFInt32  set_normalIndex
    eventIn        MFInt32  set_texCoordIndex
    exposedField   SFNode   color              NULL
    exposedField   SFNode   coord              NULL
    exposedField   SFNode   normal             NULL
    exposedField   SFNode   texCoord           NULL
    field          SFBool   ccw                TRUE
    field          MFInt32  colorIndex         []
    field          SFBool   colorPerVertex     TRUE
    field          SFBool   convex             TRUE
    field          MFInt32  coordIndex         []
    field          SFFloat  creaseAngle        0
    field          MFInt32  normalIndex        []
    field          SFBool   normalPerVertex    TRUE
```

```
    field          SFBool  solid              TRUE
    field          MFInt32 texCoordIndex      []
}
```

The **IndexedFaceSet** node represents a 3D shape formed by constructing faces (polygons) from vertices listed in the *coord* field. The *coord* field must contain a **Coordinate** node. **IndexedFaceSet** uses the indices in its *coordIndex* field to specify the polygonal faces. An index of −1 indicates that the current face has ended and the next one begins. The last face may (but does not have to be) followed by a −1. If the greatest index in the *coordIndex* field is N, then the **Coordinate** node must contain N + 1 coordinates (indexed as 0 − N). **IndexedFaceSet** is specified in the local coordinate system and is affected by parent transformations.

For descriptions of the *coord*, *normal*, and *texCoord* fields, see the **Coordinate, Normal,** and **TextureCoordinate** nodes. See Section 2.9.6, Lighting Model, for details on lighting equations and the interaction between textures, materials, and geometries.

If the *color* field is not NULL then it must contain a **Color** node with colors that are applied to the vertices or faces of the **IndexedFaceSet** as follows:

- If *colorPerVertex* is FALSE, colors are applied to each face, as follows:

  - If the *colorIndex* field is not empty, then it is used to choose one color for each face of the **IndexedFaceSet**. There must be at least as many indices in the *colorIndex* field as there are faces in the **IndexedFaceSet**. If the greatest index in the *colorIndex* field is N, then there must be N + 1 colors in the **Color** node. The *colorIndex* field must not contain any negative entries.

  - If the *colorIndex* field is empty, then the colors are applied to each face of the **IndexedFaceSet** in order. There must be at least as many colors in the **Color** node as there are faces.

- If *colorPerVertex* is TRUE, colors are applied to each vertex, as follows:

  - If the *colorIndex* field is not empty, then it is used to choose colors for each vertex of the **IndexedFaceSet** in exactly the same manner that the *coordIndex* field is used to choose coordinates for each vertex from the **Coordinate** node. The *colorIndex* field must contain at least as many indices as the *coordIndex* field and must contain end-of-face markers (−1) in exactly the same places as the *coordIndex* field. If the greatest index in the *colorIndex* field is N, then there must be N + 1 colors in the **Color** node.

  - If the *colorIndex* field is empty, then the *coordIndex* field is used to choose colors from the **Color** node. If the greatest index in the *coordIndex* field is N, then there must be N + 1 colors in the **Color** node.

If the *normal* field is NULL, then the browser should automatically generate normals using *ccw* to determine the normal vector's orientation and using *creaseAngle* to determine if and how normals are smoothed across shared vertices (see Section 2.9.2, Geometry).

If the *normal* field is not NULL, then it must contain a **Normal** node, with normals that are applied to the vertices or faces of the **IndexedFaceSet** in a manner exactly equivalent to that described for applying colors to vertices and faces. Note that the orientation of these normals should match the *ccw* field, but are not required.

If the *texCoord* field is not NULL, then it must contain a **TextureCoordinate** node. The texture coordinates in that node are applied to the vertices of the **Indexed-FaceSet** as follows:

- If the *texCoordIndex* field is not empty, then it is used to choose texture coordinates for each vertex of the **IndexedFaceSet** in exactly the same manner that the *coordIndex* field is used to choose coordinates for each vertex from the **Coordinate** node. The *texCoordIndex* field must contain at least as many indices as the *coordIndex* field and must contain end-of-face markers (−1) in exactly the same places as the *coordIndex* field. If the greatest index in the *texCoordIndex* field is N, then there must be N + 1 texture coordinates in the **TextureCoordinate** node.

- If the *texCoordIndex* field is empty, then the *coordIndex* array is used to choose texture coordinates from the **TextureCoordinate** node. If the greatest index in the *coordIndex* field is N, then there must be N + 1 texture coordinates in the **TextureCoordinate** node.

If the *texCoord* field is NULL, default texture coordinate mapping is calculated using the bounding box of the shape. The longest dimension of the bounding box defines the s coordinates, and the next longest defines the t coordinates. If two or all three dimensions of the bounding box are equal, then ties should be broken by choosing the x, y, or z dimension in that order of preference. The value of the s coordinate ranges from 0 to 1, from one end of the bounding box to the other. The t coordinate ranges between 0 and the ratio of the second greatest dimension of the bounding box to the greatest dimension. See Figure 3-30 for an illustration of default texture coordinates for a simple box-shaped **IndexedFaceSet** with a bounding box with an x dimension that is twice as large as the z dimension, which is twice as large as the y dimension.

See Section 2.9.2, Geometry, for a general description of the *ccw, solid, convex,* and *creaseAngle* fields.

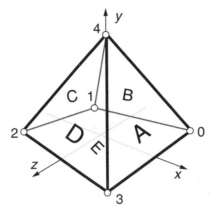

```
IndexedFaceSet {
  coord Coordinate { point [ 1 0 -1, -1 0 -1, -1 0 1, 1 0 1, 0 2 0 ] }
  coordIndex [ 0 4 3 -1        # face A, right
             1 4 0 -1        # face B, back
             2 4 1 -1        # face C, left
             3 4 2 -1        # face D, front
             0 3 2 1 -1 ]    # face E, bottom
}
```

FIGURE 3-30 *IndexedFaceSet Node*

DESIGN NOTE

IndexedFaceSet nodes are specified in the *geometry* field of **Shape** nodes. Unlike VRML 1.0, they cannot be added directly as children of grouping nodes; a **Shape** must be used to associate an appearance (material and texture) with each **IndexedFaceSet.**

Most geometry in most VRML worlds is made of **IndexedFaceSets.** In fact, most of the other geometry nodes in VRML (**Extrusion, ElevationGrid, Cube, Cone, Sphere,** and **Cylinder**) could be implemented as prototyped **IndexedFaceSets** with **Scripts** that generated the appropriate geometry.

Vertex positions, colors, normals, and texture coordinates are all specified as separate nodes (stored in the *coord, color, normal,* and *texCoord* exposedFields) to allow them to be shared between different **IndexedFaceSets.** Sharing saves bandwidth and can be very convenient. For example, you might create a model with interior parts and wish to allow the user to control whether the exterior or interior is being shown. You can put the interior and exterior in two different **Shapes** underneath a **Switch** node, but still share vertex coordinates between the interior and exterior parts.

The default texture coordinates generated by an **IndexedFaceSet** are easy to calculate and are well defined, but otherwise have very little to recommend them. If you are texturing an **IndexedFaceSet** that is anything more complicated than a square, you will almost certainly want to define better texture coordinates. Unfortunately, automatically generating good texture coordinates for each vertex is very difficult, and a good mapping depends on the texture image being used, whether the **IndexedFaceSet** is part of a larger surface, and so on. A good modeling system will provide both better automatic texture coordinate generation and precise control over how texture images are wrapped across each polygon.

Generating good default normals is a much easier task, and by setting *creaseAngle* appropriately you will almost always be able to get a good-looking surface without bloating your files with explicit normals.

The **Index* fields are not fully exposed: You can only set them; you cannot get them. This is done to help implementations that might convert the **IndexedFaceSet** to a more efficient internal representation. For example, some graphics hardware is optimized to draw triangular strips. A browser running with such hardware might triangulate the **IndexedFaceSets** given to it and create triangular strips when the VRML file is read and whenever it receives a *set_*Index* event. After doing so, it can free up the memory used by the index arrays. If those arrays were exposedFields, a much more complicated analysis would have to be done to determine whether or not their values might possibly be accessed sometime in the future.

EXAMPLE

This example shows three **IndexedFaceSets** illustrating color applied per face, indexed color applied per vertex, texture coordinates applied per vertex, and a dodecahedron (20 vertices, 12 faces, 6 colors [primaries, RGB; complements, CMY]) mapped to the faces.

```
#VRML V2.0 utf8
Viewpoint { description "Initial view" position 0 0 9 }
NavigationInfo { type "EXAMINE" }
# Three IndexedFaceSets, showing:
#   - Color applied per-face, indexed
#   - Color applied per-vertex
#   - Texture coordinates applied per-vertex

# A dodecahedron: 20 vertices, 12 faces.
# 6 colors (primaries:RGB and complements:CMY) mapped to the faces.
Transform {
  translation -1.5 0 0
  children Shape {
    appearance DEF A Appearance { material Material { } }
```

```
    geometry DEF IFS IndexedFaceSet {
      coord Coordinate {
        point [ # Coords/indices derived from "Jim Blinn's Corner"
          1 1 1, 1 1 -1, 1 -1 1, 1 -1 -1,
          -1 1 1, -1 1 -1, -1 -1 1, -1 -1 -1,
          .618 1.618 0, -.618 1.618 0, .618 -1.618 0, -.618 -1.618 0,
          1.618 0 .618, 1.618 0 -.618, -1.618 0 .618, -1.618 0 -.618,
          0 .618 1.618, 0 -.618 1.618, 0 .618 -1.618, 0 -.618 -1.618
        ]
      }
      coordIndex [
        1 8 0 12 13 -1, 4 9 5 15 14 -1, 2 10 3 13 12 -1,
        7 11 6 14 15 -1, 2 12 0 16 17 -1, 1 13 3 19 18 -1,
        4 14 6 17 16 -1, 7 15 5 18 19 -1, 4 16 0 8 9 -1,
        2 17 6 11 10 -1, 1 18 5 9 8 -1, 7 19 3 10 11 -1,
      ]
      color Color {  # Six colors:
        color [ 0 0 1, 0 1 0, 0 1 1, 1 0 0, 1 0 1, 1 1 0 ]
      }
      colorPerVertex FALSE # Applied to faces, not vertices
      # This indexing gives a nice symmetric appearance:
      colorIndex [ 0, 1, 1, 0, 2, 3, 3, 2, 4, 5, 5, 4 ]

      # Five texture coordinates, for the five vertices on each face.
      # These will be re-used by indexing into them appropriately.
      texCoord TextureCoordinate {
        point [  # These are the coordinates of a regular pentagon:
          0.654508 0.0244717,  0.0954915 0.206107
          0.0954915 0.793893,  0.654508 0.975528, 1 0.5,
        ]
      }
      # And this particular indexing makes a nice image:
      texCoordIndex [
        0 1 2 3 4 -1, 2 3 4 0 1 -1, 4 0 1 2 3 -1, 1 2 3 4 0 -1,
        2 3 4 0 1 -1, 0 1 2 3 4 -1, 1 2 3 4 0 -1, 4 0 1 2 3 -1,
        4 0 1 2 3 -1, 1 2 3 4 0 -1, 0 1 2 3 4 -1, 2 3 4 0 1 -1,
      ]
    }
  }
}
# A tetrahedron, with a color at each vertex:
Transform {
  translation 1.5 -1.5 0
  children Shape {
    appearance USE A  # Use same dflt material as dodecahedron
    geometry IndexedFaceSet {
      coord Coordinate {
        point [ # Coords/indices derived from "Jim Blinn's Corner"
```

```
          1 1 1,  1 -1 -1,  -1 1 -1,  -1 -1 1,
        ]
      }
      coordIndex [
        3 2 1 -1,  2 3 0 -1,  1 0 3 -1,  0 1 2 -1,
      ]
      color Color {  # Four colors:
        color [ 0 1 0, 1 1 1, 0 0 1, 1 0 0 ]
      }
      # Leave colorPerVertex field set to TRUE.
      # And no indices are needed, either-- each coordinate point
      # is assigned a color (or, to think of it another way, the same
      # indices are used for both coordinates and colors).
    }
  }
}
# The same dodecahedron, this time with a texture applied.
# The texture overrides the face colors given.
Transform {
  translation 1.5 1.5 0
  children Shape {
    appearance Appearance {
      texture ImageTexture { url "Pentagon.gif" }
      material Material { }
    }
    geometry USE IFS
  }
}
```

IndexedLineSet

```
IndexedLineSet {
  eventIn       MFInt32 set_colorIndex
  eventIn       MFInt32 set_coordIndex
  exposedField  SFNode  color          NULL
  exposedField  SFNode  coord          NULL
  field         MFInt32 colorIndex     []
  field         SFBool  colorPerVertex TRUE
  field         MFInt32 coordIndex     []
}
```

The **IndexedLineSet** node represents a 3D geometry formed by constructing polylines from 3D points specified in the *coord* field. **IndexedLineSet** uses the indices in its *coordIndex* field to specify the polylines by connecting points together from the *coord* field. An index of −1 indicates that the current polyline has ended and the next one begins. The last polyline may (but does not have to be) followed by a −1. **IndexedLineSet** is specified in the local coordinate system and is affected by parent transformations.

The *coord* field specifies the 3D vertices of the line set and is specified by a **Coordinate** node.

Lines are neither lit, texture mapped, nor collided with during collision detection.

If the *color* field is not NULL, it must contain a **Color** node, and the colors are applied to the line(s) as follows:

- If *colorPerVertex* is FALSE:
  - If the *colorIndex* field is not empty, then one color is used for each polyline of the **IndexedLineSet**. There must be at least as many indices in the *colorIndex* field as there are polylines in the **IndexedLineSet**. If the greatest index in the *colorIndex* field is N, then there must be N + 1 colors in the **Color** node. The *colorIndex* field must not contain any negative entries.
  - If the *colorIndex* field is empty, then the colors are applied to each polyline of the **IndexedLineSet** in order. There must be at least as many colors in the **Color** node as there are polylines.
- If *colorPerVertex* is TRUE:
  - If the *colorIndex* field is not empty, then colors are applied to each vertex of the **IndexedLineSet** in exactly the same manner that the *coordIndex* field is used to supply coordinates for each vertex from the **Coordinate** node. The *colorIndex* field must contain at least as many indices as the *coordIndex* field and must contain end-of-polyline markers (−1) in exactly the same places as the *coordIndex* field. If the greatest index in the *colorIndex* field is N, then there must be N + 1 colors in the **Color** node.
  - If the *colorIndex* field is empty, then the *coordIndex* field is used to choose colors from the **Color** node. If the greatest index in the *coordIndex* field is N, then there must be N + 1 colors in the **Color** node.

If the *color* field is NULL and there is a **Material** defined for the **Appearance** affecting this **IndexedLineSet**, then use *emissiveColor* of **Material** to draw the lines and ignore all other fields of the **Material**. See Section 2.9.5, Lighting Model, for details on lighting equations.

TIP

> **IndexedLineSet** nodes are specified in the *geometry* field of **Shape** nodes.

DESIGN NOTE

IndexedFaceSet, IndexedLineSet, and **PointSet** are the three fundamental geometry primitives that support drawing of polygons, lines, and points. Points and lines are not textured or lit. Some rendering libraries support texture mapping or lighting points and lines, but adding support for texture coordinates and normals to **IndexedLineSet** and **PointSet** would add complexity for a seldom-used feature.

EXAMPLE

The following example illustrates typical use of the **IndexedLineSet**. Note that the first **Indexed-LineSet** applies colors per polyline (one for the axes and one for the center line) and the second **IndexedLineSet** applies colors per vertex using the indices specified in the *coordIndex* (default):

```
#VRML V2.0 utf8
Transform { children [
  Shape {
    geometry IndexedLineSet {
      point [ 0 10 0, 0 0 0, 20 0 0, -1 5 0, 21 5 0 ]
      coordIndex [ 0 1 2 -1    # axes
                   3 4 ]       # centerline
      color Color { color [ 0 0 0, .2 .2 .2 ] }
      colorIndex [ 0 1 ]       # black for axes, gray for centerline
      colorPerVertex FALSE     # color per polyline
    }
  }
  Shape {
    geometry IndexedLineSet {
      point [ 2 1 0, 5 2 0, 8 1.5 0, 11 9 0, 14 7 0, 17 10 0 ]
      coordIndex [ 0 1 2 3 4 5 ]     # connect the dots
      color Color { color [ .1 .1 .1, .2 .2 .2, .15 .15 .15,
                            .9 .9 .9 , .7 .7 .7, 1 1 1   ] }
    }
  }
]} # end of children and Transform
```

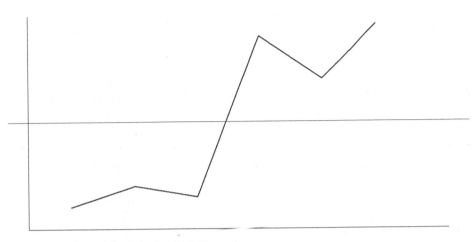

FIGURE 3-31 *IndexedLineSet Node Example*

Inline

```
Inline {
  exposedField MFString url          []
  field        SFVec3f  bboxCenter  0 0 0
  field        SFVec3f  bboxSize    -1 -1 -1
}
```

The **Inline** node is a grouping node that reads its children data from a location in the WWW. Exactly when its children are read and displayed is not defined. Reading the children may be delayed until the **Inline** is actually visible to the viewer. The *url* field specifies the URL containing the children. An **Inline** with an empty URL does nothing.

An **Inline**'s URLs shall refer to a valid VRML file that contains a list of children nodes at the top level. See Section 2.3.1, Grouping and Children Nodes, for details. The results are undefined if the URL refers to a file that is not VRML or if the file contains nonchildren nodes at the top level.

DESIGN NOTE

Because **Inline** nodes are grouping nodes, the file to which they point must not contain a scene graph fragment. For example, this is illegal:

```
Shape {
  appearance Appearance {
```

```
      # The following line is ILLEGAL; Inline is a grouping node!
      material Inline { url "http://..." }
   }
   geometry Box { }
}
```

Restricting **Inlines** to be like a **Group** with across-the-Web children makes implementing them much simpler and satisfies the need for a simple mechanism to distribute different parts of the scene graph across the Web.

If multiple URLs are specified, the browser may display a URL of a lower preference file while it is obtaining (or if it is unable to obtain) the higher preference file. See Section 2.1.3, URLs, for details on the *url* field and preference order.

The *bboxCenter* and *bboxSize* fields specify a bounding box that encloses the **Inline**'s children. This is a hint that may be used for optimization purposes. If the specified bounding box is smaller than the actual bounding box of the children at any time, then the results are undefined. A default *bboxSize* value, $(-1,-1,-1)$, implies that the bounding box is not specified and if needed must be calculated by the browser. See Section 2.3.6, Bounding Boxes, for a description of the *bboxCenter* and *bboxSize* fields.

TIP

Use **Inlines** as children of **LOD** nodes wherever possible. This ensures that the **Inline** file is only considered for download when it is within a reasonable distance from the user (and avoids unnecessary downloads for objects that are out of view).

DESIGN NOTE

Many programmers expect **Inline** nodes to act like the C/C++ "#include" directive, simply textually including the URL given into the VRML file. They don't. **Inline** nodes are grouping nodes, not a syntax-parsing directive.

If it were legal to **Inline** just a **Material,** the *bbox* fields would not make sense—**Material** nodes have no bounding box. **Inline** is meant only as an easy-to-implement, easy-to-optimize solution for a common case. The more general EXTERNPROTO/PROTO mechanism can be used to define libraries of materials or other properties.

The contents of the **Inline** node (the child nodes that are loaded across the Web) are completely opaque. Any nodes or prototypes defined inside the file to which the **Inline** points are not accessible outside of that file. Again, the more general EXTERNPROTO/PROTO mechanism can be used to create files with nonopaque interfaces. This **Inline**

```
Inline {
  url "http://....."
  bboxCenter 0 0 0
  bboxSize 10 10 10
}
```

is equivalent to

```
EXTERNPROTO _DummyName [ ]   "http://..."
Group {
  children _DummyName { }
  bboxCenter 0 0 0
  bboxSize 10 10 10
}
```

Like EXTERNPROTO, each **Inline** is unique, even if two **Inlines** point to the same URL. Since **Inline**'s cannot be changed "from the outside," the only time this matters is if the URL file contains user interface sensor nodes that might be triggered. For example, someone might define a completely self-contained Calculator object that had buttons, reacted to the user pressing the buttons, and so forth. You could include two such calculators in your world by simply doing

```
Group { children [
  Transform {
    translation 10 0 0
    children Inline {
      url "http://...../Calculator.wrl"
    }
  }
  Transform { translation -10 0 0
    children Inline {
      url "http://..../Calculator.wrl"
    }
  }
]}
```

Each of the calculators would calculate independently. You could, of course, also have the same calculator appear in two places in the world using DEF/USE:

```
Group { children [
  Transform {
    translation 10 0 0
    children DEF Calculator Inline {
      url "http://...../Calculator.wrl"
    }
  }
  Transform {
    translation -10 0 0
    children USE Calculator
  }
]}
```

DESIGN NOTE

Since **Inlines** specify separate files, the DEF/USE namespace of the current file is not inherited by the referenced file and vice versa. Therefore, you cannot DEF a node in the current file and USE it from within the **Inline**'s file, and you cannot DEF a node in an **Inline** file and USE the node later in the current file.

EXAMPLE

The following example illustrates a simple use of the **Inline** node. The file contains one **Inline** node that references the VRML file `groundPlane.wrl`. Notice that the **Inline** also specifies the bounding box for the contents of the file:

```
#VRML V2.0 utf8
Inline {
  bboxCenter 0 3 0
  bboxSize 100 6 100
  url "groundPlane.wrl"
}
Viewpoint {
  position 0 1.8 10
  description "In front of flag-pole"
}
Transform {     # Box
  translation -3 1 0
  children Shape {
    appearance Appearance {
      material Material { diffuseColor 0 0 1 }
    }
    geometry Box { }
  }
}
Transform {     # Cone
  translation 0 1 3
  children Shape {
    appearance Appearance {
      material Material { diffuseColor 0 1 0 }
    }
    geometry Cone { bottom FALSE }
  }
}
Transform {     # Sphere
  translation 3 1 0
  children Shape {
    appearance Appearance {
      material Material { diffuseColor 1 0 0 }
```

```
      }
      geometry Sphere { }
   }
}
```

groundPlane.wrl:

```
#VRML V2.0 utf8
# Bounds of this world:  (-50, 0 -50) to (50, 6, 50)
Transform { children [
  DirectionalLight { direction 0 -1 0   intensity 0.75 }
  # Grey ground-plane
  Shape {
    appearance DEF A Appearance { material Material { } }
    geometry IndexedFaceSet {
      coord Coordinate {
        point [ -50 0 -50  -50 0 50  50 0 50  50 0 -50 ]
      }
      coordIndex [ 0 1 2 3 -1 ]
    }
  }
  # Flag-pole at origin
  Shape {
    appearance USE A
    geometry IndexedFaceSet {
      coord Coordinate {
        point [ -.1 0 -.1  -.1 0 .1  .1 0 0
                -.1 6 -.1  -.1 6 .1  .1 6 0 ]
      }
      coordIndex [ 0 1 4 3 -1  1 2 5 4 -1  2 0 3 5 -1  3 4 5 -1 ]
    }
  }
  # Flag
  Shape {
    appearance Appearance {
      material Material { diffuseColor .9 0 0 }
    }
    geometry IndexedFaceSet {
      coord Coordinate {
        point [ .1 6 0  .1 5 0  1.4 5 0  1.4 6 0 ]
      }
      coordIndex [ 0 1 2 3 -1 ]
      solid FALSE
    }
  }
]}
```

LOD

```
LOD {
  exposedField MFNode   level    []
  field        SFVec3f  center   0 0 0
  field        MFFloat  range    []
}
```

The **LOD** node specifies various levels of detail or complexity for a given object, and provides hints for browsers to choose the appropriate version of the object automatically based on the distance from the user. The *level* field contains a list of nodes that represent the same object or objects at varying levels of detail, from the highest to the lowest level of detail, and the *range* field specifies the ideal distances at which to switch between the levels. See Section 2.3.1, Grouping and Children Nodes, for details on the types of nodes that are legal values for *level*.

DESIGN NOTE

It might seem strange that the "children" of an **LOD** node aren't stored in a field called *children,* but are stored in the *level* field. Grouping nodes that have a *children* field (**Anchor, Transform, Collision, Group, Billboard**) all share similar semantics. The order of the nodes in the *children* field doesn't matter and they always draw all of them. **LOD** levels have different semantics—the order of levels is critical and only one level is drawn at a time.

TIP

It is often useful to use an empty **Group** or **WorldInfo** node as the last level of an **LOD** so nothing is displayed when an object is far enough away. It can also be very useful to use an empty **Group** or **WorldInfo** as the first **LOD** level so that very large objects disappear if the user gets too close to them. For example, the exterior of a skyscraper might be modeled in several levels of detail, separately from each part of the building's interior. The center of the model is the center of the building. The highest level of detail, shown when the user is inside the building, might be nothing at all since there is no reason to show the exterior when the user is inside the building.

The *center* field is a translation offset in the local coordinate system that specifies the center of the **LOD** object for distance calculations. In order to calculate which level to display, first the distance is calculated from the viewpoint and transformed into the local coordinate space of the **LOD** node (including any scaling transformations) to the center point of the **LOD**. If the distance is less than the first value in the *range* field, then the first level of the **LOD** is drawn. If it is between the first and second values in the *range* field, the second level is drawn, and so on.

If there are N values in the *range* field, the **LOD** shall have N + 1 nodes in its *level* field. Specifying too few levels will result in the last level being used repeatedly for the lowest levels of detail; if more levels than ranges are specified, the extra levels will be ignored. The exception to this rule is to leave the *range* field empty, which is a hint to the browser that it should choose a level automatically to maintain a constant display rate. Each value in the *range* field should be greater than the previous value; otherwise, results are undefined.

Authors should set **LOD** ranges so that the transitions from one level of detail to the next are smooth. Browsers may adjust which level of detail is displayed to maintain interactive frame rates, to display an already-fetched level of detail while a higher level of detail (contained in an **Inline** node) is fetched, or might disregard the author-specified ranges for any other implementation-dependent reason. For best results, specify ranges only where necessary, and nest **LOD** nodes with and without ranges. Browsers should try to honor the hints given by authors, and authors should try to give browsers as much freedom as they can to choose levels of detail based on performance.

DESIGN NOTE

The ideal distance to switch between levels is the nearest distance at which a viewer with the default field of view (45 degrees; see the **Viewpoint** node) cannot detect the change, assuming a display device with infinite resolution being viewed by a person with 20/20 vision. Theoretically, given a set of **LOD** levels, a computer could compute the ideal distance by rendering the levels at various distances and resolutions, performing pixel comparisons on the results, and taking into account average human physiology. However, it is more practical for the scene creator to specify reasonable switching distances based on their knowledge of how much "**LOD** popping" they are willing to tolerate for each object.

For unimportant objects it is best to omit ranges entirely, allowing the browser to choose the best level it has time to render. For important objects, you might combine the two techniques. For example, there might be three representations of an object that are acceptable as close-up views when the user is within ten meters. And there might be two simpler representations (perhaps a simple **Box** and nothing at all) that are acceptable when the user is farther than ten meters. This can be expressed to the VRML browser as

```
LOD {                    # Two level LOD, near and far:
  range [ 10 ]
  level [
    LOD {                # Performance LOD:  Any of these OK when near:
      level [
```

```
            DEF HIGH Inline { url "...High.wrl" }
            DEF MEDIUM Inline { url "...Medium.wrl" }
            DEF LOW Inline { url "...Low.wrl" }
        ]
    }
    LOD {                    # Second performance LOD: these OK when far:
        level [
            USE LOW          # Lowest level OK when far away,
            Shape {          # or display a simple Box,
                geometry Box { size ... }
                appearance Appearance { material Material { ... } }
            }
            WorldInfo { }    # or, display nothing.
        ]
    }
    ]
}
```

TIP

LOD is meant to be used to optimize performance by drawing fewer or simpler polygons for objects that are far away from the viewer. Because browsers may adjust or ignore the **LOD** switching distances to maintain a reasonable frame rate, content creators should refrain from using **LODs** for other special effects. For example, if you want a door to open as the user approaches it, you should use a **ProximitySensor.** If you use an **LOD** (with the closest level being a door fully open and the farthest being a door fully closed), you may not get the behavior you expect in all implementations.

Various other types of level-of-detail schemes can be created using **ProximitySensors, Scripts,** and **Switch** nodes. For example, a **ProximitySensor** can report the orientation of the viewer with respect to the **ProximitySensor**'s coordinate system. You could give that information to a **Script** that then sets the **Switch** to display a rectangle with a prerendered texture map of the object from that viewing angle. In fact, an **LOD** that just switches based on distance can be recreated using a **ProximitySensor,** and a **Switch** node.

LOD nodes are evaluated top-down in the scene graph. Only the descendants of the currently selected level are rendered. Note that all nodes under an **LOD** node continue to receive and send events (i.e., routes) regardless of which **LOD** level is active. For example, if an active **TimeSensor** is contained within an inactive level of an **LOD**, the **TimeSensor** sends events regardless of the **LOD**'s state.

DESIGN NOTE

Actually, implementations can optimize away changes made to things that cannot be seen (or heard or otherwise detected by the user interacting with the virtual world), and might not generate events for a **TimeSensor** modifying objects underneath an **LOD** level that is not being seen. Since there are no guarantees about how often a **TimeSensor** generates events while it is active, it is perfectly legal to have unseen **TimeSensors** generate no events while they are hidden. This is the key to VRML's scalability and is what makes VRML theoretically capable of dealing with arbitrarily large worlds.

Combining **LOD** with the **Inline** node or EXTERNPROTO instances is very powerful, allowing optimization of both rendering speed and conservation of network bandwidth. If the user never gets close to an object, only a coarse representation of the object needs to be loaded from across the network and displayed. Implementations can globally optimize rendering time, figuring out which **LODs** are most important (based on the range hints given by the scene creators and any built-in heuristics) and adjusting which levels are drawn to give the best results possible. Implementations can also globally optimize network bandwidth, allocating more bandwidth to important objects (or to objects that it might predict will soon be important, perhaps based on the direction the user is moving) and less to unimportant objects. If **LOD** was not a built-in node, these kinds of global optimizations done by the browser would not be possible.

TIP

LOD is the most important node in VRML for performance tuning. Use it whenever possible to avoid unnecessary rendering complexity of objects that are far away or out of view. Note that a large percentage of the scene will be at a low **LOD** level *most* of the time. Thus, it is important to create very low-complexity versions of the objects (e.g., one to four polygons) for the lowest or second-to-lowest level of the **LOD.** Authors will find that making the lowest level invisible (e.g., **WorldInfo** node) helps performance considerably and is hardly noticed by the user (especially when used with a **Fog** node to hide popping). Three to four levels are recommended, with the lowest containing a **WorldInfo** and the second-to-lowest containing a *very* low polygon count **Shape.**

TIP

Use the **Inline** node to define the children of the more complex levels of the **LOD.** This has the nice result of delaying the download of the geometry until it is needed. Often, large portions of the scene will not be downloaded since the user restricted navigation to a small part of the world and is not penalized by waiting for the entire world to download. It is recommended that the lowest visible level of the **LOD** not be inlined. This ensures that there is always something to render whether the browser is busy downloading or not (or if the connection is down).

EXAMPLE

The following example illustrates typical use of the **LOD** node. Note that each level may contain any type of node. For example, level 0 contains a **Cone** node for maximum fidelity, while levels 1 and 2 use an **IndexedFaceSet**, level 3 uses a **Billboard,** and the last level is basically empty but uses a **WorldInfo** node as a placeholder. It is very good for performance to keep the last level empty. There are several options for creating an empty level. **WorldInfo** is the best choice since it contains no state and should have a small memory overhead. An empty **Group** node is a second option (and possibly more logical) for creating an empty level, but may incur traversal overhead.

```
#VRML V2.0 utf8
LOD {
  range [ 25, 100, 200, 400 ]
  level  [
    # level 0 - default gray, lit cone
    Transform { translation 0 1.5 0   children
      Shape {
        appearance DEF AP Appearance { material Material {} }
        geometry Cone { bottomRadius 1   height 3 }
      }
    }
    # level 1 - lit, 8 triangle cone approximation
    Shape {
      appearance USE AP
      geometry IndexedFaceSet {
        coord Coordinate {
          point [ 1 0 0, .707 0 -.707, 0 0 -1,
                  -.707 0 -.707, -1 0 0, -.707 0 .707, 0 0 1,
                  .707 0 .707, 0 3 0 ] }
          coordIndex [ 0 1 8 -1   1 2 8 -1   2 3 8 -1   3 4 8 -1
                       4 5 8 -1   5 6 8 -1   6 7 8 -1   7 0 8 -1
                       0 7 6 5 4 3 2 1 ]
        }
    }
    # level 2 - lit, tetrahedron
    Shape {
    appearance USE AP
    geometry IndexedFaceSet {
      coord Coordinate {
        point [ 1 0 0, 0 0 -1, -1 0 0, 0 0 1, 0 3 0 ] }
        coordIndex [ 0 1 4 -1   1 2 4 -1   2 3 4 -1
                     3 0 4 -1   0 3 2 1   ]
      }
    }
    # level 3 - unlit, medium gray billboarded polygon
    Billboard {
      children Shape {
        geometry IndexedFaceSet {
          coord Coordinate { point [ 1 0 0, 0 3 0, -1 0 0 ] }
```

```
        coordIndex [ 0 1 2 ]
        colorPerVertex FALSE
        color Color { color 0.5 0.5 0.5 }
      }
    }
  }
  # level 4 - empty
  WorldInfo {}
 ]
}
```

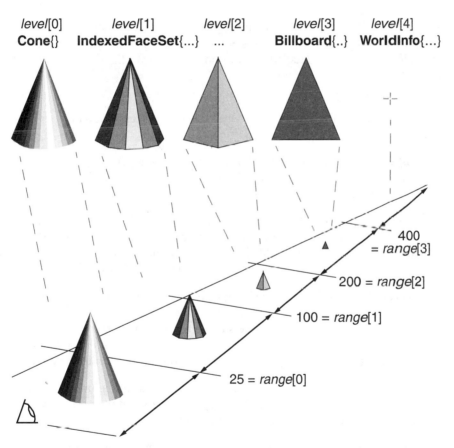

FIGURE 3-32 *LOD Node*

Material

```
Material {
  exposedField SFFloat  ambientIntensity  0.2
  exposedField SFColor  diffuseColor      0.8 0.8 0.8
  exposedField SFColor  emissiveColor     0 0 0
  exposedField SFFloat  shininess         0.2
  exposedField SFColor  specularColor     0 0 0
  exposedField SFFloat  transparency      0
}
```

The **Material** node specifies surface material properties for associated geometry nodes and are used by the VRML lighting equations during rendering. See Section 2.9.5, Lighting Model, for a detailed description of the VRML lighting model equations.

All of the fields in the **Material** node range from 0.0 to 1.0.

The fields in the **Material** node determine the way light reflects off an object to create color:

1. The *diffuseColor* field reflects all VRML light sources depending on the angle of the surface with respect to the light source. The more directly the surface faces the light, the more diffuse is light reflected.

2. The *ambientIntensity* field specifies how much ambient light from light sources this surface should reflect. Ambient light is omnidirectional and depends only on the number of light sources, not their positions with respect to the surface. Ambient color is calculated as *ambientIntensity * diffuseColor*.

3. The *specularColor* and *shininess* fields specify the specular highlights—for example, the shiny spots on an apple. When the angle from the light to the surface is close to the angle from the surface to the viewer, *specularColor* is added to the diffuse and ambient color calculations. Lower *shininess* values produce soft glows, while higher values result in sharper, smaller highlights.

4. The *emissiveColor* field models "glowing" objects. This can be useful for displaying radiosity-based models (where the light energy of the room is computed explicitly) or for displaying scientific data.

5. The *transparency* field specifies the precentage of light that is transmitted through the object with 1.0 being completely transparent and 0.0 completely opaque.

DESIGN NOTE

If *diffuseColor, specularColor,* and *ambientIntensity* are zero, browsers can recognize this as a hint to turn off lighting calculations and simply render the geometry in the *emissiveColor.*

TIP

It is rare for an object to use all of the **Material** node's parameters at the same time. Just specifying an overall *diffuseColor* is easy and gives good results. Adding specular highlights by specifying a white *specularColor* and adjusting the *shininess* field will suffice for most objects. Alternatively, you can specify a black *diffuseColor* and simply use *emissiveColor* to get full-intensity, glowing objects. If an object is purely emissive (*specularColor* and *diffuseColor* are both black), then implementations do not need to perform lighting calculations for the object at all.

Partially transparent objects can be used to create a lot of great effects. For example, very nice smoke and fire effects can be created using semitransparent, animated triangles. Unfortunately, not all systems support partial transparency, so if you want your world to be viewed by the largest number of people you should stay away from transparency values other than 0.0 (completely opaque) and 1.0 (completely transparent).

Perhaps the greatest frustration for content creators with VRML 1.0 was creating scenes that would look good on all of the various VRML browsers. Varying capabilities of the underlying rendering libraries and different interpretations of the incomplete specification resulted in vastly different appearances for identical scenes. These problems are addressed in VRML 2.0 in several different ways.

First, ideal lighting equations are given, and the interaction between lights, materials, and textures are well defined (see Section 2.9.5, Lighting Model). The VRML 1.0 specification was vague about what the ideal, correct scene would look like once rendered; VRML 2.0 is very precise. Implementations will still be forced to approximate the ideal due to hardware and software limitations, but at least now all implementations will be aiming at the same target, and results can be judged against the ideal.

VRML 1.0 allowed multiple materials to be specified in a **Material** node and allowed the materials to be applied to each face or vertex of shapes. VRML 2.0 allows only a single **Material** node, but also allows specification of multiple diffuse colors for each vertex or face, restricting the feature to a simple, common case.

The *ambientColor* field of VRML 1.0 is replaced by the VRML 2.0 *ambientIntensity* field. Specifying what fraction of the diffuse color should be visible due to ambient light is simpler and better matches the capabilities of most interactive renderers. Specifying the ambient reflected color as a fraction of the reflected diffuse color also works much better with texture colors and per-face/per-vertex colors, which are both treated as diffuse colors. It would be very strange to see texture in the lighted parts of a textured object but see nothing but the ambient color in the unlit parts of the object.

However, even with these changes, color fidelity will continue to be a problem for content creators. Three-dimensional rendering libraries and hardware are a new feature for inexpensive computers and there will continue to be fairly large variations between different implementations. Differences in display hardware—monitors and video cards—can result in different colors being displayed on different machines even if the VRML browser makes exactly the same lighting calculations and puts exactly the same value in the frame buffer. As standards for color reproduction on computer displays develop and as 3D graphics hardware and software on inexpensive machines mature, the situation will gradually improve. However, it is likely to be several years before it will be practical to decide what color you will paint your house by applying virtual paint to a virtual house and judging the color as it appears on your computer screen.

TIP

Many of the rendering libraries do not support the features offered by the VRML **Material** node. It is recommended that authors perform tests on the browser before investing time into the various features in **Material.** It is generally safe to assume that *diffuseColor* will produce the basic object color during rendering. Beyond that, experimentation with the various browsers is required.

EXAMPLE

The following example illustrates the use of the **Material** node by varying different fields in each row. The last **Sphere** in each row has identical values as the third **Sphere**, with the exception of increased *emissiveColor*. The first row increases the *diffuseColor* from left to right. The second row increases *shininess* from left to right. The third row increases *transparency* from left to right:

```
#VRML V2.0 utf8
Group { children [
  Transform {
    translation -3 2.5 0  children Shape { geometry DEF S Sphere {}
      appearance Appearance {
        material Material { diffuseColor 0.2 0.2 0.2 }
}}}
  Transform {
    translation 0 2.5 0  children Shape { geometry USE S
      appearance Appearance {
        material Material { diffuseColor .5 .5 .5 }
}}}
  Transform {
    translation 3 2.5 0  children Shape { geometry USE S
      appearance Appearance {
        material Material { diffuseColor 1 1 1 }
}}}
```

```
Transform {
  translation 6 2.5 0  children Shape { geometry USE S
    appearance Appearance {
      material Material {
        diffuseColor 1 1 1
        emissiveColor .5 .5 .5
      }
}}}
Transform {
  translation -3 0 0 children Shape { geometry USE S
    appearance Appearance {
      material Material {
        specularColor 1 1 1
        shininess 0.01
      }
}}}
Transform {
  translation 0 0 0
  children Shape { geometry USE S
    appearance Appearance {
      material Material {
        specularColor 1 1 1
        shininess 0.5
      }
}}}
Transform {
  translation 3 0 0
  children Shape { geometry USE S
    appearance Appearance {
      material Material {
        specularColor 1 1 1
        shininess 0.98
      }
}}}
Transform {
  translation 6 0 0
  children Shape { geometry USE S
    appearance Appearance {
      material Material {
        specularColor 1 1 1
        shininess 0.98
        emissiveColor 0.5 0.5 0.5
      }
}}}
Transform {
  translation -3 -2.5 0
  children Shape { geometry USE S
    appearance Appearance {
      material Material {
        specularColor 1 1 1
```

```
                shininess 0.5
                transparency 0.2
            }
  }}}
  Transform {
    translation 0 -2.5 0
    children Shape { geometry USE S
      appearance Appearance {
        material Material {
          specularColor 1 1 1
          shininess 0.5
          transparency 0.5
    }
  }}}
  Transform {
    translation 3 -2.5 0
    children Shape { geometry USE S
      appearance Appearance {
        material Material {
          specularColor 1 1 1
          shininess 0.5
          transparency 0.8
        }
  }}}
  Transform {
    translation 6 -2.5 0
    children Shape { geometry USE S
      appearance Appearance {
        material Material {
          specularColor 1 1 1
          shininess 0.5
          transparency 0.8
          emissiveColor 0.5 0.5 0.5
        }
  }}}
  Shape {
    geometry IndexedFaceSet {
      coord Coordinate {
        point [ -4 -4 -2, 7 -4 -2, 7 -3 -2, -4 -3 -2 ] }
        coordIndex [ 0 1 2 3 ]
    }
    appearance Appearance {
      texture ImageTexture { url "celtic.gif" } }
  }
  Background { skyColor 1 1 1 }
  DirectionalLight { direction -.65 0 -.85 }
  NavigationInfo { type "EXAMINE" headlight FALSE }
]}
```

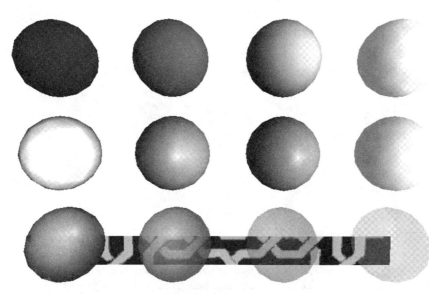

FIGURE 3-33 *Material Node Example*

MovieTexture

```
MovieTexture {
  exposedField SFBool    loop              FALSE
  exposedField SFFloat   speed             1
  exposedField SFTime    startTime         0
  exposedField SFTime    stopTime          0
  exposedField MFString  url               []
  field        SFBool    repeatS           TRUE
  field        SFBool    repeatT           TRUE
  eventOut     SFTime    duration_changed
  eventOut     SFBool    isActive
}
```

The **MovieTexture** node defines a time-dependent texture map (contained in a movie file) and parameters for controlling the movie and the texture mapping. A **MovieTexture** can also be used as the source of sound data for a **Sound** node, but in this special case is not used for rendering.

TIP

> It is most useful to use a sound-and-video **MovieTexture** as both a texture and source for a sound, so you can both see and hear it. This is easily accomplished with DEF/USE. For example:
>
> ```
> Shape {
>   appearance Appearance {
>     texture DEF MOVIE MovieTexture {
>       url "http://..."
>     }
>   }
>   geometry Box { }
> }
> Sound {
>   source USE MOVIE
> }
> ```
>
> The audio and video will be automatically synchronized, since there is only one **Movie-Texture** node and only one set of start/stop/repeat controls.

Texture maps are defined in a 2D coordinate system (*s,t*) that ranges from 0.0 to 1.0 in both directions. The bottom edge of the image corresponds to the *s*-axis of the texture map and the left edge of the image corresponds to the *t*-axis of the texture map. The lower left pixel of the image corresponds to $s = 0$, $t = 0$, and the top right pixel of the image corresponds to $s = 1$, $t = 1$.

TIP

> See Figure 3-34 for an illustration of the image space of a texture map movie (specified in the *url* field). Notice how the movie defines the 0.0 to 1.0 *s* and *t* boundaries. Regardless of the size and aspect ratio of the texture map movie, the left edge of the movie always represents $s = 0$; the right edge, $s = 1.0$; the bottom edge, $t = 0.0$; and the top edge, $t = 1.0$. Also, notice how we have illustrated the texture map infinitely repeating in all directions. This shows what happens conceptually when *s* and *t* values, specified by the **TextureCoordinate** node, are outside of the 0.0 to 1.0 range.

The *url* field that defines the movie data must support MPEG1-Systems (audio and video) or MPEG1-Video (video-only) movie file formats ("Motion Pictures Experts Group," International Organization of Standards, ISO/IEC IS 11172-1:1993, `http://www.iso.ch/isob/switch-engine-cate.pl?searchtype=refnumber&KEYWORDS=11172`). See Section 2.1.3, URLs, for details on the *url* field. It is recommended that implementations support gray-scale or alpha transparency rendering if the specific movie format being used supports these features.

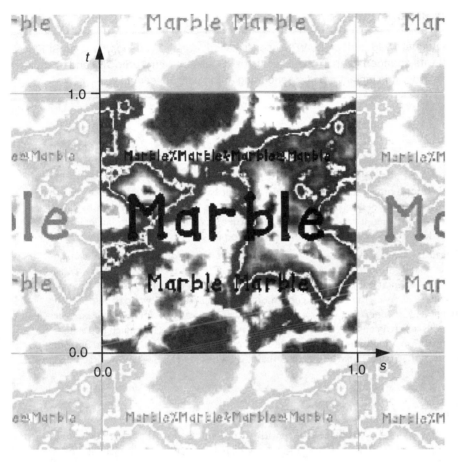

FIGURE 3-34 *Texture Map Image Space*

TIP

> The only common movie file format that currently (early 1997) supports transparency is Animated GIF (GIF89-a), and it doesn't support partial transparency.

See Section 2.9.5, Lighting Model, for details on lighting equations and the interaction between textures, materials, and geometries.

As soon as the movie is loaded, a *duration_changed* eventOut is sent. This indicates the duration of the movie, in seconds. This eventOut value can be read (for instance, by a **Script**) to determine the duration of a movie. A value of −1 implies the movie has not yet loaded or the value is unavailable for some reason.

DESIGN NOTE

In the August 1996 draft of the VRML specification, *duration_changed* was an SFFloat field. It was changed to an SFTime field to be consistent with **AudioClip** and because it was a more convenient type for performing arithmetic in a script.

TIP

Movies tend to be very large and can take a long time to load. The *duration_changed* eventOut can be very useful for giving the user feedback when you know they will have to wait for a movie to be downloaded. You might have a **Switch** with a **Text** node that displays "Movie loading, please wait . . ." and a **Script** that removes the text by changing the **Switch** when it receives the **MovieTexture**'s *duration_changed* event, indicating that the movie has been loaded and is ready to play.

Because loading a movie can be such an expensive operation, implementations might defer loading it until it is scheduled to be played. Content creators should try to help the implementations by setting the **MovieTexture**'s *startTime* field as early as possible, hopefully allowing the browser enough time to complete the download before the scheduled starting time. So, for example, if you animate a **Transform** when the user presses a button and play a movie after the animation is done, it is much better to set the *startTime* of both the animation and the movie based on the time of the button press, rather than waiting to set the **MovieTexture**'s *startTime* when the first animation is finished.

The *loop*, *startTime*, and *stopTime* exposedFields and the *isActive* eventOut, and their effects on the **MovieTexture** node, are discussed in detail in Section 2.9.7, Time-dependent Nodes. The cycle of a **MovieTexture** is the length of time in seconds for one playing of the movie at the specified speed.

If a **MovieTexture** is inactive when the movie is first loaded, then frame 0 is shown in the texture if *speed* is nonnegative. The last frame of the movie is shown if speed is negative. A **MovieTexture** will always display frame 0 if *speed* = 0. For positive values of *speed*, **MovieTexture** displays frame *f* at time *t* (i.e., in the movie's local time system with frame 0 at time 0, at *speed* = 1)

$$f = \text{fmod}(t - startTime, duration / speed)$$

If *speed* is negative, then the frame to display at time *t* is

$$f = duration + \text{fmod}(now - startTime, duration / speed)$$

When a **MovieTexture** becomes inactive, the frame corresponding to the time at which the **MovieTexture** became inactive will remain as the texture.

TIP

> If you want an object to appear as if it has no texture at all before the **Movie Texture** starts or after it finishes, either insert a single-color movie frame at the beginning or end of the movie file or use a **Script** and a **Switch** node to switch between two **Shapes** that share the same geometry (use DEF/USE to share the geometry) but have different appearances (one with a **Movie Texture** and one without).

The *speed* exposedField indicates how fast the movie should be played. A *speed* of 2 indicates the movie plays twice as fast as normal. Note that the *duration_changed* output is not affected by the *speed* exposedField. *Set_speed* events are ignored while the movie is playing. A negative *speed* implies that the movie will play backward. However, content creators should note that this may not work for streaming movies or very large movie files.

TIP

> Playing movies backward is also likely to result in very poor performance, if it works at all, because video hardware and software is optimized to play movies forward. The MPEG-2 standard, for example, relies heavily on a compression technique where the differences from one frame to the next are encoded, making it much more expensive to recreate the frames of the movie out of order.

Movie Textures can be referenced by an **Appearance** node's *texture* field (as a movie texture) and by a **Sound** node's *source* field (as an audio source only).

DESIGN NOTE

The size of a typical movie file and the memory and computational expense of supporting animating texture maps make it somewhat impractical for most VRML users. However, 3D graphics hardware and network bandwidth are getting better every year, and what is only barely achievable today will soon be commonplace. It will be interesting to see how much the VRML standard will influence the development of other graphics and networking standards. It will also be interesting to see how much VRML changes over the years because of changes in other graphics and networking standards.

TIP

> See the **Image Texture** section for important tips on texture mapping tricks.

EXAMPLE

The following example illustrates a simple case of the **MovieTexture** node. The **MovieTexture** is assigned to the texture of a rectangular polygon. A **TouchSensor** is used to trigger the movie play sequence. Each time the user clicks on the rectangle, the movie starts from the beginning (unless it is already running):

```
#VRML V2.0 utf8
Group { children [
  Shape {
    appearance Appearance {
      texture DEF MT1 MovieTexture {
        url "test.mpeg"
        loop FALSE
      }
      material DEF M Material { diffuseColor 1 1 1 }
    }
    geometry DEF IFS IndexedFaceSet {
      coord Coordinate { point [ -1.1 -1 0, 1 -1 0, 1 1 0, -1.1 1 0 ] }
      coordIndex [ 0 1 2 3 ]
    }
  }
  DEF TS1 TouchSensor {}
  Background { skyColor 1 1 1 }
]}
ROUTE TS1.touchTime TO MT1.startTime
```

NavigationInfo

```
NavigationInfo {
  eventIn      SFBool    set_bind
  exposedField MFFloat   avatarSize      [ 0.25, 1.6, 0.75 ]
  exposedField SFBool    headlight       TRUE
  exposedField SFFloat   speed           1.0
  exposedField MFString  type            "WALK"
  exposedField SFFloat   visibilityLimit 0.0
  eventOut     SFBool    isBound
}
```

The **NavigationInfo** node contains information describing the physical characteristics of the viewer and viewing model. **NavigationInfo** is a *bindable node* (see Section 2.9.1, Bindable Children Nodes) and thus there exists a **NavigationInfo** stack in the browser in which the topmost **NavigationInfo** on the stack is the currently active **NavigationInfo.** The current **NavigationInfo** is considered to be a child of the current **Viewpoint,** regardless of where it is initially located in the file. Whenever the current **Viewpoint** changes, the current **NavigationInfo** must be reparented to it. Whenever the current **NavigationInfo** changes, the new **NavigationInfo** must be reparented to the current **Viewpoint.**

DESIGN NOTE

The *avatarSize* and *speed* fields of **NavigationInfo** are interpreted in the current **Viewpoint**'s coordinate system because it works much better for worlds within worlds and it is much easier to implement. You might take a model of a house, for example, scale it down, and make it a toy house in a world you are creating. If the user binds to a **Viewpoint** that is inside the house model, the current **NavigationInfo** will be reinterpreted to be in that coordinate space (i.e., scaled), making the user's avatar smaller and making their navigation speed slower, both of which are desirable to make navigation through the toy house easy. It is also easier to implement because the browser only has to keep track of the coordinate system of the current **Viewpoint** and doesn't have to keep track of the coordinate system of the current **NavigationInfo**. Note that some VRML browsers may support multiuser scenarios and allow users to specify their own personal avatar geometry so they can see each other as they move around the virtual world. These avatar geometries must behave similarly to **NavigationInfo** and be interpreted in the coordinate space of the current **Viewpoint**.

If a TRUE value is sent to the *set_bind* eventIn of a **NavigationInfo,** it is pushed onto the **NavigationInfo** stack and activated. When a **NavigationInfo** is bound, the browser uses the fields of the **NavigationInfo** to set the navigation controls of its user interface and the **NavigationInfo** is conceptually reparented under the currently bound Viewpoint. All subsequent scaling changes to the current **Viewpoint**'s coordinate system automatically change aspects (discussed later) of the **NavigationInfo** values used in the browser (e.g., scale changes to any parent transformation). A FALSE value of *set_bind* pops the **NavigationInfo** from the stack, results in an *isBound* FALSE event, and pops to the next entry in the stack, which must be reparented to the current **Viewpoint**. See Section 2.9.1, Bindable Children Nodes, for more details on the binding stacks.

The *type* field specifies a navigation paradigm to use. Minimally, browsers shall support the following navigation types: WALK, EXAMINE, FLY, and NONE. WALK navigation is used for exploring a virtual world. It is recommended that the browser should support a notion of gravity in walk mode. FLY navigation is similar to walk except that no notion of gravity should be enforced. There should still be some notion of "up" however. EXAMINE navigation is typically used to view individual objects and often includes (but does not require) the ability to spin the object and move it closer or farther away. The NONE choice removes all navigation controls—the user navigates using only controls provided in the scene, such as guided tours. Also allowed are browser-specific navigation types. These should include a unique suffix (e.g., `_sgi.com`) to prevent conflicts.

DESIGN NOTE

It is recommended that you use your domain name for unique suffix naming of new navigation types. For example, if Foo Corporation develops a new navigation type based on a helicopter, it should be named something like: `HELICOPTER_foo.com` to distinguish it from Bar Corporation's `HELICOPTER_bar.com`.

The *type* field is multivalued so that authors can specify fallbacks in case a browser does not understand a given type. If none of the types are recognized by the browser, then the default `WALK` is used. These strings values are case sensitive (`walk` is not equal to `WALK`).

TIP

`NONE` can be very useful for taking complete control over the navigation. You can use the various sensors to detect user input and have **Scripts** that control the motion of the viewer by animating **Viewpoints.** Even "dashboard" controls—controls that are always in front of the user—are possible (see the **ProximitySensor** node for an example of how to create a heads-up display).

The *speed* field is a multiplier for the rate at which the viewer travels through a scene. Since viewers may provide mechanisms to travel faster or slower, this value represents an initial value and a hint to the viewer. If the **NavigationInfo** type is `EXAMINE`, *speed* is a multiplier on the viewer translation speed; it should have no effect on the rotation speed. The transformation hierarchy of the currently bound **Viewpoint** (discussed earlier) scales the *speed* multiplier—translations and rotations have no effect on *speed*. *Speed* must be ≥0.0, where 0.0 specifies a stationary avatar and 1.0 specifies to use the browser's defaults.

TIP

A stationary avatar's position is fixed at one location but may look around, which is sometimes useful when you want the user to be able to control their angle of view, but don't want them to be able to move to a location in which they aren't supposed to be. You might combine in-the-scene navigation to take the user from place to place, animating the position of a **Viewpoint,** but allow the user complete freedom over their orientation.

The *avatarSize* field specifies the user's physical dimensions in the world for the purpose of collision detection and terrain following. It is a multivalue field that allows several dimensions to be specified. The first value should be the allowable distance between the user's position and any collision geometry (as specified by **Collision**) before a collision is detected. The second should be the height above the terrain at which the viewer should be maintained. The third should be the height of the tallest object over which the viewer can "step." This allows staircases to be built with dimensions that can be ascended by all browsers. Additional values are *browser dependent* and all values may be ignored; but, if a browser interprets these values, the first three should be interpreted as described.

TIP

The three *avatarSize* parameters define a cylinder with a knee. The first is the cylinder's radius. It should be small enough so that viewers can pass through any doorway you've put in your world, but large enough so that they can't slip between the bars in any prison cell you've created. The second is the cylinder's height. It should be short enough so that viewers don't hit their head as they walk through doorways and tall enough so that they don't feel like an ant running around on the floor (unless you want them to feel like an ant . . .). And the third parameter is knee height. (Humans have trouble stepping onto obstacles that are higher than the height of our knees.) The knee height should be tall enough so that viewers can walk up stairs instead of running into them, but low enough so that viewers bump into tables instead of hopping up onto them. If a browser supports avatar geometry, it is up to the browser to decide how to scale that geometry to fit within the parameters given by the world author.

DESIGN NOTE

VRML 2.0 was designed to anticipate multiuser worlds, but leaves out any multiuser functionality because multiuser systems are still in the research and experimentation phase, and because producing a single-user specification with interaction and animation is a useful first step toward multiuser worlds. The *avatarSize* field was particularly difficult to design because it is important for both single-user and multiuser systems.

The problem was how much information about the user's virtual representation should be included in a VRML 2.0 world. Solutions could range from nothing at all to a complete specification of an **Avatar** node, including geometry, standard behaviors, and so forth. A middle ground was chosen that specifies just enough information so that world creators can specify the assumptions they've made about the virtual viewer's size and general shape when creating their world. No information is included about how an avatar should look or behave as it travels through the world. It is expected that each user will desire a different virtual representation, and such information does not belong in the virtual world but should be kept with the user's personal files and registered with the VRML browser(s).

For purposes of *terrain following* the browser needs a notion of the "down" direction (down vector), since gravity is applied in the direction of the down vector. This down vector should be along the negative *y*-axis in the local coordinate system of the currently bound **Viewpoint** (i.e., the accumulation of the **Viewpoint**'s parent transformations, not including the **Viewpoint**'s orientation field).

DESIGN NOTE

"Down" is a local, not a global, notion. There is not necessarily one down direction for the entire world. Simply specifying that down is the −*y*-axis of the coordinate system of the currently bound **Viewpoint** has a lot of very nice scalability benefits, and allows the creation of worlds on asteroids and space stations, where up and down can change dramatically with relatively small changes in location. This does mean that implementations need to interpret the user's navigation gestures in the coordinate system of the current **Viewpoint,** but that should be fairly easy because the implementation must already know the coordinate system of the current **Viewpoint** to correctly perform any **Viewpoint** animations that might be happening.

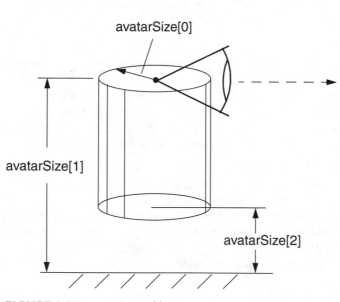

FIGURE 3-35 *avatarSize Field*

The *visibilityLimit* field sets the farthest distance the user is able to see. The browser may clip all objects beyond this limit or fade them into the background. A value of 0.0 (the default) indicates an infinite visibility limit. *VisibilityLimit* is restricted to be ≥0.0.

DESIGN NOTE

A *z-buffer* is a common mechanism for performing hidden surface elimination. The major problem with z-buffers is dealing with their limited precision. If polygons are too close together, z-buffer comparisons that should resolve one polygon being behind another will determine that they are equal, and an ugly artifact called *z-buffer tearing* will occur. Z-buffer resolution is enhanced when the near clipping plane (which should be one-half the *avatarSize;* [discussed later]) is as far away from the viewer as possible and the far clipping plane is as near to the viewer as possible.

Ideally, the proper near and far clipping planes would be constantly and automatically computed by the VRML browser based on the item at which the user was looking In practice, it is very difficult to write an algorithm that is fast enough so that it doesn't cause a noticeable degradation in performance and yet general enough that it works well for arbitrary worlds. So, the world creator can tell the browser how far the user should be able to see by using the *visibilityLimit* field. If the user is inside an enclosed space, set *visibilityLimit* to the circumference of the space to clip out any objects that might be outside the space. You might find that clipping out distant objects is less objectionable to z-buffer tearing of near, almost-coincident polygons. In this case, make *visibilityLimit* smaller to try to get better z-buffer resolution for nearby objects.

The *speed*, *avatarSize*, and *visibilityLimit* values are all scaled by the transformation being applied to a currently bound **Viewpoint.** If there is no currently bound **Viewpoint,** they are interpreted in the world coordinate system. This allows these values to be automatically adjusted when binding to a **Viewpoint** that has a scaling transformation applied to it without requiring a new **NavigationInfo** node to be bound as well. If the scale applied to the **Viewpoint** is nonuniform, the behavior is undefined.

The *headlight* field specifies whether a browser should turn on a headlight. A headlight is a directional light that always points in the direction the user is looking. Setting this field to TRUE allows the browser to provide a headlight, possibly with user interface controls to turn it on and off. Scenes that enlist precomputed lighting (e.g., radiosity solutions) can turn the headlight off. The headlight shall have *intensity* = 1, *color* = (1,1,1), *ambientIntensity* = 0.0, and *direction* = (0,0,−1).

It is recommended that the near clipping plane should be set to one-half of the collision radius as specified in the *avatarSize* field. This recommendation may be ignored by the browser, but setting the near plane to this value prevents excessive clipping of objects just above the collision volume and provides a region inside the collision volume for content authors to include geometry that should remain fixed relative to the viewer, such as icons or a HUD, but should not be occluded by geometry outside the collision volume.

DESIGN NOTE

The near clipping plane roughly corresponds to the surface of your eyeballs. In general, things don't look good if they intersect the near clipping plane, just as things don't look good when objects intersect your eye. The current **Viewpoint** position can be thought of as the center of your head. *AvatarSize[1]* specifies the distance from the center of your body to your shoulders (defining the width of an opening through which you can squeeze). Defining the near clipping plane to be one-half of the *avatarSize* roughly corresponds to a human body's physical geometry, with your eyeballs about halfway from the center of the body to the shoulders. Allowing geometry in front of the eyeballs but before the collision radius gives content creators a useful place to put geometry that should always follow the user around (see the **ProximitySensor** section for details on how to create geometry that stays fixed relative to the user).

The first **NavigationInfo** node found during reading of the world is automatically bound (receives a *set_bind* TRUE event) and supplies the initial navigation parameters.

EXAMPLE

The following example illustrates the use of the **NavigationInfo** node. It contains two **Navigation-Info** nodes, each with a corresponding **ProximitySensor** that binds and unbinds it. The idea is that within each of the two regions bounded by the **PromitySensors**, a different **NavigationInfo** is to be used. Note that the initial **NavigationInfo** will be activated by the initial location of the viewer (i.e., the first **Viewpoint**) and thus overrides the default choice of using the first **NavigationInfo** in the file:

```
#VRML V2.0 utf8
Group { children [
  DEF N1 NavigationInfo {
    type "NONE"          # all other defaults are ok
  }
  DEF N2 NavigationInfo {
    avatarSize [ .01, .06, .02 ]   # get small
    speed .1
    type "WALK"
    visibilityLimit 10.0
  }
```

```
Transform {              # Proximity of the very small room
   translation 0 .05 0
   children DEF P1 ProximitySensor { size .4 .1 .4 }
}
Transform {              # Proximity of initial Viewpoint
   translation 0 1.6 -5.8
   children DEF P2 ProximitySensor { size 5 5 5 }
}
Transform { children [ # A very small room with a cone inside
   Shape {              # The room
     appearance DEF A Appearance {
       material DEF M Material {
         diffuseColor 1 1 1 ambientIntensity .33
       }
     }
     geometry IndexedFaceSet {
       coord Coordinate {
         point [ .2 0 -.2, .2 0 .2, -.2 0 .2, -.2 0 -.2,
                 .2 .1 -.2, .2 .1 .2, -.2 .1 .2, -.2 .1 -.2 ]
       }
       coordIndex [ 0 1 5 4 -1, 1 2 6 5 -1, 2 3 7 6 -1, 4 5 6 7 ]
       solid FALSE
     }
   }
   Transform {                      # Cone in the room
     translation -.1 .025 .1
     children DEF S Shape {
       geometry Cone { bottomRadius 0.01 height 0.02 }
       appearance USE A
     }
   }
]}
Transform { children [          # Outside the room
   Shape {                      # Textured ground plane
     appearance Appearance {
       material USE M
       texture ImageTexture { url "marble.gif" }
     }
     geometry IndexedFaceSet {
       coord Coordinate { point [ 2 0 -1, -2 0 -1, -2 0 3, 2 0 3 ] }
       coordIndex [ 0 1 2 3 ]
     }
   }
]}
DEF V1 Viewpoint {
   position 0 1.6 -5.8
   orientation 0 1 0 3.14
   description "Outside the very small house"
}
```

```
  DEF V2 Viewpoint {
    position 0.15 .06 -0.19
    orientation 0 1 0 2.1
    description "Inside the very small house"
  }
  DirectionalLight { direction 0 -1 0 }
  DEF Background { skyColor 1 1 1 }
]}
ROUTE P1.isActive TO N1.set_bind
ROUTE P2.isActive TO N2.set_bind
```

Normal

```
Normal {
  exposedField MFVec3f vector   []
}
```

This node defines a set of 3D surface normal vectors to be used in the *vector* field of some geometry nodes (**IndexedFaceSet, ElevationGrid**). This node contains one multivalued field that contains the normal vectors. Normals should be unit length or results are undefined.

TIP

Use default normals whenever possible. Since normals can occupy a large amount of file size, do not specify normals if the default normals (calculated by the browser) are adequate. See Section 2.9.2, Geometry, for details on default normals calculations.

EXAMPLE

The following example illustrates three typical uses of the **Normal** node. The first **Indexed-FaceSet** defines a **Normal** node that has five normals and uses the *normalIndex* field to assign the correct normal to the corresponding vertex of each face. The second **IndexedFaceSet** defaults to using the *coordIndex* field to index into the **Normal** node. This is probably the most common use of the **Normal** node (i.e., one normal for each coordinate). The third **IndexedFaceSet** applies a **Normal** node to the faces of the geometry. This produces a faceted polygonal object and may render faster than when specifying normals per vertex:

```
#VRML V2.0 utf8
Group { children [
  Transform {
    translation -3 0 0
```

```
      children Shape {
        appearance DEF A1 Appearance {
          material Material { diffuseColor 1 1 1 }
        }
        geometry IndexedFaceSet {
          coord DEF C1 Coordinate {
            point [ 1 0 1, 1 0 -1, -1 0 -1, -1 0 1, 0 3 0 ]
          }
          coordIndex [ 0 1 4 -1,  1 2 4 -1,  2 3 4 -1,  3 0 4 ]
          normal Normal {
            vector [ .707 0  .707, .707 0 -.707, -.707 0 -.707,
                    -.707 0  .707, .707 .707 0, 0 .707 -.707,
                    -.707 .707 0, 0 .707 .707 ]
          }
          normalIndex [ 0 1 4 -1  1 2 5 -1  2 3 6 -1  3 0 7 ]
        }
      }
    }
Transform {
  children Shape {
    appearance USE A1
    geometry IndexedFaceSet {
      coord USE C1
      coordIndex [ 0 1 4 -1,  1 2 4 -1,  2 3 4 -1,  3 0 4 ]
      normal Normal {      # use coordIndex for normal indices
        vector [ .707 0  .707,  .707 0 -.707,
                -.707 0 -.707, -.707 0  .707, 0 1 0 ]
      }
    }
  }
}
Transform {
  translation 3 0 0
  children Shape {
    appearance USE A1
    geometry IndexedFaceSet {
      coord USE C1
      coordIndex [ 0 1 4 -1,  1 2 4 -1,  2 3 4 -1,  3 0 4 ]
      normal Normal {
      vector [ .707 .707 0, 0 .707 -.707, -.707 .707 0,
              0 .707 .707 ]
      }
      normalIndex [ 0, 1, 2, 3 ]
      normalPerVertex FALSE
    }
  }
}
DirectionalLight { direction 1 0 0 }
Background { skyColor 1 1 1 }
] }
```

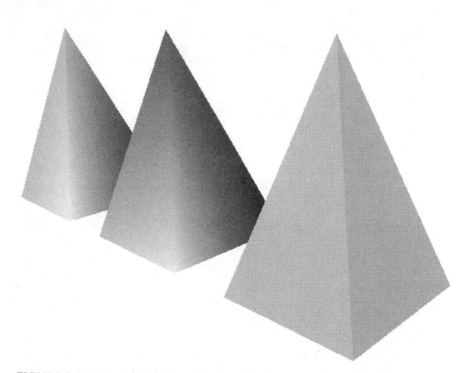

FIGURE 3-36 *Normal* Node Example

NormalInterpolator

```
NormalInterpolator {
  eventIn       SFFloat  set_fraction
  exposedField  MFFloat  key            []
  exposedField  MFVec3f  keyValue       []
  eventOut      MFVec3f  value_changed
}
```

This node interpolates among a set of multivalued MFVec3f values, suitable for transforming normal vectors. All output vectors will have been normalized by the interpolator.

The number of normals in the *keyValue* field must be an integer multiple of the number of keyframes in the *key* field. The integer multiple defines how many normals will be contained in *value_changed* events.

Normal interpolation is to be performed on the surface of the unit sphere. That is, the output values for a linear interpolation from a point P on the unit sphere to a point Q also on the unit sphere should lie along the shortest arc (on the unit sphere) connecting points P and Q. Also, equally spaced input fractions will result in arcs of equal length. Cases in which P and Q are diagonally opposing allow an infinite number of arcs. The interpolation for this case can be along any one of these arcs. Refer to Section 2.9.3, Interpolators, for a more detailed discussion of interpolators.

TIP

NomalInterpolator is an advanced node and is only used in fairly obscure cases. The **NormalInterpolator** node is needed when a **CoordinateInterpolator** is being used to morph coordinates and normals are not being automatically generated. If you have two shapes with the same topology (coordinate and normal indices), you can easily morph between them by using coordinate and normal interpolators driven by **Time-Sensors**. Various effects are also possible by varying only the normals of an object, changing the shading of the object over time.

TIP

Remember that **TimeSensor** outputs *fraction_changed* events in the 0.0 to 1.0 range, and that interpolator nodes routed *from* **TimeSensors** should restrict their *key* field values to the 0.0 to 1.0 range to match the **TimeSensor** output and thus produce a full interpolation sequence.

EXAMPLE

The following example illustrates a simple case of the **NormalInterpolator** node. A **TouchSensor** triggers the interpolation when it is clicked. The **TimeSensor** drives the **NormalInterpolator**, which in turn modifies the normals of the **IndexedFaceSet**, producing a rather strange effect:

```
#VRML V2.0 utf8
Group { children [
  DEF NI NormalInterpolator {
    key [ 0.0, 1.0 ]
    keyValue [ .707 0 .707, .707 0 -.707,
              -.707 0 -.707, -.707 0 .707, 0 1 0,
              1 0 0, 1 0 0, -1 0 0, -1 0 0, 0 1 0 ]
  }
  Shape {
    geometry IndexedFaceSet {
```

```
    coord Coordinate {
    point [ 1 0 1, 1 0 -1, -1 0 -1, -1 0 1, 0 3 0 ] }
    coordIndex [ 0 1 4 -1,  1 2 4 -1,  2 3 4 -1,  3 0 4 ]
    normal DEF N Normal {
      vector [ .707 0  .707,  .707 0 -.707,
               -.707 0 -.707, -.707 0  .707, 0 1 0 ]
    }
  }
  appearance Appearance {
    material Material { diffuseColor 1 1 1 }
  }
}
DEF T TouchSensor {}   # Click to start the morph
DEF TS TimeSensor {    # Drives the interpolator
  cycleInterval 3.0    # 3 second normal morph
  loop TRUE
}
Background { skyColor 1 1 1 }
] }
ROUTE NI.value_changed TO N.vector
ROUTE T.touchTime TO TS.startTime
ROUTE TS.fraction_changed TO NI.set_fraction
```

OrientationInterpolator

```
OrientationInterpolator {
  eventIn       SFFloat     set_fraction
  exposedField  MFFloat     key            []
  exposedField  MFRotation  keyValue       []
  eventOut      SFRotation  value_changed
}
```

This node interpolates among a set of SFRotation values. The rotations are absolute in object space and are, therefore, not cumulative. The *keyValue* field must contain exactly as many rotations as there are keyframes in the *key* field, or an error will be generated and results will be undefined.

An orientation represents the final position of an object after a rotation has been applied. An **OrientationInterpolator** will interpolate between two orientations by computing the shortest path on the unit sphere between the two orientations. The interpolation will be linear in arc length along this path. The path between two diagonally opposed orientations will be any one of the infinitely possible paths with arc length π.

If two consecutive *keyValue* values exist such that the arc length between them is greater than π, then the interpolation will take place on the arc complement. For example, the interpolation between the orientations

$$(0,1,0,0) \rightarrow (0,1,0,5.0)$$

is equivalent to the rotation between the two orientations

$$(0,1,0,2\pi) \rightarrow (0,1,0,5.0)$$

Refer to Section 2.9.3, Interpolators, for a more detailed discussion of interpolators.

TIP

The **OrientationInterpolator,** like all of the other interpolators, interpolates between a series of poses. The keyframes that define each pose do not encode any information about how the object got into that pose. This makes it tricky to create an **OrientationInterpolator** that rotates an object 180 degrees or more, because the keyframes must be thought of as a static orientation of an object, and not as an axis to rotate about and an angle rotation amount.

Confusion arises because the representation chosen for orientations is the axis and angle that the object must be rotated around to bring it from its default orientation to the desired orientation. However, that conceptual movement has no relation to the movement of an object between orientation keyframes, just like the conceptual movement of an object from (0,0,0) to a position keyframe has no relation to the movement between keyframes.

It is easy to think that an orientation keyframe of (0,1,0,6π) means "perform three complete rotations about the *y*-axis." It really means "the orientation that results when the object is rotated three complete times about the *y*-axis," which is exactly the same orientation as zero (or one or two or three) rotations about the *y*-axis, and it is exactly the same orientation as six (or zero) complete rotations about any other axis.

More than one keyframe must be specified to perform a rotation of 180 degrees (π radians) or greater. In general, to specify N complete rotations of an object you must specify 3N+1 keyframes, each spaced 120 degrees apart. For example, an **OrientationInterpolator** that rotates an object all the way around the *y*-axis as it receives *set_fraction* events from 0.0 to 1.0 can be specified as

```
OrientationInterpolator {
   key [ 0  0.333  0.666  1 ]
   keyValue [ 0 0 1 0      # Start with identity.
                           # Same as  0 1 0 0.
            0 1 0 2.09  # Oriented 120 deg Y
            0 -1 0 2.09 # Oriented 120 deg -Y
                           # Same as 0 1 0 4.18
            0 0  1 0 ]  # End up where we started
}
```

TIP

Remember that **TimeSensor** outputs *fraction_changed* events in the 0.0 to 1.0 range and that interpolator nodes routed *from* **TimeSensors** should restrict their *key* field values to the 0.0 to 1.0 range to match the **TimeSensor** output and thus produce a full interpolation sequence.

TIP

Remember that rotations in VRML are specified as an axis vector and an angle, and that the angle is specified in radians, not degrees. Radians were chosen in the Open Inventor tool kit for their programming convenience and were, unfortunately (less familiar than degrees), inherited when we created VRML.

TIP

When creating an **OrientationInterpolator**, make sure to specify *key* values (i.e., time) that produce desirable rotation velocities. For example, if you want constant rotational velocity you must choose key times that are spaced identically to the spacing of the rotations in *keyValues*. First, specify all of the *keys* to be identical to the *keyValues* and then divide each key by the maximum *keyValue*:

```
OrientationInterpolator {
  key [          0.0,        0.286,        .857,       1.0 ]
  # where key[1] = .286 = keyValue[1] / max(keyValue) = 1/3.5
  # where key[2] = .857 = keyValue[2] / max(keyValue) = 3/3.5
  keyValue [ 0 0 1 0, 0 0 1 1.0, 0 0 1 3.0, 0 0 1 3.5 ]
}
```

TIP

Remember that the **OrientationInterpolator** takes the shortest rotational path between keyframe values and that it is often necessary to insert extra keyframe values to ensure the desired rotations. For example, the following **OrientationInterpolator** will first rotate counterclockwise 0.523 radians (30 degrees) about the z-axis and then reverse direction and rotate clockwise to −0.523 radians (330 degrees):

```
OrientationInterpolator {
  key [ 0.0 0.5 1.0 ]
  keyValue [ 0 0 1 0, 0 0 1 0.523, 0 0 1 -.523 ]
}
```

However, if the desired rotation is to complete a full revolution, rather than reversing direction, an extra keyframe value must be inserted:

```
OrientationInterpolator {
  key [ 0 0.33 0.66 1.0 ]
  keyValue [ 0 0 1 0, 0 0 1 0.523, 0 0 1 3.14, 0 0 1 -.523 ]
}
```

EXAMPLE

The following example illustrates the use of the **OrientationInterpolator** node. A **TouchSensor** is used to trigger the start of the interpolation by routing to a **TimeSensor**, which is routed to the **OrientationInterpolator**. The **OrientationInterpolator** is routed to the *rotation* field of a **Transform**:

```
#VRML V2.0 utf8
Group { children [
  DEF OI OrientationInterpolator {
     key [ 0.0, 0.1, 0.3, 0.6, 0.8, 1.0 ]
     keyValue [ 0 0 1 0, 0 0 1 1.2, 0 0 1 -1.57, 0 0 1 1.5,
               0 0 1 3.15, 0 0 1 6.28 ]
  }
  DEF T Transform {
    children Shape {
      geometry Cone {}
      appearance Appearance {
        material Material { diffuseColor 1 0 0 }
      }
    }
  }
  DEF TOS TouchSensor {}  # Click to start
  DEF TS TimeSensor {     # Drives the interpolator
    cycleInterval 3.0     # 3 second interp loop
  }
  Background { skyColor 1 1 1 }
] }
ROUTE OI.value_changed TO T.rotation
ROUTE TOS.touchTime TO TS.startTime
ROUTE TS.fraction_changed TO OI.set_fraction
```

PixelTexture

```
PixelTexture {
  exposedField SFImage   image      0 0 0
  field        SFBool     repeatS    TRUE
  field        SFBool     repeatT    TRUE
}
```

The **PixelTexture** node defines a 2D, image-based texture map as an explicit array of pixel values and parameters controlling tiling repetition of the texture onto geometry.

Texture maps are defined in a 2D coordinate system (s, t) that ranges from 0.0 to 1.0 in both directions. The bottom edge of the pixel image corresponds to the s-axis of the texture map and the left edge of the pixel image corresponds to the t-axis of the texture map. The lower left pixel of the pixel image corresponds to $s = 0, t = 0$, and the top right pixel of the image corresponds to $s = 1, t = 1$.

TIP

> See Figure 3-37 for an illustration of the image space of a texture map image (specified in the *image* field). Notice how the image defines the 0.0 to 1.0 s and t boundaries. Regardless of the size and aspect ratio of the texture map image, the left edge of the image always represents $s = 0$; the right edge, $s = 1.0$; the bottom edge, $t = 0.0$; and the top edge, $t = 1.0$. Also, notice how we have illustrated the texture map infinitely repeating in all directions. This shows what happens conceptually when s and t values, specified by the **TextureCoordinate** node, are outside the 0.0 to 1.0 range.

Images may be one component (gray scale), two component (gray scale plus alpha opacity), three component (full RGB color), or four component (full RGB color plus alpha opacity). An ideal VRML implementation will use the texture image to modify the diffuse color and transparency (1 - alpha opacity) of an object's material (specified in a **Material** node), then perform any lighting calculations using the rest of the object's material properties with the modified diffuse color to produce the final image. The texture image modifies the diffuse color and transparency depending on how many components are in the image, as follows:

1. Diffuse color is multiplied by the gray-scale values in the texture image.

2. Diffuse color is multiplied by the gray-scale values in the texture image; material transparency is multiplied by transparency values in the texture image.

3. RGB colors in the texture image replace the material's diffuse color.

4. RGB colors in the texture image replace the material's diffuse color; transparency values in the texture image replace the material's transparency.

Browsers may approximate this ideal behavior to increase performance. One common optimization is to calculate lighting only at each vertex and combine the texture image with the color computed from lighting (performing the texturing after lighting). Another common optimization is to perform no lighting calculations at all when texturing is enabled, displaying only the colors of the texture image. (See Section 2.9.5, Lighting Model, for details on the VRML lighting equations and see Section 4.5, SFImage, for details on how to specify an image.)

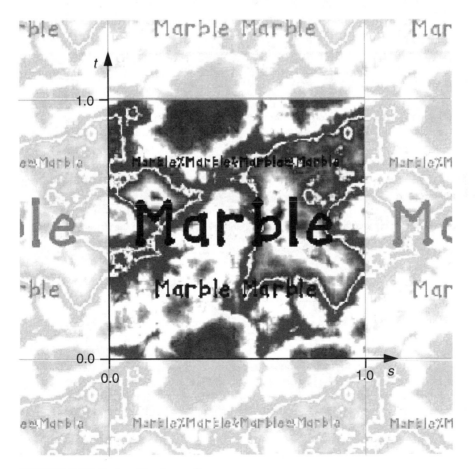

FIGURE 3-37 *Texture Map Image Space*

The *repeatS* and *repeatT* fields specify how the texture wraps in the *s* and *t* directions. If *repeatS* is TRUE (the default), the texture map is repeated outside the 0-to-1 texture coordinate range in the *s* direction so that it fills the shape. If *repeatS* is FALSE, the texture coordinates are clamped in the *s* direction to lie within the 0 to 1 range. The *repeatT* field is analogous to the *repeatS* field.

DESIGN NOTE

The SFImage format for pictures used by **PixelTexture** is intentionally very simple and is not designed for efficient transport of large images. **PixelTextures** are expected to be useful mainly as placeholders for textures that are algorithmically generated by **Script** nodes, either once in the **Script**'s `initialize()` method or repeatedly as the **Script** receives events from a **TimeSensor** to generate an animated texture. Downloading just the **Script** code to generate textures and the parameters to control the generation can be much more bandwidth efficient than transmitting a lot of texture images across the network.

TIP

See the **ImageTexture** section for important tips on texture mapping tricks.

TIP

PixelTexture can also be used to replace **ImageTexture** nodes if you want to make a VRML file self-contained. However, using the `data:` protocol (see Section 2.1.4, Data Protocol) to insert a compressed JPEG or PNG into the URL field of the **ImageTexture** will probably result in a smaller file.

EXAMPLE

The following example illustrates four variations of the **PixelTexture** node. Each of the four maps a **PixelTexture** onto a simple, rectangular **IndexedFaceSet**. The first three use the same **TextureCoordinate** node to repeat the texture three times along both axes of the rectangle. The first object shows how to specify a one-component, gray-scale texture and how the *diffuseColor* of the **Material** can be used to tint or brighten the texture. The second **PixelTexture** uses a three-component, full-color texture and illustrates how to turn lighting off (by not specifying a **Material**). The third object shows a four-component texture with lighting on. The fourth **PixelTexture** illustrates the effect of setting the *repeatS* and *repeatT* fields to FALSE:

```
#VRML V2.0 utf8
Group { children [
```

```
Transform {
  translation -2.5 0 0.5
  rotation 0 1 0 0.5
  children Shape {
    appearance Appearance {
      texture PixelTexture {    # One component (gray scale)
        image 4 4 1 0x00 0xDD 0xAA 0xFF
                    0xDD 0x00 0xDD 0x00
                    0xAA 0xDD 0x00 0x00
                    0xFF 0x00 0x00 0x00
      }
      # Notice how the diffuseColor darkens the texture
      material DEF M Material { diffuseColor .7 .7 .7 }
    }
    geometry DEF IFS IndexedFaceSet {
      coord Coordinate {
      point [ -1.1 -1 0, 1 -1 0, 1 1 0, -1.1 1 0 ] }
      coordIndex [ 0 1 2 3 ]
      texCoord TextureCoordinate { point [ 0 0, 3 0, 3 3, 0 3 ] }
    }
  }
}
Transform {
  translation 0 0 0
  children Shape {
    appearance Appearance {
      # For faster rendering, do not specify a Material
      # and avoid lighting calculations on the texture.
      texture PixelTexture {
        image 2 2 3 0xFFFFFF 0xAAAAAA 0xDDDDDD  0x000000
      }
    }
    geometry USE IFS
  }
}

Transform {
  translation 2.5 0 0
  children Shape {
    appearance Appearance {
      texture PixelTexture {
        image 2 2 4 0xFFFFFF00 0xAAAAAAA0 0xDDDDDDA0  0x000000AA
      }
      material DEF M Material {
        diffuseColor 0 0 0  # diffuseColor and transp have no
        transparency 1.0    # effect - replaced by image values.
        shininess  0.5      # All other fields work fine.
```

```
                ambientIntensity 0.0
            }
        }
        geometry USE IFS
    }
}
Transform {
    translation 5 0 0
    children Shape {
        appearance Appearance {
            texture PixelTexture {      # repeat fields
                image 4 4 1 0x00 0xDD 0xAA 0xFF
                            0xDD 0x00 0xDD 0x00
                            0xAA 0xDD 0x00 0x00
                            0xFF 0x00 0x00 0x00
                repeatS FALSE
                repeatT FALSE
            }
            material DEF M Material { diffuseColor 1 1 1 }
        }
        geometry IndexedFaceSet {
            coord Coordinate { point [ -1 -1 0, 1 -1 0, 1 1 0, -1 1 0 ] }
            coordIndex [ 0 1 2 3 ]
            texCoord TextureCoordinate {
                point [ -0.25 -0.5, 1.25 -0.5, 1.25 1.5, -0.25 1.5 ]
            }
        }
    }
}
Background {
    skyColor [ 1 1 1, 1 1 1, .5 .5 .5, 1 1 1, .2 .2 .2, 1 1 1 ]
    skyAngle [ 1.35, 1.4, 1.45, 1.5, 1.55 ]
    groundColor [ 1 1 1, 1 1 1, 0.4 0.4 0.4 ]
    groundAngle [ 1.3, 1.57 ]
}
NavigationInfo { type "EXAMINE" }
Viewpoint { position  0 1 6 orientation -.707 0 -.707 0 }
]}
```

FIGURE 3-38 *PixelTexture Node Example*

PlaneSensor

```
PlaneSensor {
  exposedField SFBool   autoOffset          TRUE
  exposedField SFBool   enabled             TRUE
  exposedField SFVec2f  maxPosition         -1 -1
  exposedField SFVec2f  minPosition         0 0
  exposedField SFVec3f  offset              0 0 0
  eventOut     SFBool   isActive
  eventOut     SFVec3f  trackPoint_changed
  eventOut     SFVec3f  translation_changed
}
```

The **PlaneSensor** maps pointing device (e.g., mouse or wand) motion into translation in two dimensions, in the *xy* plane of its local space. **PlaneSensor** uses the descendant geometry of its parent node to determine if a hit occurs.

TIP

> **PlaneSensors** allow the user to change the position of objects in the world. The world's creator controls which objects can be moved and exactly how they can be moved by inserting **PlaneSensors** into the scene, setting their fields appropriately, and routing their events to **Script** or **Transform** nodes. Like other sensors, **Plane-Sensors** are not useful by themselves.

The *enabled* exposedField enables and disables the **PlaneSensor.** If TRUE, the sensor reacts appropriately to user events; if FALSE, the sensor does not track user input or send output events. If *enabled* receives a FALSE event and *isActive* is TRUE, the sensor becomes disabled and deactivated, and outputs an *isActive* FALSE event. If *enabled* receives a TRUE event, the sensor is enabled and ready for user activation.

The **PlaneSensor** generates events if the pointing device is activated while over any descendant geometry nodes of its parent group and then moved while activated. Typically, the pointing device is a 2D device such as a mouse. The pointing device is considered to be moving within a plane at a fixed distance from the viewer and perpendicular to the line of sight. This establishes a set of 3D coordinates for the pointer. If a 3D pointer is in use, then the sensor generates events only when the pointer is within the user's field of view. In either case, the pointing device is considered to "pass over" geometry when that geometry is intersected by a line extending from the viewer and passing through the pointer's 3D coordinates. If multiple sensors' geometry intersect this line (hereafter called the *bearing*), only the nearest will be eligible to generate events.

On activation of the pointing device (e.g., mouse button down) over the sensor's geometry, an *isActive* TRUE event is sent. Dragging motion is mapped into a relative translation in the plane parallel to the sensor's local *xy* plane and coincident with the initial point of intersection. For each subsequent position of the bearing, a *translation_changed* event is output that corresponds to a relative translation from the original intersection point to the current intersection point between the bearing and the plane, plus the *offset* value. The sign of the translation is defined by the *xy* plane of the sensor's coordinate system. *TrackPoint_changed* events reflect the unclamped drag position on the surface of this plane. When the pointing device is deactivated and *autoOffset* is TRUE, *offset* is set to the last translation value and an *offset_changed* event is generated. See Section 2.9.6, Sensor Nodes, for more details.

When the sensor generates an *isActive* TRUE event, it grabs all further motion events from the pointing device until it releases and generates an *isActive* FALSE event (other pointing device sensors cannot generate events during this time). Motion of the pointing device while *isActive* is TRUE is referred to as *drag*. If a 2D pointing device is in use, *isActive* events will typically reflect the state of the primary button associated with the device (i.e., *isActive* is TRUE when the primary button is pressed and is FALSE when it is released). If a 3D pointing device (e.g., wand) is in use, *isActive* events will typically reflect whether the pointer is within or in contact with the sensor's geometry.

MinPosition and *maxPosition* may be set to clamp translation events to a range of values as measured from the origin of the *xy* plane. If the *x* or *y* component of *minPosition* is greater than the corresponding component of *maxPosition*, *translation_changed* events are not clamped in that dimension. If the *x* or *y* component of *minPosition* is equal to the corresponding component of *maxPosition,* that

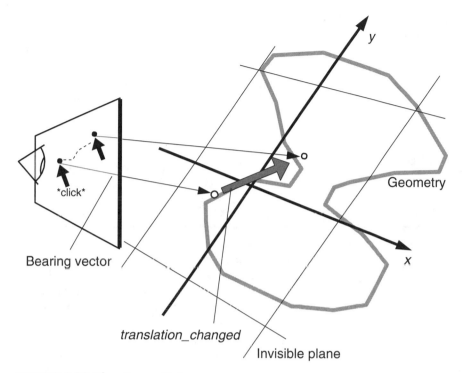

FIGURE 3-39 *PlaneSensor Node*

component is constrained to the given value. This technique provides a way to implement a line sensor that maps dragging motion into a translation in one dimension.

TIP

Setting a *minPosition* and *maxPosition* for one dimension, and setting *minPosition* = *maxPosition* for the other dimension, is the foundation for a slider user interface widget. VRML 2.0 does not define standard user interface components like sliders, buttons, and so forth. Instead, building blocks like **PlaneSensor, TouchSensor,** geometry, and **Script** are provided to allow many different types of user interface components to be built. The prototyping mechanism is provided so that these components can be easily packaged and reused once they have been built. Interaction on a 2D desktop is a well-understood problem, suitable for standardization, while user interaction in a 3D world is still in the research and experimentation stages

While the pointing device is activated, *trackPoint_changed* and *translation_changed* events are output. *TrackPoint_changed* events represent the unclamped intersection points on the surface of the local *xy* plane. If the pointing device is dragged off of the *xy* plane while activated (e.g., above the horizon line), browsers may interpret this in several ways (e.g., clamp all values to the horizon). Each movement of the pointing device, while *isActive* is TRUE, generates *trackPoint_changed* and *translation_changed* events. (See Section 2.9.6, Sensor Nodes, for more details.)

TIP

It is usually a bad idea to route a drag sensor to its own parent. Typically, the drag sensor will route to **Transform,** which does not affect the sensor. See the following examples.

DESIGN NOTE

A **PlaneSensor** that is not oriented almost perpendicular to the viewer can be very difficult to control. Small movements of the pointer can result in very large translations, because the plane and the pointing ray are almost parallel. The specification is a little bit vague about what to do about such cases, guaranteeing only that the *trackPoint* will accurately represent the last intersection of the pointing ray with the plane. Implementations are left free to experiment with schemes to control the *translation_changed* events that are generated to make it easier for users to control.

TIP

Combining **PlaneSensor** with other features produces some neat features. Putting a **PlaneSensor** underneath a **Billboard** node results in a **PlaneSensor** that always turns to face the user, which can make a user interface component built from a **PlaneSensor** much easier to control. Combining a **PlaneSensor, ProximitySensor,** and a **Transform** node can result in a **PlaneSensor** that is always in front of the user. Again, this can be very useful, since one big problem with user interface controls in a 3D world is that it is easy for the user to lose them. Combining these two techniques can give you a **PlaneSensor** that is always in front of the user and is always oriented with the computer screen. In that case, the **PlaneSensor** will produce values that are almost raw mouse *x, y* positions (almost because the positions will be off by constant scale and offset factors).

EXAMPLE

The following example illustrates a simple case of the **PlaneSensor** node. It uses three **PlaneSensors** to translate a **Cone** in a restricted rectangular area. Notice how the **Transforms** are used to rotate the **PlaneSensors** into the *xy* plane (since the default orientation for a **PlaneSensor** is the *xy* plane). The second two **PlaneSensors** illustrate how to create 1D sliders by taking advantage of the *minPosition* and *maxPosition* fields:

```
#VRML V2.0 utf8
Group { children [
  Transform {                # Create the object to be translated
    translation 0 1 0
    rotation 1 0 0 1.57     # Rotate sensor into XZ plane
    children [
      DEF PS1 PlaneSensor {
        minPosition -5 -5
        maxPosition 5 5
      }
      DEF T1 Transform {
        rotation 1 0 0 -1.57  # unrotate so that cone is upright
        children Shape {
          appearance DEF A1 Appearance {
            material Material { diffuseColor 1 1 1 }
          }
          geometry Cone { bottomRadius 1 height 2 }
        }
      }
    ]
  }
  Transform {              # Create Z slider
    translation 5 0 0
    rotation 1 0 0 1.57
    children [
      DEF PS2 PlaneSensor {
        minPosition 0 -5    # Restrict translation to Z axis
        maxPosition 0 5
      }
      DEF T2 Transform {    # Z slider's thumb geometry
        children Shape {
          geometry Box { size .5 .5 .5 }
          appearance USE A1
        }
      }
    ]
  }
  Transform {             # Create X slider
    translation 0 0 -5
    rotation 1 0 0 1.57
    children [
      DEF PS3 PlaneSensor {
        minPosition -5 0    # Restrict translation to X axis
        maxPosition 5 0
      }
      DEF T3 Transform {    # X Slider's thumb geometry
        children Shape {
          geometry Cylinder { radius 0.5 height 1 }
```

```
            appearance USE A1
        }
      }
    ]
  }
  Transform {                    # table
    translation 0 -0.1 0
    children Shape {
      geometry Box { size 10 0.2 10 }
      appearance USE A1
    }
  }
  Background { skyColor 1 1 1 }
  NavigationInfo { type "EXAMINE" }
]}
ROUTE PS1.translation_changed TO T1.set_translation
ROUTE PS2.translation_changed TO T2.set_translation
ROUTE PS2.translation_changed TO T1.set_translation
ROUTE PS3.translation_changed TO T3.set_translation
ROUTE PS3.translation_changed TO T1.set_translation
ROUTE PS2.offset_changed TO PS1.set_offset
ROUTE PS3.offset_changed TO PS1.set_offset
```

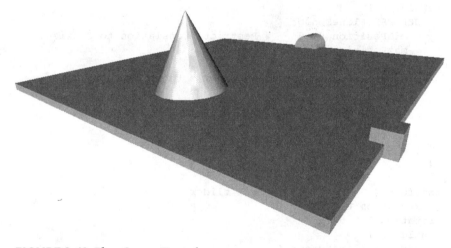

FIGURE 3-40 *PlaneSensor Example*

The Out-of-Box Experience (OOBE) was created by Silicon Graphics, Inc., to provide their users with an interactive virtual tour of their new workstation. OOBE walks the user along a guided tour that includes system setup, demonstrations, a workstation tutorial, and entertainment.

Plate 1 This image shows an overview shot of the entire world. The building in the foreground is the Entry space pavillion, where the user starts at the top of the stairs and begins the system configuration. Off in the distance the Central Plaza, System Tour, Innovation Gallery, and Jungle Island can be seen.

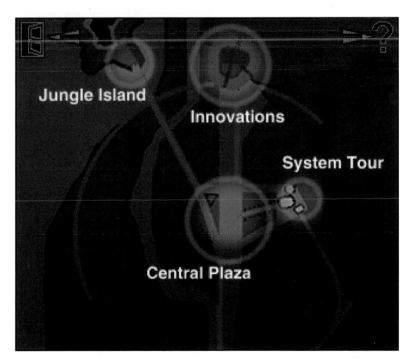

Plate 2 This is an image map of the world. It provides the user with an alternative navigation method.

Plate 3 This is the first stop in a step-by-step system setup procedure. Here users choose the language and time zone to be used by the workstation.

Plate 4 This is the second stop in the system setup. This is where users choose networking and system configuration options.

Plate 5 This image shows a wide-angle view of the world beyond the Entry space pavilion.

Plate 6 Once the system setup is complete, users are guided along to the Central Plaza of the courtyard. From here, users choose where to go next: System Tour, Innovations Gallery, or Jungle Island.

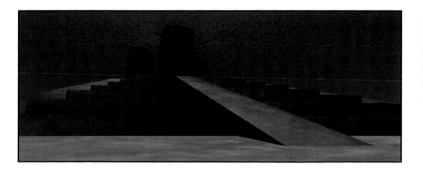

Plate 7 This image shows the front of the System Tour building, which contains an interactive tour of the workstation's hardware and software.

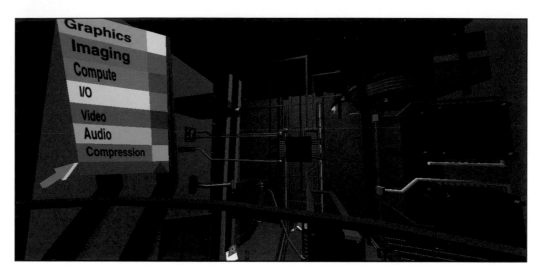

Plate 8 This image shows the interior of the System Tour building. The 3D menu illustrates how traditional user interfaces can be implemented inside 3D worlds.

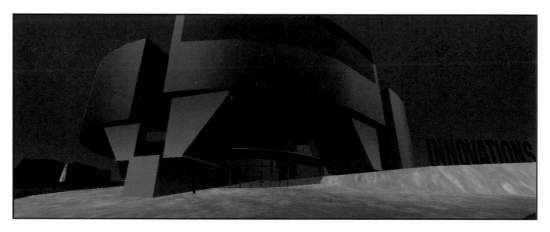

Plate 9 The Innovations Gallery contains various rooms, each dedicated to an educational demonstration.

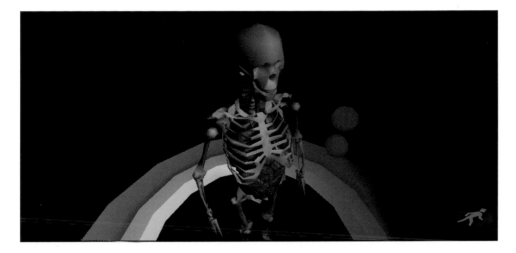

Plate 10 CyberAnatomy101 is one of the rooms inside the Innovations Gallery. It provides an interactive exploration of the human anatomy. Users can observe the motion and sound of major organs while accessing information about the various parts of the body. Each major organ and skeletal region links to a detailed HTML page.

Plate 11 CyberAstronomy is another room in the Innovations Gallery. It presents an interactive guided tour of our solar system with information on planets, moons, and other cellestial bodies. Users can follow the guided tour and click on the various objects to activate HTML pages that provide details on each topic.

Plate 12 Jungle Island is the entertainment part of the tour. It contains a variety of animations, behaviors, and sound effects. Each grass hut links to another world: CyberGourds, Raptor Builder, and Boink.

Plate 13 This image shows the first stop along the Jungle Island tour. The hut links to the CyberGourds world.

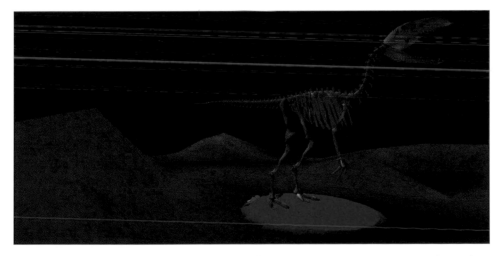

Plate 14 CyberGourds is a 3D drum machine complete with several different rhythmic styles and plant life. Users can explore the different styles of timbre and color by clicking on the gourds. The scratch pad allows the user to improvise with the music by activating a single drum beat or sound. The small balls select the various predefined sounds.

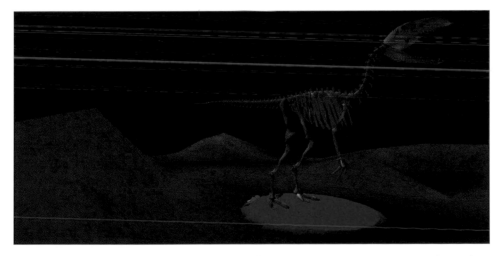

Plate 15 In the Raptor Builder, users must first collect all of the bones to activate the Raptor creature. Once constructed, the body can be interactively posed by dragging on the individual parts. A control panel provides users with an opportunity to interactively experiment with skin textures.

Plate 16 In Boink, users can customize their experience by altering the appearance of the room, objects, and lighting. Each click on an object advances it to the next predefined behavior. The lights are 3D widgets that can be interactively edited to create customized room lighting.

Plate 17 This image shows another view of the Boink world. It shows what happens if you click on the bouncing objects or drag the lights' sensors.

PointLight

```
PointLight {
    exposedField SFFloat  ambientIntensity  0
    exposedField SFVec3f  attenuation       1 0 0
    exposedField SFColor  color             1 1 1
    exposedField SFFloat  intensity         1
    exposedField SFVec3f  location          0 0 0
    exposedField SFBool   on                TRUE
    exposedField SFFloat  radius            100
}
```

The **PointLight** node specifies a point light source at a 3D location in the local coordinate system. A point source emits light equally in all directions; that is, it is omnidirectional. **PointLights** are specified in their local coordinate system and are affected by parent transformations. See Section 2.9.4, Light Sources, for a detailed description of the *ambientIntensity, color,* and *intensity* fields.

A **PointLight** may illuminate geometry within *radius* (≥0.0) meters of its *location*. Both *radius* and *location* are affected by parent transformations (scale *radius* and transform *location*).

A **PointLight**'s illumination falls off with distance as specified by three attenuation coefficients. The attenuation factor is

$$1 / (attenuation[0] + attenuation[1] \times r + attenuation[2] \times r^2)$$

where r is the distance of the light to the surface being illuminated.

The default is no attenuation. An attenuation value of (0,0,0) is identical to 1 0 0. Attenuation values must be ≥0.0. See Section 2.9.5, Lighting Model, for a detailed description of VRML's lighting equations.

TIP

Implementations typically only perform lighting at each vertex in the scene. This means that large polygons and **PointLights** tend not to work very well together. Imagine a **PointLight** at the origin with a radius of 100 m, illuminating a square that is centered at the origin and has sides 1,000 m long (perhaps the square functions as a ground plane for your world). Most implementations will perform only four lighting calculations for the square, one at each vertex. None of the vertices are lit by the **PointLight** because they are too far away. The result will be a square that is dark everywhere, instead of a square that is bright near the origin and dark near the edges.

The solution is to break the square up into multiple pieces so that more vertices are used to draw the same picture, forcing implementations to do more lighting calculations. The more it is broken up, the more accurate the lighting calculations—and the slower the scene will be rendered. Content creators must balance the need for good-looking scenes against constraints on how many lit vertices an implementation can process per second.

One common technique is to fake point and spotlights by precomputing appropriate texture maps, with lighting and shadows built-in. This works very well as long as the lights and geometry don't move relative to each other, but the number of texture maps required can quickly make this impractical for scenes that are sent across a slow network connection.

TIP

The *radius* field of **PointLight** and **SpotLight** restricts the illumination effects of these light sources. It is recommended that you minimize this field to the smallest possible value (i.e., small enough to enclose all of the **Shapes** that you intend to illuminate) in order to avoid significant impacts on rendering performance. A safe rule to live by is: "Never create a file in which the *radius* fields of the light sources exceed the bounding box enclosing all the **Shapes** in the file." This has the nice property that prevents light sources from bleeding outside the original file. Keep in mind that, during rendering, each **Shape** must perform lighting calculations at each vertex for each light source that affects it. Thus, restricting each light source to the intended radius can improve performance and create files that will compose nicely.

TIP

See the **DirectionalLight** section for general tips on light sources.

EXAMPLE

The following example illustrates a simple case of the **PointLight** node. This file contains three **PointLights.** The first light is positioned between the **Sphere** and the table and shows the effects of light attenuation with distance (i.e., slight effect on the **Box** and **Cone**). The second light is positioned to the right side of the **Cone**, but has specified no attenuation (*attenuation* (1,0,0)) and thus illuminates all three objects regardless of distance. The third **PointLight** is positioned to the left of the **Box**, specifies linear *attenuation* (0,1,0) and thus has a marginal effect on the **Sphere** and practically no visible effect on the **Cone**. Note that a **ProximitySensor** is used to turn the lights on when the user is near and to turn them off when the user leaves the vicinity. The initial **Viewpoint** locates the user outside the bounding box of the **ProximitySensor**, while the second **Viewpoint** is inside:

```
#VRML V2.0 utf8
Group { children [
  DEF PL1 PointLight {  # Between sphere and table
    location 0 -0.3 0.5 # with linear attenuation
    attenuation 0 1 0
    on FALSE
    radius 10
  }
  DEF PL2 PointLight {    # Right side - no attenuation
    location 5 2.0 1
    attenuation 1 0 0
    on FALSE
    radius 10
  }
  DEF PL3 PointLight {    # Left side close to the table
    location -5 -.1 2      # with linear attenuation
    attenuation 0 1 0
    on FALSE
    radius 10
  }
  Transform {
    translation -3 0.77 0
    rotation 0.30 0.94 -0.14 0.93
    scale 0.85 0.85 0.85
    scaleOrientation -0.36 -0.89 -0.29  0.18
    children Shape {
      appearance DEF A1 Appearance {
        material Material {
          ambientIntensity 0.34
          diffuseColor 0.85 0.85 0.85
          specularColor 1 1 1
          shininess 0.56
        }
      }
      geometry Box {}
    }
  }
  Transform {
    translation 0 0.7 0
    children Shape {
      appearance USE A1
      geometry Sphere {}
    }
  }
  Transform {
    translation 3 1.05 0
    rotation 0 0 1  0.6
    children Shape {
      appearance USE A1
```

```
          geometry Cone {}
      }
  }
  Transform {
    translation -5 -1 -2
    children Shape {
      appearance USE A1
      geometry ElevationGrid {
        height [ 0 0 0 0 0 ... 0 ]
        xDimension 11
        zDimension 5
        xSpacing 1
        zSpacing 1
      }
    }
  }
  DEF PS ProximitySensor { size 20 10 20 }
  Background { skyColor 1 1 1 }
  NavigationInfo { type "EXAMINE" headlight FALSE }
  Viewpoint {
    position 5 2 50
    orientation -.2 0 .9 0
    description "Outside the light zone"
  }
  Viewpoint {
    position 0 1 7
    orientation 0 0 -1 0
    description "Inside the light zone"
  }
]}
ROUTE PS.isActive TO PL1.on
ROUTE PS.isActive TO PL2.on
ROUTE PS.isActive TO PL3.on
```

FIGURE 3-41 *PointLight Node Example*

PointSet

```
PointSet {
  exposedField  SFNode  color  NULL
  exposedField  SFNode  coord  NULL
}
```

The **PointSet** node specifies a set of 3D points in the local coordinate system with associated colors at each point. The *coord* field specifies a **Coordinate** node (or instance of a **Coordinate** node). Results are undefined if the *coord* field specifies any other type of node. **PointSet** uses the coordinates in order. If the *coord* field is NULL, then the **PointSet** is empty.

PointSets are not lit, not texture mapped, and not collided with during collision detection.

If the *color* field is not NULL, it must specify a **Color** node that contains at least the number of points contained in the **Coordinate** node. Results are undefined if the *color* field specifies any other type of node. Colors are applied to each point in order. The results are undefined if the number of values in the **Color** node is less than the number of values specified in the **Coordinate** node.

If the *color* field is NULL and there is a **Material** defined for the **Appearance** affecting this **PointSet**, then the *emissiveColor* of the **Material** is used to draw the points. See Section 2.9.5, Lighting Model, for details on lighting equations.

DESIGN NOTE

Implementations decide how large or small the points should appear. There is no way of setting the size of the points. If there were a way of specifying how large points should be, it isn't clear what units should be used. Most rendering systems that support points allow specification of size in pixels, but the size of one pixel can vary dramatically depending on the resolution of the display device. A common problem with resolution-dependent standards is that technology keeps on making content created for a specific resolution obsolete. Applications designed for the 640 x 480-pixel screens of yesterday look postage stamp sized on today's 1000 x 1000+ screens.

Open Inventor follows the PostScript model, specifying point sizes (and line widths, another feature not in VRML 2.0) in points—1/72 of an inch—with the special size of zero interpreted to mean "as small as the display device allows." Doing something similar for VRML would be possible, perhaps using millimeters or another metric measurement to match VRML's default unit of meters. However, using any "real-world" measurement poses serious problems for immersive display systems where the user cannot hold a tape measure up to the computer screen to measure how big a **PointSet** point is because they are inside the display. One millimeter is a lot of pixels on a head-mounted display that is only a few centimeters away from your eye.

Specifying point sizes just like any other size in VRML (in the local coordinate system of the **PointSet** node) causes implementation problems, since conventional displays must then make points larger and smaller as they get closer and farther from the viewer. Typically, content creators don't want their **PointSets** to change size, either.

This issue will undoubtedly come up again, since varying line widths and point sizes is an often-requested feature and necessary for several important applications. Perhaps a measurement such as the angle subtended by a point might be used, allowing precise and efficient implementations on both immersive and nonimmersive displays.

EXAMPLE

The following example illustrates a simple case of the **PointSet** node. The first **Shape** defines a **PointSet** consisting of seven randomly located points with a color specified for each one. The second **PointSet** uses the same seven coordinates, but specifies the point color by using a **Material** node's *emissiveColor* field. Note that the all other fields of the **Material** are ignored. A **TimeSensor** routed to an **OrientationInterpolator** spins the root **Transform**:

```
#VRML V2.0 utf8
DEF T Transform { children [
  Shape {
    geometry PointSet {
      coord DEF C Coordinate {
        point [ 0 -1 2, 1 0 0, -2 3 -1, -4 0 0, -2 2 -1, 5 -2 1,
                3 -6 3  ]
      }
      color Color {
        color [ 1 0 0, 0 1 0, 1 1 0, 0 1 1, 1 1 1, 1 0 0, 1 0 0 ]
      }
    }
  }
  Transform {
    rotation 1 0 0 1.57
    children Shape {
      geometry PointSet { coord USE C }
      appearance Appearance {
        material Material {
          emissiveColor 0 1 0     # defines the point colors
          diffuseColor 1 0 0      # has no effect at all
        }
      }
    }
  }
}
```

```
    DEF TS TimeSensor {
      stopTime -1
      loop TRUE
      cycleInterval 1.0
    }
    DEF OI OrientationInterpolator {
      key [ 0 .5 1 ]
      keyValue [ 0 1 0 0, 0 1 0 3.14, 0 1 0 6.27 ]
    }
  ]}
  ROUTE TS.fraction_changed TO OI.set_fraction
  ROUTE OI.value_changed TO T.rotation
```

PositionInterpolator

```
PositionInterpolator {
  eventIn       SFFloat set_fraction
  exposedField MFFloat  key          []
  exposedField MFVec3f  keyValue     []
  eventOut      SFVec3f value_changed
}
```

This node linearly interpolates among a set of SFVec3f values. This is appropriate for interpolating a translation. The vectors are interpreted as absolute positions in object space. The *keyValue* field must contain exactly as many values as in the *key* field. Refer to Section 2.9.3, Interpolators, for a more detailed discussion of interpolators.

TIP

A **PositionInterpolator** can be used to animate any SFVec3f value, but for some values the interpolation calculation done by the **PositionInterpolator** will not give the best results. For example, you can use a **PositionInterpolator** to make an object change size by routing it to a Transform's *set_scale* eventIn. However, scaling is a logarithmic operation, and the linear interpolation done by the **PositionInterpolator** will give nonintuitive results. Imagine you are making an object go from one-quarter its normal size to four times its normal size. An interpolator that maintained a constant rate of growth would make the object normal size halfway through the animation. A **PositionInterpolator,** however, would make the object

$$.25 + (4 - .25)/2 = 2.125$$

halfway through, resulting in rapid growth at the beginning of the animation and very slow growth at the end. A **ScaleInterpolator** that would look exactly like a **PositionInterpolator** but perform a different interpolation calculation was considered, but animation of scale isn't common enough to justify adding another node to the specification.

TIP

Remember that **TimeSensor** outputs *fraction_changed* events in the 0.0 to 1.0 range, and that interpolator nodes routed *from* **TimeSensors** should restrict their *key* field values to the 0.0 to 1.0 range to match the **TimeSensor** output and thus produce a full interpolation sequence.

TIP

When creating a **PositionInterpolator** make sure to specify *key* values (e.g., time) that produce desirable velocities. For example, if you want constant velocity you must choose *key* times that are spaced proportionally to the distances between the *keyValues*. For each *key*[i], calculate the linear distance from the first *keyValue*[0] to the current *keyValue*[i] (making sure to go through all of the points between *keyValue*[0] and *keyValue*[i]), and divide this by the length of the entire *keyValue* sequence:

```
PositionInterpolator {
   key [ 0.0, .0909, 1.0 ]
   # where key[1] = .0909 = (length[i] / total length) = (9/99)
   keyValue [ 1 0 0, 10 0 0, 100 0 0 ]
}
```

EXAMPLE

The following example illustrates a simple case of the **PositionInterpolator** node. A **Position-Interpolator** is routed to a **Transform** that contains a **Cone**. When the **Cone** is clicked it fires the **TouchSensor**, which starts the **TimeSensor**, which drives one complete cycle of the **Position-Interpolator**:

```
#VRML V2.0 utf8
Group { children [
  DEF PI PositionInterpolator {
    key [ 0.0, .1, .4, .7, .9, 1.0 ]
    keyValue [ -3 0 0,  0 0 0, 0 20 -50, 0 0 -100, 0 0 0, -3 0 0 ]
  }
  DEF T Transform {
    translation -3 0 0
    children Shape {
      geometry Cone {}
      appearance Appearance {
        material Material { diffuseColor 1 0 0 }
      }
    }
  }
```

```
    DEF TOS TouchSensor {}  # Click to start
    DEF TS TimeSensor { cycleInterval 3.0 }   # 3 sec loop
    Background { skyColor 1 1 1 }
    NavigationInfo { type "EXAMINE" }
]}
ROUTE PI.value_changed TO T.translation
ROUTE TOS.touchTime TO TS.startTime
ROUTE TS.fraction_changed TO PI.set_fraction
```

ProximitySensor

```
ProximitySensor {
    exposedField SFVec3f     center       0 0 0
    exposedField SFVec3f     size         0 0 0
    exposedField SFBool      enabled      TRUE
    eventOut     SFBool      isActive
    eventOut     SFVec3f     position_changed
    eventOut     SFRotation  orientation_changed
    eventOut     SFTime      enterTime
    eventOut     SFTime      exitTime
}
```

The **ProximitySensor** generates events when the user enters, exits, and moves
within a region in space (defined by a box). A proximity sensor can be enabled or
disabled by sending it an *enabled* event with a value of TRUE or FALSE. A disabled
sensor does not send output events.

TIP

Earlier drafts of the specification had two kinds of proximity sensors, **BoxProximity-
Sensor** and **SphereProximitySensor.** Only the box version made the final specification because axis-aligned boxes are used in other places in the specification (bounding
box fields of grouping nodes), because they are more common than spheres, and
because **SphereProximitySensor** functionality can be created using a **Script** and a
BoxProximitySensor. The **BoxProximitySensor** must be large enough to enclose
the sphere, and the **Script** just filters the events that come from the box region, passing along only events that occur inside the sphere (generating appropriate enter and exit
events, etc.). This same technique can be used if you need to sense the viewer's relationship to any arbitrarily shaped region of space. Just find the box that encloses the region
and write a script that throws out events in the uninteresting regions.

A **ProximitySensor** generates *isActive* TRUE/FALSE events as the viewer enters and exits the rectangular box defined by its *center* and *size* fields. Browsers interpolate user positions and set time stamps for *isActive* events with the exact time the user first intersected the proximity region. The *center* field defines the center point of the proximity region in object space; the *size* field specifies a vector that defines the width (x), height (y), and depth (z) of the box bounding the region. All values of the *size* field must be ≥ 0.0. **ProximitySensor** nodes are affected by the hierarchical transformations of their parents.

DESIGN NOTE

Browsers move the camera in discrete steps, usually one step per frame rendered when the user is moving. How often the browser renders frames (whether ten frames per second or 60 frames per second) varies depending on how fast the computer is on which it is running and so on. It is important that content creators be able to depend on accurate times from **ProximitySensors,** which is why it is important that implementations interpolate between sampled user positions to calculate **ProximitySensor** enter and exit times. For example, you might create a "speed trap" that measures how fast the user moves between two points in the world (and gives the user a virtual speeding ticket if they are moving too quickly). This is easy to accomplish using two **Proximity-Sensors** and a **Script** that takes the two sensors' *enterTimes* and determines the user's speed as speed = distance / (*enterTime*1 − *enterTime*2). This should work even if the sensors are close together and the user is moving fast enough to travel through both of them during one frame, and it will work if the implementation performs the correct interpolation calculation.

If both the user and the **ProximitySensor** are moving, calculating the precise, theoretical time of intersection can be almost impossible. The VRML specification does not require perfection—implementations are expected only to do the best they can. A reasonable strategy is to simulate the motion of the **ProximitySensors** first, and then calculate the exact intersection of the user's previous and current position against the final position of the sensor. That will give perfect results when just the user is moving, and will give very good results even when both the user and the sensor are moving.

An *enterTime* event is generated whenever an *isActive* TRUE event is generated (a user enters the box), and an *exitTime* event is generated whenever an *isActive* FALSE event is generated (a user exits the box).

The *position_changed* and *orientation_changed* events are sent if the viewer's avatar (see **NavigationInfo**) is inside the **ProximitySensor**'s box, and if the position and orientation of the viewer changes with respect to the **ProximitySensor**'s coordinate system (this includes enter and exit times). Note that the user movement may be a result of a variety of circumstances (e.g., browser navigation, the **Proximity-Sensor**'s coordinate system changes, or the bound **Viewpoint**'s position or orientation changes). The *position_changed* and *orientation_changed* events are specified in the coordinate system of the **ProximitySensor.**

Each **ProximitySensor** behaves independently of all other **ProximitySensors.** Every enabled **ProximitySensor** that is affected by the user's movement receives and sends events, possibly resulting in multiple **ProximitySensors** receiving and sending events simultaneously. Unlike **TouchSensors,** there is no notion of a **ProximitySensor** lower in the scene graph "grabbing" events.

Instanced (DEF/USE) **ProximitySensors** use the union of all the boxes to check for enter and exit. An instanced **ProximitySensor** will detect enter and exit for all instances of the box and send output events appropriately. If instanced **Proximity-Sensors** overlap, results are undefined in the region of overlap.

DESIGN NOTE

Instancing a **ProximitySensor** makes it sense a series of box-shaped regions instead of a single box-shaped region. Results are still well defined, as long as the various instances do not overlap. Results are undefined for viewer movement in the overlapping region. For example, this instanced **ProximitySensor** overlaps in the unit cube around the origin and results are undefined for *position_changed* and *orientation_changed* events generated in that region:

```
Transform {
  translation 0 1 0
  children  DEF P ProximitySensor {
    size 1 2 1
  }
}
Transform {
  translation 0 -1 0
  children USE P
}
```

A **ProximitySensor** that surrounds the entire world will have an *enterTime* equal to the time that the world was entered and can be used to start up animations or behaviors as soon as a world is loaded. A **ProximitySensor** with a (0,0,0) *size* field cannot generate events (this is equivalent to setting the *enabled* field to FALSE).

DESIGN NOTE

ProximitySensor started as a simple feature designed for a few simple uses, but turned out to be a very powerful feature useful for a surprisingly wide variety of tasks. **ProximitySensors** were first added to VRML 2.0 as a simple trigger for tasks like opening a door or raising a platform when the user arrived at a certain location in the world.

The **ProximitySensor** design had only the *isActive* SFBool eventOut (and the *center* and *size* fields to describe the location and size of the region of interest).

Just knowing whether or not viewers are in a region of space is very useful, but sometimes it is desirable to know exactly where viewers enter the space or the orientation of viewers when they enter the space. You might want to create a doorway that only opens if viewers approach it facing forward (and stays shut if the users back into it), for example. The *position_changed* and *orientation_changed* events were added to give this information, but were defined to generate events only when the *isActive* eventOut generated events—when a viewer entered or exited the region.

While the **ProximitySensor** design was being revised, two other commonly requested features were being designed: allowing a **Script** to find out the current position and orientation of the viewer, and notifying a **Script** when the viewer moves.

The obvious solution to the first problem is to provide `getCurrentPosition()`/`getCurrentOrientation()` methods that a **Script** could call at any time to find out the current position and orientation of the viewer. The problem with this solution is that **Script** nodes are not necessarily part of the scene hierarchy and so are not necessarily defined in any particular coordinate system. For the results of a `getCurrentPosition()` call to make any sense, they must be defined in some coordinate system known to the creator of the **Script**. Requiring every **Script** to be part of the scene hierarchy just in case the **Script** makes these calls is a bad solution, since it adds a restriction that is unnecessary in most cases (most **Script** nodes will not care about the position or orientation of the viewer). Requiring some **Script** nodes to be defined in a particular coordinate system but not requiring others is also a bad solution, because it is inconsistent and error prone. And reporting positions and orientations in some world coordinate system is also a bad solution, because the world coordinate system may not be known to the author of the **Script**. VRML worlds are meant to be composable, with the world coordinate system of one world becoming just another local coordinate system when that world is included in a larger world.

The obvious solution for the second problem is allowing **Scripts** to register callback methods that the browser calls whenever the viewer's position or orientation changes. This has all of the coordinate system problems just described, plus scalability problems. Every **Script** that registered these "tell-me-when-the-viewer-moves" callbacks would make the VRML browser do a little bit of extra work. In a very large virtual world, the overhead of informing thousands or millions of **Scripts** that the viewer moved would leave the browser no time to do anything else.

The not-so-obvious solution that addressed all of these problems was to use the *position_changed* and *orientation_changed* eventOuts of the **ProximitySensor.** They were redefined to generate events whenever the viewer moved inside the region defined by the **ProximitySensor** instead of just generating events when the user crossed the boundaries of the region, making it easy to ROUTE them to a **Script** that wants to be informed whenever the viewer's position or orientation changes. The coordinate system problems are solved because **ProximitySensors** define a particular region of the world, and so must be part of the scene hierarchy and exist in some coordinate system.

The scalability problem is solved by requiring world creators to define the region in which they're interested. As long as they define reasonably sized regions, browsers will be able to generate events efficiently only for **ProximitySensors** that are relevant. If world creators don't care about scalability, they can just define a very, very large **ProximitySensor** (size 1e25 1e25 1e25 should be big enough; assuming the default units of meters, it is about the size of the observable universe and is still much smaller than the largest legal floating point value, which is about 1e38).

Scripts that just want to know the current position (or orientation) of the user can simply read the *position_changed* (or *orientation_changed*) eventOut of a **ProximitySensor** whenever convenient. If the *position_changed* eventOut does not have any ROUTEs coming from it, the browser does not have to update it until a **Script** tries to read from it, making this solution just as efficient as having the **Script** call a getCurrentPosition() method.

TIP

An unanticipated use for **ProximitySensors** is creating "dashboard" geometry that stays in a fixed position on the computer's screen. Putting a **ProximitySensor** and a **Transform** node in the same coordinate system and routing the sensor's *position_changed* and *orientation_changed* eventOuts to the **Transform**'s *set_translation* and *set_rotation* eventIns, like this

```
Group {
  children [
    DEF PS ProximitySensor { size ... }
    DEF T Transform { children [ ... dashboard geometry... ] }
  ]
  ROUTE PS.position_changed TO T.set_translation
  ROUTE PS.orientation_changed TO T.set_rotation
}
```

will make the **Transform** follow the viewer. Any geometry underneath the **Transform** will therefore stay fixed with respect to the viewer.

There are a couple of potential problems with this solution. First, you must decide on a size for the **ProximitySensor.** If you want your dashboard to be visible anywhere in your world, you must make the **ProximitySensor** at least as large as your world. If you don't care about your world being composed into a larger world, just give the **ProximitySensor** a huge size (e.g., size 1e25 1e25 1e25).

Second, precise placement of geometry on the screen is only possible if you know the dimensions of the window into which the VRML browser is rendering and the viewer's field of view. A preferred field of view can be specified in the **Viewpoint** node, but the VRML specification provides no way to set the dimensions of the browser's window. Instead, you must use the HTML <EMBED> or <OBJECT> tags to specify the window's dimensions and put the VRML world inside an HTML Web page.

Finally, usually it is desirable for dashboard geometry to always appear on top of other geometry in the scene. This must be done by putting the dashboard geometry inside the empty space between the viewer's eye and the navigation collision radius (set using a **NavigationInfo** node). Geometry put there should always be on top of any geometry in the scene, since the viewer shouldn't be able to get closer than the collision radius to any scene geometry. However, putting geometry too close to the viewer's eye causes the implementation problem known as "z-buffer tearing," so it is recommended that you put any dashboard geometry between half the collision radius and the collision radius. For example, if the collision radius is 0.1 m (10 cm), place dashboard geometry between 5 and 10 cm away from the viewer (and, of course, the dashboard geometry should be underneath a **Collision** group that turns off collisions with the dashboard).

EXAMPLE

The following example illustrates the use of the **ProximitySensor** node. The file contains three **ProximitySensor** nodes. The first one, PS1, illustrates how to create a simple HUD by defining the sensor's bounding box to enclose the entire world (probably a good idea to put some walls up) and then track the position and orientation of the user's avatar during navigation. Then, adjust the HUD geometry (a **Sphere** with a **TouchSensor**) to stay in view. Clicking down on the **Sphere-Sensor/TouchSensor** binds to a **Viewpoint**, V2, and unbinds on release. The second **Proximity-Sensor**, PS2, encloses the small pavilion on the left side of the scene. On entering the sensor's bounding box, an **AudioClip** greeting is started. The third **ProximitySensor**, PS3, encloses the identical pavilion on the right side. On entering this pavilion, a **Cone** floating inside begins a looping animation and stops when the user exits the pavilion:

```
#VRML V2.0 utf8
Group { children [
  Collision {
    collide FALSE
    children [
      DEF PS1 ProximitySensor { size 100 10 100 }
      DEF T1 Transform {
        children Transform {
          translation 0.05 -0.05 -.15   # Relative to viewer
          children  [
            DEF TS TouchSensor {}
            Shape {
              appearance DEF A1 Appearance {
                material Material { diffuseColor 1 .5 .5 }
              }
```

```
                  geometry Sphere { radius 0.005 }
             }
]}}]}
Transform {
  translation -7 1 0
  children [
    DEF PS2 ProximitySensor { center 2.5 1 -2.5 size 5 2 5 }
    Sound {
      location 2.5 1 2.5
      maxBack 5 minBack 5
      maxFront 5 minFront 5
      source DEF AC AudioClip {
        description "Someone entered the room."
        url "enterRoom.wav"
      }
    }
    DEF G Group { children [
      DEF S Shape {
        geometry Box { size 0.2 2 0.2 }
        appearance DEF A2 Appearance {
          material Material { diffuseColor 1 1 1 }
        }
      }
      Transform { translation 5 0 0 children USE S }
      Transform { translation 5 0 -5 children USE S }
      Transform { translation 0 0 -5 children USE S }
      Transform {
        translation 2.5 2 -2.5
        children Shape {
          appearance USE A1
          geometry Cone { bottomRadius 5.0 height 1.2 }
        }
      }
}]}]}
Transform {
  translation 7 1 0
  children [
    DEF PS3 ProximitySensor { center 2.5 1 -2.5 size 5 2 5 }
    USE G
    DEF T Transform {
      translation 2.5 0 -2.5
      children Shape {
        geometry Cone { bottomRadius 0.3 height 0.5 }
        appearance USE A1
      }
    }
    DEF TIS TimeSensor {}
    DEF OI OrientationInterpolator {
      key [ 0.0, .5, 1.0 ]
```

```
            keyValue [ 0 0 1 0, 0 0 1 3.14, 0 0 1 6.28 ]
        }
      ]
    }
    Transform {                 # Floor
      translation -20 0 -20
      children Shape {
        appearance USE A2
        geometry ElevationGrid {
          height [ 0 0 0 0 0 0 0 0 0 0 0 0 0 0 0 0 0 0 0 0 0 0 0 0 0 ]
          xDimension 5
          zDimension 5
          xSpacing 10
          zSpacing 10
        }
      }
    }
    DirectionalLight { direction -.707 -.707 0 intensity 1 }
    Background { skyColor 1 1 1 }
    NavigationInfo { type "WALK" }
    DEF V1 Viewpoint {
      position 5 1.6 18
      orientation -.2 0 .9 0
      description "Initial view"
    }
    DEF V2 Viewpoint {
      position 10 1.6 10
      orientation -.707 0 -.707 0
      description "View of the pavilions"
    }
  ]}
ROUTE TS.isActive TO V2.set_bind
ROUTE PS1.orientation_changed TO T1.rotation
ROUTE PS1.position_changed TO T1.translation
ROUTE PS2.enterTime TO AC.startTime
ROUTE PS3.isActive TO TIS.loop
ROUTE PS3.enterTime TO TIS.startTime
ROUTE TIS.fraction_changed TO OI.set_fraction
ROUTE OI.value_changed TO T.rotation
```

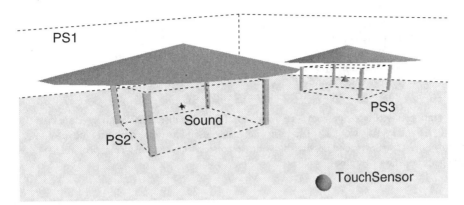

FIGURE 3-42 *ProximitySensor Node Example*

ScalarInterpolator

```
ScalarInterpolator {
    eventIn        SFFloat set_fraction
    exposedField MFFloat key         []
    exposedField MFFloat keyValue    []
    eventOut       SFFloat value_changed
}
```

This node linearly interpolates among a set of SFFloat values. This interpolator is appropriate for any parameter defined using a single floating point value (e.g., *width*, *radius*, *intensity*, etc.). The *keyValue* field must contain exactly as many numbers as there are keyframes in the *key* field. Refer to Section 2.9.3, Interpolators, for a more detailed discussion of interpolators.

TIP

One nonobvious use for a **ScalarInterpolator** is to modify the *fraction_changed* values of a **TimeSensor** before they are sent to another interpolator. Normally the *fraction_changed* events will range from 0 to 1 in a linear ramp, but a **ScalarInterpolator** can be used to modify them in interesting ways. For example, you can map the normal 0 to 1 "sawtooth" ramp of a **TimeSensor** into a 0 to 1 to 0 "triangle" ramp by doing this:

```
DEF TS TimeSensor { }
DEF SI ScalarInterpolator {
```

```
   key [ 0, 0.5, 1 ]
   keyValue [ 0, 1, 0 ]
}
DEF PI PositionInterpolator { ... }
ROUTE TS.fraction_changed TO SI.set_fraction
ROUTE SI.value_changed TO PI.set_fraction
```

Generating events that run from 1 to 0 instead of 0 to 1 is just as easy. Simply use *keys* of [0, 1] and *keyValues* of [1, 0]. Ease-in and ease-out effects (where objects move slowly when starting, speed up, then slow down to stop) are also easy to approximate using appropriate keyframes.

TIP

Remember that **TimeSensor** outputs *fraction_changed* events in the 0.0 to 1.0 range, and that interpolator nodes routed *from* **TimeSensors** should restrict their *key* field values to the 0.0 to 1.0 range to match the **TimeSensor** output and thus produce a full interpolation sequence.

EXAMPLE

The following simple example illustrates the **ScalarInterpolator** node. A **TouchSensor** is used to trigger a **TimeSensor,** which drives the **ScalarInterpolator.** The output from the **ScalarInterpolator** modifies the *transparency* field of the **Cone's Material** node:

```
#VRML V2.0 utf8
Group { children [
  DEF SI ScalarInterpolator {
    key [ 0.0, .5, 1.0 ]
    keyValue [ 0, .9, 0 ]
  }
  DEF T Transform {
    translation -3 0 0
    children Shape {
      geometry Cone {}
      appearance Appearance { .
        material DEF M Material { diffuseColor 1 0 0 }
      }
    }
  }
DEF TOS TouchSensor {}  # Click to start
DEF TS TimeSensor { loop TRUE cycleInterval 3.0 } # 3 sec loop
Background { skyColor 1 1 1 }
```

```
     NavigationInfo { type "EXAMINE" }
]}
ROUTE SI.value_changed TO M.transparency
ROUTE TOS.touchTime TO TS.startTime
ROUTE TS.fraction_changed TO SI.set_fraction
```

Script

```
Script {
   exposedField MFString url              []
   field           SFBool    directOutput   FALSE
   field           SFBool    mustEvaluate   FALSE
   # And any number of:
   eventIn         eventTypeName eventName
   field           fieldTypeName fieldName initialValue
   eventOut        eventTypeName eventName
}
```

The **Script** node is used to program behavior in a scene. **Script** nodes typically receive events that signify a change or user action, contain a program module that performs some computation, and effect change somewhere else in the scene by sending output events. Each **Script** node has associated programming language code (referenced by the *url* field) that is executed to carry out the **Script** node's function. That code will be referred to as "the script" in the rest of this description.

Browsers are not required to support any specific language. See Section 2.7, Scripting, for detailed information on scripting languages. Browsers are required to adhere to the language bindings of languages specified in annexes of the specification. See Section 2.1.3, URLs, for details on the *url* field.

When the script is created, any language-dependent or user-defined initialization is performed. The script is able to receive and process events that are sent to it. Each event that can be received must be declared in the **Script** node using the same syntax as is used in a prototype definition:

```
eventIn type name
```

The type can be any of the standard VRML fields (see Chapter 4, Field and Event Reference), and the name must be an identifier that is unique for this **Script** node.

The **Script** node should be able to generate events in response to the incoming events. Each event that can be generated must be declared in the **Script** node using the following syntax:

```
eventOut type name
```

Script nodes cannot have exposedFields. The implementation ramifications of exposedFields is far too complex and thus not allowed.

DESIGN NOTE

Defining exactly what it means for a **Script** to have an exposedField gets complicated. It isn't enough to say that an exposedField is equivalent to an eventIn, field, and event Out. For example, if the following **Script** were legal

```
DEF ILLEGAL Script {
  exposedField SFBool foo FALSE
}
```

and considered equivalent to

```
Script {
  field SFBool foo FALSE
  eventIn SFBool set_foo
  eventOut SFBool foo_changed
}
```

a variety of difficult questions would need to be addressed. Is the **Script**'s code required to generate *foo_changed* events when a *set_foo event* is received, or is that done automatically for the **Script** by the browser? If it is done automatically by the browser (which would certainly be convenient for the person writing the **Script**), is the **Script**'s code also allowed to send *foo_changed* events or change the *foo* field? And if it is done automatically by the browser, then will it be done automatically in the second previous example (where *foo, set_foo,* and *foo_changed* are declared individually instead of as an exposedField)?

If *foo_changed* events are not automatically generated when *set_foo* events are received, is the **Script** required to generate them? If not, then *foo* isn't really an exposedField, since the definition of an exposedField involves both syntax (it is syntactically equivalent to a field + eventIn + eventOut) and semantics (an exposedField's semantics are that it generates *_changed* events and sets the field whenever a *set_* event is received).

ExposedFields in **Script** nodes are a design issue that will probably be revisited at some time in the future. Allowing a **Script** read-only access to its exposedFields and allowing only the browser to generate *_changed* events would be a good solution, but requires that the notion of a read-only variable be supported somehow in each scripting language. For VRML 2.0, the simple and conservative solution of just not allowing **Script** nodes to have exposedFields was chosen.

If the **Script** node's *mustEvaluate* field is FALSE, the browser can delay sending input events to the script until its outputs are needed by the browser. If the *mustEvaluate* field is TRUE, the browser should send input events to the **Script** as soon as possible, regardless of whether the outputs are needed. The *mustEvaluate* field should be set to TRUE only if the **Script** has effects that are not known to the browser (such as sending information across the network); otherwise, poor performance may result.

DESIGN NOTE

Executing a **Script** might be a fairly expensive operation, possibly involving communication with a language interpreter that may be running as a separate process. Therefore, VRML 2.0 was designed so that browsers can queue up multiple events and give them to a **Script** node at the same time. The *mustEvaluate* flag is a hint to the browser that it should execute the **Script** as soon as possible after it receives events, which is less efficient than waiting as long as possible to execute the **Script.**

Once the script has access to a VRML node (via an SFNode or MFNode value either in one of the **Script** node's fields or passed in as an eventIn), the script is able to read the contents of that node's exposedFields. If the **Script** node's *directOutput* field is TRUE, the script may also send events directly to any node to which it has access, and may dynamically establish or break routes. If *directOutput* is FALSE (the default), then the script may only affect the rest of the world via events sent through its eventOuts.

A script is able to communicate directly with the VRML browser to get the current time, the current world URL, and so on. This is strictly defined by the API for the specific language being used. It is expected that all other functionality (such as networking capabilities, multithreading capabilities, etc.) will be provided by the scripting language.

The location of the **Script** node in the scene graph has no effect on its operation. For example, if a parent of a **Script** node is a **Switch** node with *whichChoice* set to −1 (i.e., ignore its children), the **Script** continues to operate as specified (receives and sends events).

DESIGN NOTE

A couple of generalizations for the **Script** node were considered but did not make it into the final VRML 2.0 specification. One was the ability for a **Script** to add or remove fields, eventIns, and eventOuts from itself dynamically while it was running. Combined with the browser `addRoute()` and `deleteRoute()` methods, this would sometimes be useful. However, it might be difficult to implement and will be easy to add later if necessary.

Another generalization along the same line is allowing a **Script** to declare that it can receive events of any type, with the type determined by the **Script** as it runs. This would require additional syntax (perhaps an "SFAny" field pseudotype) and would affect the design of several other features (such as PROTO and EXTERNPROTO). Again, this might make implementation of the VRML specification significantly more difficult and can be added later if it becomes clear that it is necessary.

TIP

At present, there are two scripting languages supported in the VRML specification: Java and JavaScript. There has been an endless and raging debate in the VRML community on which language is "better." The pro-Java camp believes that Java is a "real" programming language and has much more power, flexibility, infrastructure, and industry acceptance. These points are all true. The JavaScript proponents state that JavaScript is much easier to learn and use, especially if you are not a hard-core programmer. This is also a reasonable position (debated strongly by Java programmers, though). In general, when choosing a programming language, you should first assess the problem you are trying to solve; second, consider your own programming skills and experience; and then, choose the language that best fits these two parameters. A gross generalization is that Java is more capable of solving the difficult or serious programming problems, such as network access, database integration, multiusers, and so forth, while JavaScript is more suitable for simple behavior scripting, such as "a combination lock," "turn on the lights when ...," and so on. Another common generalization is that Java is a better choice for full-time programmers (due to strong object-oriented architecture and deep system libraries), while JavaScript is a good choice for the part-time or amateur programmer (due to forgiving syntax and lack of types). Also, it is important to note that the VRML specification does not require either scripting language to be supported. Therefore, it is important to verify that the scripting languages you choose to use in your content are supported by the browsers you intend to use.

EXAMPLE

The following example illustrates use of the **Script** node. This world defines a toggle button prototype, **Button**, and a simple combination lock that composes three **Button** nodes together with a **Script** node that verifies the combination. Note that the first **Script** node is defined within the prototype **Button**. This example is illustrated in both Java and JavaScript:

```
#VRML V2.0 utf8
PROTO Button [
    exposedField SFNode geom NULL
    eventOut SFInt32 state_changed ]
{
  Group { children [
    DEF TOS TouchSensor {}
    DEF Toggle Script {
      eventIn SFTime touch
      eventOut SFInt32 which_changed IS state_changed
```

```
        url [ "javascript:
          function initialize() {
            // Initialize to 0th child at load time
            which_changed = 0;
          }
          function touch(value, time) {
            // Toggle the button value
            which_changed = !which_changed;
          }"
          # Or Java:
          "ToggleScript.class" ]
      }
    DEF SW Switch {
      whichChoice 0
      choice [
        Shape {      # child 0 - "off"
          geometry IS geom
          appearance DEF A2 Appearance {
            material Material { diffuseColor .3 0 0 }
          }
        }
        Shape {      # choice 1 - "on"
          geometry IS geom
          appearance DEF A1 Appearance {
            material Material { diffuseColor 1 0 0 }
          }
        }
      ]
    }
  ]}
  ROUTE TOS.touchTime TO Toggle.touch
  ROUTE Toggle.which_changed TO SW.set_whichChoice
} # end of Toggle prototype

# Now, create 3 Buttons and wire together with a Script
Transform {
  translation -3 0 0
  children DEF B1 Button { geom Box {} }
}
DEF B2 Button { geom Sphere {} }
Transform {
  translation 3 0 0
  children DEF B3 Button { geom Cone {} }
}
DEF ThreeButtons Script {
  field SFInt32 b1 0
  field SFInt32 b2 0
  field SFInt32 b3 0
  eventIn SFInt32 set_b1
```

```
      eventIn SFInt32 set_b2
      eventIn SFInt32 set_b3
      eventOut SFTime startTime
      url [ "javascript:
        function set_b1(value, time) {
          b1 = value;
          if ((b1 == 1) && (b2 == 0) && (b3 == 1)) startTime = time;
        }
        function set_b2(value, time) {
          b2 = value;
          if ((b1 == 1) && (b2 == 0) && (b3 == 1)) startTime = time;
        }
        function set_b3(value, time) {
          b3 = value;
          if ((b1 == 1) && (b2 == 0) && (b3 == 1)) startTime = time;
        }"
        # Or Java:
        "ScriptLogic.class" ]
}
DEF T Transform { children [              # Explosion effect
  Shape { geometry Sphere {  radius 0.1 } }  # Hidden inside
  DEF SI PositionInterpolator {
    key [ 0.0 1.0 ]
    keyValue [ 0.01 0.01 0.01, 300.0 300.0 300.0 ]
  }
  DEF TS TimeSensor { }
  NavigationInfo { type "EXAMINE" }
] }
ROUTE B1.state_changed TO ThreeButtons.set_b1
ROUTE B2.state_changed TO ThreeButtons.set_b2
ROUTE B3.state_changed TO ThreeButtons.set_b3
ROUTE ThreeButtons.startTime TO TS.startTime
ROUTE TS.fraction_changed TO SI.set_fraction
ROUTE SI.value_changed TO T.set_translation


  ToggleScript.java:
/*
 * ToggleScript.java
 * Toggles an integer between 0 to 1 every time a time event is received
 */
import vrml.*;
import vrml.field.*;
import vrml.node.*;
public class ToggleScript extends Script {
  SFInt32 which_changed;
  public void initialize() {
    which_changed  = (SFInt32) getEventOut("which_changed");
```

```java
      which_changed.setValue(0);
  }
  public void processEvent( Event e ) {
    String name = e.getName();
    if ( name.equals( "touch" )) {
      which_changed.setValue(1 - which_changed.getValue());
    }
  }
}


   ScriptLogic.java:
/*
 * ScriptLogic.java
 * Receives set_b1/2/3 events, when correct combination is received outputs
 *   a startTime event.
 */
import vrml.*;
import vrml.field.*;
import vrml.node.*;
public class ScriptLogic extends Script {
  int b1;
  int b2;
  int b3;
  SFTime startTime;
  public void initialize() {
    startTime  = (SFTime) getEventOut("startTime");
  }
  public void processEvent( Event e ) {
    String name = e.getName();
    if ( name.equals( "set_b1" )) {
      b1 = ((ConstSFInt32)e.getValue()).getValue();
    } else if ( name.equals( "set_b2" )) {
      b2 = ((ConstSFInt32)e.getValue()).getValue();
    } else if ( name.equals( "set_b3" )) {
      b3 = ((ConstSFInt32)e.getValue()).getValue();
    }
    if ((b1 == 1) && (b2 == 0) && (b3 == 1))
      startTime.setValue(e.getTimeStamp());
  }
}
```

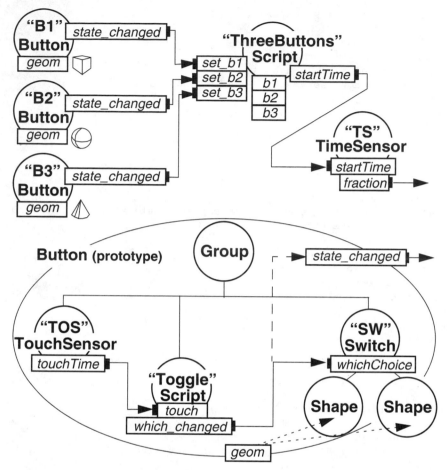

FIGURE 3-43 *Script Node Example*

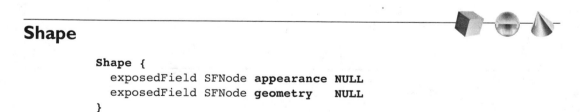

Shape

```
Shape {
  exposedField SFNode appearance NULL
  exposedField SFNode geometry  NULL
}
```

The **Shape** node has two fields—*appearance* and *geometry*—that are used to create rendered objects in the world. The *appearance* field contains an **Appearance** node that specifies the visual attributes (e.g., material and texture) to be applied to the geometry. The *geometry* field specifies a geometry node. The specified geometry node is rendered with the specified **Appearance** nodes applied. (See Section 2.9.5, Lighting Model, for details of the VRML lighting model and the interaction between **Appearance** and geometry nodes.) If the *geometry* field is NULL, the object is not drawn.

EXAMPLE

The following simple example illustrates the **Shape** node:

```
#VRML V2.0 utf8
Group { children [
  Transform {
    translation -3 0 0
    children Shape {
      geometry Box {}
      appearance Appearance {
        material Material { diffuseColor 1 0 0 }
      }
    }
  }
  Transform {
    children Shape {
      geometry Sphere {}
      appearance Appearance {
        material Material { diffuseColor 0 1 0 }
      }
    }
  }
  Transform {
    translation 3 0 0
    children Shape {
      geometry Cone {}
      appearance Appearance {
        material Material { diffuseColor 0 0 1 }
      }
    }
  }
]}
```

Sound

```
Sound {
  exposedField SFVec3f   direction   0 0 1
  exposedField SFFloat   intensity   1
```

```
    exposedField SFVec3f   location      0 0 0
    exposedField SFFloat   maxBack       10
    exposedField SFFloat   maxFront      10
    exposedField SFFloat   minBack       1
    exposedField SFFloat   minFront      1
    exposedField SFFloat   priority      0
    exposedField SFNode    source        NULL
    field        SFBool    spatialize    TRUE
}
```

The **Sound** node describes the positioning and spatial presentation of a sound in a VRML scene. The sound may be located at a point and emit sound in a spherical or ellipsoid pattern, in the local coordinate system. The ellipsoid is pointed in a particular direction and may be shaped to provide more or less directional focus from the location of the sound. The **Sound** node may also be used to describe an ambient sound that tapers off at a specified distance from the **Sound** node.

The **Sound** node also enables ambient background sound to be created by setting *maxFront* and *maxBack* to the radius of the area for the ambient noise. If ambient noise is required for the whole scene, then these values should be set to at least cover the distance from the location to the farthest point in the scene from that point (including effects of **Transforms**).

TIP

> To create an ambient background sound track, set the *maxFront* and *maxBack* fields as described (to the desired radius of influence) and set the **AudioClip** node's *loop* field to TRUE. If *stopTime* is less than or equal to *startTime*, the audio will play when the world is loaded. Also, avoid overlapping ambient **Sounds,** since browsers will have a hard limit (e.g., 3) on how many audio tracks can be played simultaneously.

The *source* field specifies the sound source for the **Sound** node. If there is no source specified, the **Sound** will emit no audio. The *source* field shall specify either an **AudioClip** or a **MovieTexture** node. Furthermore, the **MovieTexture** node must refer to a movie format that supports sound (e.g., MPEG1-Systems "Motion Pictures Experts Group," International Organization of Standards, ISO/IEC IS 11172-1:1993, `http://www.iso.ch/isob/switch-engine-cate.pl?searchtype=refnumber&KEYWORDS=11172`).

The *intensity* field adjusts the volume of each sound source. The *intensity* is an SFFloat that ranges from 0.0 to 1.0. An *intensity* of 0 is silence and an *intensity* of 1 is the full volume of the sound in the sample or the full volume of the MIDI clip.

The *priority* field gives the author some control over which sounds the browser will choose to play when there are more sounds active than sound channels available.

The *priority* varies between 0.0 and 1.0, with 1.0 being the highest priority. For most applications *priority* 0.0 should be used for a normal sound and 1.0 should be used only for special event or cue sounds (usually of short duration) that the author wants the user to hear even if they are farther away and perhaps of lower intensity than some other ongoing sounds. Browsers should make as many sound channels available to the scene as is efficiently possible.

If the browser does not have enough sound channels to play all of the currently active sounds, it is recommended that the browser sort the active sounds into an ordered list using the following sort keys:

1. Decreasing *priority*

2. For sounds with *priority* >0.5, increasing (*now − startTime*)

3. Decreasing *intensity* at viewer location (*intensity*/(distance^2))

where *now* represents the current time, and *startTime* is the *startTime* field of the audio source node specified in the *source* field.

It is important that sort key #2 be used for the high-priority (event and cue) sounds so that new cues will be heard even when the channels are "full" of currently active high-priority sounds. Sort key #2 should not be used for normal-priority sounds, so selection among them will be based on sort key #3: intensity and distance from the viewer.

The browser should play as many sounds from the beginning of this sorted list as it has available channels. On most systems the number of concurrent sound channels is distinct from the number of concurrent MIDI streams. On these systems the browser may maintain separate, ordered lists for sampled sounds and MIDI streams.

A sound's *location* in the scene graph determines its spatial location (the sound's location is transformed by the current transformation) and whether or not it can be heard. A sound can only be heard while it is part of the traversed scene. **Sound** nodes that are descended from **LOD, Switch,** or any grouping or prototype node that disables traversal (i.e., drawing) of its children will not be audible unless they are traversed. If a sound is silenced for a time under a **Switch** or **LOD** node, and it later becomes part of the traversal again, the sound picks up where it would have been had it been playing continuously.

Around the location of the emitter, *minFront* and *minBack* determine the extent of the full-intensity region in front of and behind the sound. If the location of the sound is taken as a focus of an ellipsoid, the *minBack* and *minFront* values, in combination with the *direction* vector, determine the two foci of an ellipsoid bounding the ambient region of the sound. Similarly, *maxFront* and *maxBack* determine the limits of audibility in front of and behind the sound; they describe a second, outer

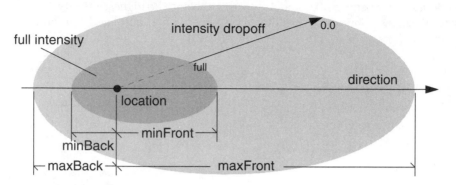

FIGURE 3-44 *The Sound* Node

ellipsoid. If *minFront* equals *minBack* and *maxFront* equals *maxBack,* the sound is omnidirectional, the direction vector is ignored, and the minimum and maximum ellipsoids become spheres centered around the **Sound** node. The fields *minFront, maxFront, minBack,* and *maxBack* are scaled by the parent transformations—these values must be ≥0.0.

The inner ellipsoid defines a space of full intensity for the sound. Within that space the sound will play at the intensity specified in the **Sound** node. The outer ellipsoid determines the maximum extent of the sound. Outside that space, the sound cannot be heard at all. In between the two ellipsoids, the intensity drops off proportionally with the inverse square of the distance. With this model, a **Sound** will usually have smooth changes in intensity over the entire extent in which it can be heard. However, if at any point the maximum is the same as or inside the minimum, the sound is cut off immediately at the edge of the minimum ellipsoid.

The ideal implementation of the sound attenuation between the inner and outer ellipsoids is an inverse power drop-off. A reasonable approximation to this ideal model is a linear drop-off in decibel value. Since an inverse power drop-off never actually reaches zero, it is necessary to select an appropriate cutoff value for the outer ellipsoid so that the outer ellipsoid contains the space in which the sound is truly audible and excludes space where it would be negligible. Keeping the outer ellipsoid as small as possible will help limit resources used by nearly inaudible sounds. Experimentation suggests that a 20-dB drop-off from the maximum intensity is a reasonable cutoff value that makes the bounding volume (the outer ellipsoid) contain the truly audible range of the sound. Since actual physical sound drop-off in an anechoic environment follows the inverse square law, using this algorithm it is possible to mimic real-world sound attenuation by making the maximum ellipsoid ten times larger than the minimum ellipsoid. This will yield an inverse square drop-off between them.

Browsers should support spatial localization of sound as much as their underlying sound libraries will allow. The *spatialize* field is used to indicate to browsers that they should try to locate this sound. If the *spatialize* field is TRUE, the sound should be treated as a monaural sound coming from a single point. A simple spatialization mechanism just places the sound properly in the pan of the stereo (or multichannel) sound output. Sounds are faded out over distance as described. Browsers may use more elaborate sound spatialization algorithms if they wish.

Authors can create ambient sounds by setting the *spatialize* field to FALSE. In that case, stereo and multichannel sounds should be played using their normal separate channels. The distance to the sound and the minimum and maximum ellipsoids (discussed earlier) should affect the intensity in the normal way. Authors can create ambient sound over the entire scene by setting *minFront* and *minBack* to the maximum extents of the scene.

DESIGN NOTE

The basic design for the **Sound** node came from a proposal from the RSX (Realistic Sound Experience) group at Intel. Their original proposal can be found at: `http://www.intel.com/ial/rsx/links/vrmlnode.htm`. It contains in-depth explanations of the sound model and justifications for their design.

TIP

For better performance, specify *minBack, minFront, maxBack,* and *maxFront* values that restrict the **Sound** to the smallest space possible. This will limit the effects of the **Sound** node only to the regions where it is needed, and prepare the file for future compatibility and reuse (e.g., if you **Inline** this file from another file, it will not hurt the performance). A good rule to live by is: "Limit the effects of all **Sound** nodes in a file to the bounding box that encloses all the **Shapes** in the file." Also, use the following high-performance settings whenever possible:

1. Set *spatialize* to FALSE if the direction of the sound source is not important.

2. Set *minBack = minFront* and *maxBack = maxFront* to produce directionless sounds that fade with distance from the source.

3. Set *minBack = minFront = maxBack = maxFront* to produce directionless sounds that emit at constant volume regardless of the distance to the source. This is a good choice for sound effects and ambient sounds.

These tips are especially important for looping **Sounds** (since they are running continuously!).

EXAMPLE

The following example illustrates three typical applications of the **Sound** node. The first **Sound** is an ambient background track that loops continuously. The min/max fields specify a sphere that encloses the entire world and plays the audio at a constant intensity regardless of the location or orientation of the user. The second **Sound** node is an example of a directionless sound effect that is triggered by a user event. In this case, the user clicks on the **TouchSensor** to play one cycle of the audio track, and the user's orientation has no effect on the perceived volume of the sound (*minFront = maxFront* and *minBack = maxBack*). The third **Sound** node is an example of a continuously looping directional sound (i.e., the user's orientation affects perceived volume).

```
#VRML V2.0 utf8
Group { children [
  DEF S1 Sound {          # Ambient background music
    maxBack 20            # Surround floor area
    minBack 20            # Constant sound within the sphere
    maxFront 20
    minFront 20
    spatialize FALSE      # No spatialization for ambient sound
    intensity 0.2
    source AudioClip {
      description "Ambient background music is playing..."
      url "doodoo.aiff"
      loop TRUE
    }
  }
  Transform {             # Button (triggers the sound effect)
    translation -5 0 0
    children [
      DEF TS TouchSensor {}
      Shape {
        geometry Box {}
        appearance Appearance {
          material Material { diffuseColor 0 0 1 }
        }
      }
      Transform {
        translation -2.2 1.1 0
        children Shape {
          geometry Text {
            string "Click here."
            fontStyle FontStyle {}
          }
        }
      }
    }
    DEF S2 Sound {        # Sound triggered by TouchSensor
      location 0 1 0
      priority 1.0
      minFront 1          # Omni-directional (sphere) sound
```

```
      minBack 1
      maxFront 10
      maxBack 10
      source DEF AC AudioClip {
        description "Sound effect is playing once."
        url "forgive.wav"
      }
    }
  ]
}
Transform {
  translation 8 0 0
  children [
    DEF S3 Sound {              # Spatialized speaker
      location 0 2 0
      priority 0.5
      minBack .5
      minFront 8
      maxBack 5
      maxFront 25
      source AudioClip {
        description "A looping spatialized sound track/"
        url "here.wav"
        loop TRUE
      }
    }
    Transform {                 # Speaker geometry
      translation 0 2 0
      rotation 1 0 0 -1.57
      children Shape {
        geometry Cone { bottomRadius 0.2 height .5 }
        appearance Appearance {
          material Material { diffuseColor 1 1 0 }
        }
      }
    }
    Transform {                 # Speaker post
      translation 0 1 0
      children Shape {
        geometry Cylinder { radius 0.05 height 2 }
        appearance Appearance {
          material Material { diffuseColor 1 0 0 }
        }
      }
    }
  ]
}
```

```
Transform {                   # Floor
  translation -20 0 -20
  children Shape {
    geometry ElevationGrid {
      height [ 0 0 0 0 0 0 0 0 0 0 0 0 0 0 0 0 0 0 0 0 0 0 0 0 0 ]
      xDimension 5
      zDimension 5
      xSpacing 10
      zSpacing 10
    }
    appearance Appearance { material Material {} }
  }
}
DirectionalLight { direction -.707 -.707 0 intensity 0.5 }
NavigationInfo { type "WALK" }
Viewpoint {
  position 0 1.6 15
  description "Initial view"
}
]}
ROUTE TS.touchTime TO AC.startTime
```

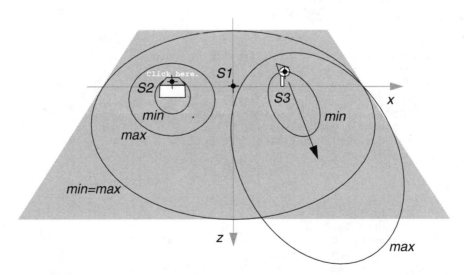

FIGURE 3-45 *Sound* Node Example

Sphere

```
Sphere {
   field SFFloat radius   1
}
```

The **Sphere** node specifies a sphere centered at (0,0,0) in the local coordinate system. The *radius* field specifies the radius of the sphere and must be ≥0.0.

When a texture is applied to a sphere, the texture covers the entire surface, wrapping counterclockwise from the back of the sphere. The texture has a seam at the back where the *yz* plane intersects the sphere. **TextureTransform** affects the texture coordinates of the **Sphere**.

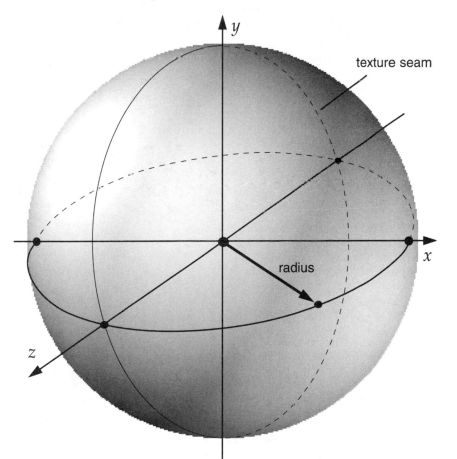

FIGURE 3-46 *Sphere Node*

The **Sphere** geometry is considered to be solid and thus requires outside faces only. When viewed from the inside, the results are undefined.

TIP

Sphere nodes belong in the geometry field of a **Shape** node; they may not be children of a **Transform** or **Group** node.

Browser implementors will make different compromises between rendering speed and the quality of spheres (and cones and cylinders and text). They may choose to display very coarse-looking spheres to make scenes render faster, which is good if you want your world to display smoothly on a wide variety of machines, but is bad if you want to guarantee that your world maintains a certain image quality. If maintaining quality is important, describe your shapes using the polygon-based primitives. To minimize file transmission time, you can generate the polygons using a **Script.** For example, this prototype will generate an approximation of a one-unit-radius **Sphere,** given the number of latitude and longitude samples:

```
#VRML V2.0 utf8
PROTO LatLongSphere [
  field SFInt32 numLat 4
  field SFInt32 numLong 4 ]
{
  # Empty IndexedFaceSet, filled in by Script based on PROTO fields6
  DEF IFS IndexedFaceSet {
    coord DEF C Coordinate { }
    texCoord DEF TC TextureCoordinate { }
    creaseAngle 3.14
  }
  DEF S Script {
    field SFInt32 numLat IS numLat
    field SFInt32 numLong IS numLong
    eventOut MFVec3f c_changed
    eventOut MFVec2f tc_changed
    eventOut MFInt32 ci_changed
    url "javascript:
      function initialize() {
        var r, angle, x, y, z;
        var i, j, polyIndex;
        // Compute coordinates, texture coordinates:
        for (i = 0; i < numLat; i++) {
          y = 2 * ( i / (numLat-1) ) - 1;
          r = Math.sqrt( 1 - y*y );
          for (j = 0; j < numLong; j++) {
            angle = 2 * Math.PI * j / numLong;
            x = -Math.sin(angle)*r;
            z = -Math.cos(angle)*r;
            c_changed[i*numLong+j] = new SFVec3f(x,y,z);
```

```
            tc_changed[i*numLong+j] =
                 new SFVec2f( j/numLong, i/(numLat-1) );
      }
    }
    // And compute indices:
    for (i = 0; i < numLat-1; i++) {
      for (j = 0; j < numLong; j++) {
        polyIndex = 5*(i*numLong+j);
        ci_changed[polyIndex+0] = i*numLong+j;
        ci_changed[polyIndex+1] = i*numLong+(j+1)%numLong;
        ci_changed[polyIndex+2] = (i+1)*numLong+(j+1)%numLong;
        ci_changed[polyIndex+3] = (i+1)*numLong+j;
        ci_changed[polyIndex+4] = -1;  // End-of-polygon
      }
    }
  }"
}
ROUTE S.c_changed TO C.set_point
ROUTE S.tc_changed TO TC.set_point
ROUTE S.ci_changed TO IFS.set_coordIndex
}
Shape {
  appearance Appearance { material Material { } }
  geometry LatLongSphere { numLat 16 numLong 16 }
}
```

TIP

To create ellipsoid shapes, enclose a **Sphere** in a **Transform** and modify the *scale* field of the **Transform**.

EXAMPLE

The following example illustrates a simple use of the **Sphere** node. Notice how the last two **Spheres**, "carrot" and "hat rim," use the *scale* field of a **Transform** to deform the sphere:

```
#VRML V2.0 utf8
Group { children [
  Transform {              # Base of snowman
    translation 0 1 0
    children Shape {
      geometry Sphere { radius 1 }
```

```
      appearance DEF A1 Appearance {
        material Material {
          diffuseColor 1 1 1
          emissiveColor .3 .3 .3
        }
      }
    }
  }
}
Transform {              # Middle of snowman
  translation 0 2.333 0
  children Shape {
    geometry Sphere { radius 0.66 }
    appearance USE A1
  }
}
Transform {              # Head of snowman
  translation 0 3.2 0
  children Shape {
    geometry Sphere { radius 0.4 }
    appearance USE A1
  }
}
Transform {              # Left eye stone
  translation .16 3.4 .3
  children Shape {
    geometry DEF S1 Sphere { radius 0.05 }
    appearance DEF A2 Appearance {
      material Material { diffuseColor 0 0 0 }
    }
  }
}
Transform {              # Right eye stone
  translation -.17 3.43 .3
  children Shape {
    geometry USE S1
    appearance Appearance {
      material Material { diffuseColor 0.2 0.2 0.2 }
    }
  }
}
Transform {              # Carrot nose
  translation 0 3.3 .5
  scale 0.5 0.5 2
  children Shape {
    geometry Sphere { radius 0.1 }
    appearance Appearance {
      material Material { diffuseColor 1.0 0.3 0.1 }
    }
  }
}
```

```
   Transform {              # Hat cap
     translation 0 3.5 0
     children Shape {
       geometry Sphere { radius .2 }
       appearance Appearance {
         material Material { diffuseColor 1.0 0.0 0.0 }
       }
     }
   }
   Transform {              # Hat rim
     translation 0 3.55 0
     scale 2 .01 2
     children Shape {
       geometry Sphere { radius .4 }
       appearance Appearance {
         material Material { diffuseColor 1.0 0.0 0.0 }
       }
     }
   }
   Background { skyColor 1 1 1 }
   NavigationInfo { type "EXAMINE" }
 ] }
```

FIGURE 3-47 *Sphere Node Example*

SphereSensor

```
SphereSensor {
  exposedField SFBool      autoOffset         TRUE
  exposedField SFBool      enabled            TRUE
  exposedField SFRotation  offset             0 1 0 0
  eventOut     SFBool      isActive
  eventOut     SFRotation  rotation_changed
  eventOut     SFVec3f     trackPoint_changed
}
```

The **SphereSensor** maps pointing device (e.g., mouse or wand) motion into spherical rotation about the center of its local space. **SphereSensor** uses the descendant geometry of its parent node to determine if a hit occurs. The feel of the rotation is as if you were rolling a ball.

The *enabled* exposedField enables and disables the **SphereSensor.** If TRUE, the sensor reacts appropriately to user events; if FALSE, the sensor does not track user input or send output events. If *enabled* receives a FALSE event and *isActive* is TRUE, the sensor becomes disabled and deactivated, and outputs an *isActive* FALSE event. If *enabled* receives a TRUE event, the sensor is enabled and ready for user activation.

The **SphereSensor** generates events if the pointing device is activated while over any descendant geometry nodes of its parent group and then moved while activated. Typically, the pointing device is a 2D device such as a mouse. The pointing device is considered to be moving within a plane at a fixed distance from the viewer and perpendicular to the line of sight (this establishes a set of 3D coordinates for the pointer). If a 3D pointer is in use, then the sensor generates events only when the pointer is within the user's field of view. In either case, the pointing device is considered to "pass over" geometry when that geometry is intersected by a line extending from the viewer and passing through the pointer's 3D coordinates. If multiple sensors' geometry intersect this line (hereafter called the *bearing*), only the nearest will be eligible to generate events.

On activation of the pointing device (e.g., mouse button down) over the sensor's geometry, an *isActive* TRUE event is sent. The vector defined by the initial point of intersection on the **SphereSensor**'s geometry and the local origin determine the radius of the sphere used to map subsequent pointing device motion while dragging. The virtual sphere defined by this radius and the local origin at the time of activation is used to interpret subsequent pointing device motion and is not affected by any changes to the sensor's coordinate system while the sensor is active. For each position of the bearing, a *rotation_changed* event is output that corresponds to a relative rotation from the original intersection, plus the *offset* value. The sign of the rotation is defined by the local coordinate system of the sensor.

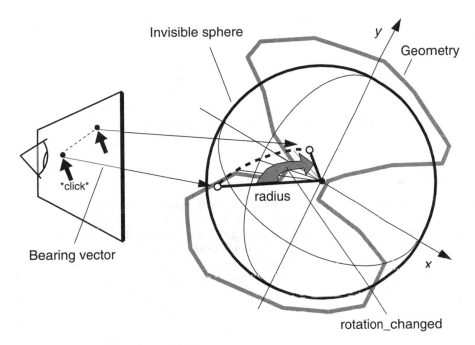

Invisible sphere

Geometry

click

Bearing vector

radius

rotation_changed

FIGURE 3-48 *SphereSensor Node*

TrackPoint_changed events reflect the unclamped drag position on the surface of this sphere. When the pointing device is deactivated and *autoOffset* is TRUE, *offset* is set to the last rotation value and an *offset_changed* event is generated. See Section 2.9.6, Sensor Nodes, for more details.

When the sensor generates an *isActive* TRUE event, it grabs all further motion events from the pointing device until it releases and generates an *isActive* FALSE event (other pointing device sensors cannot generate events during this time). Motion of the pointing device while *isActive* is TRUE is referred to as *drag*. If a 2D pointing device is in use, *isActive* events will typically reflect the state of the primary button associated with the device (i.e., *isActive* is TRUE when the primary button is pressed and FALSE when released). If a 3D pointing device (e.g., wand) is in use, *isActive* events will typically reflect whether the pointer is within or in contact with the sensor's geometry.

While the pointing device is activated, *trackPoint_changed* and *rotation_changed* events are output. *TrackPoint_changed* events represent the unclamped intersection points on the surface of the invisible sphere. If the pointing device is dragged off the sphere while activated, browsers may interpret this in several ways (e.g., clamp all values to the sphere, continue to rotate as the point is dragged away from the sphere, etc.). Each movement of the pointing device, while *isActive* is TRUE, generates *trackPoint_changed* and *rotation_changed* events. See Section 2.9.6, Sensor Nodes, for more details.

TIP

It is usually a bad idea to route a drag sensor to its own parent. Typically, the drag sensor will route to **Transform,** which does not affect the sensor. See the following examples.

EXAMPLE

The following example illustrates the **SphereSensor** node. The first **SphereSensor**, ss1, affects all of the children contained by the first **Transform** node, and is used to rotate both the **Sphere** and **Cone** about the **Sphere**'s center. The second **SphereSensor**, ss2, affects only the **Cone** and is used to rotate the **Cone** about its center. The third **SphereSensor**, ss3, acts as a user interface widget that rotates both itself (the **Box**) and the **Sphere/Cone** group. The fourth **SphereSensor**, ss4, acts as a user interface widget that rotates itself (the **Cylinder**) and the **Cone**:

```
#VRML V2.0 utf8
Group { children [
  Transform { children [
    DEF SS1 SphereSensor {}
    DEF T1 Transform { children [
      Shape {
        geometry Sphere {}
        appearance DEF A1 Appearance {
          material Material { diffuseColor 1 1 1 }
        }
      }
      Transform {
        translation 3.5 0 0
        children [
          DEF SS2 SphereSensor {}
          DEF T2 Transform {
            children Shape {
              geometry Cone { bottomRadius 0.5 height 1 }
              appearance USE A1
            }
          }
        }
    ]}]}]}
  Transform {
    translation 5 0 0
    children [
      DEF SS3 SphereSensor {}
      DEF T3 Transform {
        children Shape {
```

```
               geometry Box { size 0.5 0.25 0.5 }
               appearance USE A1
           }
       }
   ]}
   Transform {
     translation -5 0 0
     children [
       DEF SS4 SphereSensor {}
       DEF T4 Transform {
         children Shape {
             geometry Cylinder { radius .25 height .5 }
             appearance USE A1
         }
       }
   ]}
   Background { skyColor 1 1 1 }
   NavigationInfo { type "EXAMINE" }
]}
ROUTE SS1.rotation_changed TO T1.set_rotation
ROUTE SS1.rotation_changed TO T3.set_rotation
ROUTE SS1.offset TO T3.rotation
ROUTE SS1.offset TO SS3.offset
ROUTE SS2.rotation_changed TO T2.set_rotation
ROUTE SS2.rotation_changed TO T4.set_rotation
ROUTE SS2.offset TO T4.rotation
ROUTE SS2.offset TO SS4.offset
ROUTE SS3.rotation_changed TO T1.set_rotation
ROUTE SS3.rotation_changed TO T3.set_rotation
ROUTE SS3.offset_changed TO SS1.set_offset
ROUTE SS4.rotation_changed TO T2.set_rotation
ROUTE SS4.rotation_changed TO T4.set_rotation
ROUTE SS4.offset_changed TO SS2.set_offset
```

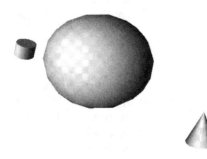

FIGURE 3-49 *SphereSensor Node Example*

SpotLight

```
SpotLight {
  exposedField SFFloat  ambientIntensity  0
  exposedField SFVec3f  attenuation       1 0 0
  exposedField SFFloat  beamWidth         1.570796
  exposedField SFColor  color             1 1 1
  exposedField SFFloat  cutOffAngle       0.785398
  exposedField SFVec3f  direction         0 0 -1
  exposedField SFFloat  intensity         1
  exposedField SFVec3f  location          0 0 0
  exposedField SFBool   on                TRUE
  exposedField SFFloat  radius            100
}
```

The **SpotLight** node defines a light source that emits light from a specific point along a specific direction vector and constrained within a solid angle. **Spotlights** may illuminate geometry nodes that respond to light sources and intersect the solid angle. **Spotlights** are specified in their local coordinate system and are affected by parent transformations.

See Section 2.9.4, Light Sources, for a detailed description of the *ambientIntensity, color,* and *intensity* fields. See Section 2.9.5, Lighting Model, for a detailed description of the VRML lighting equations.

The *location* field specifies a translation offset of the center point of the light source from the light's local coordinate system origin. This point is the apex of the solid angle that bounds light emission from the given light source. The *direction* field specifies the direction vector of the light's central axis defined in its own local coordinate system. The *on* field specifies whether the light source emits light. If TRUE, then the light source is emitting light and may illuminate geometry in the scene; if FALSE, it does not emit light and does not illuminate any geometry. The *radius* field specifies the radial extent of the solid angle and the maximum distance from a location that may be illuminated by the light source (the light source does not emit light outside this radius). The *radius* must be ≥0.0.

The *cutOffAngle* field specifies the outer bound of the solid angle. The light source does not emit light outside of this solid angle. The *beamWidth* field specifies an inner solid angle in which the light source emits light at uniform full intensity. The light source's emission intensity drops off from the inner solid angle (*beamWidth*) to the outer solid angle (*cutOffAngle*). The drop-off function from the inner angle to the outer angle is a cosine raised to a power function. The following equations specify the multiplier to be applied to the light source intensity based on angle (see Section 2.9.5, Lighting Models, for details):

angle = the angle between the **SpotLight**'s *direction* vector and the vector from the
    SpotLight center to the point to be illuminated

If: angle ≥ cutOffAngle,

    multiplier = 0 (no light outside cutOffAngle)

Else if: angle < beamWidth,

    multiplier = 1 (no angle attenuation)

Else:

    multiplier = 1 – (cos(beamWidth) – cos(angle))/
                (cos(beamWidth) – cos(cutOffAngle))
    (cosine fall-off)

If *beamWidth* > *cutOffAngle,* then *beamWidth* is assumed to be equal to *cutOffAngle* and the light source emits full intensity within the entire solid angle defined by *cutOffAngle.* Both *beamWidth* and *cutOffAngle* must be greater than 0.0 and less than or equal to π/2. See Figure 3-50 for an illustration of the **SpotLight**'s field semantics (note: this example uses the default attenuation).

TIP

Typically, *beamWidth* > *cutOffAngle* will produce faster rendering (and "harder" spotlight effects) than *beamWidth* < *cutOffAngle*. Also, note that some implementations ignore *beamWidth*. It is recommended that you test this feature on your intended browser before using it.

DESIGN NOTE

The default *beamWidth* (1.570796 radians) was chosen to be greater than the default *cutOffAngle* (0.785398 radians) for performance reasons. If *beamWidth* is less than the *cutOffAngle,* the lighting equations must perform extra calculations (i.e., cosine drop-off) and will slow down rendering. The default field values were chosen so that the default **SpotLights** render as fast as possible, and if the author sets *cutOffAngle* (and not *beamWidth*), the **SpotLight** continues to render quickly without *beamWidth* performance impacts.

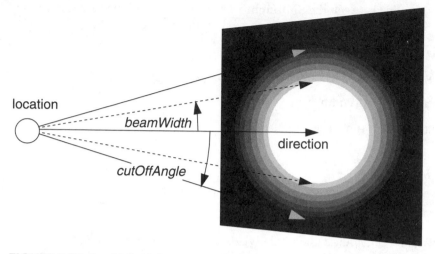

FIGURE 3-50 *SpotLight Node*

The light's illumination falls off with distance as specified by three attenuation coefficients. The attenuation factor is $1 / (attenuation[0] + attenuation[1] \times r + attenuation[2] \times r^2)$, where r is the distance of the light to the surface being illuminated. The default is no attenuation. An attenuation value of 0 0 0 is identical to 1 0 0. Attenuation values must be ≥0.0.

TIP

In order to produce soft penumbras, it will be necessary to generate a large number of vertices in the geometry (remember that lighting calculations are typically performed only at the vertices!). This can have the undesirable effect of slowing rendering and increasing download time. For faster rendering performance, in cases where the light source is not moving, consider using an **ImageTexture** with lighting effects "painted" on, rather than render the effect at each frame.

TIP

The *radius* field of **PointLight** and **SpotLight** restricts the illumination effects of these light sources. It is recommended that you minimize this field to the smallest possible value (i.e., small enough to enclose all of the **Shapes** that you intend to illuminate) in order to avoid significant impacts on rendering performance. A safe rule to live by is: "Never create a file in which the *radius* fields of the light sources exceed the bounding box enclosing all the **Shapes** in the file." This has the nice property that prevents light sources from bleeding outside of the original file. Keep in mind that, during rendering, each **Shape** must perform lighting calculations at each vertex for each light source that affects it. Thus, restricting each light source to the intended radius can improve performance and create files that will compose nicely.

TIP

See the **DirectionalLight** section in this chapter for general tips on light sources.

EXAMPLE

The following example illustrates the **SpotLight** node. This file contains three **SpotLights**. The first, **L1**, is directed at the **Sphere**; the second, **L2**, is directed at a corner of the **Box**; and the third, **L3**, is directed at the **Cone**. Notice the amount of vertices that the **ElevationGrid** required to produce a soft penumbra effect:

```
#VRML V2.0 utf8
Group { children [
  DEF L1 SpotLight {
    location 0.0 3.8 3
    direction 0.035 -0.84 -0.55
    beamWidth 0.017
    cutOffAngle 1.5708
  }
  DEF L2 SpotLight {
    location -3 3.4 2.6
    direction 0.06 -0.85 -0.51
    beamWidth 0.017
    cutOffAngle 1.5708
  }
  DEF L3 SpotLight {
    location 2.2 4 2
    direction 0.34 -0.91 -0.24
    beamWidth 0.017
    cutOffAngle 1.5708
  }
  Transform {
    translation -3 0.77 0
    rotation 0.301025 0.943212 -0.140478  0.93
    scale 0.85 0.85 0.85
    scaleOrientation -0.317855 0.939537 -0.127429  0.960173
    children Shape {
      appearance DEF A1 Appearance {
```

```
      material Material {
        ambientIntensity .5
        diffuseColor 0.85 0.85 0.85
        specularColor 1 1 1
        shininess 0.56
      }
    }
    geometry Box {}
  }
}
Transform {
  translation 0 0.7 0
  children Shape {
    appearance USE A1
    geometry Sphere {}
  }
}
Transform {
  translation 3 1.05 0
  rotation 0 0 1 0.6
  children Shape {
    appearance USE A1
    geometry Cone {}
  }
}
Transform {
  translation -2.71582 -1 -0.785248
  children Shape {
    appearance USE A1
    geometry ElevationGrid {
      height [ 0, 0, 0, 0, ..., 0 ]
      xDimension 20
      xSpacing 0.2
      zDimension 10
      zSpacing 0.1
    }
  }
}
Background { skyColor 1 1 1 }
NavigationInfo { headlight FALSE type "EXAMINE" }
]}
```

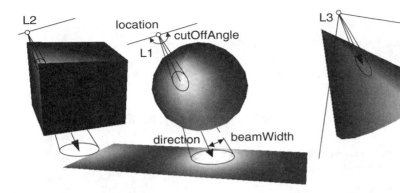

FIGURE 3-51 *SpotLight Node Example*

Switch

```
Switch {
  exposedField    MFNode   choice        []
  exposedField    SFInt32  whichChoice  -1
}
```

The **Switch** grouping node traverses zero or one of the nodes specified in the *choice* field. See Section 2.3.1, Grouping and Children Nodes, which describes children nodes, for details on the types of nodes that are legal values for *choice*.

The *whichChoice* field specifies the index of the child to traverse, where the first child has index 0. If *whichChoice* is >0 or greater than the number of nodes in the *choice* field, then nothing is chosen.

Note that all nodes under a **Switch** continue to receive and send events (i.e., routes) regardless of the value of *whichChoice*. For example, if an active **TimeSensor** is contained within an inactive choice of a **Switch**, the **TimeSensor** sends events regardless of the **Switch**'s state.

DESIGN NOTE

Note that the **Switch** node is a grouping node, so it can't be used in place of an **Appearance** or **Material** node to switch between different appearances or textures. Allowing a node to act like several different node types causes implementation difficulties, especially for object-oriented implementations that create a hierarchy of node classes. If **Switch** could appear anywhere in the scene, implementations would have to be prepared to treat it as a group *or* a geometry *or* a material *or* any other node class.

TIP

A **Switch** node can be used to hide or "comment-out" parts of the scene, which can be useful when you are creating a world and want to turn parts of it off quickly. Just replace any **Group** or **Transform** with

```
Switch { choice Group/Transform ... }
```

The default value for the *whichChoice* field is −1, so the **Group/Transform** will not be displayed.

If you need to switch between different textures or materials for a **Shape,** there are a couple of ways of doing it. The obvious way

```
# THIS EXAMPLE IS ILLEGAL!
Shape {
  appearance Appearance {
    material DEF ILLEGAL Switch {  # Switch is NOT a material!
      choice [
        # Materials are NOT legal children!
        DEF M1 Material { ... }
        DEF M2 Material { ... }
      ]
    }
  }
  geometry IndexedFaceSet ...
}
```

does not work, because **Switch** nodes are not materials, and **Material** nodes are not legal children nodes. Instead, you can switch between two different shapes that share parts that aren't changing with DEF/USE, like this:

```
Switch {
  choice [
    Shape {
      appearance Appearance {
        material DEF M1 Material { ... }
      }
      geometry DEF IFS IndexedFaceSet ...
    }
    Shape {
      appearance Appearance {
        material DEF M2 Material { ... }
      }
      geometry USE IFS  # Same geometry, different material
    }
  ]
}
```

Or, alternatively, you can write a **Script** that changes the **Material** node directly. For example, here is a prototype that encapsulates a **Script** that just toggles a **Material** between two different colors based on an SFBool eventIn:

```
PROTO ToggleMaterial [
  field SFColor color1 1 1 1  # White and
  field SFColor color2 0 0 0  # black by default
  eventIn SFBool which ]
{
  DEF M Material { }
  DEF S Script {
    field SFColor color1 IS color1
    field SFColor color2 IS color2
    eventIn SFBool which IS which
    eventOut SFColor color_changed
    url "javascript:
      function initialize() {
        color_changed = color1;
      }
      function which(value) {
        if (value) color_changed = color2;
        else color_changed = color1;
      }"
  }
  ROUTE S.color_changed TO M.set_diffuseColor
}
# Use like this:
Group {
  children [
    Shape {
      appearance Appearance {
        material DEF TM ToggleMaterial {
          color1 1 0 0  color2 0 1 0
        }
      }
      geometry Cube { }
    }
    DEF TS TouchSensor { }
  ]
  ROUTE TS.isOver TO TM.which
}
```

TIP

Bindable nodes (**Background, Fog,** and **NavigationInfo**) are *not* bound by setting their parent **Switch**'s *whichChoice* field and have no effect on whether a bindable node is active or not. For example, the following file excerpt has a **Switch** node that has activated the second choice (`whichChoice 1`). However, the first choice is the first encountered **Background** node in the file and is bound at load time (i.e., *whichChoice* has no effect on binding):

```
...
Switch {
  whichChoice 1       # sets second choice, B2, as active
  choice [
    DEF B1 Background { ... }  # choice 0 bound at load time
    DEF B2 Background { ... }  # choice 1 not bound at load time
    DEF B3 Background { ... }  # choice 2
    ...
  ]
}
...
```

EXAMPLE

The following example illustrates a simple use of the **Switch** node. A **TouchSensor** is routed to a **Script,** which cycles through the *whichChoice* field of the **Switch** node:

```
#VRML V2.0 utf8
Group { children [
  DEF SW Switch {
    whichChoice 0  # set by Script
    choice [
      Shape {                  # choice 0
        geometry Box {}
        appearance DEF A1 Appearance {
          material Material { diffuseColor 1 0 0 }
        }
      }
      Shape {                  # choice 1
        geometry Sphere {}
        appearance DEF A1 Appearance {
          material Material { diffuseColor 0 1 0 }
        }
      }
      Shape {                  # choice 2
        geometry Cone {}
```

```
          appearance DEF A1 Appearance {
            material Material { diffuseColor 0 0 1 }
          }
        }
      ]
    }
  DEF TS TouchSensor {}
  DEF SCR Script {              # Switches the choice
    eventIn SFTime touchTime
    eventOut SFInt32 whichChoice
    url "javascript:
      function initialize() {
        whichChoice = 0;
      }
      function touchTime( value, time) {
        if ( whichChoice == 2 ) whichChoice = 0;
        else ++whichChoice;
      }"
  }
  NavigationInfo { type "EXAMINE" }
]}
ROUTE TS.touchTime TO SCR.touchTime
ROUTE SCR.whichChoice TO SW.whichChoice
```

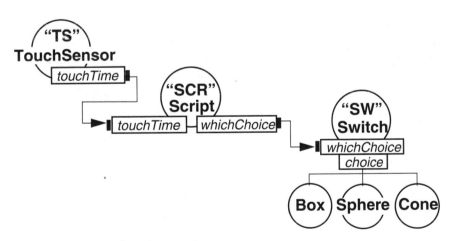

FIGURE 3-52 *Switch Node Example*

Text

```
Text {
    exposedField   MFString  string    []
    exposedField   SFNode    fontStyle NULL
    exposedField   MFFloat   length    []
    exposedField   SFFloat   maxExtent 0.0
}
```

The **Text** node specifies a two-sided, flat text string object positioned in the *xy* plane of the local coordinate system based on values defined in the *fontStyle* field (see the **FontStyle** node section in this chapter). **Text** nodes may contain multiple text strings specified using the UTF-8 encoding as specified by the ISO 10646-1: 1993 standard (`http://www.iso.ch/cate/d18741.html`). Due to the drastic changes in Korean Jamo language, the character set of the UTF-8 will be based on ISO 10646-1:1993 plus pDAM 1–5 (including the Korean changes). Text strings are stored in visual order.

The text strings are contained in the *string* field. The *fontStyle* field contains one **FontStyle** node that specifies the font size, font family and style, direction of the text strings, and any specific language rendering techniques that must be used for the text.

The *maxExtent* field limits and fits all of the text strings if the length of the maximum string is longer than the maximum extent, as measured in the local coordinate space. If the text string with the maximum length is shorter than the *maxExtent,* then there is no scaling. The maximum extent is measured horizontally for horizontal text (**FontStyle** node: *horizontal* = TRUE) and vertically for vertical text (**FontStyle** node: *horizontal* = FALSE). The *maxExtent* field must be ≥0.0.

The *length* field contains an MFFloat value that specifies the length of each text string in the local coordinate space. If the string is too short, it is stretched (either by scaling the text or by adding space between the characters). If the string is too long, it is compressed (either by scaling the text or by subtracting space between the characters). If a *length* value is missing (for example, if there are four strings but only three *length* values), the missing values are considered to be 0.

For both the *maxExtent* and *length* fields, specifying a value of 0 indicates that the string may be any length.

Textures are applied to text as follows. The texture origin is at the origin of the first string, as determined by the justification. The texture is scaled equally in both *s* and *t* dimensions, with the font height representing one unit. *S* increases to the right and *t* increases up.

Characters in ISO 10646 are encoded in multiple octets. Code space is divided into four units:

- Group octet
- Plane octet
- Row octet
- Cell octet

ISO 10646-1:1993 allows two basic forms for characters:

1. UCS-2 (Universal Coded Character Set-2), also known as the Basic Multi-lingual Plane (BMP). Characters are encoded in the lower two octets (row and cell). Predictions are that this will be the most commonly used form of 10646.

2. UCS-4 (Universal Coded Character Set-4). Characters are encoded in the full four octets. In addition, three transformation formats are accepted: UTF-7, UTF-8, and UTF-16. Each represents the nature of the transformation—7 bit, 8 bit, and 16 bit, respectively. UTF-7 and UTF-16 can be referenced in the Unicode Standard 2.0 book.

UTF 8 maintains transparency for all of the ASCII code values (0 . . . 127). It allows ASCII text (0x0..0x7F) to appear without any changes and encodes all characters from 0x80..0x7FFFFFFF into a series of six or fewer bytes.

If the most significant bit of the first character is 0, then the remaining seven bits are interpreted as an ASCII character. Otherwise, the number of leading one bits will indicate the number of bytes following. There is always a zero bit between the count bits and any data.

As depicted in Table 3-5, the first byte could be one of the following. The X indicates bits available to encode the character.

TABLE 3-5 *UTF-8 encoding*

Encoding	Number of bytes	Description
0XXXXXXX	One byte	0..0x7F (ASCII)
110XXXXX	Two bytes	Maximum character value is 0x7FF
1110XXXX	Three bytes	Maximum character value is 0xFFFF
11110XXX	Four bytes	Maximum character value is 0x1FFFFF
111110XX	Five bytes	Maximum character value is 0x3FFFFFF
1111110X	Six bytes	Maximum character value is 0x7FFFFFFF

All of the following bytes have this format: 10XXXXXX.

A two-byte example: The symbol for a registered trademark is ® or 174 in ISO/Latin-1 (8859/1). It is encoded as 0x00AE in UCS-2 of ISO 10646. In UTF-8, it has the following two-byte encoding: 0xC2, 0xAE.

DESIGN NOTE

Typically, browsers must consider three parameters when choosing which system font best matches the requested font in the VRML file: the UTF-8 character set contained in **Text**'s *string* field, and the *family* and *style* fields specified in **FontStyle.** Browsers shall adhere to the following order of priority when choosing the font: character set, then *family,* then *style.*

See Section 2.9.5, Lighting Model, for details on VRML lighting equations and how **Appearance, Material** and textures interact with lighting.

The **Text** node does not perform collision detection.

DESIGN NOTE

Significant performance opportunities exist for implementations that avoid generating polygons when rendering the **Text** node. One approach is to generate two-component (luminance plus alpha with a **Material** node for color) or four-component (full color plus alpha) texture maps, and apply the generated texture to a rectangle, instead of rendering the explicit polygons at each frame.

A second, potentially complementary, approach is to manage the visible complexity of the text adaptively as a function of distance from the user. A simple method is to generate multiple levels of detail for the text automatically, ranging from high to low resolution plus a very low resolution via "greeking" methods, and lastly to generate an empty level. An even better optimization might combine the texture map generation scheme with the adaptive complexity technique.

And finally, implementations will find it necessary to implement a caching scheme to avoid regenerating the polygons or texture maps at each frame.

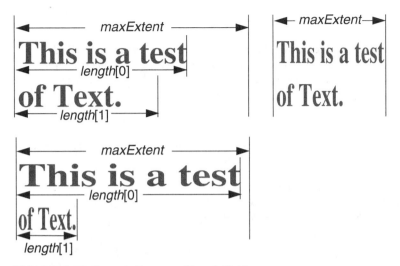

FIGURE 3-53 *Text maxExtent and length Fields*

TIP

> The **Text** node is *the* most dangerous performance sink in VRML since it is easy to create objects that generate large amounts of polygons. Typically, each character of the **Text** node generates a set of polygons that can quickly become the limiting factor in your scene's rendering time. Use this node *sparingly* and limit the strings to short, simple labels.
>
> If you need to present a lot of text to the user, put your VRML world inside a Web page that also contains HTML, or use **ImageTexture** nodes to display the text. As of this writing (early 1997), The World Wide Web Consortium is in the middle of standardizing the HTML tags used to do this. See their web site for details—http://www.w3.org/; information on HTML can be found at http://www.w3.org/pub/WWW/MarkUp/ Activity.
>
> Even though the VRML standard calls for internationalized text, VRML browsers will probably not be able to display every possible international character due to the lack of complete international fonts.

TIP

> Use **LOD** nodes as parents of **Text** to reduce rendering load when **Text** is not important.

TIP

Use the *emissiveColor* field of the **Material** node to set the **Text** color, and set all other material properties to zero. This produces more readable text (i.e., not subject to lighting effects) and thus significant performance gains in implementations that recognize the hint

```
Shape {
  appearance Appearance {
    material Material {      # Hint to browser to ignore lighting
      diffuseColor 0 0 0     # black
      specularColor 0 0 0    # black
      ambientIntensity 0.0   # black
      shininess 0.0          # none
      emissiveColor 1 1 1    # white or whatever
    }
  }
  geometry Text { string "testing" }
}
```

TIP

Combine a **Text** node with a screen-aligned **Billboard** node (i.e., *axisOfRotation* (0,0,0)) to create **Text** that is readable from any direction. This is especially effective for labels that follow the user's gaze:

```
Billboard {
  axisOfRotation 0 0 0
  children Shape {
    geometry Text { string "Smart Label" }
  }
}
```

EXAMPLE

The following example illustrates three typical cases of the **Text** node. The first **Text** node shows fully lit 3D text floating over a **Box**. The text is fixed in space and is readable when the user navigates to face the text. Notice that this text is illuminated by the light source and becomes unreadable when the light shines directly on it (fades into background). The second **Text** node is combined with a screen-aligned **Billboard** to face the user at all times. The **Material** node turns off lighting and results in improved text readability. The third **Text** node also combines with a **Billboard** and turns lighting off, but billboards around the *y*-axis to face the user:

```
#VRML V2.0 utf8
Group { children [
  Transform {
    translation -5 0 0
    children [
      Shape {
        geometry Box {}
        appearance DEF A1 Appearance {
          material Material { diffuseColor 1 1 1 }
        }
      }
      Transform {
        translation 0 2.5 0
        children Shape {
          geometry Text {
            string [ "This is a Box.", "Need I say more?" ]
            fontStyle DEF FS FontStyle {
              size 0.5
              family "SERIF"
              style "ITALIC"
              justify "MIDDLE"
            }
          }
          appearance USE A1
}}]]
  Billboard {
    axisOfRotation 0 0 0     # Screen-aligned
    children [
      Shape { geometry Sphere {} appearance USE A1 }
      Transform {
        translation 0 2.5 0
        children Shape {
          appearance DEF A2 Appearance {
            material Material {      # Hint to render fast
              diffuseColor 0 0 0
              ambientIntensity 0
              emissiveColor 0 0 0
            }
          }
          geometry Text {
            string [ "This is a", "Sphere." ]
            fontStyle USE FS
          }
}}]}
  Transform {
    translation 5 0 0
    children Billboard {
      axisOfRotation 0 1 0       # Billboard around Y-axis
      children [
```

```
        Shape { geometry Cone {} appearance USE A1 }
        Transform {
          translation 0 2.5 0
            children Shape {
              appearance USE A2
              geometry Text {
                string [ "This is a", "Cone." ]
                fontStyle USE FS
              }
  }}}]}
  Background { skyColor 1 1 1 }
 NavigationInfo { type "EXAMINE" }

]}
```

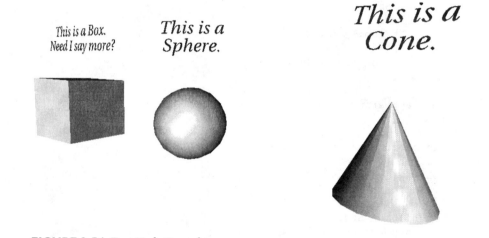

FIGURE 3-54 *Text Node Example*

TextureCoordinate

```
TextureCoordinate {
  exposedField MFVec2f point   []
}
```

The **TextureCoordinate** node specifies a set of 2D texture coordinates used by vertex-based geometry nodes (e.g., **IndexedFaceSet** and **ElevationGrid**) to map from textures to the vertices. Textures are 2D color functions that given an *s* and *t* pair return a color value. Texture map parameter values range from 0.0 to 1.0 in *s* and *t*. However, **TextureCoordinate** values, specified by the *point* field, can range from −*infinity* to +*infinity*. Texture coordinates identify a location (and thus a color value) in the texture map. The horizontal coordinate, *s,* is specified first, followed by the vertical coordinate, *t.*

If the texture map is repeated in a given direction (*s* or *t*), then a texture coordinate *c* is mapped into a texture map that has N pixels in the given direction as follows:

```
Location = (C - floor(C)) × N
```

If the texture is not repeated

```
Location = (C > 1.0 ? 1.0 : (C < 0.0 ? 0.0 : C)) × N
```

See texture nodes (**ImageTexture, MovieTexture, PixelTexture**) for details on repeating textures.

TIP

> See Figure 3-55 for an illustration of how **TextureCoordinate** values are used to map points in a texture map image into points in 3D space (e.g., on a polygon). Notice that the texture map image repeats infinitely in both the *s* and *t* directions, and thus **TextureCoordinate** values can range from −infinity to +infinity.

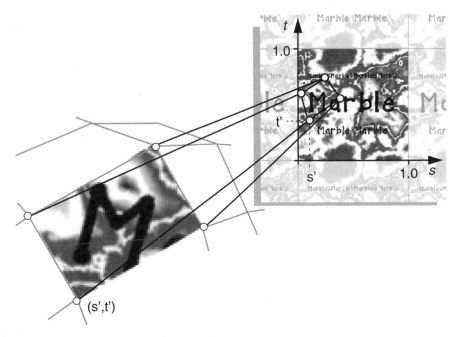

FIGURE 3-55 *TextureCoordinate Node*

TIP

See Figure 3-27 for a conceptual illustration of how texture coordinates map into the texture map space.

TIP

TextureCoordinate nodes are specified in the *texCoord* field of **IndexedFaceSet** or **ElevationGrid** nodes.

Animating texture coordinates can produce interesting effects. However, there is no equivalent of the **CoordinateInterpolator** node for texture coordinates, so you must write a **Script** to perform the animation interpolation.

EXAMPLE

The following example illustrates three cases of the **TextureCoordinate** node. The first **Texture-Coordinate** node repeats the texture map in a reversed *x* direction across the rectangle. It illustrates what happens when **TextureCoordinate** values exceed the 0.0 to 1.0 boundaries of the texture map. The second **TextureCoordinate** is the simplest and most common. It applies the texture map to a rectangle with no distortion or stretching. In this case, it is important for the aspect ratio of the rectangle to match the aspect ratio of the texture map.

```
#VRML V2.0 utf8
Group { children [
  Transform {
    translation -2.5 0 0.5
    rotation 0 1 0 0.5
    children Shape {
      appearance DEF A1 Appearance {
        texture ImageTexture { url "marble2.gif" }
        material Material { diffuseColor 1 1 1 }
      }
      geometry IndexedFaceSet {
        coord DEF C Coordinate {
          point [ -1 -1 0, 1 -1 0, 1 1 0, -1 1 0 ]
        }
        coordIndex [ 0 1 2 3 ]
        texCoord TextureCoordinate { point [ 3 0, 0 0, 0 3, 3 3 ] }
      }
    }
  }
  Shape {
    appearance USE A1
    geometry IndexedFaceSet {
      coord USE C
```

```
          coordIndex [ 0 1 2 3 ]
          texCoord TextureCoordinate {
            point [ 0 0, 1 0, 1 1, 0 1 ]
          }
        }
      }
    }
    Transform {
      translation 2.5 0 0.5
      rotation 0 1 0 -0.5
      children Shape {
        appearance USE A1
        geometry IndexedFaceSet {
          coord USE C
          coordIndex [ 0 1 2 3 ]
          texCoord TextureCoordinate {
            point [ .3 .3, .6 .3, .6 .6, .3 .6 ]
          }
        }
      }
    }
    Background { skyColor 1 1 1 }
    NavigationInfo { type "EXAMINE" }
]}
```

FIGURE 3-56 *TextureCoordinate* Node Example

TextureTransform

```
TextureTransform {
  exposedField SFVec2f  center       0 0
  exposedField SFFloat  rotation     0
  exposedField SFVec2f  scale        1 1
  exposedField SFVec2f  translation  0 0
}
```

The **TextureTransform** node defines a 2D transformation that is applied to texture coordinates (see **TextureCoordinate**). This node affects the way textures are applied to the surface of geometry. The transformation consists of (in order) a translation, a rotation about a center point, and a nonuniform scale about a center point. This allows for changes to the size, orientation, and position of textures on shapes. Note that these changes appear reversed when viewed on the surface of geometry. For example, a *scale* value of 2 2 will scale the texture coordinates and have the net effect of shrinking the texture size by a factor of two (texture coordinates are twice as large and thus cause the texture to repeat). A *translation* of 0.5 0.0 translates the texture coordinates +.5 units along the s-axis and has the net effect of translating the texture −0.5 along the s-axis on the geometry's surface. A *rotation* of $\pi/2$ of the texture coordinates results in a $-\pi/2$ rotation of the texture on the geometry.

The *center* field specifies a translation offset in texture coordinate space about which the *rotation* and *scale* fields are applied. The *scale* field specifies a scaling factor in s and t of the texture coordinates about the center point; *scale* values may be in the range −infinity to +infinity. The *rotation* field specifies a rotation in radians of the texture coordinates about the center point after the scale has taken place. The *translation* field specifies a translation of the texture coordinates.

Given a 2D texture coordinate *Tc* and a **TextureTransform** node, *Tc* is transformed into coordinate *Tc'* by a series of intermediate transformations. In matrix-transformation notation, where *C* (center), *T* (translation), *R* (rotation), and *S* (scale) are the equivalent transformation matrices

$$Tc' = -C \times S \times R \times C \times T \times Tc$$

where *Tc* is a column vector

Note that this order is opposite to the **Transform** node's matrix order. This reversal is because the transformation is applied to the texture coordinates, not the texture. This, in effect, transforms the texture's coordinate system instead of the texture.

TIP

TextureTransform should have been named **TextureCoordinateTransform**, since it does not transform texture maps, but transforms texture coordinates. This is a subtle yet critical distinction that must be understood before using this node. In short, all operations have the inverse effect on the resulting texture.

Texture coordinates are very much like vertex coordinates. They are specified in a local coordinate system, can be transformed (using a **TextureTransform** node), and the transformed coordinates specify a particular location in some space. One difference is that vertex coordinates are transformed into "world space"—the xyz space in which the virtual world is constructed. Texture coordinates are transformed into "texture image space"—the 0 to 1st space of a texture image. However, it is difficult to think in terms of the texture coordinates being transformed, because the texture image is transformed (warped) to be displayed on the screen. To think in terms of the texture image being transformed first by the **TextureTransform** and then by the given **TextureCoordinates,** everything must be reversed, resulting in the nonintuitive behavior that specifying a scale of two for a **TextureTransform** results in a half-size texture image.

DESIGN NOTE

Animating a **TextureTransform** can produce interesting effects such as flowing water or billowing curtains. However, animating **TextureTransforms** is not a common enough operation to justify the inclusion of special 2D interpolator nodes, so you must write a **Script** node to interpolate the SFVec2f values of a **TextureTransform**'s *translation, scale,* or *center* fields.

EXAMPLE

The following example illustrates the **TextureTransform** node. All five rectangles share an identical geometry, material, and texture map while varying the values of the **TextureTransform**. The first rectangle illustrates the rectangle with no **TextureTransform** applied. Notice how the **TextureCoordinate** node repeats the texture. The second rectangle sets the *scale* field of the **TextureTransform**. Notice that *scale* values greater than 1.0 reduce the resulting texture on the rectangle because **TextureTransform** transforms the texture coordinates, not the texture map (and conversely, *scale* values <1.0 will enlarge the resulting texture). The third rectangle sets the *translation* field of **TextureTransform** and has the net effect of translating the texture to the left and down (rather than to the right and up, as might be expected). The last rectangle shows the combined effect of the *scale, rotation,* and *translation* fields:

```
#VRML V2.0 utf8
Group { children [
  Transform {
    translation -5 0 0
    children Shape {
      appearance Appearance {
        texture DEF IT ImageTexture { url "marble2.gif" }
        material DEF M Material { diffuseColor 1 1 1 }
      }
      geometry DEF IFS IndexedFaceSet {
        coord Coordinate { point [ -1 -1 0, 1 -1 0, 1 1 0, -1 1 0 ] }
        coordIndex [ 0 1 2 3 ]
        texCoord TextureCoordinate { point [ 0 0, 3 0, 3 3, 0 3 ] }
      }
    }
  }
}
```

```
  Transform {
    translation -2.5 0 0
    children Shape {
      geometry USE IFS
      appearance Appearance {
        material USE M
        texture USE IT
        textureTransform TextureTransform {
          scale 2 2
        }
}}}
  Transform {
    translation 0 0 0
    children Shape {
      geometry USE IFS
      appearance Appearance {
        material USE M
        texture USE IT
        textureTransform TextureTransform {
          translation .5 .5
        }
}}}
  Transform {
    translation 2.5 0 0
    children Shape {
      geometry USE IFS
      appearance Appearance {
        material USE M
        texture USE IT
        textureTransform TextureTransform {
          rotation .785
        }
}}}
  Transform {
    translation 5 0 0
    children Shape {
      geometry USE IFS
      appearance Appearance {
        material USE M
        texture USE IT
        textureTransform TextureTransform {
          translation .5 .5
          rotation .7
          scale 0.25 0.25
        }
}}}
  Background { skyColor 1 1 1 }
]}
```

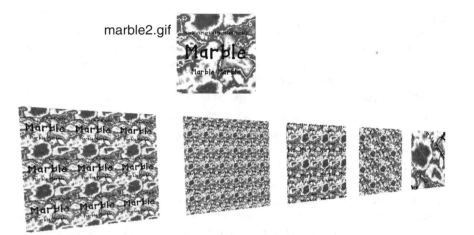

marble2.gif

FIGURE 3-57 *TextureTransform Node Example*

TimeSensor

```
TimeSensor {
    exposedField SFTime    cycleInterval 1
    exposedField SFBool    enabled       TRUE
    exposedField SFBool    loop          FALSE
    exposedField SFTime    startTime     0
    exposedField SFTime    stopTime      0
    eventOut     SFTime    cycleTime
    eventOut     SFFloat   fraction_changed
    eventOut     SFBool    isActive
    eventOut     SFTime    time
}
```

TimeSensors generate events as time passes. They can be used to drive continuous simulations and animations, periodic activities (e.g., one per minute), and single occurrence events such as an alarm clock. **TimeSensor** discrete eventOuts include *isActive,* which becomes TRUE when the **TimeSensor** begins running and FALSE when it stops running, and *cycleTime,* a time event at *startTime* and at the beginning of each new cycle (useful for synchronization with other time-based objects). The remaining outputs generate continuous events and consist of *fraction_changed,* which is an SFFloat in the closed interval [0,1] representing the completed fraction of the current cycle, and *time,* which is an SFTime event specifying the absolute time for a given simulation tick.

DESIGN NOTE

More time was spent refining the design of the **TimeSensor** node than any other node in the VRML 2.0 specification. That's not unreasonable; **TimeSensors** are important. With the exception of **Sounds** and **MovieTextures,** all animation in VRML worlds is driven by **TimeSensors,** and **TimeSensors** implement VRML's model of time.

It might have been simpler to define two types of **TimeSensors:** one that generated a (conceptually) continuous stream of events and one that generated a series of discrete events. Much of the work of defining the behavior of the **TimeSensor** was specifying exactly when discrete (*isActive, cycleTime*) and continuous (*fraction_changed, time*) eventOuts are generated, relative to the events that come in and relative to each other. **TimeSensor** generates both discrete and continuous events because synchronizing discrete events (such as starting an audio clip) with continuous events (such as animating the position of an object) is very important. Even if two separate nodes had been defined it would still be necessary to define precisely how they interact, which would be as difficult as defining the behavior of the combined **TimeSensor.**

If the *enabled* exposedField is TRUE, the **TimeSensor** is enabled and may be running. If a *set_enabled* FALSE event is received while the **TimeSensor** is running, then the sensor should evaluate and send all relevant outputs, send a FALSE value for *isActive,* and disable itself. However, events in the exposedFields of the **Time-Sensor** (such as *set_startTime*) are processed and their corresponding eventOuts (*startTime_changed*) are sent regardless of the state of *enabled.* The remaining discussion assumes *enabled* is TRUE.

The *loop, startTime,* and *stopTime* exposedFields; the *isActive* eventOut; and their effects on the **TimeSensor** node are discussed in detail in Section 2.9.7, Time-dependent Nodes. The "cycle" of a **TimeSensor** lasts for *cycleInterval* seconds. The value of *cycleInterval* must be greater than 0 (a value ≥0 produces undefined results). Because **TimeSensor** is more complex than the abstract Time Dependent node and generates continuous eventOuts, some of the information in Section 2.9.7, Time-dependent Nodes, is repeated here.

A *cycleTime* eventOut can be used for synchronization purposes (e.g., sound with animation). The value of a *cycleTime* eventOut will be equal to the time at the beginning of the current cycle. A *cycleTime* eventOut is generated at the beginning of every cycle, including the cycle starting at *startTime.* The first *cycleTime* eventOut for a **TimeSensor** node can be used as an alarm (single pulse at a specified time).

TIP

The easiest way to set up a **TimeSensor** as an "alarm clock" that produces an event at a specific time in the future is to specify that time as the *startTime,* specify *loop* FALSE, and ROUTE from the **TimeSensor**'s *cycleTime* eventOut. Theoretically, it doesn't matter what value you give for *cycleInterval,* since you're only using the *cycleTime* event generated at *startTime.* However, it is a good idea to use an arbitrarily small value as the *cycleInterval* (0.001 s should work well), because some browsers may generate *fraction_changed* and *time* events during the *cycleInterval* regardless of whether or not they are being used.

The easiest way to have one **TimeSensor** start when another has stopped is to write a little **Script** that sends the second **TimeSensor** a *startTime* event when it receives an *isActive* FALSE event from the first **TimeSensor,** like this:

```
DEF TS1 TimeSensor { }
DEF TS2 TimeSensor { }
DEF S Script {
  eventIn SFBool isActive
  eventOut SFTime startTime_changed
  url "javascript:
    function isActive(value, timestamp) {
      if (value == false) startTime_changed = timestamp;
    }"
}
ROUTE TS1.isActive TO S.isActive
ROUTE S.startTime_changed TO TS2.set_startTime
```

However, it is better to set the second **TimeSensor**'s *startTime* as early as possible, so the browser knows in advance when it will start and thus it has a better chance of downloading any textures, sounds, or **Inline** geometry that might be needed once the second animation starts. This is also fairly easy, because the first **TimeSensor** will end at time *startTime + cycleInterval:*

```
DEF TS1 TimeSensor { }
DEF TS2 TimeSensor { }
DEF S Script {
  eventIn SFTime startTime_changed
  field SFTime start 0
  eventIn SFTime cycleInterval_changed
  field SFTime interval 0
  eventOut SFTime set_startTime
  url "javascript:
   function startTime_changed(value) { start = value; }
   function cycleInterval_changed(value) { interval = value; }
   function eventsProcessed() { set_startTime = start+interval; }"
}
```

```
ROUTE TS1.startTime_changed TO S.startTime_changed
ROUTE TS1.cycleInterval_changed TO S.cycleInterval_changed
ROUTE S.set_startTime TO TS2.set_startTime
```

When a **TimeSensor** becomes active, it will generate an *isActive* TRUE event and will begin generating *time, fraction_changed,* and *cycleTime* events, which may be routed to other nodes to drive animation or simulated behaviors (behavior at read time is discussed later). The *time* event outputs the absolute time for a given tick of the **TimeSensor** (*time* fields and events represent the number of seconds since midnight GMT January 1, 1970). *Fraction_changed* events output a floating point value in the closed interval [0, 1], where 0 corresponds to *startTime* and 1 corresponds to *startTime* + N × *cycleInterval*, where N = 1, 2, ... That is, the *time* and *fraction_changed* eventOuts can be computed as

time = now

f = fmod(now - *startTime, cycleInterval*)

If: (f == 0.0 && now > *startTime*)
        fraction_changed = 1.0

Else:

        fraction_changed = f / *cycleInterval*

A **TimeSensor** can be set up to be active at read time by specifying *loop* TRUE (not the default) and *stopTime* ≤ *startTime* (satisfied by the default values). The *time* events output absolute times for each tick of the **TimeSensor**; *times* must start at *startTime* and end with either *startTime* + *cycleInterval, stopTime,* or *loop* forever depending on the values of the other fields. An active **TimeSensor** must stop at the first simulation tick when time *now* ≥ *stopTime* > *startTime*.

No guarantees are made with respect to how often a **TimeSensor** will generate time events, but a **TimeSensor** should generate events at least at every simulation tick. **TimeSensors** are guaranteed to generate final *time* and *fraction_changed* events. If *loop* is FALSE, the final *time* event will be generated with a value of (*startTime* + *cycleInterval*) or *stopTime* (if *stopTime* > *startTime*), whichever value is less. If *loop* is TRUE at the completion of every cycle, then the final event will be generated as evaluated at *stopTime* (if *stopTime* > *startTime*) or never.

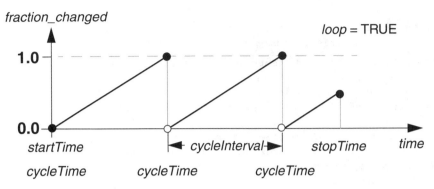

FIGURE 3-58 *TimeSensor Node*

An active **TimeSensor** ignores *set_cycleInterval* and *set_startTime* events. An active **TimeSensor** also ignores *set_stopTime* events for *set_stopTime* < *startTime*. For example, if a *set_startTime* event is received while a **TimeSensor** is active, then that *set_startTime* event is ignored (the *startTime* field is not changed and a *startTime_changed* eventOut is not generated). If an active **TimeSensor** receives a *set_stopTime* event that is less than *now* and greater than or equal to *startTime,* it behaves as if the *stopTime* requested is *now* and sends the final events based on *now* (note that *stopTime* is set as specified in the eventIn).

TIP

Ignoring *set_* events while a **TimeSensor** is running makes creating simple animations much easier, because for most simple animations you want the animation played to completion before it can be restarted. If you do need to stop and restart a **TimeSensor** while it is running, send it both a *stopTime* and a *startTime* event. The *stopTime* event will stop the sensor and the *startTime* event will restart it immediately. For example, this fragment will result in the **TimeSensor** immediately restarting when the **TouchSensor** is activated:

```
DEF TOUCHS TouchSensor { ... }
DEF TIMES TimeSensor { ... }
ROUTE TOUCHS.touchTime TO TIMES.set_stopTime
ROUTE TOUCHS.touchTime TO TIMES.set_startTime
```

TIP

There are two cases of the **TimeSensor** that are most common. The first case uses a **TimeSensor** to drive a single cycle of an animation or behavior. Typically, another node that has a SFTime eventOut (e.g., **Script, TouchSensor,** or **ProximitySensor**) routes to the **TimeSensor**'s *startTime* eventIn (setting it to *now* or *now + delay*), which in turn routes its *fraction_changed* eventOut to another node's *set_fraction* eventIn.

The second common case of a **TimeSensor** is a continuously looping animation or behavior. In this case, the **TimeSensor**'s *loop* field is TRUE, *stopTime* is 0, *startTime* is 0, and *cycleTime* is the length of the intended sequence. This has the effect of starting the sequence in 1970 and looping forever. Be aware that looping **TimeSensors** can slow down rendering performance if too many are active simultaneously, and should be used only when necessary. It is recommended that you restrict the effect of looping **Time-Sensors** by coupling them with a **ProximitySensor**, **VisibilitySensor**, **Script**, or **LOD** that disables the **TimeSensor** when out of range or not relevant.

EXAMPLE

The following example illustrates the **TimeSensor**. The first **TimeSensor** defines a continuously running animation that is enabled and disabled by a **ProximitySensor**. The second **TimeSensor** is triggered by a **TouchSensor** and fires one cycle of an animation each time it is triggered:

```
#VRML V2.0 utf8
Group { children [
  DEF PS ProximitySensor { size 30 30 30 }
  DEF TS1 TimeSensor {
    enabled FALSE
    loop TRUE
  }
  DEF T1 Transform {
    translation 0 0 -.5
    rotation .707 -.707 0 1.57
    children Shape {
      geometry Box {}
      appearance DEF A Appearance {
        material Material { diffuseColor 1 1 1 }
      }
    }
  }
  DEF OI OrientationInterpolator {
    key [ 0, 0.33, 0.66, 1.0 ]
    keyValue [ .707 .707 0 0,     .707 .707 0 2.09,
               .707 .707 0 4.18, .707 .707 0 6.28 ]
  }
  DEF T2 Transform {
    translation -4 0 0
    children [
      Shape {
        geometry Sphere { radius 0.5 }
        appearance USE A
      }
```

```
        DEF TOS TouchSensor {}
        DEF TS2 TimeSensor { cycleInterval 0.75 }
        DEF PI PositionInterpolator {
          key [ 0, .2, .5, .8, 1 ]
          keyValue [ -4 0 0, 0 4 0, 4 0 0, 0 -4 0, -4 0 0 ]
        }
      ]
    }
    Viewpoint { position 0 0 50 description "Animation off"}
    Viewpoint { position 0 0 10 description "Animation on"}
  ] }
ROUTE PS.isActive TO TS1.enabled
ROUTE TS1.fraction_changed TO OI.set_fraction
ROUTE OI.value_changed TO T1.rotation
ROUTE TOS.touchTime TO TS2.startTime
ROUTE TS2.fraction_changed TO PI.set_fraction
ROUTE PI.value_changed TO T2.translation
```

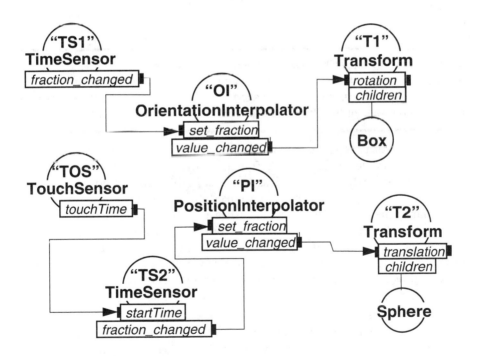

FIGURE 3-59 *TimeSensor Node Example*

TouchSensor

```
TouchSensor {
  exposedField SFBool   enabled TRUE
  eventOut      SFVec3f hitNormal_changed
  eventOut      SFVec3f hitPoint_changed
  eventOut      SFVec2f hitTexCoord_changed
  eventOut      SFBool  isActive
  eventOut      SFBool  isOver
  eventOut      SFTime  touchTime
}
```

A **TouchSensor** tracks the location and state of the pointing device and detects
when the user points at geometry contained by the **TouchSensor**'s parent group.
This sensor can be enabled or disabled by sending it an *enabled* event with a value
of TRUE or FALSE. If the **TouchSensor** is disabled, it does not track user input or
send output events.

DESIGN NOTE

TouchSensor was originally called **ClickSensor,** and was specified in a "mouse-
centric" way. Sam Denton, a regular contributor to the *www-vrml* mailing list, rewrote
this section so that it was easier to map alternative input devices (e.g., 3D wands and
gloves) into the semantics of the **TouchSensor.**

The **TouchSensor** generates events as the pointing device "passes over" any geometry nodes that are descendants of the **TouchSensor**'s parent group. Typically, the
pointing device is a 2D device, such as a mouse. In this case, the pointing device is
considered to be moving within a plane a fixed distance from the viewer and perpendicular to the line of sight (this establishes a set of 3D coordinates for the
pointer). If a 3D pointer is in use, then the **TouchSensor** generates events only
when the pointer is within the user's field of view. In either case, the pointing
device is considered to pass over geometry when that geometry is intersected by a
line extending from the viewer and passing through the pointer's 3D coordinates. If
multiple surfaces intersect this line (hereafter called the *bearing*), only the nearest
will be eligible to generate events.

The *isOver* eventOut reflects the state of the pointing device with regard to whether
it is over the **TouchSensor**'s geometry or not. When the pointing device changes
state from a position such that its bearing does not intersect any of the **TouchSensor**'s geometry to one in which it does intersect geometry, an *isOver* TRUE event is
generated. When the pointing device moves from a position such that its bearing
intersects geometry to one in which it no longer intersects the geometry, or some

other geometry is obstructing the **TouchSensor**'s geometry, an *isOver* FALSE event is generated. These events are generated only if the pointing device has both moved and has changed the *"over"* state; events are not generated if the geometry itself is animating and moving underneath the pointing device unless the pointing device is also moving.

TIP

> The *isOver* event makes it easy to implement a technique called *locate highlighting*. Locate highlighting means making an active user interface widget change color or shape when the mouse moves over it, and lets the user know that something will happen if they press the mouse button. User interaction inside a 3D scene is something with which users are not familiar, and they probably will not be able to tell which objects are "hot" and which are just decoration just by looking at the scene. Writing a **Script** that takes *isOver* events and changes the geometry's color (or activates a **Switch** that displays a "Click Me" message on top of the sensor's geometry, or starts a **Sound** of some kind, or does all three!) will make user interaction much easier and more fun for the user.

As the user moves the bearing over the **TouchSensor**'s geometry, the point of intersection (if any) between the bearing and the geometry is determined. Each movement of the pointing device, while *isOver* is TRUE, generates *hitPoint_changed*, *hitNormal_changed*, and *hitTexCoord_changed* events. *HitPoint_changed* events contain the 3D point on the surface of the underlying geometry, specified in the **TouchSensor**'s coordinate system. *HitNormal_changed* events contain the surface normal vector at the intersection point specified in the **TouchSensor**'s coordinate system. *HitTexCoord_changed* events contain the texture coordinates at the intersection point, which can be used to support the 3D equivalent of an image map.

If *isOver* is TRUE, the user may activate the pointing device to cause the **TouchSensor** to generate *isActive* events (e.g., press the primary mouse button). When the **TouchSensor** generates an *isActive* TRUE event, it grabs all further motion events from the pointing device until it releases and generates an *isActive* FALSE event (other pointing device sensors will not generate events during this time). Motion of the pointing device while *isActive* is TRUE is referred to as *drag*. If a 2D pointing device is in use, *isActive* events will typically reflect the state of the primary button associated with the device (i.e., *isActive* is TRUE when the primary button is pressed and FALSE when it is released). If a 3D pointing device is in use, *isActive* events will typically reflect whether the pointer is within or in contact with the **TouchSensor**'s geometry.

TIP

> The combination of *isActive* and *isOver* gives four possible states in which a **Touch-Sensor** can exist:
>
> *isOver* FALSE, *isActive* FALSE: The user has clicked on some other object or the user hasn't clicked at all and the mouse isn't over this sensor's geometry.
>
> *isOver* TRUE, *isActive* FALSE: The mouse is over this sensor's geometry but the user hasn't clicked yet. If something will happen when the user clicks, it is a good idea to provide some locate-highlighting feedback indicating this.
>
> *isOver* TRUE, *isActive* TRUE: The user has clicked down on the geometry and is still holding the button down, and is still over the geometry. Further feedback at this point is a good idea, but it is also a good idea to allow the user to abort the click by moving the mouse off the geometry.
>
> *isOver* FALSE, *isActive* TRUE: The user clicked down on the geometry and is still holding down the button, but has moved the mouse off the geometry. Feedback to the user that they are aborting the operation is appropriate.

The *touchTime* eventOut is generated when all three of the following conditions are true:

1. The pointing device was over the geometry when it was initially activated (*isActive* is TRUE)

2. The pointing device is currently over the geometry (*isOver* is TRUE)

3. The pointing device is deactivated (*isActive* FALSE event is also generated)

See Section 2.9.6, Sensor Nodes, for more details.

DESIGN NOTE

TouchSensor is designed to be abstract enough to apply to a variety of input devices (e.g., wand, glove) and simple enough for the lowest common denominator hardware found on general-purpose computers today—a pointing device with a single button. The success of Apple's Macintosh proves that multiple buttons aren't necessary to create a really good user interface, and since minimalism was one of the design goals for VRML 2.0, only one-button support is required.

EXAMPLE

The following example illustrates the **TouchSensor**. The first **TouchSensor** is used to move a small **Box** on the surface of a **Sphere**. The **TouchSensor**'s *hitPoint_changed* eventOut is routed to the *translation* field of the **Transform** affecting the **Box.** This has the net effect of translating the **Box** to the intersection point with the **TouchSensor**'s geometry, the **Sphere.** Note, however, that the second **TouchSensor** is used as a toggle button to activate and deactivate the first **TouchSensor.** This is accomplished with a simple **Script** node that is routed to the first **TouchSensor**'s *enabled* field. The **Switch** nodes are used to change the color of the toggle button (**Cone**) and the **Box,** based on the activation state (on or off):

```
#VRML V2.0 utf8
Transform { children [
  Transform { children [
    # Sphere on which the box is moved.
    DEF TOS1 TouchSensor { enabled FALSE }
    Shape {
      geometry Sphere {}
      appearance Appearance {
        material Material { diffuseColor 1 0 1 }
      }
    }
  ]}
  DEF T1 Transform { children [
    # Box that moves and changes activation color.
    DEF SW1 Switch {
      whichChoice 0
      choice [
        Shape {    # choice 0 = off state
          geometry DEF B Box { size 0.25 0.25 0.25 }
          appearance Appearance {
            material Material { diffuseColor 0.2 0.2 0 }
          }
        }
        Shape {    # choice 1 = on state
          geometry USE B
          appearance Appearance {
            material Material { diffuseColor 1 1 0.2 }
          }
        }
      ]
    }
  ]}
  Transform {
    # toggle button which turns box on/off.
    translation -3 0 0
    children [
      DEF TOS2 TouchSensor {}
      DEF SW2 Switch {
        whichChoice 0
        choice [
```

```
          Shape {    # choice 0 = off state
            geometry DEF C Cone {}
            appearance Appearance {
              material Material { diffuseColor 0.8 0.4 0.4 }
            }
          }
          Shape {    # choice 1 = on state
            geometry USE C
            appearance Appearance {
              material Material { diffuseColor 1.0 0.2 0.2 }
            }
          }
        ]
      }
    DEF S2 Script {
      eventIn SFTime touchTime
      field SFBool enabled FALSE
      eventOut SFBool onOff_changed
      eventOut SFInt32 which_changed
      url "javascript:
        function initialize() {
          // Initialize to off state.
          whichChoice = 0;
          onOff_changed = false;
        }
        function touchTime( value, time ) {
          # Toggle state on each click.
          enabled = !enabled;
          onOff_changed = enabled;
          which_changed = enabled;
        }"
    }
  ]
  }
]}
ROUTE TOS2.touchTime TO S2.touchTime
ROUTE S2.onOff_changed TO TOS1.enabled
ROUTE S2.which_changed TO SW1.whichChoice
ROUTE S2.which_changed TO SW2.whichChoice
ROUTE TOS1.hitPoint_changed TO T1.set_translation
```

Transform

```
Transform {
  eventIn       MFNode        addChildren
  eventIn       MFNode        removeChildren
  exposedField  SFVec3f       center          0 0 0
```

```
exposedField  MFNode       children         []
exposedField  SFRotation   rotation         0 0 1  0
exposedField  SFVec3f      scale            1 1 1
exposedField  SFRotation   scaleOrientation 0 0 1  0
exposedField  SFVec3f      translation      0 0 0
field         SFVec3f      bboxCenter       0 0 0
field         SFVec3f      bboxSize         -1 -1 -1
}
```

A **Transform** is a grouping node that defines a coordinate system for its children that is relative to the coordinate systems of its parents. See also Section 2.3.4, Coordinate Systems and Transformations.

See Section 2.3.1, Grouping and Children Nodes, for a description of the *children, addChildren,* and *removeChildren* fields and eventIns.

The *bboxCenter* and *bboxSize* fields specify a bounding box that encloses the **Transform**'s children. This is a hint that may be used for optimization purposes. If the specified bounding box is smaller than the actual bounding box of the children at any time, then the results are undefined. A default *bboxSize* value, (−1,−1,−1), implies that the bounding box is not specified and if needed must be calculated by the browser. See Section 2.3.6, Bounding Boxes, for a description of the *bboxCenter* and *bboxSize* fields.

The *translation, rotation, scale, scaleOrientation,* and *center* fields define a geometric 3D transformation consisting of, in order, a nonuniform scale about an arbitrary point, a rotation about an arbitrary point and axis, and a translation. The *center* field specifies a translation offset from the local coordinate system's origin, (0,0,0). The *rotation* field specifies a rotation of the coordinate system. The *scale* field specifies a nonuniform scale of the coordinate system; *scale* values must be >0.0. The *scaleOrientation* field specifies a rotation of the coordinate system before the scale (to specify scales in arbitrary orientations). The *scaleOrientation* field applies only to the scale operation. The *translation* field specifies a translation to the coordinate system.

TIP

The translation/rotation/scale operations performed by the **Transform** node occur in the "natural" order—each operation is independent of the other. For example, if the **Transform**'s translation field is (1, 0, 0), then the objects underneath the **Transform** will be translated one unit to the right, regardless of the **Transform**'s *rotation and scale* fields. If you want to apply a series of translate/rotate/scale operations in some other order, you can either use nested **Transform** nodes or figure out the combined transformation and express that as a single **Transform** node. As long as all of your scaling operations are uniform scales (scale equally about x-, y-, z-axes), then any series of scale/rotate/translate operations can be expressed as a single **Transform** node.

Note that negative scale values are not allowed, so the common trick of defining one-half of an object and then mirroring it (using a negative scale and USE-ing the geometry again) will not work. Interactive programs will still provide mirroring operations, of course, but when saving to a VRML file the program will have to duplicate the mirrored polygons to avoid the negative scale.

Given a 3D point P and **Transform** node, P is transformed into point P' in its parent's coordinate system by a series of intermediate transformations. In matrix-transformation notation, where C (center), SR (scaleOrientation), T (translation), R (rotation), and S (scale) are the equivalent transformation matrices

$$P' = T \times C \times R \times SR \times S \times -SR \times -C \times P$$

The **Transform** node

```
Transform {
  center           C
  rotation         R
  scale            S
  scaleOrientation SR
  translation      T
  children         [...]
}
```

is equivalent to the nested sequence of

```
Transform {
  translation T
  children transform { translation C
   children transform { rotation R
    children transform { rotation SR
     children transform { scale S
      children transform { rotation -SR
       children transform { translation -C
             ...
}}}}}}}
```

DESIGN NOTE

VRML 1.0 included special-purpose versions of **Transform—Scale, Rotate,** and **Translate** nodes—and the more general **MatrixTransform** node. The special-purpose nodes were dropped from VRML 2.0 because they are equivalent to a **Transform** node with some of its fields left as default values. If their absence bothers you, their prototype definitions are trivial. For example:

```
PROTO Translate [ exposedField SFVec3f translation ] {
  Transform { translation IS translation }
}
```

Dropping **MatrixTransform** was much more controversial. Allowing arbitrary matrix transformations was a very powerful feature that is almost impossible to support in its full generality. The arbitrary 4×4 matrix of the **MatrixTransform** allows specification of perspective transformations that have singularities and degenerate matrices that cannot be inverted, both of which cause major implementation headaches. Lighting operations, for example, typically rely on transforming normal vectors by the inverse transpose of the transformation matrix, which is a big problem if the matrix cannot be inverted. And picking operations (determining which geometry is underneath the pointing device) are best done by transforming a picking ray into the object's coordinate space, which, again, is impossible if there is a degenerate or perspective transformation in the transformation stack. No VRML 1.0 browser completely implements the **MatrixTransform** node.

Restricting the legal values of a **MatrixTransform** was suggested, but doing that makes **MatrixTransform** just another representation for the **Transform** node. Since that representation is both more verbose (16 numbers, four of which would always be (0, 0, 0, 1) versus the ten for a simple translate/rotate/scale **Transform** node), conversion back and forth between the two representations is possible (see the Graphics Gems series of books by Academic Press for several approaches). **MatrixTransform** was used in relatively few VRML 1.0 worlds, and one of the design goals for VRML 2.0 was minimalism. For all of these reasons, **MatrixTransform** is not part of the VRML 2.0 specification.

TIP

To use the **Transform** node properly, it is important to understand the order of the transformation operations as they accumulate. The first step is the *center* field. It translates the local origin of the object to a new position before all the other operations take place. It does *not* translate the object and will have no effect if no other operations are specified. Think of this operation as specifying the location of the object's center point to be used for subsequent operations (e.g., rotation). For example, the default **Box** node is centered at (0,0,0), and represents a cube that spans −1 to +1 along all three axes. In the following file excerpt, the **Box** is parented by a **Transform** that specifies a *center* of (−3,0,0) and a *rotation* of +180 degrees about the z-axis of the modified center. The result is an upside-down box centered at (−6,0,0):

```
Transform {
  center -3 0 0
  rotation 0 0 1 3.14
  children Shape { geometry Box {} }
}
```

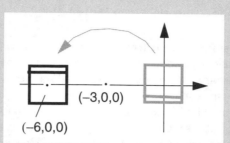

The second operation, in order, is the *scaleOrientation*. This operation is the most obscure and is rarely used. The *scaleOrientation* temporarily rotates the object's coordinate system (i.e., local origin) in preparation for the third operation, *scale*, and rotates back after the *scale* is performed. This is sometimes handy when you wish to scale your object along a direction that is not aligned with the object's local coordinate system (e.g., skewing).

The fourth operation is *rotation*. It specifies an axis about which to rotate the object and the angle (in radians) to rotate. Remember that positive rotations produce counterclockwise rotations when viewed down the positive axis. This is sometimes referred to as the *right-hand rule* (see any computer graphics or VRML tutorial book for an explanation).

The last operation is *translation*. It specifies a translation to be applied to the object. Remember that translation will occur along the local axes of the object's coordinate system.

TIP

Another important concept to understand is the order in which nested **Transforms** operate. Within a single **Transform** the operation order occurs as described, but when a **Transform** parents another **Transform**, the lowest level **Transform** is applied first and each subsequent parent's operations are applied in "upward" order. For example, the following excerpt defines two **Transforms**, T1 and T2. The first **Transform**, T1, performs a *translation* and a *scale* operation, and has a child T2. The **Transform** T2 performs a *scale* and a *rotation* operation. Therefore, the order of operations is: T2 *scale*, T2 *rotation*, T1 *scale*, and finally T1 *translation*. It is important to notice that T1's *scale* operation scales the rotated object (and produces a skew):

```
DEF T1 Transform {
  scale 1 2 1                     # Stretch along Y
  translation 0 0 -3              # Translate back in Z
  children DEF T2 Transform {
    scale  1 1 10                 # Stretch in Z
    rotation 1 0 0 0.785          # Rotate 45 degrees about X axis
    children Shape { geometry Box {} }
  }
}
```

EXAMPLE

The following example illustrates the **Transform** node. The first **Transform**, T1, is the parent transformation for all subsequent objects in the file. The second **Transform**, T2, uses default values and is transformed by its parent's transformations. The third **Transform**, T3, specifies a new center point and a rotation about that center point. Note that these operations take place before the T1's *scale* and *translation*. The fourth **Transform**, T4, scales and translates the object, and of course is also transformed by T1.

```
#VRML V2.0 utf8
DEF T1 Transform {          # Parent transform for entire file
  translation 0 0 -100      # Translates entire file down Z
  scale 1 2 1               # Scales entire file in Y
  children [
    DEF T2 Transform {      # Default transform at origin
      children Shape {
        geometry Box {}
        appearance Appearance {
          material Material { diffuseColor 1 0 0 }
    }}}
    DEF T3 Transform {      # Re-centered and rotated
      center -3 0 0
      rotation 0 0 1 3.14
      children Shape {
        geometry Cone {}
        appearance Appearance {
          material Material { diffuseColor 0 1 0 }
    }}}
    DEF T4 Transform {      # Scaled (half) and translated +X
      scale 0.5 0.5 0.5
      translation 3 0 0
      children Shape {
        geometry Cylinder {}
        appearance Appearance {
          material Material { diffuseColor 0 0 1 }
    }}}
  ]
}
```

Viewpoint

```
Viewpoint {
  eventIn        SFBool      set_bind
  exposedField   SFFloat     fieldOfView      0.785398
  exposedField   SFBool      jump             TRUE
```

```
    exposedField SFRotation orientation     0  0  1   0
    exposedField SFVec3f    position         0  0  10
    field        SFString   description      " "
    eventOut     SFTime     bindTime
    eventOut     SFBool     isBound
}
```

The **Viewpoint** node defines a specific location in a local coordinate system from which the user might view the scene. **Viewpoints** are *bindable children nodes* (see Section 2.9.1, Bindable Children Nodes) and thus there exists a **Viewpoint** stack in the browser in which the topmost **Viewpoint** on the stack is the currently active **Viewpoint**. If a TRUE value is sent to the *set_bind* eventIn of a **Viewpoint,** it is moved to the top of the **Viewpoint** stack and thus activated. When a **Viewpoint** is at the top of the stack, the user's view is conceptually reparented as a child of the **Viewpoint.** All subsequent changes to the **Viewpoint**'s coordinate system change the user's view (e.g., changes to any parent transformation nodes or to the **View-point**'s *position* or *orientation* fields). Sending a *set_bind* FALSE event removes the **Viewpoint** from the stack and results in *isBound* FALSE and *bindTime* events. If the popped **Viewpoint** is at the top of the **Viewpoint** stack, the user's view is reparented to the next entry in the stack. See Section 2.9.1, Bindable Children Nodes, for more details on the binding stacks. When a **Viewpoint** is moved to the top of the stack, the existing top-of-stack **Viewpoint** sends an *isBound* FALSE event and is pushed onto the stack.

DESIGN NOTE

Viewpoints follow the binding stack paradigm because they are like a global property—the viewer's position and orientation are determined by, at most, one **Viewpoint** at a time.

It may seem strange that the viewer's position or orientation is changed by binding to and then modifying a **Viewpoint,** but a completely different node (**ProximitySensor**) is used to determine the viewer's current position or orientation. This asymmetry makes sense, because reporting the viewer's position and orientation is *not* like a global property. The viewer's position and orientation can be reported in any local coordinate system, and there may be multiple **Scripts** tracking the movements of the viewer at the same time.

An author can automatically move the user's view through the world by binding the user to a **Viewpoint** and then animating either the **Viewpoint** or the transformations above it. Browsers shall allow the user view to be navigated relative to the coordinate system defined by the **Viewpoint** (and the transformations above it), even if the **Viewpoint** or its parent transformations are being animated.

TIP

> If you want to control completely how the viewer may move through your world, bind to a **NavigationInfo** node that has its type field set to NONE. When the navigation type is NONE, browsers should remove all out-of-scene navigation controls and not allow the user to move away from the currently bound **Viewpoint**.

The *bindTime* eventOut sends the time at which the **Viewpoint** is bound or unbound. This can happen during loading, when a *set_bind* event is sent to the **Viewpoint**, or when the browser binds to the **Viewpoint** via its user interface.

The *position* and *orientation* fields of the **Viewpoint** node specify relative locations in the local coordinate system. *Position* is relative to the coordinate system's origin (0,0,0), while *orientation* specifies a rotation relative to the default orientation (on the −z-axis looking down toward the origin with +x to the right and +y up). **Viewpoints** are affected by the transformation hierarchy.

Navigation types (see the **NavigationInfo** section in this chapter) that require a definition of a down vector (e.g., terrain following) shall use the negative y-axis of the coordinate system of the currently bound **Viewpoint**. Likewise, navigation types that require a definition of an up vector shall use the positive y-axis of the coordinate system of the currently bound **Viewpoint**. Note that the *orientation* field of the **Viewpoint** does not affect the definition of the down or up vectors. This allows the author to separate the viewing direction from the gravity direction.

TIP

> The distinction between the gravity direction (which way is down) and the **Viewpoint's** orientation (which way the user happens to be looking) allows you to create interesting effects, but also requires you to be careful when animating **Viewpoint** orientations. For example, if you create an animation that moves the viewer halfway up a mountain, with the final orientation looking up toward the top of the mountain, you should animate the fields of the **Viewpoint** and *not* a **Transform** node above the **Viewpoint**. If you do animate the coordinate system of the **Viewpoint** (a **Transform** node above it), then you are changing the down direction, and if the user happens to step off a bridge over a chasm you placed on the mountain, they will fall in the wrong direction. Note that all of this is assuming that the VRML browser being used implements terrain following—keeping users on the ground as they move around the world. Although not required by the VRML specification, it is expected that most VRML browsers will support terrain following because it makes moving through a 3D world so much easier.

The *jump* field specifies whether the user's view "jumps" to the position and orientation of a bound **Viewpoint** or remains unchanged. The jump is instantaneous and discontinuous; no collisions are performed and no **ProximitySensors** are checked between the starting point (current user's view) and ending point (**Viewpoint**'s position and orientation). If the user's position before the jump is inside a **ProximitySensor**, the **ProximitySensor** shall send an *exitTime* event with a time stamp equal to the bind's time stamp. If the **Viewpoint** is inside a **ProximitySensor**, the **ProximitySensor** shall send an *enterTime* event with a time stamp equal to the bind's time stamp (assuming that *jump* is TRUE).

Regardless of the value of *jump* at bind time, the relative viewing transformation between the user's view and the current **Viewpoint** shall be stored with the current **Viewpoint** for later use when unjumping. The following is a restatement of the general bind stack rules described in Section 2.9.1, Bindable Children Nodes, with additional rules specific to **Viewpoints** in bold print:

1. During read

   - The first encountered **Viewpoint** is bound by pushing it to the top of the **Viewpoint** stack

     – Nodes contained within **Inlines** are not candidates for the first encountered **Viewpoint.**

     – The first node within a prototype is a valid candidate for the first encountered **Viewpoint.**

   - The first encountered **Viewpoint** sends an *isBound* TRUE event

2. When a *set_bind* TRUE eventIn is received by a **Viewpoint**

   - If it is not on the top of the stack

     – **The relative transformation from the current top-of-stack** Viewpoint **to the user's view is stored with the current top of stack** Viewpoint

     – The current top-of-stack node sends an *isBound* FALSE eventOut

     – The new node is moved to the top of the stack and becomes the currently bound **Viewpoint**

     – The new **Viewpoint** (top of stack) sends an *isBound* TRUE eventOut

     – **If** *jump* **is TRUE for the new** Viewpoint, **then the user's view is "jumped" to match the values in the** *position* **and** *orientation* **fields of the new** Viewpoint

   - If the node is already at the top of the stack, then this event has no effect.

3. When a *set_bind* FALSE eventIn is received by a **Viewpoint**

   - It is removed from the stack

   - If it is on the top of the stack

- It sends an *isBound* FALSE eventOut

- The next node in the stack becomes the currently bound **Viewpoint** (i.e., pop) and issues an *isBound* TRUE eventOut

- **If its *jump* is TRUE, the user's view is "jumped" to the *position* and *orientation* of the next** Viewpoint **in the stack with the stored relative transformation applied**

4. If a *set_bind* FALSE eventIn is received by a node not in the stack, the event is ignored and *isBound* events are not sent.

5. When a node replaces another node at the top of the stack, the *isBound* TRUE and FALSE eventOuts from the two nodes are sent simultaneously (i.e., identical time stamps).

6. If a bound node is deleted, then it behaves as if it received a *set_bind* FALSE event (see #3).

Note that the *jump* field may change after a **Viewpoint** is bound—the rules just described still apply. If *jump* was TRUE when the **Viewpoint** was bound, but changed to FALSE before the *set_bind* FALSE was sent, then the **Viewpoint** does not unjump during unbind. If *jump* was FALSE when the **Viewpoint** was bound, but changed to TRUE before the *set_bind* FALSE was sent, then the **Viewpoint** does perform the unjump during unbind.

TIP

The rules for properly implementing the *jump* field are pretty complicated, but it is really a pretty simple concept. If *jump* is TRUE, then the viewer will be teleported to the **Viewpoint** as soon as the **Viewpoint** is bound (they will jump there instantaneously). If *jump* is FALSE, then the viewer will not appear to move at all when the **Viewpoint** is bound; the viewer will move only when the **Viewpoint** changes.

Discontinuous movements can be disorienting for the user. It is as if they are suddenly blindfolded, taken to another place, and unblindfolded. It is generally better to animate viewers to a new location smoothly so that they have a sense of where they are relative to where they were. Combining a **Viewpoint** with its *jump* field set to FALSE with a **ProximitySensor** to detect the user's position and orientation, and some interpolators to move the viewer smoothly to a new position and orientation, is a good technique. For example, here is a prototype that will smoothly move the user to a new position and orientation at a given *startTime*:

```
#VRML V2.0 utf8
PROTO SmoothMove [ exposedField SFTime howLong 1
                   eventIn SFTime set_startTime
                   field SFVec3f newPosition 0 0 0
                   field SFRotation newOrientation 0 0 1 0 ]
{
```

```
# Group is just a convenient way of holding the necessary
# ProximitySensor and Viewpoint:
Group {
  children [
    # ProximitySensor to detect where the user is.
    DEF PS ProximitySensor { size 1e10 1e10 1e10 }
    # This Viewpoint is bound when the TimeSensor goes active,
    # animated, and then unbound when the TimeSensor finishes.
    DEF V Viewpoint { jump FALSE }
  ]
}
# TimeSensor drives the interpolators to give smooth animation.
DEF TS TimeSensor {
  set_startTime IS set_startTime
  cycleInterval IS howLong
}
DEF PI PositionInterpolator {
  key [ 0, 1 ]
  # These are dummy keyframes; real keyframes set by Script node
  # when the TimeSensor becomes active.
  keyValue [ 0 0 0, 0 0 0 ]
}
DEF OI OrientationInterpolator {
  key [ 0, 1 ]
  keyValue [ 0 0 1 0, 0 0 1 0 ]
}
DEF S Script {
  field SFVec3f newPosition IS newPosition
  field SFRotation newOrientation IS newOrientation
  field SFNode p_sensor USE PS
  eventIn SFTime startNow
  eventOut MFVec3f positions
  eventOut MFRotation orientations
  url "javascript:
    function startNow() {
      // Starting: setup interpolators (direct ROUTE from
      // TimeSensor.isActive to Viewpoint.set_bind binds the
      // Viewpoint for us)

      positions[0] = p_sensor.position_changed;
      positions[1] = newPosition;
      orientations[0] = p_sensor.orientation_changed;
      orientations[1] = newOrientation;
    }"
}
ROUTE TS.isActive TO V.set_bind
ROUTE TS.fraction_changed TO PI.set_fraction
ROUTE TS.fraction_changed TO OI.set_fraction
```

```
     ROUTE OI.value_changed TO V.set_orientation
     ROUTE TS.cycleTime TO S.startNow
     ROUTE S.positions TO PI.keyValue
     ROUTE S.orientations TO OI.keyValue
     ROUTE PI.value_changed TO V.set_position
}
# Example use:  Touch cube, move to new position/orientation
Group {
  children [
    Shape {
      appearance Appearance { material
        Material { diffuseColor 0.8 0.2 0.4 }
      }
      geometry Box { }
    }
    DEF SM SmoothMove {
      howLong 5
      newPosition 0 0 10
      newOrientation 0 1 0  .001
    }
    DEF TS TouchSensor { }
  ]
}
ROUTE TS.touchTime TO SM.set_startTime
```

The *fieldOfView* field specifies a preferred field of view from this **Viewpoint**, in radians. A small field of view roughly corresponds to a telephoto lens; a large field of view roughly corresponds to a wide-angle lens. The field of view should be greater than zero and smaller than π. The default value corresponds to a 45-degree field of view. The value of *fieldOfView* represents the maximum viewing angle in any direction axis of the view. For example, a browser with a rectangular viewing projection shall use an angle of *fieldOfView* for the larger direction (depending on aspect ratio) and *fieldOfView* divided by the aspect ratio in the smaller direction. If the aspect ratio is 2:1 (i.e., horizontal twice the vertical) and the *fieldOfView* is 1.0, the horizontal viewing angle would be 1.0 and the vertical viewing angle would be 0.5. *FieldOfView* is a hint to the browser and may be ignored.

TIP

A small field of view is like a telephoto lens on a camera and will make distant objects look bigger. Changing the field of view can give interesting effects, but browsers may choose to implement a fixed field of view for the very good reason that display devices such as head-mounted displays have an inherent field of view and overriding it can result in the user becoming disoriented or even sick. If you want to zoom in on some part of your world, it is better to move the **Viewpoint** closer rather than changing its field of view.

The *description* field identifies **Viewpoints** that are recommended to be publicly accessible through the browser's user interface (e.g., **Viewpoints** menu). The string in the *description* field should be displayed if this functionality is implemented. If *description* is empty, then the **Viewpoint** should not appear in any public user interface. It is recommended that the browser bind and jump to a **Viewpoint** when its *description* is selected. Once the new position is reached, both the *isBound* and *bindTime* eventOuts are sent.

The URL syntax `".../scene.wrl#ViewpointName"` specifies the user's initial **Viewpoint** when entering `scene.wrl` to be the first **Viewpoint** in that file that appears as `DEF ViewpointName Viewpoint {...}`. This overrides the default behavior (see Section 2.9.1, Bindable Children Nodes) in which the first **Viewpoint** encountered in the file is used as the initial user view. If the `#Viewpoint-Name` is not found, the default behavior is used. The URL syntax `#ViewpointName` may be used by the **Anchor** or **Script** node to bind to a **Viewpoint** within the existing file.

DESIGN NOTE

This "#name" URL syntax comes directly from HTML, where specifying a URL of the form `page.html#name` jumps to a specific (named) location in a given page.

TIP

The easiest way to move the viewer between viewpoints in the world is to use an **Anchor** node and the `#ViewpointName` URL syntax. For example, this VRML file format fragment will take users to the viewpoint named MOUNTAIN_TOP when they click on the **Box:**

```
Anchor {
  children Shape {
    appearance Appearance {
      material Material { }
    }
    geometry Box { }
  }
  url "#MOUNTAIN_TOP"
}
```

If a **Viewpoint** is bound (*set_bind*) and is the child of an **LOD, Switch,** or any node or prototype that disables its children, then the result is undefined. If a **Viewpoint** is bound and results in a collision with geometry, then the browser performs its self-defined navigation adjustments as if the user navigated to this point (see the **Collision** section in this chapter).

TIP

You will almost always want to name a **Viewpoint** node using DEF, because **Viewpoints** don't do much by themselves. You will either ROUTE events to them or will use the URL #ViewpointName syntax.

You should be careful when you use the USE feature with **Viewpoints**. USE can make the same object appear in multiple places in the world at the same time. For example, you might create just a few different cars and then USE them many times to create a traffic jam. However, what would happen if you put a **Viewpoint** named "DRIVER" inside one of the cars and then bound the viewer to that **Viewpoint?** The car would be in multiple places in the world at the same time—something that is OK for a virtual world, but can never happen in the real world. And since the person looking at the virtual world is a real person who can look at the virtual world from only one place at a time, there is a problem. What happens is undefined. Browsers can do whatever they wish, including completely ignoring the DRIVER **Viewpoint** or randomly picking one of the locations of the car and putting the viewer there.

To avoid problems, you should make sure that each **Viewpoint** is the child of exactly one grouping node. And that any of the **Viewpoint's** parent grouping nodes is the child of only one grouping node, too.

EXAMPLE

The following example illustrates the **Viewpoint** node. This example demonstrates a couple of typical uses of **Viewpoints**. Click on one of the shapes (**Box, Cone, Sphere**) to move yourself to a **Viewpoint** on their platform. Navigate yourself onto the moving white platform, which will then bind you to a **Viewpoint** on that platform and move you along with it. Move off the platform to unbind yourself from that **Viewpoint:**

```
#VRML V2.0 utf8
# Three fixed viewpoints
DEF V1 Viewpoint {
  position 0 1.8 -12
  orientation 0 1 0   3.1416
  description "View: green platform"
}
DEF V2 Viewpoint {
  position -10.4 1.8 6
  orientation 0 1 0   -1.047
  description "View: red platform"
}
```

```
DEF V3 Viewpoint {
  position 10.4 1.8 6
  orientation 0 1 0  1.047
  description "View: blue platform"
}
# A moving Viewpoint.  This Transform rotates, taking the
# Viewpoint, ProximitySensor and children with it:
DEF VT Transform { children [
  Transform {
    translation 0 -.1 -4
    children [
      DEF V4 Viewpoint {
        position 0 1.3 1.8       # Edge of platform
        orientation 0 1 0  0  # Looking out
        jump FALSE
        description "View: moving platform"
      }
      Shape {  # Octagonal platform
        appearance Appearance { material Material { } }
        geometry  IndexedFaceSet {
          coord Coordinate {
            point [ 1 0 2, 2 0 1, 2 0 -1, 1 0 -2,
                   -1 0 -2, -2 0 -1, -2 0 1, -1 0 2 ]
          }
          coordIndex [ 0, 1, 2, 3, 4, 5, 6, 7, -1 ]
        }
      }
      # When this ProximitySensor is activated, viewer bound to V4:
      DEF PS ProximitySensor {
        center 0 2 0
        size 4 4 4
      }
    ]
  }
  DEF OI OrientationInterpolator {
    # It takes 18 seconds to go all the way around.
    # Four-second 120-degree rotation, two second pause, repeated
    # three times.
    # These keytimes are 18'ths:
    key [ 0,    .056, .167, .22,
         .33,  .389, .5,   .556,
         .667, .722, .833, .889,
         1 ]
    # Rotate a total of 2 PI radians.  Keys are given at 1/8 and 7/8
    # of each one-third rotation to make the rot smoother (slow
    # in-out animation); that's why these angles are multiples of
    # 1/24'th (PI/12 radians) rotation:
    keyValue [
      0 1 0  0,       0 1 0  .262,  0 1 0  1.833,  0 1 0  2.094,
```

```
          0 1 0   2.094,   0 1 0   2.356,   0 1 0   3.927,   0 1 0   4.189,
          0 1 0   4.189,   0 1 0   4.45,    0 1 0   6.021,   0 1 0   0,
          0 1 0   0
        ]
      }
    DEF TS TimeSensor {
      loop TRUE   startTime 1
      cycleInterval 18
    }
  ]}
#Routes for platform animation:
ROUTE TS.fraction_changed TO OI.set_fraction
ROUTE OI.value_changed TO VT.set_rotation
# And bind viewer to V4 when they're on the moving platform:
ROUTE PS.isActive TO V4.set_bind
# Some geometry to look at:
DirectionalLight { direction 0 -1 0 }
Transform {
  translation 0 0 -9
  children [
    Shape {
      appearance DEF A1 Appearance {
        material Material { diffuseColor 0 0.8 0 }
      }
      geometry DEF IFS IndexedFaceSet {
        coord Coordinate {
          point [ 0 0 -6, -5.2 0 3,  5.2 0 3 ]
        }
        coordIndex [ 0, 1, 2, -1 ]
        solid FALSE
      }
    }
    Anchor {
      url "#V1"
      children
      Transform {
        translation 0 0.5 0
        children Shape {
          appearance USE A1
          geometry Box { size 1 1 1 }
        }
}}]}
Transform {
  translation -7.8 0 4.5
  children [
    Shape {
      geometry USE IFS
      appearance DEF A2 Appearance {
        material Material { diffuseColor 0.8 0 0 }
    }}
```

```
    Anchor {
      url "#V2"
      children Transform {
        translation 0 .5 0
        children Shape {
          appearance USE A2
          geometry Sphere { radius .5 }
}}}]}
Transform {
  translation 7.8 0 4.5
  children [
    Shape {
      geometry USE IFS
      appearance DEF A3 Appearance {
        material Material { diffuseColor 0 0 0.8 }
      }
    }
    Anchor {
      url "#V3"
      children Transform {
        translation 0 .5 0
        children Shape {
          appearance USE A3
          geometry Cone { bottomRadius .5  height 1 }
}}}]}
```

VisibilitySensor

```
VisibilitySensor {
  exposedField SFVec3f  center    0 0 0
  exposedField SFBool   enabled   TRUE
  exposedField SFVec3f  size      0 0 0
  eventOut     SFTime   enterTime
  eventOut     SFTime   exitTime
  eventOut     SFBool   isActive
}
```

The **VisibilitySensor** detects visibility changes of a rectangular box as the user navigates the world. **VisibilitySensor** is typically used to detect when the user can see a specific object or region in the scene, and to activate or deactivate some behavior or animation in order to attract the user or improve performance.

TIP

A **VisibilitySensor** detects whether a box-shaped region of the world is visible or not. If you need to find out if an object is visible or not, it is up to you to set the **Visibility-Sensor**'s *center* and *size* field so that the **VisibilitySensor** surrounds the object.

The *enabled* field enables and disables the **VisibilitySensor.** If *enabled* is set to FALSE, the **VisibilitySensor** does not send output events. If *enabled* is TRUE, then the **VisibilitySensor** detects changes to the visibility status of the box specified and sends events through the *isActive* eventOut. A TRUE event is output to *isActive* when any portion of the box impacts the rendered view, and a FALSE event is sent when the box has no effect on the view. Browsers shall guarantee that if *isActive* is FALSE, then the box has absolutely no effect on the rendered view. Browsers may error liberally when *isActive* is TRUE (e.g., *maybe* it does effect the rendering).

DESIGN NOTE

In other words, it is not OK for a browser to say that something is invisible when it can be seen, but it is OK for a browser to say that something is visible when it actually isn't. The reason the rules are written this way is to allow browser implementors to decide how accurate to make their visibility computations. For example, one implementation might simply calculate whether or not the visibility region is inside or outside the viewer's field of view, while another might go further and compute whether or not there is an object in front of the visibility region that completely hides it.

The *center* and *size* exposedFields specify the object space location of the box center and the extents of the box (i.e., width, height, and depth). The **Visibility-Sensor**'s box is affected by hierarchical transformations of its parents.

The *enterTime* event is generated whenever the *isActive* TRUE event is generated, and *exitTime* events are generated whenever *isActive* FALSE events are generated.

Each **VisibilitySensor** behaves independently of all other **VisibilitySensors**. Every enabled **VisibilitySensor** that is affected by the user's movement receives and sends events, possibly resulting in multiple **VisibilitySensors** receiving and sending events simultaneously. Unlike **TouchSensors** there is no notion of a **Visibility-Sensor** lower in the scene graph "grabbing" events. Instanced (DEF/USE) **VisibilitySensors** use the union of all the boxes defined by their instances to check for enter and exit. An instanced **VisibilitySensor** will detect enter, motion, and exit for all instances of the box and send output events appropriately.

TIP

> The **VisibilitySensor** node is an excellent tool for managing behavior complexity and rendering performance of your scene. Use the **VisibilitySensor** to disable interpolators or **Scripts** when not in view. For example, imagine a file that contains several butterfly swarms that flutter around various flower patches (guided by either interpolators or a **Script**). Each butterfly swarm can be managed by a **VisibilitySensor** that encloses the entire swarm and disables the swarm movement when out of view. This is also a good technique for building into behavioral objects or prototypes that you intend to reuse in other files. It establishes good composability principles (objects that manage themselves and do not arbitrarily impact overall world performance).

EXAMPLE

The following illustrates a simple example of a **VisibilitySensor**. Two **TimeSensors** are used to move a **Cylinder**: one gives it a large motion and one gives it a small motion. A **VisibilitySensor** is used to disable the small-motion **TimeSensor** when the object is out of view:

```
#VRML V2.0 utf8
DEF T1 Transform {  # Large motion transform
  children [
    DEF VS VisibilitySensor {
      # Must be big enough to enclose object plus small motion:
      size 1.6 4.6 1.6
    }
    DEF T2 Transform { # Small motion transform
      children [
        Shape {
          appearance Appearance { material Material { } }
          geometry Cylinder { }
        }
      ]
    }
  ]
}
DEF TS1 TimeSensor { # Large motion TimeSensor
  loop TRUE
  cycleInterval 50
}
DEF PI1 PositionInterpolator { # Gross movement around scene
  key [ 0, .1, .2, .3, .4, .5, .6, .7, .8, .9, 1 ]
  keyValue [ 0 0 -30,  -10 5 -20,  -20 0 -10,  -30 -5 10,
            -20 7 20,  -10 4 10,  0 6 20,  20 4 0,  30 2 -20,
            10 0 -20,  0 0 -30 ]
}
```

```
ROUTE TS1.fraction_changed TO PI1.set_fraction
ROUTE PI1.value_changed TO T1.set_translation
DEF TS2 TimeSensor { # Small motion
  loop TRUE
  cycleInterval 5
}
DEF PI2 PositionInterpolator { # Fine movement
  key [ 0, .2, .4, .6, .8, 1 ]
  keyValue [ 0 0 0, 0 1 0, 0 2 0, 0 3 0, 0 1.8 0, 0 0 0 ]
}
DEF OI OrientationInterpolator { # More fine movement:
  # One full rotation requires at least 4 keyframes to avoid
  # indeterminate rotation:
  key [ 0, .33, .66, 1 ]
  keyValue [ 1 0 0  0,  1 0 0  2.09,  1 0 0  4.19, 1 0 0  0 ]
}
DEF V Viewpoint {
  description "Initial View"
  position 0 1.6 15
}
ROUTE TS2.fraction_changed TO PI2.set_fraction
ROUTE TS2.fraction_changed TO OI.set_fraction
ROUTE PI2.value_changed TO T2.set_translation
ROUTE OI.value_changed TO T2.set_rotation
# Only perform fine motion when cylinder is visible:
ROUTE VS.isActive TO TS2.set_enabled
```

WorldInfo

```
WorldInfo {
  field MFString info  []
  field SFString title ""
}
```

The **WorldInfo** node contains information about the world. This node has no effect on the visual appearance or behavior of the world. It is strictly for documentation purposes. The *title* field is intended to store the name or title of the world so that browsers can present this to the user (e.g., in their window border). Any other information about the world can be stored in the *info* field (e.g., the scene author, copyright information, and public domain information).

TIP

You can use **WorldInfo** nodes to save title, copyright, credit, statistical, and authoring data. This can be included in the final published file or stripped out in the last step. It is recommended that you place this information at the top of the file, so that others notice it. Typically, only the first **WorldInfo** node in the file specifies the *title* field. If you have information that applies to a specific object in the file, create a **Group** node, insert a **WorldInfo** as the first child in the **Group**, and add the relevant nodes as subsequent children (see the following example).

EXAMPLE

The following example illustrates a few simple uses of the **WorldInfo** node. The first **WorldInfo** specifies the world's title, overall credits, legal information, and authoring data pertaining to the entire file. The second **WorldInfo** is used as a lightweight stand-in node for an empty level of an **LOD** node. The third **WorldInfo** documents a specific object in the scene (the **Cone**). In this case, the author has specified that if anyone wishes to reuse this data, they must retain the **WorldInfo** node and thus give credit to the original author. The third example also illustrates how an authoring system can store technical data for future editing sessions. It is recommended that authors (and authoring systems) strip out this extra data during the publishing step to reduce download time:

```
#VRML V2.0 utf8
WorldInfo {     # Title and documentation for this file
  title "The Annotated VRML Reference Manual world"
  info [ "Copyright (c) 1997 by Rikk Carey and Gavin Bell",
         "Published by Addison-Wesley Publishing Co., Inc.",
         "All rights reserved.  etc.",
         "Created using XYZ Author: version 4.3 ..." ]
}
Group {
  children [
    LOD {
      range [ 10 ]
      level [
        Shape { geometry Sphere { radius 2 } }
        WorldInfo {}        # Empty level standin
      ]
    }
    Group {
      children [
        WorldInfo {           # Documentation for this object
          info [ "DO NOT REMOVE THIS INFORMATION.",
                 "Copyright (c) by John Smith",
                 "The following object was created ...",
                 "Modeling information: x=123.45 y=42, a=666 ...",
                 "Tips: This object is centered at 0,0,0..." ]
```

```
        }
        Shape {
          geometry Cone {}
          appearance Appearance { material Material {} }
        }
      ]
    }
  ]
}
```

Field and Event Reference

This chapter describes the syntax and general semantics of fields and events—the elemental data types used by VRML nodes to define objects (see Chapter 3, Node Ref erence). Nodes are composed of fields and events (see Section 2.2, Nodes, Fields, and Events). The types defined in this annex are used by both fields and events.

4.1 Introduction

There are two general classes of fields and events: one that contains a *single* value (where a value may be a single number, a vector, or even an image) and one that contains *multiple* values. Single-valued fields and events have names that begin with SF. Multivalued fields and events have names that begin with MF.

Multivalued fields and events are written as a series of values enclosed in square brackets and are separated by whitespace (e.g., commas). If the field or event has zero values then only the square brackets ("[ ]") are written. The last value may be optionally followed by whitespace (e.g., comma). If the field has exactly one value, the brackets may be omitted and just the value written. For example, all of the following are valid for a multivalued MFInt32 field named *foo* containing the single integer value 1:

```
foo 1
foo [1,]
foo [ 1 ]
```

DESIGN NOTE

There are some "missing" MF field types. For example, there is an SFBool field type but no MFBool type. Only the field types used by the 54 nodes in the specification are defined. The practical, immediate benefits of making implementations a little bit smaller were judged to be more important than the intangible benefits of having a more symmetric design or the possible future benefits to language extensions defined using EXTERNPROTO.

The design of the field types is not as conceptually "clean" as it could be. The problem is that some of the field types define only the syntax or structure of the values they contain, while others define both the syntax and the semantics of the values they contain. For example, an SFVec3f field can contain any triple of floating point numbers, regardless of how they are used. An SFColor field is syntactically identical to an SFVec3f field, but it implies something about the semantics of the numbers in the field—they must be between 0.0 and 1.0, and they represent RGB intensities. The field types would be more consistent if either there was no SFColor field type or if the SFVec3f field type was replaced with field types with specific uses—perhaps SFPosition (for a point in space) and SFUnitVector (for a unit vector such as a polygon normal).

It isn't clear which design would be better—one with fewer field types that define only the structure of the fields or one with more field types that define the semantics of the fields. The mix of both found in the current specification works pretty well in practice.

4.2 SFBool

SFBool is a field or event containing a single Boolean value. SFBools are specified as TRUE or FALSE. For example

```
fooBool FALSE
```

is an SFBool field, *fooBool,* defining a FALSE value. The initial value of an SFBool eventOut is FALSE.

TIP

> It is annoying, but VRML uses "TRUE" and "FALSE" for Boolean values, while Java and JavaScript use "true" and "false." Just remember to use TRUE/FALSE when you are writing the VRML file format, but always use true/false when you are writing Java or JavaScript code.

4.3 SFColor and MFColor

SFColor defines one RGB color triple and MFColor defines zero or more RGB triples. Each color is specified as an RGB triple of floating point numbers in ANSI C floating point format, in the range 0.0 to 1.0. For example

```
fooColor [ 1.0 0. 0.0, 0 1 0, 0 0 1 ]
```

is an MFColor field, *fooColor,* containing the three primary colors red, green, and blue.

The initial value of an SFColor eventOut is (0,0,0). The initial value of an MFColor eventOut is [ ].

TIP

> Each component (R,G,B) of a color is expressed in VRML as a floating point number (0.0 to 1.0), but most VRML implementations will convert them internally into, at most, 256 discrete levels. So writing out colors with more than three significant digits of precision just makes your VRML files unnecessarily large. Users will not be able to distinguish between color (.005199 .12345 0) and color (.005 .123 0).

4.4 SFFloat and MFFloat

SFFloat defines one single-precision floating point number and MFFloat defines zero or more single-precision floating point numbers. SFFloats and MFFloats are specified in ANSI C floating point format. For example

```
fooFloat [ 3.1415926, 12.5e-3, .0001 ]
```

is an MFFloat field, *fooFloat,* containing three floating point values.

The initial value of an SFFloat eventOut is 0.0. The initial value of an MFFloat eventOut is [ ].

TIP

Legal values for single-precision floating point values range from 1.0e38 to −1.0e38, with more than seven significant decimal digits of accuracy. Seven digits of accuracy means you can model something 10 km big with about plus or minus 1-mm accuracy. Usually you won't need such high accuracy and you can make your VRML files much smaller by writing out floating point values with less precision.

4.5 SFImage

The SFImage field or event defines a single, uncompressed, 2D pixel image. SFImage fields and events are specified as three integers representing the width, height, and number of components in the image, followed by width × height hexadecimal or integer values representing the pixels in the image, separated by whitespace:

```
fooImage <width> <height> <num components> <pixels values>
```

A one-component image specifies one-byte hexadecimal or integer values representing the intensity of the image. For example, `0xFF` is full intensity and `0x00` is no intensity. A two-component image puts the intensity in the first (high) byte and the alpha (opacity) in the second (low) byte. Pixels in a three-component image have the red component in the first (high) byte, followed by the green and blue components (`0xFF0000` is red). Four-component images put the alpha byte after RGB (`0x0000FF80` is semitransparent blue). A value of `0x00` is completely transparent; `0xFF` is completely opaque.

Each pixel is read as a single unsigned number. For example, a three-component pixel with value `0x0000FF` may also be written as `0xFF` or `255` (decimal). Pixels are specified from left to right, bottom to top. The first value is the lower left pixel and the last value is the upper right pixel. For example

```
fooImage 1 2 1 0xFF 0x00
```

is a 1-pixel-wide-by-2-pixel-high one-component (i.e., gray-scale) image, with the bottom pixel white and the top pixel black. And

```
fooImage 2 4 3 0xFF0000 0xFF00 0 0 0 0 0xFFFFFF 0xFFFF00
                # red      green  black.. white    yellow
```

is a 2-pixel-wide-by-4-pixel-high RGB image, with the bottom left pixel red, the bottom right pixel green, the two middle rows of pixels black, the top left pixel white, and the top right pixel yellow.

The initial value of an SFImage eventOut is (0,0,0).

TIP

The SFImage field is used only by the **PixelTexture** node and is meant to be used only for small images or images that are algorithmically generated by a **Script** node. For larger images it is generally much better to use **ImageTexture** nodes and store the images in PNG, JPEG, or GIF files, since those file formats can compress the images, making them much faster to transmit across the network.

4.6 SFInt32 and MFInt32

The SFInt32 field and event define one 32-bit integer, and the MFInt32 field and event define zero or more 32-bit integers. SFInt32 and MFInt32 fields and events are specified as an integer in decimal or hexadecimal (beginning with **0x**) format. For example

```
fooInt32 [ 17, -0xE20, -518820 ]
```

is an MFInt32 field containing three values.

The initial value of an SFInt32 eventOut is 0. The initial value of an MFInt32 eventOut is [ ].

TIP

A 32-bit integer can hold a value that ranges from about negative two billion to positive two billion.

4.7 SFNode and MFNode

The SFNode field and event define a VRML node, and the MFNode field and event define zero or more nodes. The following example illustrates valid syntax for an MFNode field, *fooNode*, defining four nodes:

```
fooNode [ Transform { translation 1 0 0 }
         DEF CUBE Box { }
         USE CUBE
         USE SOME_OTHER_NODE ]
```

The SFNode and MFNode fields and events may contain the keyword NULL to indicate that it is empty.

The initial value of an SFNode eventOut is NULL. The initial value of an MFNode eventOut is [ ].

TIP

SFNode and MFNode are used whenever a node needs to include the definition of another node in order to define itself. The syntax of SFNode and MFNode is identical to standard VRML file syntax—you simply specify the node definition as the field value. The most common use of SFNode/MFNode is in grouping nodes that contain children nodes. For example, the **Group** node has an exposed MFNode field named *children*. This field contains a list of node definitions that represent the child nodes that the **Group** encapsulates. Remember that node definitions may contain DEF names or USE instantiations. In the following file excerpt, the **Group** node specifies five children nodes in the *children* field. Note that the last two children are specified through the USE syntax:

```
...
DEF S1 Shape { geometry Sphere {} }
Group {
  children [    # This is an MFNode exposedField
    Shape { geometry Cone {} }   # first child
    Shape { geometry Box {} }    # second child
    DEF T1 Transform { ... }     # third child (named)
    USE S1                       # fourth child (instance of S1)
    USE T1                       # fifth child (instance of T1)
  ]
}
```

4.8 SFRotation and MFRotation

The SFRotation field and event define one arbitrary rotation, and the MFRotation field and event define zero or more arbitrary rotations. SFRotations and MFRotations are specified as four floating point values separated by whitespace. The first three values specify a normalized rotation axis vector about which the rotation takes place. The fourth value specifies the amount of right-handed rotation about that axis, in radians. For example, an SFRotation containing a 180-degree rotation about the y-axis is

```
fooRot 0.0 1.0 0.0  3.14159265
```

The initial value of an SFRotation eventOut is (0,0,1,0). The initial value of an MFRotation eventOut is [ ].

DESIGN NOTE

It might have been better to name these fields SF/MFOrientation, because they really represent a "final" orientation of something and do *not* imply anything about how it might have been rotated to get to that orientation. A common VRML 1.0 extension was a **Rotor** node that used an SFRotation field to define how the object should rotate. A very common error was to use a zero rotation angle about a desired rotation axis to define the rotation. Browsers that stored rotations internally as quaternions or matrices would immediately convert the SFRotation into their internal representation and lose the desired rotation axis. The end result was a rotation about (usually) the *z*-axis and a very frustrated user.

If you are writing extension nodes or **Scripts** that truly require a rotation axis and a rotation angle, do *not* use an SFRotation field. Instead, store the axis in an SFVec3f field and store the angle in an SFFloat field. The **Rotor** node would have worked perfectly if the desired rotation axis was specified as an SFVec3f field.

TIP

Be careful. One rotation has multiple equivalent representations in the axis-plus-angle form chosen by VRML to represent rotations. Zero rotations can be especially troublesome; (1,0,0,0) and (0,1,0,0) are equivalent (and are equivalent to *any* rotation of the form (x,y,z, 0)). Similarly, a rotation (x,y,z, angle) is equivalent to the rotation (−x,−y,−z, −angle).

This means that you must not assume that the particular values you choose for the axis and angle to represent a rotation will be preserved by a browser. For example, a browser may read in an SFRotation value of (1,0,0,0), but may write the value back out (or return it to a **Script** node) as (0,0,1,0). They are equivalent rotations, but if you were expecting to get exactly the same axis and angle, you will be surprised.

Also note that these fields cannot store multiple rotations about an axis, for exactly the same reason: A rotation (x,y,z, angle) is the same as (x,y,z, i×2π×angle), for any positive or negative integer i.

4.9 SFString and MFString

The SFString and MFString fields and events contain strings formatted with the UTF-8 universal character set (ISO/IEC 10646-1:1993, `http://www.iso.ch/cate/d18741.html`). The SFString defines a single string and the MFString defines zero or more strings. Strings are specified as a sequence of UTF-8 octets enclosed in double quotes (e.g., "string").

Due to the drastic changes in Korean Jamo language, the character set of the UTF-8 will be based on ISO 10646-1:1993 plus pDAM 1–5 (including the Korean changes). The text strings are stored in visual order.

Any characters (including newlines and #) may appear within the quotes. To include a double quote character within the string, precede it with a backslash. To include a backslash character within the string, type two backslashes. For example

```
fooString [ "One, Two, Three", "He said, \"Immel did it!\"" ]
```

is an MFString field, *fooString*, with two valid strings.

The initial value of an SFString eventOut is `""`. The initial value of an MFRotation eventOut is [ ].

4.10 SFTime and MFTime

The SFTime field and event define a single time value, and the MFTime field and event define zero or more time values. Time values are specified as a double-precision floating point number in the ANSI C floating point format. Time values are specified as the number of seconds from a specific time origin. Typically, SFTime fields and events represent the number of seconds since January 1, 1970, 00:00:00 GMT.

The initial value of an SFTime eventOut is −1. The initial value of an MFTime eventOut is [ ].

DESIGN NOTE

Time must be written as double-precision values to represent absolute times accurately that are 20 years past the time origin. About 800 million seconds have elapsed since 1970, so an accuracy of one part in 800 million (about 1e-9) is required to represent absolute times in the present with one-second accuracy—beyond the seven digit accuracy given by single-precision floating points.

4.11 SFVec2f and MFVec2f

An SFVec2f field or event specifies one 2D vector. An MFVec2f field or event defines zero or more 2D vectors. SFVec2fs and MFVec2fs are specified as a pair of floating point values separated by whitespace. For example

```
fooVec2f [ 42 666, 7, 94 ]
```

is an MFVec2f field, *fooVec2f*, with two valid vectors.

The initial value of an SFVec2f eventOut is (0,0). The initial value of an MFVec2f eventOut is [ ].

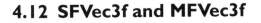

4.12 SFVec3f and MFVec3f

An SFVec3f field or event defines one 3D vector. An MFVec3f field or event defines zero or more 3D vectors. SFVec3fs and MFVec3fs are specified as three floating point values separated by whitespace. For example

```
fooVec3f [ 1 42 666, 7, 94, 0 ]
```

is an MFVec3f field, *fooVec3f*, with two valid vectors.

The initial value of an SFVec3f eventOut is (0,0,0). The initial value of an MFVec3f eventOut is [ ].

Conformance and Minimum Support Requirements

CHAPTER 5

This chapter includes the VRML 2.0 conformance guidelines. These specifications define the minimum feature set that all VRML applications must support. This information is useful to both implementors and authors.

5.1 Introduction

5.1.1 Objectives

This chapter addresses conformance of VRML files, VRML generators, and VRML browsers. The primary objectives of the specifications in this chapter are

1. To promote interoperability by eliminating arbitrary subsets of or extensions to VRML

2. To promote uniformity in the development of conformance tests

3. To facilitate automated test generation

TIP

> This chapter is mostly intended for those writing VRML browsers and authoring systems. However, the details described provide a good idea of what features a user can expect to find in *all* browsers. If you are creating VRML files and wish to ensure that they run on as many browsers as possible, use only the features described (and avoid features that are allowed to be "ignored").

5.1.2 Scope

Conformance is defined for VRML files and for VRML browsers. For VRML generators, guidelines are presented for enhancing the likelihood of successful interoperability.

A concept of *basic conformance* is defined to ensure interoperability of VRML generators and VRML browsers. Basic conformance is based on a set of limits and minimal requirements. Basic conformance is intended to provide a functional level of reasonable utility for VRML generators while limiting the complexity and resource requirements of VRML browsers. Basic conformance may not be adequate for all uses of VRML.

This chapter addresses the VRML data stream and implementation requirements. Implementation requirements include the latitude allowed for VRML generators and VRML browsers. This chapter does not directly address the environmental, performance, or resource requirements of the generator or browser.

This chapter does not define the application requirements or dictate application functional content within a VRML file.

The scope of this chapter is limited to rules for the open interchange of VRML content.

5.2 Conformance

5.2.1 Conformance of VRML Files

A VRML file is syntactically correct according to the VRML specification if the following conditions are met:

1. The VRML file contains as its first element a VRML header comment (see Section 2.1.1, Syntax Basics)

2. All entities contained therein match the functional specification of the corresponding entities of VRML 2.0 (The VRML file shall obey the relationships defined in the formal grammar and all other syntactic requirements.)

3. The sequence of entities in the VRML file obeys the relationships specified in the VRML specification producing the structure specified in the specification

4. All field values in the VRML file obey the relationships specified in the VRML specification producing the structure specified in the VRML specification

5. No nodes appear in the VRML file other than those specified in the VRML specification unless required for the encoding technique or those defined by the PROTO or EXTERNPROTO entities

6. The VRML file is encoded according to the rules of the VRML specification

A VRML file is basic conforming if

1. It is syntactically correct

2. It meets the restrictions of Table 5-1

5.2.2 Conformance of VRML Generators

Unlike VRML files and VRML browsers, conformance of VRML generators is not specifically defined. However, the probability of successful interoperability of a VRML generator with basic conforming VRML browsers (see Section 5.2.3, Conformance of VRML Browsers) is significantly improved if the generator is capable of operating in a mode of generating only basic conforming VRML files.

5.2.3 Conformance of VRML Browsers

A VRML browser is basic conforming if

1. It is able to read any basic conforming VRML file

2. It presents the graphical and audio characteristics of the VRML nodes in any basic conforming VRML file, within the latitude defined in this chapter

3. It correctly handles user interaction and generation of events as specified in the VRML specification, within the latitude defined in this chapter

4. It satisfies the requirements of Section 5.3.2, Minimum Support Requirements for Browsers

5.3 Specific Support Requirements

5.3.1 Minimum Support Requirements for Generators

There is no minimum complexity that is required of or appropriate for VRML generators. Any compliant set of nodes may be generated of arbitrary complexity, as appropriate, to represent application content.

DESIGN NOTE

The easiest way to test your generator (i.e., authoring system) is to read the VRML output into the most conforming VRML browsers that are available.

5.3.2 Minimum Support Requirements for Browsers

This section defines the minimum complexity that must be supported by a VRML browser. Browser implementations may choose to support greater limits but may not reduce the limits described in Table 5-1. When the VRML file contains nodes that exceed the limits implemented by the browser, the results are undefined. Where latitude is specified in Table 5-1 for a particular node, full support is required for other aspects of that node.

5.3.3 Basic Conforming VRML Requirements

In Table 5-1, the first column defines the item for which conformance is being defined. In some cases, general limits are defined, but are overridden in specific cases by more restrictive limits. The second column defines the requirements for a basic conforming VRML file. If a file contains any items that exceed these limits, it may not be possible for a basic conforming VRML browser to parse that file successfully. The third column defines the minimum complexity for a VRML scene that a basic conforming VRML browser must be able to present to the user. The word *ignore* in the minimum browser support column refers only to the display of the item. In particular, *set_* events to ignored exposedFields must still generate corresponding *_changed* events.

TABLE 5-1 *Basic, conforming VRML specifications*

Item (node/field/ statement)	File limit	Minimum browser support
All groups	500 children	500 children; ignore *bboxCenter* and *bboxSize*
All interpolators	1,000 key value pairs	1,000 key value pairs
All lights	8 simultaneous lights	8 simultaneous lights
Names for DEF/PROTO/field	50 utf8 octets	50 UTF-8 octets
All URL fields	10 URLs	10 URLs; URNs ignored
PROTO/EXTERNPROTO	30 fields, 30 eventIns, 30 eventOuts, 30 exposedFields	30 fields, 30 eventIns, 30 eventOuts, 30 exposedFields
PROTO definition nesting depth	5 levels	5 levels
SFBool	No restrictions	Full support
SFColor	No restrictions	Full support
SFFloat	No restrictions	Full support
SFImage	256 width; 256 height	256 width; 256 height
SFInt32	No restrictions	Full support
SFNode	No restrictions	Full support
SFRotation	No restrictions	Full support
SFString	30,000 utf8 octets	30,000 utf8 octets
SFTime	No restrictions	Full support
SFVec2f	15,000 values	15,000 values
SFVec3f	15,000 values	15,000 values
MFColor	15,000 values	15,000 values
MFFloat	1,000 values	1,000 values
MFInt32	20,000 values	20,000 values
MFNode	500 values	500 values
MFRotation	1,000 values	1,000 values

TABLE 5-1 *Basic, conforming VRML specifications (Continued)*

Item (node/field/statement)	File limit	Minimum browser support
MFString	30,000 utf8 octets per string; 10 strings	30,000 utf8 octets per string; 10 strings
MFTime	1,000 values	1,000 values
MFVec2f	15,000 values	15,000 values
MFVec3f	15,000 values	15,000 values
Anchor	No restrictions	Ignore parameter; ignore description
Appearance	No restrictions	Full support
AudioClip	30-second uncompressed PCM WAV	30-second uncompressed PCM WAV; ignore description
Background	No restrictions	One *skyColor;* one *groundColor;* panoramicimages as per **ImageTexture**
Billboard	Restrictions as for all groups	Full support except as for all groups
Box	No restrictions	Full support
Collision	Restrictions as for all groups	Full support except as for all groups; any navigation behavior acceptable when collision occurs
Color	15,000 colors	15,000 colors
ColorInterpolator	Restrictions as for all interpolators	Full support except as for all interpolators
Cone	No restrictions	Full support
Coordinate	15,000 points	15,000 points
CoordinateInterpolator	15,000 coordinates per *keyValue;* restrictions as for all interpolators	15,000 coordinates per *keyValue;* support except as for all interpolators
Cylinder	No restrictions	Full support
CylinderSensor	No restrictions	Full support
DirectionalLight	No restrictions	Not scoped by parent **Group** or **Transform**
ElevationGrid	16,000 heights	16,000 heights

TABLE 5-1 *Basic, conforming VRML specifications (Continued)*

Item (node/field/ statement)	File limit	Minimum browser support
Extrusion	(*#crossSection* points) × (*#spine* points) ≤2,500	(*#crossSection* points) × (*#spine* points) ≤2,500
Fog	No restrictions	EXPONENTIAL treated as LINEAR
FontStyle	No restrictions	If the values of the text aspects character set, family, and *style* cannot be simultaneously supported, the order of precedence shall be character set, *family,* and *style;* browser must display all characters in ISO 8859-1 character set
Group	Restrictions as for all groups	Full support except as for all groups
ImageTexture	JPEG and PNG format; restrictions as for **PixelTexture**	JPEG and PNG format; support as for **PixelTexture**
IndexedFaceSet	10 vertices per face; 5,000 faces; 15,000 indices in any index field	10 vertices per face; 5,000 faces; 15,000 indices in any index field
IndexedLineSet	15,000 total vertices; 15,000 indices in any index field	15,000 total vertices; 15,000 indices in any index field
Inline	No restrictions	Full support except as for all groups
LOD	Restrictions as for all groups	At least first four-*level/range* pairs interpreted, and support as for all groups; implementations may disregard *level* distances
Material	No restrictions	Ignore *ambientIntensity;* ignore *specularColor;* ignore *emissiveColor;* One-bit transparency; *transparency* values ≥0.5 transparent
MovieTexture	MPEG1-Systems and MPEG1-Video formats	MPEG1-Systems and MPEG1-Video formats; display one active movie texture; ignore *speed* field
NavigationInfo	No restrictions	Ignore *avatarSize;* ignore *visibilityLimit*
Normal	15,000 normals	15,000 normals
NormalInterpolator	15,000 normals per *keyValue;* restrictions as for all interpolators	15,000 normals per *keyValue;* support as for all interpolators

TABLE 5-1 *Basic, conforming VRML specifications (Continued)*

Item (node/field/ statement)	File limit	Minimum browser support
OrientationInterpolator	Restrictions as for all interpolators	Full support except as for all interpolators
PixelTexture	256 width; 256 height	256 width; 256 height; display fully transparent and fully opaque pixels
PlaneSensor	No restrictions	Full support
PointLight	No restrictions	Ignore *radius*; linear attenuation
PointSet	5,000 points	5,000 points
PositionInterpolator	Restrictions as for all interpolators	Full support except as for all interpolators
ProximitySensor	No restrictions	Full support
ScalarInterpolator	Restrictions as for all interpolators	Full support except as for all interpolators
Script	25 eventIns; 25 eventOuts; 25 fields	25 eventIns; 25 eventOuts; 25 fields
Shape	No restrictions	Full support
Sound	No restrictions	2 active sounds; linear distance attenuation; no spatialization
Sphere	No restrictions	Full support
SphereSensor	No restrictions	Full support
SpotLight	No restrictions	Ignore *beamWidth*; ignore *radius*; linear attenuation.
Switch	Restrictions as for all groups	Full support except as for all groups
Text	100 characters per string; 100 strings	100 characters per string; 100 strings
TextureCoordinate	15,000 coordinates	15,000 coordinates
TextureTransform	No restrictions	Full support
TimeSensor	No restrictions	Ignored if *cycleInterval* <0.01
TouchSensor	No restrictions	Full support

TABLE 5-1 *Basic, conforming VRML specifications (Continued)*

Item (node/field/statement)	File limit	Minimum browser support
Transform	Restrictions as for all groups	Full support except as for all groups
Viewpoint	No restrictions	Ignore *fieldOfView;* ignore *description*
VisibilitySensor	No restrictions	Always visible
WorldInfo	No restrictions	Full support

VRML Grammar Definition   APPENDIX A

This appendix provides a detailed definition of grammar rules for VRML syntax. It begins with a brief introduction and follows with specific grammar rules for general syntax, nodes, and fields and events.

A.1 Introduction

It is not possible to parse VRML files using context-free grammar. Semantic knowledge of the names and types of fields, eventIns, and eventOuts for each node type (either built in or user defined using PROTO or EXTERNPROTO) shall be used during parsing so that the parser knows which field type is being parsed.

The # (0x23) character begins a comment wherever it appears outside quoted SFString or MFString fields. The # character and all characters until the next carriage return or linefeed comprise the comment and are treated as whitespace.

The carriage return (0x0d), linefeed (0x0a), space (0x20), tab (0x09), and comma (0x2c) characters are whitespace characters wherever they appear outside quoted SFString or MFString fields. Any number of whitespace characters and comments may be used to separate the syntactic entities of a VRML file. All reserved keywords are displayed in bold type.

Chapter 3, Node Reference, contains a description of the allowed fields, eventIns, and eventOuts for all predefined node types. Some of the basic types that typically will be handled by a lexical analyzer (sffloatValue, sftimeValue, sfint32Value, and sfstringValue) have not been formally specified. Chapter 4, Field and Event Reference, contains a more complete description of their syntax.

The following conventions are used in the context-free grammar specified in this clause:

- Terminal symbols, which appear literally in the VRML file, are specified in bold type.

- Nonterminal symbols used in the grammar are specified in italic type.

- Production rules begin with a nonterminal symbol and the sequence of characters ::= and end with a semicolon (;).

- Alternation for production rules is specified using the vertical bar symbol (|).

A.2 General

The following grammar definitions specify the top-level rules for parsing VRML files:

```
vrmlScene ::=
    statements ;
statements ::=
    statement |
    statement statements |
    empty ;
statement ::=
    nodeStatement |
    protoStatement |
    routeStatement ;
nodeStatement ::=
    node |
    DEF nodeNameId node |
    USE nodeNameId ;
protoStatement ::=
    proto |
    externproto ;
protoStatements ::=
    protoStatement |
    protoStatement protoStatements |
    empty ;
```

```
proto ::=
     PROTO nodeTypeId [ interfaceDeclarations ] { protoBody } ;
protoBody ::=
     protoStatements node statements ;
interfaceDeclarations ::=
     interfaceDeclaration |
     interfaceDeclaration interfaceDeclarations |
     empty ;
restrictedInterfaceDeclaration ::=
     eventIn fieldType eventInId |
     eventOut fieldType eventOutId |
     field fieldType fieldId fieldValue ;
interfaceDeclaration ::=
     restrictedInterfaceDeclaration |
     exposedField fieldType fieldId fieldValue ;
externproto ::=
     EXTERNPROTO nodeTypeId [ externInterfaceDeclarations ]
     URLList ;
externInterfaceDeclarations ::=
     externInterfaceDeclaration |
     externInterfaceDeclaration externInterfaceDeclarations |
     empty ;
externInterfaceDeclaration ::=
     eventIn fieldType eventInId |
     eventOut fieldType eventOutId |
     field fieldType fieldId |
     exposedField fieldType fieldId ;
routeStatement ::=
     ROUTE nodeNameId . eventOutId TO nodeNameId . eventInId ;
URLList ::=
     mfstringValue ;
empty ::=
     ;
```

A.3 Nodes

The following grammar definitions specify the rules for parsing nodes:

```
node ::=
     nodeTypeId { nodeBody } |
     Script { scriptBody } ;
nodeBody ::=
     nodeBodyElement |
     nodeBodyElement nodeBody |
     empty ;
```

```
scriptBody ::=
    scriptBodyElement |
    scriptBodyElement scriptBody |
    empty ;
scriptBodyElement ::=
    nodeBodyElement |
    restrictedInterfaceDeclaration |
    eventIn fieldType eventInId IS eventInId |
    eventOut fieldType eventOutId IS eventOutId |
    field fieldType fieldId IS fieldId ;
nodeBodyElement ::=
    fieldId fieldValue |
    fieldId IS fieldId |
    eventInId IS eventInId |
    eventOutId IS eventOutId |
    routeStatement |
    protoStatement ;
nodeNameId ::=
    Id ;
nodeTypeId ::=
    Id ;
fieldId ::=
    Id ;
eventInId ::=
    Id ;
eventOutId ::=
    Id ;
Id ::=
    IdFirstChar |
    IdFirstChar IdRestChars ;
IdFirstChar ::=
    Any ISO-10646 character encoded using UTF-8 except: 0x30
    0x39, 0x0-0x20, 0x22, 0x23, 0x27, 0x2c, 0x2e, 0x5b, 0x5c,
    0x5d, 0x7b, 0x7d.
IdRestChars ::=
    Any number of ISO-10646 characters except: 0x0-0x20, 0x22,
    0x23, 0x27, 0x2c, 0x2e, 0x5b, 0x5c, 0x5d, 0x7b, 0x7d.
```

A.4 Fields and Events

The following grammar definitions specify the rules for parsing fields and events:

```
fieldType ::=
    MFColor |
    MFFloat |
```

```
            MFInt32 |
            MFNode |
            MFRotation |
            MFString |
            MFTime |
            MFVec2f |
            MFVec3f |
            SFBool |
            SFColor |
            SFFloat |
            SFImage |
            SFInt32 |
            SFNode |
            SFRotation |
            SFString |
            SFTime |
            SFVec2f |
            SFVec3f ;
fieldValue ::=
            sfboolValue |
            sfcolorValue |
            sffloatValue |
            sfimageValue |
            sfint32Value |
            sfnodeValue |
            sfrotationValue |
            sfstringValue |
            sftimeValue |
            sfvec2fValue |
            sfvec3fValue |
            mfcolorValue |
            mffloatValue |
            mfint32Value |
            mfnodeValue |
            mfrotationValue |
            mfstringValue |
            mftimeValue |
            mfvec2fValue |
            mfvec3fValue ;
sfboolValue ::=
            TRUE |
            FALSE ;
sfcolorValue ::=
            float float float ;
sffloatValue ::=
            ... floating point number in ANSI C floating point format
```

```
sfimageValue ::=
    int32 int32 int32 int32 ...
sfint32Value ::=
    [0-9]+ |
    0x[0-9A-F]+ ;
sfnodeValue ::=
    nodeStatement |
    NULL ;
sfrotationValue ::=
    float float float float ;
sfstringValue ::=
    ".*" ... double-quotes must be \", backslashes must be \\
sftimeValue ::=
    ... double-precision number in ANSI C floating point format
mftimeValue ::=
    sftimeValue |
    [ ] |
    [ sftimeValues ] ;
sftimeValues ::=
    sftimeValue |
    sftimeValue sftimeValues ;
sfvec2fValue ::=
    float float ;
sfvec3fValue ::=
    float float float ;
mfcolorValue ::=
    sfcolorValue |
    [ ] |
    [ sfcolorValues ] ;
sfcolorValues ::=
    sfcolorValue |
    sfcolorValue sfcolorValues ;
mffloatValue ::=
    sffloatValue |
    [ ] |
    [ sffloatValues ] ;
sffloatValues ::=
    sffloatValue |
    sffloatValue sffloatValues ;
mfint32Value ::=
    sfint32Value |
    [ ] |
    [ sfint32Values ] ;
sfint32Values ::=
    sfint32Value |
    sfint32Value sfint32Values ;
```

```
mfnodeValue ::=
     nodeStatement |
     [ ] |
     [ nodeStatements ] ;
nodeStatements ::=
     nodeStatement |
     nodeStatement nodeStatements ;
mfrotationValue ::=
     sfrotationValue |
     [ ] |
     [ sfrotationValues ] ;
sfrotationValues ::=
     sfrotationValue |
     sfrotationValue sfrotationValues ;
mfstringValue ::=
     sfstringValue |
     [ ] |
     [ sfstringValues ] ;
sfstringValues ::=
     sfstringValue |
     sfstringValue sfstringValues ;
mfvec2fValue ::=
     sfvec2fValue |
     [ ] |
     [ sfvec2fValues] ;
sfvec2fValues ::=
     sfvec2fValue |
     sfvec2fValue sfvec2fValues ;
mfvec3fValue ::=
     sfvec3fValue |
     [ ] |
     [ sfvec3fValues ] ;
sfvec3fValues ::=
     sfvec3fValue |
     sfvec3fValue sfvec3fValues ;
```

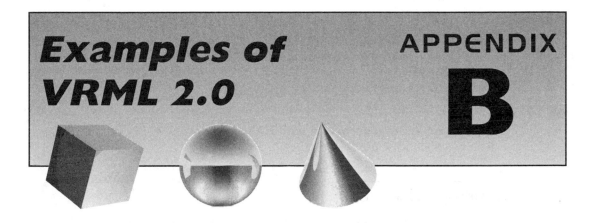

Examples of VRML 2.0

B.1 Simple Example:
"Red Sphere Meets Blue Box"

This file contains a simple scene defining a view of a red sphere and a blue box, lit by a directional light:

```
#VRML V2.0 utf8
Transform {
  children [
    NavigationInfo { headlight FALSE }
    DirectionalLight {        # First child
      direction 0 0 -1        # Light illuminating the scene
    }
    Transform {               # Second child - a red sphere
      translation 3 0 1
      children [
        Shape {
          geometry Sphere { radius 2.3 }
```

```
          appearance Appearance {
            material Material { diffuseColor 1 0 0 }    # Red
          }
        }
      ]
    }
    Transform {                # Third child - a blue box
      translation -2.4 .2 1
      rotation     0 1 1  .9
      children [
        Shape {
          geometry Box {}
          appearance Appearance {
            material Material { diffuseColor 0 0 1 }  # Blue
          }
        }
      ]
    }
  ] # end of children for world
}
```

B.2 Instancing (Sharing)

Reading the following file results in three spheres being drawn. The first sphere defines a unit sphere at the original, named **Joe**, the second sphere defines a smaller sphere translated along the +*x*-axis, and the third sphere is a reference to the second sphere and is translated along the −*x*-axis. If any changes occur to the second sphere (e.g., radius changes), then the third sphere (which is really a reference to the second) will change too:

```
#VRML V2.0 utf8
Transform {
  children [
    DEF Joe Shape { geometry Sphere {} }
    Transform {
      translation 2 0 0
      children DEF Joe Shape { geometry Sphere { radius .2 } }
    }
    Transform {
      translation -2 0 0
      children USE Joe
    }
  ]
}
# Note that the spheres are unlit because no appearance
# was specified.
```

B.3 Prototype Example

A simple chair with variable colors for the legs and seat might be prototyped as

```
#VRML V2.0 utf8
PROTO TwoColorStool [
  field SFColor legColor   .8 .4 .7
  field SFColor seatColor .6 .6 .1 ]
{
  Transform {
    children [
      Transform {   # stool seat
        translation 0 0.6 0
        children
          Shape {
            appearance Appearance {
              material Material { diffuseColor IS seatColor }
            }
            geometry Box { size 1.2 0.2 1.2 }
          }
      }
      Transform {   # first stool leg
        translation -.5 0 -.5
        children
          DEF Leg Shape {
            appearance Appearance {
              material Material { diffuseColor IS legColor }
            }
            geometry Cylinder { height 1 radius .1 }
          }
      }
      Transform {   # another stool leg
        translation .5 0 -.5
        children USE Leg
      }
      Transform {   # another stool leg
        translation -.5 0 .5
        children USE Leg
      }
      Transform {   # another stool leg
        translation .5 0 .5
        children USE Leg
      }
    ] # End of root Transform's children
  } # End of root Transform
} # End of prototype
```

```
# The prototype is now defined.
# Although it contains a number of nodes, only the legColor
# and seatColor fields are public. Instead of using the
# default legColor and seatColor, this instance of the stool
# has red legs and a green seat:

TwoColorStool {
  legColor 1 0 0 seatColor 0 1 0
}
NavigationInfo { type "EXAMINE" }        # Use the Examine viewer
```

B.4 Scripting Example

This **Script** node decides whether or not to open a bank vault given *openVault* and *combinationEntered* messages. To do this, it remembers whether or not the correct combination has been entered. Note that the *openVault* eventIn and the *vaultUnlocked* eventOut are of type SFTime. This is so they can be wired directly to a **TouchSensor** and **TimeSensor**, respectively. The **TimeSensor** can output into an interpolator, which performs an opening door animation:

```
DEF OpenVault Script {
  # Declarations of what's in this Script node:
  eventIn SFTime   openVault
  eventIn SFBool   combinationEntered
  eventOut SFTime vaultUnlocked
  field SFBool     unlocked FALSE

  # Implementation of the logic:
  url "javascript:
    function combinationEntered(value) { unlocked = value; }
    function openVault(value) {
      if (unlocked) vaultUnlocked = value;
    }"
}
```

B.5 Geometric Properties

The following **IndexedFaceSet** (contained in a **Shape** node) uses all four of the geometric property nodes to specify vertex coordinates, colors per vertex, normals per vertex, and texture coordinates per vertex (note that the **Material** sets the overall transparency):

```
Shape {
  geometry IndexedFaceSet {
```

```
      coordIndex [ 0, 1, 3, -1, 0, 2, 5, -1, ...]
      coord Coordinate { point [ 0.0 5.0 3.0, ...] }
      color Color { rgb [ 0.2 0.7 0.8, ...] }
      normal Normal { vector [ 0.0 1.0 0.0, ...] }
      texCoord TextureCoordinate { point [ 0 1.0, ...] }
  }
  appearance Appearance {
    material Material { transparency 0.5 }
  }
}
```

B.6 Transforms and Leaves

This example has two parts. The first is an example of a simple VRML 1.0 scene. It contains a red cone, a blue sphere, and a green cylinder with a hierarchical transformation structure. The second part is the same example using the VRML 2.0 **Transforms** and leaves syntax.

```
#VRML V1.0 ascii
Separator {
  Transform {
    translation 0 2 0
  }
  Material {
    diffuseColor 1 0 0
  }
  Cone { }

  Separator {
    Transform {
      scaleFactor 2 2 2
    }
    Material {
      diffuseColor 0 0 1
    }
    Sphere { }

    Transform {
      translation 2 0 0
    }
    Material {
      diffuseColor 0 1 0
    }
    Cylinder { }
  }
}
```

```
#VRML V2.0 utf8
Transform {
  translation 0 2 0
  children [
    Shape {
      appearance Appearance {
        material Material {
          diffuseColor 1 0 0
        }
      }
      geometry Cone { }
    }
    Transform {
      scale 2 2 2
      children [
        Shape {
          appearance Appearance {
            material Material {
              diffuseColor 0 0 1
            }
          }
          geometry Sphere { }
        }
        Transform {
          translation 2 0 0
          children [
            Shape {
              appearance Appearance {
                material Material {
                  diffuseColor 0 1 0
                }
              }
              geometry Cylinder { }
            }
          ]
        }
      ]
    }
  ]
}
```

Note that the default **Viewpoint** will not have the objects centered in the view.

B.7 Transform

Here is an example that illustrates the order in which the elements of a **Transform** are applied:

```
Transform {
  translation T1
  rotation R1
  scale S
  scaleOrientation R2
  center T2
  ...
}
```

The previous syntax is equivalent to the nested sequence of

```
Transform { translation T1
 children [ Transform { translation T2
  children [ Transform { rotation R1
   children [ Transform { rotation R2
    children [ Transform { scale S
     children [ Transform { rotation -R2
      children [ Transform { translation -T2
              ...
    }]
   }]
  }]
 }]
 }]
 }]
}
```

B.8 Prototypes and Alternate Representations

VRML 2.0 has the capability to define new nodes. VRML 1.0 had the ability to add nodes using the *fields* field and *isA* keyword. The prototype feature can duplicate all the features of the 1.0 node definition capabilities. Take the example of a **Refractive-Material.** This is just like a **Material** node, but it adds an *indexOfRefraction* field. This field can be ignored if the browser cannot render refraction. In VRML 1.0, this would be specified as

```
...
RefractiveMaterial {
```

```
  fields [
    SFColor ambientColor, MFColor diffuseColor,
    SFColor specularColor, MFColor emissiveColor,
    SFFloat shininess, MFFloat transparency,
    SFFloat indexOfRefraction, MFString isA ]
  isA "Material"
}
```

If the browser had been hard coded to understand a **RefractiveMaterial**, the *index-OfRefraction* would be used; otherwise, it would be ignored and **RefractiveMaterial** would behave just like a **Material** node. In VRML 2.0, this would be specified as

```
...
PROTO RefractiveMaterial [
  field SFFloat ambientIntensity 0
  field MFColor diffuseColor 0.5 0.5 0.5
  field SFColor specularColor 0 0 0
  field MFColor emissiveColor 0 0 0
  field SFFloat shininess 0
  field MFFloat transparency 0 0 0
  field SFFloat indexOfRefraction 0.1 ]
{
  Material {
    ambientIntensity IS ambientIntensity
    diffuseColor IS diffuseColor
    specularColor IS specularColor
    emissiveColor IS emissiveColor
    shininess IS shininess
    transparency IS transparency
  }
}
```

While this is more wordy, notice that the default values were given in the proto-type. These are different than the defaults for the standard **Material.** So this allows you to change defaults on a standard node. The EXTERNPROTO capability allows the use of alternative implementations of a node:

```
...
EXTERNPROTO RefractiveMaterial [
  field SFFloat ambientIntensity
  field MFColor diffuseColor
  field SFColor specularColor
  field MFColor emissiveColor
  field SFFloat shininess
  field MFFloat transparency
  field SFFloat indexOfRefraction ]
[ http://www.myCompany.com/vrmlNodes/RefractiveMaterial.wrl,
  http://somewhere.else/MyRefractiveMaterial.wrl ]
```

This will choose from one of three possible sources of **RefractiveMaterial.** If the browser has this node hard coded, it will be used. Otherwise the first URL will be requested and a prototype of the node will used from there. If that fails, the second will be tried.

B.9 Anchor

The target parameter is used by the **Anchor** node to send a request to load a URL into another frame:

```
Anchor {
  url "http://somehost/somefile.html"
  parameter [ "target=name_of_frame" ]
  ...
}
```

An **Anchor** may be used to bind the viewer to a particular viewpoint in a virtual world by specifying a URL ending with #ViewpointName, where ViewpointName is the DEF name of a viewpoint defined in the world. For example

```
Anchor {
  url "http://www.school.edu/vrml/someScene.wrl#OverView"
  children Shape { geometry Box {} }
}
```

specifies an **Anchor** that puts the viewer in the someScene world bound to the **Viewpoint** named OverView when the **Box** is chosen (note that OverView is the name of the **Viewpoint,** not the value of the **Viewpoint'**s *description* field). If no world is specified, then the current scene is implied. For example

```
Anchor {
  url "#Doorway"
  children Shape { Sphere {} }
}
```

binds you to the **Viewpoint** with the DEF name Doorway in the current scene.

B.10 Directional Light

A directional light source illuminates only the objects in its enclosing grouping node. The light illuminates everything within this coordinate system, including the objects that precede it in the scene graph. For example:

```
Transform {
  children [
```

```
      DEF UnlitShapeOne Shape { ... }
      DEF LitParent Transform {
        children [
          DEF LitShapeOne Shape { ... }
          # Lights the shapes under LitParent
          DirectionalLight { .... }
          DEF LitShapeTwo Shape { ... }
        ]
      }
      DEF UnlitShapeTwo Shape { ... }
    ]
}
```

B.11 PointSet

This simple example defines a **PointSet** composed of three points. The first point is red (1,0,0), the second point is green (0,1,0), and the third point is blue (0,0,1). The second **PointSet** instances the **Coordinate** node defined in the first **PointSet**, but defines different colors:

```
Shape {
  geometry PointSet {
    coord DEF mypts Coordinate {
      point [ 0 0 0, 2 2 2, 3 3 3 ]
    }
    color Color { color [ 1 0 0, 0 1 0, 0 0 1 ] }
  }
}
Shape {
  geometry PointSet {
    coord USE mypts
    color Color { color [ .5 .5 0, 0 .5 .5, 1 1 1 ] }
  }
}
```

B.12 Level of Detail

The **LOD** node is typically used for switching between different versions of geometry at specified distances from the viewer. However, if the *range* field is left at its default value, the browser selects the most appropriate child from the list. It can make this selection based on performance or perceived importance of the object. Children should be listed with the most detailed version first, just as for the normal case. This performance LOD feature can be combined with the normal **LOD** function to give the browser a selection of children from which to choose at each distance.

In this example, the browser is free to choose either a detailed or a less detailed version of the object when the viewer is closer than 100 m (as measured in the coordinate space of the **LOD**). The browser should display the less detailed version of the object if the viewer is between 100 and 1,000 m, and should display nothing at all if the viewer is farther than 1,000 m. Browsers should try to honor the hints given by authors, and authors should try to give browsers as much freedom as they can to choose levels of detail based on performance.

```
LOD {
  range [100, 1000]
  level [
    LOD {
      level [
        Transform { ... detailed version... }
        DEF LoRes Transform { ... less detailed version... }
      ]
    }
    USE LoRes,
    WorldInfo { } # Display nothing
  ]
}
```

For best results, specify ranges only where necessary, and nest **LOD** nodes with and without ranges.

B.13 ColorInterpolator

This example interpolates from red to green to blue in a ten-second cycle:

```
DEF myColor ColorInterpolator {
  key [ 0.0, 0.5, 1.0 ]
  keyValue [ 1 0 0, 0 1 0, 0 0 1 ] # red, green, blue
}
DEF myClock TimeSensor {
  cycleInterval 10.0      # 10 second animation
  loop           TRUE     # infinitely cycling animation
}
ROUTE myClock.fraction_changed TO myColor.set_fraction
```

B.14 TimeSensor

The **TimeSensor** is very flexible. Here are some of the many ways in which it can be used:

- A **TimeSensor** can be triggered to run continuously by setting *cycleInterval* > 0 and *loop* = TRUE, and then routing a time output from another node that triggers the loop (e.g., the *touchTime* eventOut of a **TouchSensor** can then be routed to the **TimeSensor**'s *startTime* to start the **TimeSensor** running).

- A **TimeSensor** can be made to run continuously on reading by setting *cycleInterval* > 0, *startTime* > 0, *stopTime* = 0, and *loop* = TRUE.

Here are three examples of **TimeSensor**:

1. Animate a box when the user clicks on it:

```
DEF XForm Transform { children [
  Shape { geometry Box {} }
  DEF Clicker TouchSensor {}
  DEF TimeSource TimeSensor { cycleInterval 2.0 } # Run once 2s
  # Animate one full turn about Y axis:
  DEF Animation OrientationInterpolator {
    key      [ 0,      .33,       .66,        1.0 ]
    keyValue [ 0 1 0 0, 0 1 0 2.1, 0 1 0 4.2, 0 1 0 0 ]
  }
]}
ROUTE Clicker.touchTime TO TimeSource.startTime
ROUTE TimeSource.fraction_changed TO Animation.set_fraction
ROUTE Animation.value_changed TO XForm.rotation
```

2. Play "Westminster Chimes" once an hour:

```
#VRML V2.0 utf8
Group { children [
  DEF Hour TimeSensor {
    loop           TRUE
    cycleInterval 3600.0    # 60*60 seconds == 1 hour
  }
  Sound {
    source DEF Sounder AudioClip {
      url "http://...../westminster.mid" }
  }
}
]}
ROUTE Hour.cycleTime TO Sounder.startTime
```

3. Make a grunting noise when the user runs into a wall:

```
#VRML V2.0 utf8
DEF Walls Collision { children [
  Transform {
    #... geometry of walls...
  }
  Sound {
    source DEF Grunt AudioClip {
      url "http://...../grunt.wav"
    }
  }
]}
ROUTE Walls.collideTime TO Grunt.startTime
```

B.15 Shuttles and Pendulums

Shuttles and pendulums are great building blocks for composing interesting animations. This shuttle translates its children back and forth along the *x*-axis from −1 to 1. The pendulum rotates its children about the *y*-axis from 0 to 3.14159 radians and back again.

```
PROTO Shuttle [
  exposedField SFBool enabled TRUE
  field SFFloat rate 1
  eventIn SFBool moveRight
  eventOut SFBool isAtLeft
  field MFNode children [] ]
{
  DEF F Transform { children IS children }
  DEF T TimeSensor {
    cycleInterval IS rate
    enabled IS enabled
  }
  DEF S Script {
    eventIn   SFBool   enabled IS set_enabled
    field     SFFloat  rate IS rate
    eventIn   SFBool   moveRight IS moveRight
    eventIn   SFBool   isActive
    eventOut  SFBool   isAtLeft IS isAtLeft
    eventOut  SFTime   start
    eventOut  SFTime   stop
    field     SFNode   timeSensor USE T
    url "javascript:
      // constructor: send initial isAtLeft eventOut
```

```
              function initialize() {
                isAtLeft = true;
              }
              function moveRight(move, ts) {
                if (move) {
                  // want to start move right
                  start = ts;
                  stop = ts + rate / 2;
                }
                else {
                  // want to start move left
                  start = ts - rate / 2;
                  stop = ts + rate / 2;
                }
              }
              function isActive(active) {
                if (!active) isAtLeft = !moveRight;
              }
              function set_enabled(value, ts) {
                if (value) {
                  // continue from where we left off
                  start = ts - (timeSensor.stopTime - start);
                  stop  = ts - (timeSensor.stopTime - stop);
                }
              }"
          }
          DEF I PositionInterpolator {
            key [ 0, 0.5, 1 ]
            value [ -1 0 0, 1 0 0, -1 0 0 ]
          }
          ROUTE T.fraction_changed TO I.set_fraction
          ROUTE T.isActive TO S.isActive
          ROUTE I.value_changed TO F.set_translation
          ROUTE S.start TO T.set_startTime
          ROUTE S.stop TO T.set_stopTime
      }
      PROTO Pendulum [
        exposedField SFBool enabled TRUE
        field SFFloat rate 1
        field SFFloat maxAngle
        eventIn SFBool moveCCW
        eventOut SFBool isAtCW
        field MFNode children [] ]
      {
        DEF F Transform { children IS children }
```

```
DEF T TimeSensor {
  cycleInterval IS rate
  enabled IS enabled
}
DEF S Script {
  eventIn   SFBool     enabled IS set_enabled
  field     SFFloat    rate IS rate
  field     SFFloat    maxAngle IS maxAngle
  eventIn   SFBool     moveCCW IS moveCCW
  eventIn   SFBool     isActive
  eventOut  SFBool     isAtCW IS isAtCW
  eventOut  SFTime     start
  eventOut  SFTime     stop
  eventOut  MFRotation rotation
  field     SFNode     timeSensor USE T
  url "javascript:
    function initialize() {
      // constructor:setup interpolator,
      // send initial isAtCW eventOut
      isAtCW = true;
      rot[0] = 0; rot[1] = 1; rot[2] = 0;
      rot[3] = 0;
      rotation[0] = rot;
      rotation[2] = rot;
      rot[3] = maxAngle;
      rotation[1] = rot;
    }
    function moveCCW(move, ts) {
      if (move) {
        // want to start CCW half (0.0 - 0.5) of move
        start = ts;
        stop = start + rate / 2;
      }
      else {
        // want to start CW half (0.5 - 1.0) of move
        start = ts - rate / 2;
        stop = ts + rate / 2;
      }
    }
    function isActive(active) {
      if (!active) isAtCW = !moveCCW;
    }
    function set_enabled(value, ts) {
      if (value) {
        // continue from where we left off
        start = ts - (timeSensor.stopTime - start);
```

```
                    stop  = ts - (timeSensor.stopTime - stop);
                }
            }"
    }
    DEF I OrientationInterpolator {
      key [ 0, 0.5, 1 ]
    }
    ROUTE T.fraction_changed TO I.set_fraction
    ROUTE I.value_changed TO F.set_rotation
    ROUTE T.isActive TO S.isActive
    ROUTE S.start TO T.set_startTime
    ROUTE S.stop TO T.set_stopTime
    ROUTE S.rotation TO I.set_keyValue
}
```

In use, the **Shuttle** can have its *isAtRight* output wired to its *moveLeft* input to give a continuous shuttle. The **Pendulum** can have its *isAtCw* output wired to its *moveCCW* input to give a continuous **Pendulum** effect.

B.16 Robot

Here's a simple implementation of a robot. This robot has very simple body parts: a cube for his head, a sphere for his body, and cylinders for arms (it hovers, so it has no feet!). It is something of a sentry—it walks forward, turns around, and walks back. It does this whenever the viewer is near. This makes use of the **Shuttle** and **Pendulum**:

```
DEF Walk Shuttle {
  enabled FALSE
  rate 10
  children [
    DEF Near ProximitySensor { size 10 10 10 }
    DEF Turn Pendulum {
      enabled FALSE
      children [
        # The Robot
        Shape { geometry Box { } } # head
        Transform {
          scale 1 5 1
          translation 0 -5 0
          children Shape { geometry Sphere { } } # body
        }
        DEF Arm Pendulum {
          maxAngle 0.52 # 30 degrees
          enabled FALSE
```

```
          children Transform {
            scale 1 7 1
            translation 1 -5 0
            rotation 1 0 0 4.45 # rotate so swing
                                # centers on Y axis
            center 0 3.5 0
            children Shape { geometry Cylinder { } }
          }
        }
        # duplicate arm on other side and flip so it swings
        # in opposition
        Transform {
          rotation 0 1 0 3.14159
          translation 10 0 0
          children USE Arm
        }
      ]
    }
  ]
}
# Hook up the sentry. The arms will swing indefinitely. It walks
# along the shuttle path, then turns, then walks back, etc.
ROUTE Near.isActive TO Arm.enabled
ROUTE Near.isActive TO Walk.enabled
ROUTE Arm.isAtCW TO Arm.moveCCW
ROUTE Walk.isAtLeft TO Turn.moveCCW
ROUTE Turn.isAtCW TO Walk.moveRight
```

B.17 Chopper

Here is an example of how to do simple animation triggered by a **TouchSensor**. It uses an EXTERNPROTO to include a **Rotor** node from the Net, which will do the actual animation:

```
EXTERNPROTO Rotor [
  eventIn MFFloat Spin
  field MFNode children []
] "http://somewhere/Rotor.wrl"
PROTO Chopper [
  field SFFloat maxAltitude 30
  field SFFloat rotorSpeed 1 ]
{
  Group { children [
    DEF Touch TouchSensor { } # Gotta get touch events
    Shape { ... body... }
```

```
        DEF Top Rotor { ... geometry ... }
        DEF Back Rotor { ... geometry ... }
    ]}
      DEF SCRIPT Script {
        eventIn SFBool startOrStopEngines
        field maxAltitude IS maxAltitude
        field rotorSpeed IS rotorSpeed
        field SFNode topRotor USE Top
        field SFNode backRotor USE Back
        field SFBool bEngineStarted FALSE
        url "chopper.js"
      }
      ROUTE Touch.isActive TO SCRIPT.startOrStopEngines
    }
    DEF MyScene Group {
      DEF MikesChopper Chopper { maxAltitude 40 }
    }
```

chopper.js:

```
function startOrStopEngines(value, ts) {
  // Don't do anything on mouse-down:
  if (value) return;
  // Otherwise, start or stop engines:
  if (!bEngineStarted) { StartEngine(); }
  else { StopEngine(); }
 }
function SpinRotors(fInRotorSpeed, fSeconds) {
  rp[0] = 0;
  rp[1] = fInRotorSpeed;
  rp[2] = 0;
  rp[3] = fSeconds;
  TopRotor.Spin = rp;
  rp[0] = fInRotorSpeed;
  rp[1] = 0;
  rp[2] = 0;
  rp[3] = fSeconds;
  BackRotor.Spin = rp;
}
function StartEngine() {
  // Sound could be done either by controlling a PointSound
  // (put into another SFNode field) OR by adding/removing a
  // PointSound from the Separator (in which case the Separator
  // would need to be passed in an SFNode field).
  SpinRotors(fRotorSpeed, 3);
  bEngineStarted = TRUE;
}
```

```
function StopEngine() {
  SpinRotors(0, 6);
  bEngineStarted = FALSE;
}
```

B.18 Guided Tour

VRML 2.0 has facilities to put the viewer's camera under control of a script. This is useful for things such as guided tours, merry-go-round rides, and transportation devices such as buses and elevators. These next two examples show a couple of ways to use this feature.

The first example is a simple guided tour through the world. On entry, a guide orb hovers in front of you. Click on this and your tour through the world begins. The orb follows you around on your tour. Perhaps a **PointSound** node can be embedded to point out the sights. A **ProximitySensor** ensures that the tour is started only if the user is close to the initial starting point. Note that this is done without scripts thanks to the *touchTime* output of the **TouchSensor**:

```
Group { children [
  # <geometry for the world>
  DEF GuideTransform Transform {
    children [
      DEF TourGuide Viewpoint { jump FALSE }
      DEF ProxSensor ProximitySensor { size 10 10 10 }
      DEF StartTour TouchSensor { }
      Shape { geometry Sphere { } } # the guide orb
    ]
  }
]}
DEF GuidePI PositionInterpolator {
  key [ ... ]
  keyValue [ ... ]
}
DEF GuideRI RotationInterpolator {
  key [ ... ]
  keyValue [ ... ]
}
DEF TS TimeSensor { cycleInterval 60 } # 60 second tour
ROUTE ProxSensor.isActive TO StartTour.enabled
ROUTE StartTour.touchTime TO TS.startTime
ROUTE TS.isActive TO TourGuide.bind
ROUTE TS.fraction TO GuidePI.set_fraction
ROUTE TS.fraction TO GuideRI.set_fraction
ROUTE GuidePI.value_changed TO GuideTransform.set_translation
ROUTE GuideRI.value_changed TO GuideTransform.set_rotation
```

B.19 Elevator

Here's another example of animating the camera. This time the example is an elevator that facilitates access to a multistory building. For this example we'll just show a two-story building and will assume that the elevator is already at the ground floor. To go up, you just step inside. A **ProximitySensor** fires and starts the elevator moving up automatically.

```
Group { children [
  DEF ETransform Transform {
    children [
      DEF EViewpoint Viewpoint { }
      DEF EProximity ProximitySensor { size 2 2 2 }
      # <geometry for the elevator:
      # a unit cube about the origin with a doorway>
    ]
  }
]}
DEF ElevatorPI PositionInterpolator {
  key [ 0, 1 ]
  keyValue [ 0 0 0, 0 4 0 ] # a floor is 4 meters high
}
DEF TS TimeSensor { cycleInterval 10 } # 10 second travel time
DEF S Script {
  field SFNode viewpoint USE EViewpoint
  eventIn SFBool active
  eventIn SFBool done
  eventOut SFTime start
  url "Elevator.class"
}
ROUTE EProximity.enterTime TO TS.startTime
ROUTE TS.isActive TO EViewpoint.bind
ROUTE TS.fraction_changed TO ElevatorPI.set_fraction
ROUTE ElevatorPI.value_changed TO ETransform.set_translation
```

Java Scripting Reference

APPENDIX C

*This appendix describes the Java classes and methods that allow **Script** nodes (see Chapter 3, Node Reference, Script) to interact with VRML objects and worlds. See Section 2.7, Scripting, for a general description of scripting languages in VRML.*

DESIGN NOTE

Support for Java inside **Script** nodes is not required, but if a browser does support Java inside **Script** nodes, it is required to follow the classes and methods presented in this appendix.

Java inside **Script** nodes is not required by the VRML specification mainly because of concerns that it might be impossible to implement this legally without obtaining a source code license for Java from Sun Microsystems. Freely usable implementations of Java (in source code form to allow easy incorporation into VRML browsers on any platform) would address these concerns, but as of this writing freely usable implementations of Java are not available.

There are many existing languages that have freely available implementations that could be used with VRML; however, it is assumed that people creating VRML will also be creating 2D Web pages. They will therefore already be familiar with Java and/or JavaScript. They are not willing to learn yet another scripting language (such as SafeTCL or Python or Scheme, to name three common languages occasionally championed as a better solution than JavaScript or Java) just for VRML.

Also, both Java and JavaScript were designed with a networked environment like the Internet in mind, and both deal with concerns such as the security of your personal machine as you download and execute arbitrary code.

TIP

Java has several advantages over JavaScript, the other scripting language binding defined in the VRML 2.0 specification. Java is compiled into a machine-independent byte-code representation, making execution of Java faster than other scripting languages. That also means that the source code for your **Scripts** isn't transmitted across the network. Instead, the compiled byte-code form is sent. This makes it more difficult for someone to take your code and modify it for their own purposes.

Java is also much more powerful than most other scripting languages, especially when used with the standard Java packages such as the Abstract Windowing Toolkit user interface tool kit or the networking package.

However, Java is harder to learn than JavaScript, and harder to use because you must compile your **Script** code using a Java compiler before using the result with a VRML browser. For tiny scripts that don't do very much, JavaScript is probably the right solution; for large scripts that do complicated calculations or access the windowing system or network, Java is the better solution. Hopefully in the near future all VRML browsers will support both, allowing you to choose the best language for your task.

C.1 Language

Java is an object-oriented, platform-independent, multithreaded, general-purpose programming environment developed at Sun Microsystems, Inc. See the Java Web site for a full description of the Java programming language (`http://java.sun.com/`). This appendix describes the Java bindings of VRML to the **Script** node.

DESIGN NOTE

This appendix was initially spearheaded by Chris Marrin, and was enhanced and evolved by Kouichi Matsuda, Hiroyuki Sugino, Ben Wing, and a variety of contributors on the *vrml-java* email list.

C.2 Supported Protocol in the Script Node's *url* Field

The *url* field of the **Script** node contains the URL of a file containing the Java byte code. For example:

```
Script {
  url "http://foo.co.jp/Example.class"
  eventIn SFBool start
}
```

C.2.1 File Extension

The file extension for Java byte code is `.class`.

C.2.2 MIME Type

The MIME type for Java byte code is defined as `application/x-java`.

C.3 EventIn Handling

Events to the **Script** node are passed to the corresponding Java method (`processEvent()` or `processEvents()`) in the script. It is necessary to specify the script in the *url* field of the **Script** node.

If a Java byte-code file is specified in the *url* field, the following three conditions must hold:

1. It must contain the class definition with a name that is exactly the same as the body of the file name.

2. It must be a subclass of the **Script** class (see "`vrml.node` Package" in Section C.8.2.)

3. It must be declared as "public."

For example, the following **Script** node has one eventIn field with a name of *start*:

```
Script {
  url "http://foo.co.jp/Example.class"
  eventIn SFBool start
}
```

This node points to the script file `Example.class`. Its source (`Example.java`) looks like this:

```
import vrml.*;
import vrml.field.*;
import vrml.node.*;
public class Example extends Script {
  ...
  // This method is called when any event is received
  public void processEvent (Event e) {
  // ... perform some operation ...
  }
}
```

In the previous example when the *start* eventIn is sent, the `processEvent()` method is executed and receives the eventIn.

C.3.1 Parameter Passing and the EventIn Field/Method

When a **Script** node receives an eventIn, a `processEvent()` or `processEvents()` method in the file specified in the *url* field of the **Script** node is called, which receives the eventIn as Java objects (`Event` object). See Section C.3.2 **Process-Events()** and `processEvent()` Methods, for details.

The **Event** object has three parameters associated with it: name, value, and time stamp of the eventIn. These can be retrieved using the corresponding method on the **Event** object:

```
public class Event implements Cloneable {
  public String getName();
  public ConstField getValue();
  public double getTimeStamp();
  // other methods
}
```

Suppose that the eventIn type is SFXXX and eventIn name is *eventInYYY*, then

- `getName()` should return *eventInYYY*
- `getValue()` should return `ConstField`
- `getTimeStamp()` should return the time stamp when the eventIn occurred

In the previous example, the eventIn name would be *start* and the eventIn value could be cast to be `ConstSFBool`. Also, the time stamp for the time when the eventIn occurred is available as a double. These are passed as an **Event** object to a `processEvent()` method:

```
public void processEvent (Event e) {
  if (e.getName().equals("start")) {
    ConstSFBool v = (ConstSFBool)e.getValue();
    if(v.getValue()==true){
      // ... perform some operation ...
    }
  }
}
```

C.3.2 `ProcessEvents()` and `processEvent()` Methods

Authors can define a `processEvents()` method within a class that is called when the script receives some set of events. The prototype of the `processEvents()` method is

> **`public void processEvents(int count, Event events[]);`**

Here **count** indicates the number of events delivered and **events** is the array of events delivered. Its default behavior is to iterate over each event, calling `processEvent()` on each one as follows:

```
public void processEvents(int count, Event events[])
{
  for (int i = 0; i < count; i++) { processEvent( events[i] ); }
}
```

Although authors could change this operation by giving a user-defined **process-Events()** method, in most cases they would only change the `processEvent()` method and `eventsProcessed()` method described later.

When multiple eventIns with identical time stamps are routed to single **Script** node, `processEvents()` receives multiple events as the event array. Otherwise, each coming event invokes separate `processEvents()`.

For example, the `processEvents()` method receives two events in the following case:

```
Transform {
  children [
    DEF TS TouchSensor {}
    Shape { geometry Cone {} }
  ]
}
DEF SC Script {
  url      "Example.class"
  eventIn SFBool isActive
  eventIn SFTime touchTime
}
ROUTE TS.isActive  TO SC.isActive
ROUTE TS.touchTime TO SC.touchTime
```

Authors can define a `processEvent()` method within a class. The prototype of `processEvent()` is

```
public void processEvent(Event event);
```

Its default behavior is no operation.

C.3.3 `EventsProcessed()` Method

Authors can define an `eventsProcessed()` method within a class that is called after some set of events has been received. It allows **Scripts** that do not rely on the ordering of events received to generate fewer events than an equivalent **Script** that generates events whenever events are received. It is called after every invocation of `processEvents()`.

Events generated from an `eventsProcessed()` method are given the time stamp of the last event processed.

The prototype of the `eventsProcessed()` method is

```
public void eventsProcessed();
```

Its default behavior is no operation.

C.3.4 `Shutdown()` Method

Authors can define a `shutdown()` method within a class that is called when the corresponding **Script** node is deleted.

The prototype of `shutdown()` method is

```
public void shutdown();
```

Its default behavior is no operation.

C.3.5 `Initialize()` Method

Authors can define an `initialize()` method within a class that is called before any event is generated. The various methods in **Script** such as `getEventIn()`, `getEventOut()`, `getExposedField()`, and `getField()` are not guaranteed to return correct values before the call to `initialize()` (i.e., in the constructor). The `initialize()` method is called once during the life of a **Script**.

The prototype of `initialize()` method is

```
public void initialize();
```

Its default behavior is no operation.

C.4 Accessing Fields and Events

The fields, eventIns, and eventOuts of a **Script** node are accessible from their corresponding Java classes.

C.4.1 Accessing Fields, EventIns, and EventOuts of the Script

Each field defined in the **Script** node is available to the script by using its name. Its value can be read or written. This value is persistent across function calls. EventOuts defined in the **Script** node can also be read.

Accessing fields of the **Script** node can be done by using `Script` class methods. The `Script` class has several methods to do that: `getField()`, `getEventOut()`, and `getEventIn()`.

Field getField(String fieldName)

gets the reference to the **Script** node's field with the name *fieldName*. The return value can be converted to an appropriate Java **Field** class.

Field getEventOut(String eventName)

gets the reference to the **Script** node's eventOut with the name *eventName*. The return value can be converted to an appropriate Java **Field** class.

Field getEventIn(String eventName)

gets the reference to the **Script** node's eventIn with the name *eventName*. The return value can be converted to an appropriate Java **Field** class. When you call a `getValue()` method on a field object obtained by a `getEventIn()` method, the return value is unspecified. Therefore, you can not rely on it. EventIn is a write-only field.

When you call a `setValue()`, `set1Value()`, `addValue()`, or `insertValue()` method on a field object obtained by the `getField()` method, the value specified as an argument is stored in the corresponding VRML node's field.

When you call a `setValue()`, `set1Value()`, `addValue()`, or `insertValue()` method on a field object obtained by the `getEventOut()` method, the value specified as an argument generates an event in VRML scene. The effect of this event is specified by the associated ROUTE in the VRML scene.

When you call a `setValue()`, `set1Value()`, `addValue()`, or `insertValue()` method on a field object obtained by the `getEventIn()` method, the value specified as an argument generates an event to the **Script** node. For example, the following **Script** node defines an eventIn, *start;* a field, *state;* and an eventOut, *on.* The `initialize( )` method is invoked before any events are received and the **pro-cessEvent( )** method is invoked when *start* receives an event:

```
Script {
  url       "Example.class"
  eventIn   SFBool start
  eventOut  SFBool on
  field     SFBool state TRUE
}
```

Example.class:

```
import vrml.*;
import vrml.field.*;
import vrml.node.*;
public class Example extends Script {
  private SFBool state;
  private SFBool on;
  public void initialize() {
    state = (SFBool) getField("state");
    on = (SFBool) getEventOut("on");
  }
  public void processEvent(Event e) {
    if(state.getValue()==true){
      on.setValue(true);    // set true to eventOut 'on'
      state.setValue(false);
    }
    else {
      on.setValue(false); // set false to eventOut 'on'
      state.setValue(true);
    }
  }
}
```

C.4.2 Accessing Fields, EventIns, and EventOuts of Other Nodes

If a script has access to a node, the eventIns, eventOuts, and exposedFields of that node are accessible by using the **getEventIn( )**, **getEventOut( )**, or **getExposedField( )** method defined on the node's class (see Section C.5, Exposed Classes and Methods for Nodes and Fields).

Typically, a script will access another VRML node through an SFNode field that provides a reference to the other node. The following example shows how this is done:

```
DEF SomeNode Transform { }
Script {
  field SFNode node USE SomeNode
```

```
    eventIn SFVec3f pos
    url "Example.class"
}

Example.class:

import vrml.*;
import vrml.field.*;
import vrml.node.*;
public class Example extends Script {
  private SFNode node;
  private SFVec3f trans;
  public void initialize() {
    node = (SFNode) getField("node");
  }
  public void processEvent(Event e) {
    // gets the ref to 'translation' field of Transform
    trans = (SFVec3f)((Node) node.getValue())
                .getExposedField("translation");
    trans.setValue((ConstSFVec3f)e.getValue());
  }
}
```

C.4.3 Sending EventIns or EventOuts

Sending eventOuts from a script is done by setting a value to the reference to the eventOut of the script by the **setValue()**, **set1Value()**, **addValue()**, or **insertValue()** methods. Sending eventIns from a script is done by setting a value to the reference to the eventIn by the **setValue()**, **set1Value()**, **addValue()**, or **insertValue()** methods.

C.5 Exposed Classes and Methods for Nodes and Fields

Java classes for VRML are defined in the packages **vrml**, **vrml.node**, and **vrml.field** (see Section C.8.2, VRML Packages).

The **Field** class extends Java's **Object** class by default; thus, **Field** has the full functionality of the **Object** class, including the **getClass()** method. The rest of the package defines a **Const** read-only class for each VRML field type, with a **getValue()** method for each class, and another read/write class for each VRML field type, with both **getValue()** and **setValue()** methods for each class. A **getValue()** method converts a VRML-type value into a Java-type value. A **set-Value()** method converts a Java-type value into a VRML-type value and sets it to the VRML field.

Most of the `setValue()` methods and `set1Value()` methods are listed as "throws exception," meaning that errors are possible. You may need to write exception handlers (using Java's `catch()` method) when you use those methods. Any method not listed as "throws exception" is guaranteed to generate no exceptions. Each method that throws an exception includes a prototype showing which exceptions can be thrown.

C.5.1 `Field` Class and `ConstField` Class

All VRML data types have equivalent classes in Java. The `Field` class is the root of all field types. The public abstract `Field` class implements

```
Cloneable {
  // methods
}
```

This class has two subclasses: read-only classes and writable classes

Read-only Classes

These types of classes support the `getValue()` method. In addition, some classes support some convenient methods to get values from the object:

- ConstSFBool
- ConstSFColor
- ConstSFFloat
- ConstSFImage
- ConstSFInt32
- ConstSFNode
- ConstSFRotation
- ConstSFString
- ConstSFTime
- ConstSFVec2f
- ConstSFVec3f
- ConstMFColor
- ConstMFFloat
- ConstMFInt32
- ConstMFNode
- ConstMFRotation
- ConstMFString

- `ConstMFTime`
- `ConstMFVec2f`
- `ConstMFVec3f`

Writable Classes

These types of classes support both `getValue()` and `setValue()` methods. If the class name is prefixed with MF, it is a multivalued `field` class. The class also supports the `set1Value()`, `addValue()`, and `insertValue()` methods. In addition, some classes support some convenient methods to get and set values from the object:

- `SFBool`
- `SFColor`
- `SFFloat`
- `SFImage`
- `SFInt32`
- `SFNode`
- `SFRotation`
- `SFString`
- `SFTime`
- `SFVec2f`
- `SFVec3f`
- `MFColor`
- `MFFloat`
- `MFInt32`
- `MFNode`
- `MFRotation`
- `MFString`
- `MFTime`
- `MFVec2f`
- `MFVec3f`

The Java `Field` class and its subclasses have several methods to get and set values: `getSize()`, `getValue()`, `get1Value()`, `setValue()`, `set1Value()`, `addValue()`, `insertValue()`, `clear()`, `delete()`, or `toString()`.

Note: All instances that are typed as the `BaseNode` class must be an instance of the class that extends the `BaseNode` class. The concrete class is implementation dependent and up to browser implementation.

`getSize()`

returns the number of elements of each multivalued `Field` class (MF class)

`getValue()`

converts a VRML-type value into a Java-type value and returns it

`get1Value(int index)`

converts a VRML-type value (index-th element) into a Java-type value and returns it. The index of the first element is 0. Getting the element beyond the existing elements throws an exception.

`setValue(value)`

converts a Java-type value into a VRML-type value and sets it to the VRML field

`set1Value(int index, value)`

converts from a Java-type value to a VRML-type value and sets it to the index-th element

`addValue(value)`

converts from a Java-type value to a VRML-type value and adds it to the last element

`insertValue(int index, value)`

converts from a Java-type value to a VRML-type value and inserts it to the index-th element. The index of the first element is 0. Setting the element beyond the existing elements throws an exception.

`clear()`

clears the element so that it has no more elements in it

`delete(int index)`

deletes the index-th element

`toString()`

returns the browser-dependent information of the field

These methods—`getSize()`, `get1Value()`, `set1Value()`, `addValue()`, `insertValue()`, `clear()`, and `delete()`—are only available for multivalued `Field` classes (MF classes). See "`vrml` Package" in Section C.8.2 for each class's methods definition.

Some constructors and methods of the `Field` classes take an array as an argument.

A Single-Dimensional Array

Some constructors and methods of the following classes take a single-dimensional array as an argument. The array is treated as follows:

`ConstSFColor`, `ConstMFColor`, `SFColor`, and `MFColor`

> **`float colors[]`**
>
> `colors[]` consists of a set of three float values (representing red, green, and blue).

`ConstSFRotation`, `ConstMFRotation`, `SFRotation`, and `MFRotation`

> **`float rotations[]`**
>
> `rotations[]` consists of a set of four float values (representing x-axis, y-axis, z-axis, and angle)

`ConstSFVec2f`, `ConstMFVec2f`, `SFVec2f`, and `MFVec2f`

> **`float vec2s[]`**
>
> `vec2s[]` consists of a set of two float values (representing x and y)

`ConstSFVec3f`, `ConstMFVec3f`, `SFVec3f`, and `MFVec3f`

> **`float vec3s[]`**
>
> `vec3s[]` consists of a set of three float values (representing x, y, and z)

A Single Integer and a Single-Dimensional Array

Some constructors and other methods take a single integer value (called *size*) and a single-dimensional array as arguments (e.g., `MFFloat(int size, float values[])`). The *size* field specifies the number of valid elements in the array (from 0-th element to (*size* - 1)-th element); all other values are ignored. This means that the method may be passed an array of *size* or larger.

An Array of Arrays

Some constructors and methods of the following classes take an array of arrays as an argument. The array is treated as follows:

`ConstMFColor` and `MFColor`

float colors[][]

`colors[][]` consists of an array of three float values (representing red, green, and blue)

ConstMFRotation and MFRotation

float rotations[][]

`rotations[][]` consists of an array of four float values (representing *x*-axis, *y*-axis, *z*-axis, and angle)

ConstMFVec2f and MFVec2f

float vec2s[][]

`vec2s[][]` consists of an array of two float values (representing *x* and *y*)

ConstMFVec3f and MFVec3f

float vec3s[][]

`vec3s[][]` consists of an array of three float values (representing *x*, *y*, and *z*).

Array Details

The following sections describe how arrays are interpreted in detail. Suppose *NA* represents the number of elements in the array and *NT* represents the number of elements that the target object requires or has. For example, if the target object is **SFColor**, it requires or has exactly three float values.

In the following description, suppose SF* represents subclasses of the **Field** class, ConstSF* represents subclasses of the **ConstField** class, MF* represents subclasses of the **MField** class, and ConstMF* represents subclasses of the **ConstM-Field** class.

A Single-Dimensional Array

In the following description, if the target object is

- **SFColor** and **ConstSFColor**, *NT* is exactly three
- **MFColor** and **ConstMFColor**, *NT* is a multiple of three and *NA* is rounded down to a multiple of three
- **SFRotation** and **ConstSFRotation**, *NT* is exactly four
- **MFRotation** and **ConstMFRotation**, *NT* is a multiple of four and *NA* is rounded down to a multiple of four
- **SFVec2f** and **ConstSFVec2f**, *NT* is exactly two
- **MFVec2f** and **ConstMFVec2f**, *NT* is a multiple of two and *NA* is rounded down to a multiple of two

- `SFVec3f` and `ConstSFVec3f`, *NT* is exactly three
- `MFVec3f` and `ConstMFVec3f`, *NT* is a multiple of three and *NA* is rounded down to a multiple of three

For SF* Objects and ConstSF* Objects

NA must be larger than or equal to *NT*. If *NA* is larger than *NT*, the elements from the 0-th to the (*NT* − 1)-th element are used and the remaining elements are ignored. Otherwise, `exception(ArrayIndexOutOfBoundsException)` is thrown. For example, when the array is used as an argument of `setValue()` for `SFColor`, the array must contain greater than or equal to three float values. If the array contains five float values, the first three values are used.

For MF* Objects and ConstMF* Objects

For the constructor, the same rule for SF* and ConstSF* objects are applied. For example, when the array is used as an argument of the constructor for `MFColor`, the array must contain greater than or equal to a multiple of three float values. If the array contains seven float values, the first six values are used.

For `setValue()` method

If *NT* is smaller than or equal to *NA*, *NT* is increased to *NA* and then all elements of the target object are set. If *NT* is larger than *NA*, *NT* is decreased to *NA* and then all elements of the target object are set.

For `getValue()` method

If *NT* is smaller than or equal to *NA*, all elements of the target object are copied. If *NT* is larger than *NA*, an exception is thrown.

For `set1Value()` method

The target element (the index-th element) is treated as an SF* object, so the same rule for SF* and ConstSF* objects is applied.

For `get1Value()` method

The target element (the index-th element) is treated as an SF* or ConstSF* object, so the same rule for SF* and ConstSF* objects is applied.

For `addValue()` and `insertValue()` method

The corresponding SF* object is created with the argument and then added to or inserted into the target object.

A Single Integer and a Single-Dimensional Array

Some constructors and other methods take a single integer value (called *size*) and a single-dimensional array as an argument (e.g., `MFFloat(int size, float` `values[])`). The *size* field specifies the number of valid elements in the array (from 0-th element to (*size* −1)-th element); all other values are ignored. This means that the method may be passed an array of *size* or larger.

The valid elements are copied to a virtually new array and the rules for a single-dimensional array are applied to the new array.

An Array of Arrays

This argument is used only for MF* objects and ConstMF* objects. In the following case, suppose *NA* is the number of arrays (for example for `float f[4][3]`, *NA* is four) and *NT* is the return value of the `getSize()` method of each object.

For constructor

The object that has *NA* elements is created.

For `setValue()` method

If *NT* is less than or equal to *NA*, *NT* is increased to *NA* and then all elements of the target object are set. If *NT* is larger than *NA*, *NT* is decreased to *NA* and then all elements of the target object are set.

For `getValue()` method

If *NT* is less than or equal to *NA*, all elements of the target object are copied. If *NT* is smaller than *NA*, `exception(ArrayIndexOutOfBoundsException)` is thrown.

C.5.2 Node Class

`Node` class has several methods: `getType()`, `getEventOut()`, `getEventIn()`, `getExposedField()`, `getBrowser()`, and `toString()`.

`String getType()`

   returns the type of the node

`ConstField getEventOut(String eventName)`

   gets the reference to the node's eventOut with the name *eventName*. The return value can be converted to an appropriate Java `Field` class (see Section C.5.1, `Field` Class and `ConstField` Class).

`Field getEventIn(String eventName)`

   gets the reference to the node's eventIn with the name *eventName*. The return value can be converted to an appropriate Java `Field` class. When you call the `getValue()` method on a field object obtained by the `getEventIn()` method, the return value is unspecified. Therefore, you cannot rely on it. EventIn is a write-only field.

`Field getExposedField(String eventName)`

gets the reference to the node's exposedField with the name *eventName*. The return value can be converted to an appropriate Java **`Field`** class.

`Browser getBrowser()`

gets the browser in which this node is contained. See Section C.5.3, **`Browser`** Class.

`String toString()`

returns the browser-dependent information of the node

When you call the **`setValue()`**, **`set1Value()`**, **`addValue()`**, or **`insertValue()`** methods on a field object obtained by the **`getEventIn()`** method, the value specified as an argument generates an event to the node.

When you call the **`setValue()`**, **`set1Value()`**, **`addValue()`**, or **`insertValue()`** methods on a field object obtained by the **`getExposedField()`** method, the value specified as an argument generates an event in the VRML scene. The effect of this event is specified by the associated ROUTE in the VRML scene.

C.5.3 Browser Class

This section lists the public Java interfaces to the **`Browser`** class, which allows scripts to get and set browser information. For descriptions of the following methods see Section 2.7.10, Browser Script Interface.

Return value	Method name
`String`	`getName()`
`String`	`getVersion()`
`float`	`getCurrentSpeed()`
`float`	`getCurrentFrameRate()`
`String`	`getWorldURL()`
`void`	`replaceWorld(BaseNode[] nodes)`
`BaseNode[]`	`createVrmlFromString(String vrmlSyntax)`
`void`	`createVrmlFromURL(String[] url, BaseNode node, String event)`
`void`	`addRoute(BaseNode fromNode, String fromEventOut, BaseNodetoNode, String toEventIn)`
`void`	`deleteRoute(BaseNode fromNode, String fromEventOut, BaseNode toNode, String toEventIn)`
`void`	`loadURL(String[] url, String[] parameter)`
`void`	`setDescription(String description)`

See "**vrml** Package" in Section C.8.2 for each method's definition.

Note: All instances that are typed as the **BaseNode** class must be an instance of the class that extends the **BaseNode** class. The concrete class is implementation dependent and up to browser implementation.

TABLE C-1 *Conversion table from the types used in the* **Browser** *class to Java type*

VRML type	Java type
SFString	String
SFFloat	float
MFString	String[]
MFNode	BaseNode[]

When a relative URL is specified as an argument of **BaseNode[]**, the path is relative to the VRML file that contains the **Script** node.

C.5.4 User-defined Classes and Packages

The Java classes defined by a user can be used in the Java program. They are searched from the directories specified in the **CLASSPATH** environment variable and then the directory in which the Java program is placed. If the Java class is in a package, this package is searched from the directories specified in the **CLASSPATH** environment variable and then the directory in which the Java program is placed.

C.5.5 Standard Java Packages

Java programs have access to the full set of classes available in **java.***. The security model will be browser specific. Threads are required to work as normal for Java.

C.6 Exceptions

Java methods may throw the following exceptions:

InvalidFieldException
   is thrown at the time **getField()** is executed and the field name is invalid

Example   **417**

InvalidEventInException

> is thrown at the time getEventIn() is executed and the eventIn name is invalid

InvalidEventOutException

> is thrown at the time getEventOut() is executed and the eventOut name is invalid

InvalidExposedFieldException

> is thrown at the time getExposedField() is executed and the exposedField name is invalid

InvalidVRMLSyntaxException

> is thrown at the time createVrmlFromString(), createVrmlFromURL(), or loadURL() is executed and the VRML string is invalid

InvalidRouteException

> is thrown at the time addRoute() or deleteRoute() is executed and one (or more) of the arguments is invalid

InvalidFieldChangeException

> may be thrown as a result of all sorts of illegal field changes (e.g., adding a node from one world as the child of a node in another world; creating a circularity in a scene graph; setting an invalid string on enumerated fields, such as the *fogType* field of the **Fog** node). It is not guaranteed that such exceptions will be thrown, but a browser should do the best job it can.

ArrayIndexOutOfBoundsException

> is generated at the time setValue(), set1Value(), addValue(), or insertValue() is executed and the index is out of bounds (see Section C.5.1, **Field** Class and **ConstField** Class). This is the standard exception defined in the Java **Array** class.

If exceptions are not redefined by authors, a browser's behavior is unspecified (see Section C.9, Example of Exception Class).

C.7 Example

Here's an example of a **Script** node that determines whether a given color contains a lot of red. The **Script** node exposes a *color* field, an eventIn, and an eventOut:

```
Script {
  field SFColor currentColor 0 0 0
  eventIn SFColor colorIn
  eventOut SFBool  isRed
  url "ExampleScript.class"
}
```

Here's the source code for the **ExampleScript.java** file that gets called every time an eventIn is routed to the previous **Script** node:

```
import vrml.*;
import vrml.field.*;
import vrml.node.*;
public class ExampleScript extends Script {
  // Declare field(s)
  private SFColor currentColor;
  // Declare eventOut field(s)
  private SFBool isRed;
  // buffer for  SFColor.getValue().
  private float colorBuff[] = new float[3];
  public void initialize() {
    currentColor = (SFColor) getField("currentColor");
    isRed = (SFBool) getEventOut("isRed");
  }
  public void processEvent(Event e) {
    // This method is called when a colorIn event is received
    currentColor.setValue((ConstSFColor)e.getValue());
  }
    public void eventsProcessed() {
      currentColor.getValue(colorBuff);
      if (colorBuff[0] >= 0.5)
        // if red is at or above 50%
        isRed.setValue(true);
  }
}
```

For details on when the methods defined in **ExampleScript.java** are called, see Section 2.4.3, Execution Model.

The following are **Browser** class examples:

createVrmlFromUrl() method:

```
DEF Example Script {
  url "Example.class"
  field    MFString target_url "foo.wrl"
  eventIn MFNode    nodesLoaded
  eventIn SFBool    trigger_event
}
```

Example   **419**

Example.class:

```
import vrml.*;
import vrml.field.*;
import vrml.node.*;
public class Example extends Script {
  private MFString target_url;
  private Browser browser;
  public void initialize() {
    target_url = (MFString)getField("target_url");
    browser = this.getBrowser();
  }
  public void processEvent(Event e) {
    if (e.getName().equals("trigger_event")) {
      // do something and then fetch values
      String[] urls;
      urls = new String[target_url.getSize()];
      target_url.getValue(urls);
    browser.createVrmlFromURL(urls, this, "nodesLoaded");
    }
    if (e.getName().equals("nodesLoaded")) {
      // do something
    }
  }
}
```

addRoute() method:

```
DEF Sensor TouchSensor {}
DEF Example Script {
  url "Example.class"
  field   SFNode fromNode USE Sensor
  eventIn SFBool clicked
  eventIn SFBool trigger_event
}
```

Example.class:

```
import vrml.*;
import vrml.field.*;
import vrml.node.*;
public class Example extends Script {
  private SFNode fromNode;
  private Browser browser;
  public void initialize() {
    fromNode = (SFNode) getField("fromNode");
    browser = this.getBrowser();
  }
```

```
      public void processEvent(Event e) {
        if ( e.getName().equals("trigger_event") ) {
          // do something and then add routing
          browser.addRoute( fromNode.getValue(), "isActive", this,
                            "clicked");
        }
        if (e.getName().equals("clicked")) {
          // do something
        }
      }
    }
```

C.8 Class Definitions

C.8.1 Class Hierarchy

The classes are divided into three packages: `vrml`, `vrml.field`, and `vrml.node`.

```
java.lang.Object
    |
    +- vrml.Event
    +- vrml.Browser
    +- vrml.Field
    |        +- vrml.field.SFBool
    |        +- vrml.field.SFColor
    |        +- vrml.field.SFFloat
    |        +- vrml.field.SFImage
    |        +- vrml.field.SFInt32
    |        +- vrml.field.SFNode
    |        +- vrml.field.SFRotation
    |        +- vrml.field.SFString
    |        +- vrml.field.SFTime
    |        +- vrml.field.SFVec2f
    |        +- vrml.field.SFVec3f
    |        |
    |        +- vrml.MField
    |        |     +- vrml.field.MFColor
    |        |     +- vrml.field.MFFloat
    |        |     +- vrml.field.MFInt32
    |        |     +- vrml.field.MFNode
    |        |     +- vrml.field.MFRotation
    |        |     +- vrml.field.MFString
    |        |     +- vrml.field.MFTime
    |        |     +- vrml.field.MFVec2f
    |        |     +- vrml.field.MFVec3f
```

```
    |        |
    |        +- vrml.ConstField
    |              +- vrml.field.ConstSFBool
    |              +- vrml.field.ConstSFColor
    |              +- vrml.field.ConstSFFloat
    |              +- vrml.field.ConstSFImage
    |              +- vrml.field.ConstSFInt32
    |              +- vrml.field.ConstSFNode
    |              +- vrml.field.ConstSFRotation
    |              +- vrml.field.ConstSFString
    |              +- vrml.field.ConstSFTime
    |              +- vrml.field.ConstSFVec2f
    |              +- vrml.field.ConstSFVec3f
    |              |
    |              +- vrml.ConstMFField
    |                    +- vrml.field.ConstMFColor
    |                    +- vrml.field.ConstMFFloat
    |                    +- vrml.field.ConstMFInt32
    |                    +- vrml.field.ConstMFNode
    |                    +- vrml.field.ConstMFRotation
    |                    +- vrml.field.ConstMFString
    |                    +- vrml.field.ConstMFTime
    |                    +- vrml.field.ConstMFVec2f
    |                    +- vrml.field.ConstMFVec3f
    |
    +- vrml.BaseNode
    +- vrml.node.Node
    +- vrml.node.Script

java.lang.Exception
     java.lang.RuntimeException
            vrml.InvalidRouteException
            vrml.InvalidFieldException
            vrml.InvalidEventInException
            vrml.InvalidEventOutException
            vrml.InvalidExposedFieldException
            vrml.InvalidFieldChangeException
     vrml.InvalidVRMLSyntaxException
```

C.8.2 VRML Packages

vrml Package

```
package vrml;
public abstract class Field implements Cloneable
{
  public Object clone();
}
```

```
public abstract class ConstField extends Field { }
public abstract class ConstMField extends ConstField
{
  public abstract int getSize();
}
public abstract class MField extends Field
{
  public abstract int getSize();
  public abstract void clear();
  public abstract void delete(int index);
}
public class Event implements Cloneable
{
  public String getName();
  public double getTimeStamp();
  public ConstField getValue();
  public Object clone();
  // This overrides a method in Object
  public String toString();
}
public class Browser
{
  private Browser();
  // This overrides a method in Object
  public String toString();
  // Browser interface
  public String getName();
  public String getVersion();
  public float getCurrentSpeed();
  public float getCurrentFrameRate();
  public String getWorldURL();
  public void replaceWorld(BaseNode[] nodes);
  public BaseNode[] createVrmlFromString(String vrmlSyntax)
    throws InvalidVRMLSyntaxException;
  public void createVrmlFromURL(String[] url, BaseNode node,
    String event)
  public void addRoute(BaseNode fromNode, String fromEventOut,
    BaseNode toNode, String toEventIn);
  public void deleteRoute(BaseNode fromNode, String fromEventOut,
    BaseNode toNode, String toEventIn);
  public void loadURL(String[] url, String[] parameter)
  public void setDescription(String description);
}
//
// This is the general BaseNode class
//
```

```
public abstract class BaseNode {
  // Returns the type of the node.  If the node is a prototype
  //   it returns the name of the prototype.
  public String getType();
  // Get the Browser that this node is contained in.
  public Browser getBrowser();
}
```

vrml.field Package

```
package vrml.field;
public class ConstSFBool extends ConstField {
  public ConstSFBool(boolean value);
  public boolean getValue();
  // This overrides a method in Object
  public String toString();
}
public class ConstSFColor extends ConstField
{
  public ConstSFColor(float red, float green, float blue);
  public void getValue(float colors[]);
  public float getRed();
  public float getGreen();
  public float getBlue();
  // This overrides a method in Object
  public String toString();
}
public class ConstSFFloat extends ConstField
 {
    public ConstSFFloat(float value);
    public float getValue();
    // This overrides a method in Object
    public String toString();
 }
public class ConstSFImage extends ConstField
{
    public ConstSFImage( int width, int height, int components,
                         byte pixels[] );
    public int getWidth();
    public int getHeight();
    public int getComponents();
    public void getPixels(byte pixels[]);
    // This overrides a method in Object
    public String toString();
}
public class ConstSFInt32 extends ConstField
```

```
{
    public ConstSFInt32(int value);
    public int getValue();
    // This overrides a method in Object
    public String toString();
}
public class ConstSFNode extends ConstField
{
    public ConstSFNode(BaseNode node);
    public BaseNode getValue();
    // This overrides a method in Object
    public String toString();
}
public class ConstSFRotation extends ConstField
{
    public ConstSFRotation( float axisX, float axisY, float axisZ,
                            float angle);
    public void getValue(float rotations[]);
    // This overrides a method in Object
    public String toString();
}
public class ConstSFString extends ConstField
{
    public ConstSFString(String value);
    public String getValue();
    // This overrides a method in Object
    public String toString();
}
public class ConstSFTime extends ConstField
{
    public ConstSFTime(double time);
    public double getValue();
    // This overrides a method in Object
    public String toString();
}
public class ConstSFVec2f extends ConstField
{
    public ConstSFVec2f(float x, float y);
    public void getValue(float vec2s[]);
    public float getX();
    public float getY();
    // This overrides a method in Object
    public String toString();
}
public class ConstSFVec3f extends ConstField
```

```
{
    public ConstSFVec3f(float x, float y, float z);
    public void getValue(float vec3s[]);
    public float getX();
    public float getY();
    public float getZ();
    // This overrides a method in Object
    public String toString();
}
public class ConstMFColor extends ConstMField
{
    public ConstMFColor(float colors[][]);
    public ConstMFColor(float colors[]);
    public ConstMFColor(int size, float colors[]);
    public void getValue(float colors[][]);
    public void getValue(float colors[]);
    public void get1Value(int index, float colors[]);
    public void get1Value(int index, SFColor color);
    // This overrides a method in Object
    public String toString();
}
public class ConstMFFloat extends ConstMField
{
    public ConstMFFloat(int size, float values[]);
    public ConstMFFloat(float values[]);
    public void getValue(float values[]);
    public float get1Value(int index);
    // This overrides a method in Object
    public String toString();
}
public class ConstMFInt32 extends ConstMField
{
    public ConstMFInt32(int size, int values[]);
    public ConstMFInt32(int values[]);
    public void getValue(int values[]);
    public int get1Value(int index);
    // This overrides a method in Object
    public String toString();
}
public class ConstMFNode extends ConstMField
{
    public ConstMFNode(int size, BaseNode node[]);
    public ConstMFNode(BaseNode node[]);
    public void getValue(BaseNode node[]);
    public BaseNode get1Value(int index);
    // This overrides a method in Object
    public String toString();
}
```

```java
public class ConstMFRotation extends ConstMField
{
    public ConstMFRotation(float rotations[][]);
    public ConstMFRotation(float rotations[]);
    public ConstMFRotation(int size, float rotations[]);
    public void getValue(float rotations[][]);
    public void getValue(float rotations[]);
    public void get1Value(int index, float rotations[]);
    public void get1Value(int index, SFRotation rotation);
    // This overrides a method in Object
    public String toString();
}
public class ConstMFString extends ConstMField
{
    public ConstMFString(int size, String s[]);
    public ConstMFString(String s[]);
    public void getValue(String values[]);
    public String get1Value(int index);
    // This overrides a method in Object
    public String toString();
}
public class ConstMFTime extends ConstMField
{
    public ConstMFTime(int size, double times[]);
    public ConstMFTime(double times[]);
    public void getValue(double times[]);
    public double get1Value(int index);
    // This overrides a method in Object
    public String toString();
}
public class ConstMFVec2f extends ConstMField
{
    public ConstMFVec2f(float vec2s[][]);
    public ConstMFVec2f(float vec2s[]);
    public ConstMFVec2f(int size, float vec2s[]);
    public void getValue(float vec2s[][]);
    public void getValue(float vec2s[]);
    public void get1Value(int index, float vec2s[]);
    public void get1Value(int index, SFVec2f vec);
    // This overrides a method in Object
    public String toString();
}
public class ConstMFVec3f extends ConstMField
{
    public ConstMFVec3f(float vec3s[][]);
    public ConstMFVec3f(float vec3s[]);
```

```
    public ConstMFVec3f(int size, float vec3s[]);
    public void getValue(float vec3s[][]);
    public void getValue(float vec3s[]);
    public void get1Value(int index, float vec3s[]);
    public void get1Value(int index, SFVec3f vec);
    // This overrides a method in Object
    public String toString();
}
public class SFBool extends Field
{
    public SFBool();
    public SFBool(boolean value);
    public boolean getValue();
    public void setValue(boolean b);
    public void setValue(ConstSFBool b);
    public void setValue(SFBool b);
    // This overrides a method in Object
    public String toString();
}
public class SFColor extends Field
{
    public SFColor();
    public SFColor(float red, float green, float blue);
    public void getValue(float colors[]);
    public float getRed();
    public float getGreen();
    public float getBlue();
    public void setValue(float colors[]);
    public void setValue(float red, float green, float blue);
    public void setValue(ConstSFColor color);
    public void setValue(SFColor color);
    // This overrides a method in Object
    public String toString();
}
public class SFFloat extends Field
{
    public SFFloat();
    public SFFloat(float f);
    public float getValue();
    public void setValue(float f);
    public void setValue(ConstSFFloat f);
    public void setValue(SFFloat f);
    // This overrides a method in Object
    public String toString();
}
public class SFImage extends Field
```

```
{
    public SFImage();
    public SFImage(int width, int height, int components,
                   byte pixels[]);
    public int getWidth();
    public int getHeight();
    public int getComponents();
    public void getPixels(byte pixels[]);
    public void setValue(int width, int height, int components,
                         byte pixels[]);
    public void setValue(ConstSFImage image);
    public void setValue(SFImage image);
    // This overrides a method in Object
    public String toString();
}
public class SFInt32 extends Field
{
    public SFInt32();
    public SFInt32(int value);
    public int getValue();
    public void setValue(int i);
    public void setValue(ConstSFInt32 i);
    public void setValue(SFInt32 i);
    // This overrides a method in Object
    public String toString();
}
public class SFNode extends Field
{
    public SFNode();
    public SFNode(BaseNode node);
    public BaseNode getValue();
    public void setValue(BaseNode node);
    public void setValue(ConstSFNode node);
    public void setValue(SFNode node);
    // This overrides a method in Object
    public String toString();
}
public class SFRotation extends Field
{
    public SFRotation();
    public SFRotation(float axisX, float axisY, float axisZ,
                      float angle);
    public void getValue(float rotations[]);
    public void setValue(float rotations[]);
    public void setValue(float axisX, float axisY, float axisZ,
                         float angle);
```

```
        public void setValue(ConstSFRotation rotation);
        public void setValue(SFRotation rotation);
        // This overrides a method in Object
        public String toString();
}
public class SFString extends Field
{
        public SFString();
        public SFString(String s);
        public String getValue();
        public void setValue(String s);
        public void setValue(ConstSFString s);
        public void setValue(SFString s);
        // This overrides a method in Object
        public String toString();
}
public class SFTime extends Field
{
        public SFTime();
        public SFTime(double time);
        public double getValue();
        public void setValue(double time);
        public void setValue(ConstSFTime time);
        public void setValue(SFTime time);
        // This overrides a method in Object
        public String toString();
}
public class SFVec2f extends Field
{
        public SFVec2f();
        public SFVec2f(float x, float y);
        public void getValue(float vec2s[]);
        public float getX();
        public float getY();
        public void setValue(float vec2s[]);
        public void setValue(float x, float y);
        public void setValue(ConstSFVec2f vec);
        public void setValue(SFVec2f vec);
        // This overrides a method in Object
        public String toString();
}
public class SFVec3f extends Field
{
        public SFVec3f();
        public SFVec3f(float x, float y, float z);
        public void getValue(float vec3s[]);
```

```
    public float getX();
    public float getY();
    public float getZ();
    public void setValue(float vec3s[]);
    public void setValue(float x, float y, float z);
    public void setValue(ConstSFVec3f vec);
    public void setValue(SFVec3f vec);
    // This overrides a method in Object
    public String toString();
}
public class MFColor extends MField
{
    public MFColor();
    public MFColor(float colors[][]);
    public MFColor(float colors[]);
    public MFColor(int size, float colors[]);
    public void getValue(float colors[][]);
    public void getValue(float colors[]);
    public void setValue(float colors[][]);
    public void setValue(float colors[]);
    public void setValue(int size, float colors[]);
    /***************************************************
      color[0] ... color[size - 1] are used as color data
         in the way that color[0], color[1], and color[2]
         represent the first color. The number of colors
         is defined as "size / 3".
      ***************************************************/
    public void setValue(MFColor colors);
    public void setValue(ConstMFColor colors);
    public void get1Value(int index, float colors[]);
    public void get1Value(int index, SFColor color);
    public void set1Value(int index, ConstSFColor color);
    public void set1Value(int index, SFColor color);
    public void set1Value(int index, float red, float green,
                          float blue);
    public void addValue(ConstSFColor color);
    public void addValue(SFColor color);
    public void addValue(float red, float green, float blue);
    public void insertValue(int index, ConstSFColor color);
    public void insertValue(int index, SFColor color);
    public void insertValue(int index, float red, float green,
                            float blue);
    // This overrides a method in Object
    public String toString();
}
public class MFFloat extends MField
```

```
{
    public MFFloat();
    public MFFloat(int size, float values[]);
    public MFFloat(float values[]);
    public void getValue(float values[]);
    public void setValue(float values[]);
    public void setValue(int size, float values[]);
    public void setValue(MFFloat value);
    public void setValue(ConstMFFloat value);
    public float get1Value(int index);
    public void set1Value(int index, float f);
    public void set1Value(int index, ConstSFFloat f);
    public void set1Value(int index, SFFloat f);
    public void addValue(float f);
    public void addValue(ConstSFFloat f);
    public void addValue(SFFloat f);
    public void insertValue(int index, float f);
    public void insertValue(int index, ConstSFFloat f);
    public void insertValue(int index, SFFloat f);
    // This overrides a method in Object
    public String toString();
}
public class MFInt32 extends MField
{
    public MFInt32();
    public MFInt32(int size, int values[]);
    public MFInt32(int values[]);
    public void getValue(int values[]);
    public void setValue(int values[]);
    public void setValue(int size, int values[]);
    public void setValue(MFInt32 value);
    public void setValue(ConstMFInt32 value);
    public int get1Value(int index);
    public void set1Value(int index, int i);
    public void set1Value(int index, ConstSFInt32 i);
    public void set1Value(int index, SFInt32 i);
    public void addValue(int i);
    public void addValue(ConstSFInt32 i);
    public void addValue(SFInt32 i);
    public void insertValue(int index, int i);
    public void insertValue(int index, ConstSFInt32 i);
    public void insertValue(int index, SFInt32 i);
    // This overrides a method in Object
    public String toString();
}
public class MFNode extends MField
```

```
{
    public MFNode();
    public MFNode(int size, BaseNode node[]);
    public MFNode(BaseNode node[]);
    public void getValue(BaseNode node[]);
    public void setValue(BaseNode node[]);
    public void setValue(int size, BaseNode node[]);
    public void setValue(MFNode node);
    public void setValue(ConstMFNode node);
    public BaseNode get1Value(int index);
    public void set1Value(int index, BaseNode node);
    public void set1Value(int index, ConstSFNode node);
    public void set1Value(int index, SFNode node);
    public void addValue(BaseNode node);
    public void addValue(ConstSFNode node);
    public void addValue(SFNode node);
    public void insertValue(int index, BaseNode node);
    public void insertValue(int index, ConstSFNode node);
    public void insertValue(int index, SFNode node);
    // This overrides a method in Object
    public String toString();
}
public class MFRotation extends MField
{
    public MFRotation();
    public MFRotation(float rotations[][]);
    public MFRotation(float rotations[]);
    public MFRotation(int size, float rotations[]);
    public void getValue(float rotations[][]);
    public void getValue(float rotations[]);
    public void setValue(float rotations[][]);
    public void setValue(float rotations[]);
    public void setValue(int size, float rotations[]);
    public void setValue(MFRotation rotations);
    public void setValue(ConstMFRotation rotations);
    public void get1Value(int index, float rotations[]);
    public void get1Value(int index, SFRotation rotation);
    public void set1Value(int index, ConstSFRotation rotation);
    public void set1Value(int index, SFRotation rotation);
    public void set1Value(int index, float axisX, float axisY,
                          float axisZ, float angle);
    public void addValue(ConstSFRotation rotation);
    public void addValue(SFRotation rotation);
    public void addValue(float axisX, float axisY, float axisZ,
                         float angle);
    public void insertValue(int index, ConstSFRotation rotation);
```

```
        public void insertValue(int index, SFRotation rotation);
        public void insertValue(int index, float axisX, float axisY,
                            float axisZ, float angle);
        // This overrides a method in Object
        public String toString();
}
public class MFString extends MFField
{
        public MFString();
        public MFString(int size, String s[]);
        public MFString(String s[]);
        public void getValue(String s[]);
        public void setValue(String s[]);
        public void setValue(int size, String s[]);
        public void setValue(MFString s);
        public void setValue(ConstMFString s);
        public String get1Value(int index);
        public void set1Value(int index, String s);
        public void set1Value(int index, ConstSFString s);
        public void set1Value(int index, SFString s);
        public void addValue(String s);
        public void addValue(ConstSFString s);
        public void addValue(SFString s);
        public void insertValue(int index, String s);
        public void insertValue(int index, ConstSFString s);
        public void insertValue(int index, SFString s);
        // This overrides a method in Object
        public String toString();
}
public class MFTime extends MFField
{
        public MFTime();

        public MFTime(int size, double times[]);
        public MFTime(double times[]);
        public void getValue(double times[]);
        public void setValue(double times[]);
        public void setValue(int size, double times[]);
        public void setValue(MFTime times);
        public void setValue(ConstMFTime times);
        public double get1Value(int index);
        public void set1Value(int index, double time);
        public void set1Value(int index, ConstSFTime time);
        public void set1Value(int index, SFTime time);
        public void addValue(double time);
        public void addValue(ConstSFTime time);
```

```
        public void addValue(SFTime time);
        public void insertValue(int index, double time);
        public void insertValue(int index, ConstSFTime time);
        public void insertValue(int index, SFTime time);
        // This overrides a method in Object
        public String toString();
}
public class MFVec2f extends MField
{
        public MFVec2f();
        public MFVec2f(float vec2s[][]);
        public MFVec2f(float vec2s[]);
        public MFVec2f(int size, float vec2s[]);
        public void getValue(float vec2s[][]);
        public void getValue(float vec2s[]);
        public void setValue(float vec2s[][]);
        public void setValue(float vec2s[]);
        public void setValue(int size, float vec2s[]);
        public void setValue(MFVec2f vecs);
        public void setValue(ConstMFVec2f vecs);
        public void get1Value(int index, float vec2s[]);
        public void get1Value(int index, SFVec2f vec);
        public void set1Value(int index, float x, float y);
        public void set1Value(int index, ConstSFVec2f vec);
        public void set1Value(int index, SFVec2f vec);
        public void addValue(float x, float y);
        public void addValue(ConstSFVec2f vec);
        public void addValue(SFVec2f vec);
        public void insertValue(int index, float x, float y);
        public void insertValue(int index, ConstSFVec2f vec);
        public void insertValue(int index, SFVec2f vec);
        // This overrides a method in Object
        public String toString();
}
public class MFVec3f extends MField
{
        public MFVec3f();
        public MFVec3f(float vec3s[][]);
        public MFVec3f(float vec3s[]);
        public MFVec3f(int size, float vec3s[]);
        public void getValue(float vec3s[][]);
        public void getValue(float vec3s[]);
        public void setValue(float vec3s[][]);
        public void setValue(float vec3s[]);
        public void setValue(int size, float vec3s[]);
        public void setValue(MFVec3f vecs);
```

```
      public void setValue(ConstMFVec3f vecs);
      public void get1Value(int index, float vec3s[]);
      public void get1Value(int index, SFVec3f vec);
      public void set1Value(int index, float x, float y, float z);
      public void set1Value(int index, ConstSFVec3f vec);
      public void set1Value(int index, SFVec3f vec);
      public void addValue(float x, float y, float z);
      public void addValue(ConstSFVec3f vec);
      public void addValue(SFVec3f vec);
      public void insertValue(int index, float x, float y, float z);
      public void insertValue(int index, ConstSFVec3f vec);
      public void insertValue(int index, SFVec3f vec);
      // This overrides a method in Object
      public String toString();
}
```

vrml.node Package

```
package vrml.node;

// This is the general Node class
// public abstract class Node extends BaseNode
{
   // Get an EventIn by name. Return value is write-only.
   //   Throws an InvalidEventInException if eventInName isn't a
   //   valid event in name for a node of this type.
   public final Field getEventIn(String fieldName);

   // Get an EventOut by name. Return value is read-only.
   //   Throws an InvalidEventOutException if eventOutName isn't a
   //   valid event out name for a node of this type.
   public final ConstField getEventOut(String fieldName);

   // Get an exposed field by name.
   //   Throws an InvalidExposedFieldException if fieldName isn't a
   //   valid exposed field name for a node of this type.
   public final Field getExposedField(String fieldName);

   // This overrides a method in Object
    public String toString();
}

// This is the general Script class, to be subclassed by all
// scripts. Note that the provided methods allow the script
// author to explicitly throw tailored exceptions in case
// something goes wrong in the script.
```

```
public abstract class Script extends BaseNode
{
  // This method is called before any event is generated
  public void initialize();

  // Get a Field by name.
  //   Throws an InvalidFieldException if fieldName isn't a valid
  //   event in name for a node of this type.
  protected final Field getField(String fieldName);

  // Get an EventOut by name.
  //   Throws an InvalidEventOutException if eventOutName isn't a
  //   valid event out name for a node of this type.
  protected final Field getEventOut(String fieldName);

  // Get an EventIn by name.
  //   Throws an InvalidEventInException if eventInName isn't a
  //   valid event out name for a node of this type.
  protected final Field getEventIn(String fieldName);

  // processEvents() is called automatically when the script
  //   receives some set of events. It should not be called
  //   directly except by its subclass.   count indicates the
  //   number of events delivered.
  public void processEvents(int count, Event events[]);

  // processEvent() is called automatically when the script
  // receives an event.
  public void processEvent(Event event);

  // eventsProcessed() is called after every invocation of
  // processEvents().
  public void eventsProcessed()

  // shutdown() is called when this Script node is deleted.
  public void shutdown();

  // This overrides a method in Object
  public String toString();
}
```

C.9 Example of Exception Class

```
public class InvalidEventInException
    extends IllegalArgumentException {
```

```java
  // Constructs an InvalidEventInException with no detail
  //  message.
  public InvalidEventInException() {
    super();
  }

  // Constructs an InvalidEventInException with the specified
  // detail message.  A detail message is a String that
  // describes this particular exception.  @param s the detail
  // message
  public InvalidEventInException(String s) {
    super(s);
  }
}

public class InvalidEventOutException
    extends IllegalArgumentException {
  public InvalidEventOutException(){
    super();
  }
  public InvalidEventOutException(String s){
    super(s);
  }
}

public class InvalidFieldException
    extends IllegalArgumentException {
  public InvalidFieldException(){
    super();
  }
  public InvalidFieldException(String s){
    super(s);
  }
}

public class InvalidExposedFieldException
    extends IllegalArgumentException
{
  public InvalidExposedFieldException(){
    super();
  }
  public InvalidExposedFieldException(String s){
    super(s);
  }
}
```

```java
public class InvalidVRMLSyntaxException extends Exception {
  public InvalidVRMLSyntaxException(){
    super();
  }
  public InvalidVRMLSyntaxException(String s){
    super(s);
  }

  // This overrides a method in Exception
  public String getMessage();
}

public class InvalidRouteException
    extends IllegalArgumentException {
  public InvalidRouteException(){
    super();
  }
  public InvalidRouteException(String s){
    super(s);
  }
}

public class InvalidFieldChangeException
    extends IllegalArgumentException {
  public InvalidFieldChangeException(){
    super();
  }
  public InvalidFieldChangeException(String s){
    super(s);
  }
}
```

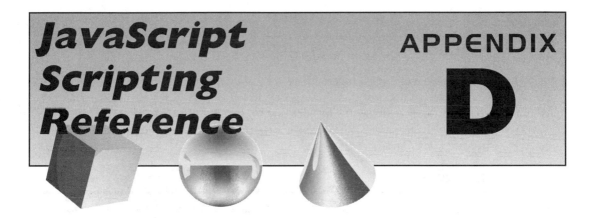

JavaScript Scripting Reference

APPENDIX D

This appendix describes the use of JavaScript with the **Script** node. Section 2.7, Scripting, contains a general overview of scripting in VRML while the Script section of Chapter 3, Node Reference, describes the **Script** node.

DESIGN NOTE

Support for JavaScript inside **Script** nodes is not required, but if a browser does support JavaScript inside **Script** nodes, it is required to adhere to the specifications in this appendix.

> **Note:** As of this writing (early 1997), some browsers support a subset of the JavaScript language, called VRMLScript. It is likely that these browsers will support the full JavaScript specification in future releases.

TIP

JavaScript is generally easier to learn and use than Java, because it is weakly typed and does not require code to be run through a compiler. Simple **Scripts** written in Java-Script are generally smaller than the equivalent script written in Java (the minimum size for a Java .class file is about 200 bytes), and putting the script's code directly into the VRML file means the VRML browser has to make fewer HTTP fetch requests. However, Java is more powerful than JavaScript and will execute large scripts much faster.

D.1 Introduction

JavaScript is a compact, object-based scripting language for creating client and server Internet applications and was developed by Netscape Communications Corporation. See the JavaScript Web site for general information on using the language: (`http:home.netscape.com/eng/mozilla/3.0/handbook/javascript/index.html`).

DESIGN NOTE

This appendix was initially created by Chris Marrin, and was enhanced and evolved by Jan Hardenbergh, Jim Kent, and a variety of contributors on the *www-vrml* email list.

D.2 Language

Netscape JavaScript was created by Netscape Communications Corporation (`http://home.netscape.com`). JavaScript is a programmable API that allows cross-platform scripting of events, objects, and actions. *JavaScript Specification, Version 1.1,* can be found at: `http://home.netscape.com/eng/javascript`. It is expected that JavaScript, version 1.2, will be the scripting language of a **Script** node when JavaScript is standardized. JavaScript is currently undergoing standardization through ECMA.

The `Math` object is required to be supported by the JavaScript implementation. This includes the constants `E`, `LN10`, `LN2`, `PI`, `SQRT1_2`, and `SQRT2`, and the methods `abs()`, `acos()`, `asin()`, `atan()`, `atan2()`, `ceil()`, `cos()`, `exp()`, `floor()`, `log()`, `max()`, `min()`, `pow()`, `random()`, `round()`, `sin()`, `sqrt()`, and `tan()`.

D.3 Supported Protocol in the Script Node's *url* Field

D.3.1 Access

The *url* field of the **Script** node may contain a URL that references JavaScript code:

```
Script { url "http://foo.com/myScript.js" }
```

The `javascript:` protocol allows the script to be placed inline as follows:

```
Script { url "javascript: function foo() { ... }"    }
```

The *url* field may contain multiple URLs and thus reference a remote file or inline code:

```
Script {
  url [ "http://foo.com/myScript.js",
        "javascript: function foo() { ... }" ]
}
```

D.3.2 File Extension

The file extension for JavaScript source code is `.js`.

D.3.3 MIME Type

The MIME type for JavaScript source code is defined as `application/x-javascript`.

D.4 EventIn Handling

D.4.1 Receiving EventIns

Events sent to the **Script** node are passed to the corresponding JavaScript function in the script. The script is specified in the *url* field of the **Script** node. The function's name is the same as the eventIn and is passed two arguments: the event value and its time stamp (see Section D.4.2, Parameter Passing and the eventIn Function). If there is no corresponding JavaScript function in the script, the browser's behavior is undefined. For example, the following **Script** node has one eventIn field with the name *start*:

```
Script {
  eventIn SFBool start
  url "javascript: function start(value, timestamp) {...}"
}
```

In this example, when the *start* eventIn is sent, the `start()` function is executed.

D.4.2 Parameter Passing and the EventIn Function

When a **Script** node receives an eventIn, a corresponding method in the file specified in the *url* field of the **Script** node is called. This method has two arguments.
The value of the eventIn is passed as the first argument and the time stamp of the
eventIn is passed as the second argument. The type of the value is the same as the type
of the eventIn and the type of the time stamp is a JavaScript numeric value corresponding to an SFTime. See Section D.6.1, VRML Field-to-JavaScript Variable
Conversion, for a description of how VRML types appear in JavaScript. The **Script**
may not refer to an eventIn field.

D.4.3 `EventsProcessed()` Method

Authors may define a function named `eventsProcessed()` that is to be called
after some set of events has been received. Some implementations call this function
after the return from each eventIn function, while others call it only after processing a number of eventIn functions. In the latter case, an author can improve performance by placing lengthy processing algorithms that do not need to execute for
every event received into the `eventsProcessed()` function.

The following example illustrates the use of eventIns: The author needs to compute
a complex inverse kinematics operation at each time step of an animation
sequence. The sequence is single-stepped using a **TouchSensor** and button geometry. Normally the author would have an eventIn function execute whenever the
button is pressed. This function would increment the time step, then run the
inverse kinematics algorithm. But, this would execute the complex algorithm at
every button press and the user could easily get ahead of the algorithm by clicking
on the button rapidly. To solve this, the eventIn function can be changed simply to
increment the time step and the inverse kinematics algorithm can be moved to an
`eventsProcessed()` function. In an efficient implementation, the clicks would
be queued. When the user clicks quickly, the time step would be incremented once
for each button click but the complex algorithm will be executed only once. In this
way the animation sequence will keep up with the user.

The `eventsProcessed()` function takes no parameters. Events generated from it
are given the time stamp of the last event processed.

D.4.4 `Initialize()` Method

Authors may define a function named `initialize()`, which is invoked at some
time after the VRML file containing the corresponding **Script** node has been loaded
and before any events are processed. This allows initialization tasks to be performed prior to events being received. These might include such actions as constructing geometry or initializing external mechanisms.

The `initialize()` function takes no parameters. Events generated from it are
given the time stamp of when the **Script** node was loaded.

D.4.5 `Shutdown()` Method

Authors may define a function named `shutdown()`, which is invoked when the corresponding **Script** node is deleted or when the world containing the **Script** node is unloaded or replaced by another world. This function can be used to send events informing external mechanisms that the **Script** node is being deleted so they can clean up allocated resources.

The `shutdown()` function has no parameters. Events generated from it are given the time stamp of when the **Script** node was deleted.

D.5 Accessing Fields

D.5.1 Accessing Fields and EventOuts of the Script

The fields and eventOuts of a **Script** node are accessible from its JavaScript functions. As in all other nodes, the fields are accessible only within the **Script**. The eventIns are not accessible. The **Script**'s eventIns can be routed to and its eventOuts can be routed from. Another **Script** node with a pointer to this node can access its eventIns and eventOuts as for any other node.

A field defined in the **Script** node is available to the script by using its name. Its value can be read or written. This value is persistent across function calls. EventOuts defined in the **Script** node can also be read. The value is the last value assigned.

D.5.2 Accessing Fields and EventOuts of Other Nodes

The script can access any exposedField, eventIn, or eventOut of any node to which it has a pointer:

```
DEF SomeNode Transform { }
  Script {
    field SFNode node USE SomeNode
    eventIn SFVec3f pos
    directOutput TRUE
    url "javascript:
      function pos(value) {
        node.set_translation = value;
      }"
}
```

This example sends a *set_translation* eventIn to the **Transform** node. An eventIn on a passed node can appear only on the left side of the assignment. An eventOut in the passed node can appear only on the right side, which reads the last value sent out. Fields in the passed node cannot be accessed. However, exposedFields can either send an event to the *set_* eventIn or read the current value of the *_changed* eventOut. This follows the routing model of the rest of VRML.

Events generated by setting an eventIn on a node are sent at the completion of the currently executing function. The eventIn must be assigned a value of the same data type. No partial assignments are allowed. For example, one cannot assign the red value of an SFColor eventIn. Since eventIns are strictly write-only, the remainder of the partial assignment would have invalid fields. Assigning to the eventIn field multiple times during one execution of the function still only sends one event and that event is the last value assigned.

D.5.3 Sending EventOuts

Assigning to an eventOut sends that event at the completion of the currently executing function. Assigning to the eventOut multiple times during one execution of the function still only sends one event and that event is the value of the eventOut at the completion of script execution.

D.6 JavaScript Objects

D.6.1 VRML-Field-to-JavaScript Variable Conversion

JavaScript native data types consist of boolean, numeric, and string. The language is not typed, so data types are implicit on assignment. The VRML 2.0 SFBool is mapped to the JavaScript boolean. In addition to the JavaScript true and false constants, the VRML 2.0 TRUE and FALSE values may be used. The VRML 2.0 SFInt32, SFFloat, and SFTime fields are mapped to the numeric data type. It will maintain double-precision accuracy. They will be passed by value in function calls. All other VRML 2.0 fields are mapped to JavaScript objects. JavaScript objects are passed by reference.

The JavaScript boolean, numeric, and string data types are automatically converted to other data types when needed.

In JavaScript, assigning a new value to a variable gives the variable the data type of the new value, in addition to the value. Scalar values (boolean and numeric) are assigned by copying the value. Other objects are assigned by reference.

When assignments are made to eventOuts and fields, the values are converted to the VRML field type. Scalar values (boolean and numeric) are assigned by copying the value. Other objects are assigned by reference.

The SF objects will be assigned as references, except for assigning to or from eventOut, fields, and MF objects. The exceptions for eventOut, field, and MF objects are at the interface between VRML field values and JavaScript variables. The VRML fields are maintained in the correct data type and must be copied at assignment.

For eventOut objects, assignment copies the value to the eventOut, which will be sent on completion of the current function. Assigning an eventOut to an internal variable creates a new object of the same type as the eventOut with the current value of the eventOut. Field objects behave identically to eventOut objects, except that no event is sent on completion of the function.

Assigning an element of an MF object to an SF object creates a new object of the corresponding SF object type with the current value of the specified MF element. Assigning an SF object to an element of an MF object (which must be of the corresponding type) copies the value of the SF object into the dereferenced element of the MF object.

D.6.2 Browser Object

This subclause lists the functions available in the browser object that allow scripts to get and set browser information. Return values and parameters are shown typed using VRML data types for clarity. Descriptions of the methods are provided in Section 2.7.10, Browser Script Interface.

Return value	Method Name
String	getName()
String	getVersion()
numeric	getCurrentSpeed()
numeric	getCurrentFrameRate()
String	getWorldURL()
void	replaceWorld(MFNode nodes)
MFNode	createVrmlFromString(String vrmlSyntax)
void	createVrmlFromURL(MFString url, Node node, String event)
void	addRoute(SFNode fromNode, String fromEventOut, SFNode toNode, String toEventIn)
void	deleteRoute(SFNode fromNode, String fromEventOut, SFNode toNode, String toEventIn)
void	loadURL(MFString url, MFString parameter)
void	setDescription(String description)

D.6.3 SFColor Object

The SFColor object corresponds to a VRML 2.0 SFColor field. All properties are accessed using the syntax sfColorObjectName.<property>, where sfColor-ObjectName is an instance of an SFColor object. The properties may also be accessed by the indices `[0]` for red, `[1]` for green, and `[2]` for blue. All methods are invoked using the syntax `sfColorObjectName.method(<argument-list>)`, where `sfColorObjectName` is an instance of an `SFColor` object.

Instance Creation Methods

`sfColorObjectName = new SFColor(r, g, b)`

> `r`, `g`, and `b` are scalar values with the red, green, and blue values of the color. Missing values will be filled by 0.

Properties

`r`

> red component of the color

`g`

> green component of the color

`b`

> blue component of the color

Methods

`setHSV(h, s, v)`

> sets the value of the color by specifying the scalar values of hue (`h`), saturation (`s`), and value (`v`)

`getHSV()`

> returns the value of the color in a three element numeric array, with hue at index 0, saturation at index 1, and value at index 2

`toString()`

> returns a `String` containing the values of `r`, `g`, and `b`.

D.6.4 `SFImage` Object

The `SFImage` object corresponds to a VRML 2.0 SFImage field.

Instance Creation Methods

`sfImageObjectName = new SFImage(x, y, comp, array)`

> `x` is the *x* dimension of the image; `y` is the *y* dimension of the image; `comp` is the number of components of the image: 1 for gray scale, 2 for gray scale + alpha,

3 for RGB, 4 for RGB + alpha. All these values are scalar. `array` is an MFInt32 field containing the `x*y` values for the pixels of the image. The format of each pixel is the same as the **PixelTexture** file format.

Properties

x

the *x* dimension of the image

y

the *y* dimension of the image

comp

the number of components of the image (1 for gray scale, 2 for gray scale + alpha, 3 for RGB, 4 for RGB + alpha)

array

the image data

Methods

toString()

returns a `String` containing the value of `x`, `y`, `comp`, and `array`

D.6.5 `SFNode` Object

The `SFNode` object corresponds to a VRML 2.0 SFNode field.

Instance Creation Methods

sfNodeObjectName = new SFNode(vrmlstring)

`vrmlstring` is an ASCII string containing the definition of a VRML 2.0 node

Properties

Each node may assign values to its eventIns and obtain the last output values of its eventOuts using the **sfNodeObjectName.eventName** syntax.

Methods

toString()

returns a **String** containing the UTF-8 VRML 2.0 equivalent of the node or, if that is not available, the empty string

D.6.6 `SFRotation` Object

The `SFRotation` object corresponds to a VRML 2.0 SFRotation field. It has four numeric properties: *x, y, z* (the axis of rotation), and angle. These may also be addressed by indices [0] through [3].

Instance Creation Methods

`sfRotationObjectName = new SFRotation(x, y, z, angle)`

`x`, `y`, and `z` are the axis of the rotation; `angle` is the angle of the rotation (in radians). All values are scalar. Missing values will default to 0, except `y`, which defaults to 1.

`sfRotationObjectName = new SFRotation(axis, angle)`

`axis` is an `SFVec3f` object with a value that is the axis of rotation; `angle` is the scalar angle of the rotation (in radians)

`sfRotationObjectName = new SFRotation(fromVector, toVector)`

`fromVector` and `toVector` are `SFVec3f`-valued objects. These vectors are normalized and the rotation value that would rotate from the `fromVector` to the `toVector` is stored in the object.

Properties

`x`

returns the first value of the axis vector

`y`

returns the second value of the axis vector

`z`

returns the third value of the axis vector

`angle`

an `SFFloat` corresponding to the angle of the rotation (in radians)

Methods

`getAxis()`

returns the axis of rotation as an `SFVec3f` object

inverse()

returns an `SFRotation` object with a value that is the inverse of this object's rotation

multiply(rotation)

returns an `SFRotation` with a value that is the object multiplied by the passed `SFRotation`

multVec(vec)

returns an `SFVec3f` with a value that is the `SFVec3f vec` multiplied by the matrix corresponding to this object's rotation

setAxis(vec)

sets the axis of rotation to the vector passed in **vec**

slerp(destRotation, t)

Returns an `SFRotation` with a value that is the spherical linear interpolation between this object's rotation and `destRotation` at value $0 \leq t \leq 1$. For **t** = 0, the value is this object's rotation. For **t** = 1, the value is `destRotation`.

toString()

returns a `String` containing the value of **x**, **y**, **z**, and **angle**

D.6.7 `SFVec2f` Object

The `SFVec2f` object corresponds to a VRML 2.0 SFVec2f field. Each component of the vector can be accessed using the **x** and **y** properties or using C-style array dereferencing (i.e., `sfVec2fObjectName[0]` or `sfVec2fObjectName[1]`).

Instance Creation Methods

sfVec2fObjectName = new SFVec2f(number1, number2)

where **number1** and **number2** are scalar expressions. Missing values will be filled by 0.

Properties

x

returns the first value of the vector

y

returns the second value of the vector

Methods

add(vec)

returns an **SFVec2f** with a value that is the passed **SFVec2f** added, component-wise, to the object

divide(number)

returns an **SFVec2f** with a value that is the object divided by the passed numeric value

dot(vec)

returns the dot product of this vector and **SFVec2f vec**

length()

returns the geometric length of this vector

multiply(number)

returns an **SFVec2f** with a value that is the object multiplied by the passed numeric value

negate()

returns an **SFVec2f** with a value that is the component-wise negation of the object

normalize()

returns an **SFVec2f** of object converted to unit length

subtract(vec)

returns an **SFVec2f** with a value that is the passed **SFVec2f** subtracted, component-wise, from the object

toString()

returns a **String** containing the value of **x** and **y**

D.6.8 **SFVec3f Object**

The **SFVec3f** object corresponds to a VRML 2.0 SFVec3f field. Each component of the vector can be accessed using the **x**, **y**, and **z** properties or using C-style array dereferencing (i.e., **sfVec3fObjectName[0]**, **sfVec3fObjectName[1]** or **sfVec3fObjectName[2]**).

Instance Creation Methods

sfVec3fObjectName = new SFVec3f(number1, number2, number3)

where **number1**, **number2**, and **number3** are scalar expressions. Missing values will be filled by 0.

Properties

x

returns the first value of the vector

y

returns the second value of the vector

z

returns the third value of the vector

Methods

add(vec)

returns an **SFVec3f** with a value that is the passed **SFVec3f** added, component-wise, to the object

cross(vec)

returns the cross product of the object and the passed **SFVec3f**

divide(number)

returns an **SFVec3f** with a value that is the object divided by the passed numeric value

dot(vec)

returns the dot product of this vector and **SFVec3f vec**

length()

returns the geometric length of this vector

multiply(number)

returns an **SFVec3f** with a value that is the object multiplied by the passed numeric value

negate()

returns an `SFVec3f` with a value that is the component-wise negation of the object

normalize()

returns an `SFVec3f` of object converted to unit length

subtract(vec)

returns an `SFVec3f` with a value that is the passed `SFVec3f` subtracted, component-wise, from the object

toString()

returns a `String` containing the value of `r`, `g`, and `b`

D.6.9 `MFColor` Object

The `MFColor` object corresponds to a VRML 2.0 MFColor field. It is used to store a 1D array of `SFColor` objects. Individual elements of the array can be referenced using the standard C-style dereferencing operator (e.g., `mfColorObjectName[index]`, where `index` is an integer-valued expression with $0 \leq$ `index` $<$ `length` and `length` is the number of elements in the array). Assigning to an element with `index` $>$ `length` results in the array being dynamically expanded to contain length elements. All elements not explicitly initialized are set to `SFColor(0, 0, 0)`.

Instance Creation Methods

mfColorObjectName = new MFColor([SFColor, SFColor, ...])

can be passed 0 or more `SFColor`-valued expressions to initialize the elements of the array

Properties

length

is the integer field for getting/setting the number of elements in the array

Methods

toString()

returns a `String` containing the value of `MFColor` array

D.6.10 `MFFloat` Object

The `MFFloat` object corresponds to a VRML 2.0 MFFloat field. It is used to store a 1D array of `SFFloat` objects. Individual elements of the array can be referenced using the standard C-style dereferencing operator (e.g., `mfFloatObject-Name[index]`, where `index` is an integer-valued expression with $0 \leq$ `index` $<$ `length` and `length` is the number of elements in the array). Assigning to an element with `index` > `length` results in the array being dynamically expanded to contain length elements. All elements not explicitly initialized are set to 0.

Instance Creation Methods

`mfFloatObjectName = new MFFloat([number, number...])`

> can be passed zero or more numeric-valued expressions to initialize the elements of the array

Properties

`length`

> is the integer field for getting/setting the number of elements in the array

Methods

`toString()`

> returns a `String` containing the value of `MFFloat` array

D.6.11 `MFInt32` Object

The `MFInt32` object corresponds to a VRML 2.0 MFInt32 field. It is used to store a 1D array of `SFInt32` objects. Individual elements of the array can be referenced using the standard C-style dereferencing operator (e.g., `mfInt32Object-Name[index]`, where `index` is an integer-valued expression with $0 \leq$ `index` $<$ `length` and `length` is the number of elements in the array). Assigning to an element with `index` > `length` results in the array being dynamically expanded to contain length elements. All elements not explicitly initialized are set to 0.

Instance Creation Methods

`mfInt32ObjectName = new MFInt32([number, number, ...])`

> can be passed zero or more integer-valued expressions to initialize the elements of the array

Properties

length

> is the integer field for getting/setting the number of elements in the array

Methods

toString()

> returns a **String** containing the value of **MFInt32** array

D.6.12 **MFNode** Object

The **MFNode** object corresponds to a VRML 2.0 MFNode field. It is used to store a 1D array of **SFNode** objects. Individual elements of the array can be referenced using the standard C-style dereferencing operator (e.g., **mfNodeObjectName[index]**, where **index** is an integer-valued expression with $0 \leq$ **index** $<$ **length** and **length** is the number of elements in the array). Assigning to an element with **index** $>$ **length** results in the array being dynamically expanded to contain **length** elements. All elements not explicitly initialized are set to **NULL**.

Instance Creation Methods

mfNodeObjectName = new MFNode([SFNode, SFNode, ...])

> can be passed zero or more **SFNode**-valued expressions to initialize the elements of the array

Properties

length

> is the integer field for getting/setting the number of elements in the array

Methods

toString()

> returns a **String** containing the VRML 2.0 UTF-8 representation of each node or an empty **MFNode** **"[]"**

D.6.13 **MFRotation** Object

The **MFRotation** object corresponds to a VRML 2.0 MFRotation field. It is used to store a 1D array of **SFRotation** objects. Individual elements of the array can be referenced using the standard C-style dereferencing operator (e.g., `mfRotation-ObjectName[index]`, where `index` is an integer-valued expression with $0 \leq index < length$ and `length` is the number of elements in the array). Assigning to an element with `index > length` results in the array being dynamically expanded to contain `length` elements. All elements not explicitly initialized are set to `SFRotation(0, 0, 1, 0)`.

Instance Creation Methods

```
mfRotationObjectName = new MFRotation(
                            [MFRotation, MFRotation, ...])
```

can be passed zero or more `SFRotation`-valued expressions to initialize the elements of the array

Properties

`length`

is the integer field for getting/setting the number of elements in the array

Methods

`toString()`

returns a `String` containing the value of `MFRotation` array

D.6.14 `MFString` Object

The `MFString` object corresponds to a VRML 2.0 MFString field. It is used to store a 1D array of `SFString` objects. Individual elements of the array can be referenced using the standard C-style dereferencing operator (e.g., `mfStringObject-Name[index]`, where `index` is an integer-valued expression with $0 \leq index < length$ and `length` is the number of elements in the array). Assigning to an element with `index > length` results in the array being dynamically expanded to contain `length` elements. All elements not explicitly initialized are set to the empty string.

Instance Creation Methods

```
mfStringObjectName = new MFString([SFString, SFString, ...])
```

can be passed zero or more `SFString`-valued expressions to initialize the elements of the array

Properties

length

> is the integer field for getting/setting the number of elements in the array

Methods

toString()

> returns a `String` containing the value of `MFString` array

D.6.15 MFVec2f Object

The `MFVec2f` object corresponds to a VRML 2.0 MFVec2f field. It is used to store a 1D array of `SFVec2f` objects. Individual elements of the array can be referenced using the standard C-style dereferencing operator (e.g., `mfVec2fObject-Name[index]`, where `index` is an integer-valued expression with $0 \leq$ `index` $<$ `length` and `length` is the number of elements in the array). Assigning to an element with `index` $>$ `length` results in the array being dynamically expanded to contain `length` elements. All elements not explicitly initialized are set to `SFVec2f(0, 0)`.

Instance Creation Methods

mfVec2fObjectName = new MFVec2f([SFVec2f, SFVec2f, ...])

> can be passed zero or more `SFVec2f`-valued expressions to initialize the elements of the array

Properties

length

> is the integer field for getting/setting the number of elements in the array

Methods

toString()

> returns a `String` containing the value of `MFVec2f` array

D.6.16 MFVec3f Object

The `MFVec3f` object corresponds to a VRML 2.0 MFVec3f field. It is used to store a 1D array of `SFVec3f` objects. Individual elements of the array can be referenced using the standard C-style dereferencing operator (e.g., `mfVec3fObject-`

`Name[index]`, where `index` is an integer-valued expression with $0 \leq \text{index} <$ `length` and `length` is the number of elements in the array). Assigning to an element with `index` > `length` results in the array being dynamically expanded to contain `length` elements. All elements not explicitly initialized are set to `SFVec3f(0, 0, 0)`.

Instance Creation Methods

mfVec3fObjectName = new MFVec3f([SFVec3f, SFVec3f,...])

can be passed zero or more `SFVec3f`-valued expressions to initialize the elements of the array

Properties

length

is the integer field for getting/setting the number of elements in the array

Methods

toString()

returns a `String` containing the value of `MFVec3f` array

D.6.17 VrmlMatrix Object

The `VrmlMatrix` object provides many useful methods for performing manipulations on 4×4 matrices. Each element of the matrix can be accessed using C-style array dereferencing (i.e., `vrmlMatrixObjectName[0][1]` is the element in row 0, column 1). The results of dereferencing a `VrmlMatrix` object using a single index (i.e., `vrmlMatrixObjectName[0]`) are undefined. The translation elements will be in the fourth row. For example, `vrmlMatrixObjectName[3][0]` is the X offset.

Instance Creation Methods

VrmlMatrixObjectName = new VrmlMatrix(f11, f12, f13, f14, f21, f22, f23, f24, f31, f32, f33, f34, f41, f42, f43, f44)

creates and returns a new matrix initialized with the values in `f11` through `f44`. The translation values will be `f41`, `f41`, and `f42`.

VrmlMatrixObjectName = new VrmlMatrix()

creates and returns a new matrix initialized with the identity matrix

Properties

`none`

Methods

`setTransform( translation, rotation, scale, scaleOrientation, center )`

sets the `VrmlMatrix` to the passed values. The `translation` value is an `SFVec3f` object, `rotation` is an `SFRotation` object, `scale` is an `SFVec3f` object, `scaleOrientation` is an `SFRotation` object, and **center** is an `SFVec3f` object. Any of the rightmost parameters can be omitted. In other words, the method can take from 0 to 5 parameters. For example, you can specify 0 parameters (resulting in an identity matrix), 1 parameter (a translation), 2 parameters (a translation and a rotation), 3 parameters (a translation, rotation, and a scale), and so on. Any unspecified parameter is set to its default as specified in the **Transform** node section of the VRML 2.0 specification.

`getTransform(translation, rotation, scale)`

decomposes the `VrmlMatrix` and returns the components in the passed `translation` (`SFVec3f`), `rotation` (`SFRotation`), and `scale` (`SFVec3f`) objects. The types of these passed objects is the same as the first three arguments to `setTransform`. If any passed object is not sent, that value is not returned. Any projection or shear information in the matrix is ignored.

`inverse()`

returns a `VrmlMatrix` with a value that is the inverse of this object

`transpose()`

returns a `VrmlMatrix` with a value that is the transpose of this object

`multLeft(matrix)`

returns a `VrmlMatrix` with a value that is the object multiplied by the passed matrix on the left

`multRight(matrix)`

returns a `VrmlMatrix` with a value that is the object multiplied by the passed matrix on the right

`multVecMatrix(vec)`

returns an `SFVec3f` with a value that is the object multiplied by the passed row vector

Example **459**

multMatrixVec(vec)

returns an `SFVec3f` with a value that is the object multiplied by the passed column vector

toString()

returns a `String` containing the values of the `VrmlMatrix`

D.7 Example

The following is an example of a **Script** node that determines whether a given color contains a lot of red. The **Script** node exposes a *color* field, an eventIn, and an eventOut:

```
Script {
    field    SFColor currentColor 0 0 0
    eventIn  SFColor colorIn
    eventOut SFBool  isRed
    url "javascript:
      function colorIn(newColor, ts) {
        // This method is called when a colorIn event is received
        currentColor = newColor;
      }
      function eventsProcessed() {
        if (currentColor[0] >= 0.5)
          // if red is at or above 50%
          isRed = true;
      }"
}
```

Details on when the methods defined in the **Script** are called are provided in Section 2.4.3, Execution Model.

The following examples illustrate the use of browser access:

`createVrmlFromURL()` method:

```
DEF Example Script {
  field    SFNode myself USE Example
  field    MFString url "foo.wrl"
  eventIn MFNode    nodesLoaded
  eventIn SFBool    trigger_event
  url "javascript:
    function trigger_event(value, ts) {
      // do something and then fetch values
      browser.createVRMLFromURL( url, myself, "nodesLoaded" );
    }
```

```
      function nodesLoaded(value, timestamp){
        // do something
      }"
}
```

addRoute() method:

```
DEF Sensor TouchSensor {}
DEF Baa Script {
  field   SFNode myself USE Baa
  field   SFNode fromNode USE Sensor
  eventIn SFBool clicked
  eventIn SFBool trigger_event
  url "javascript:
    function trigger_event(eventIn_value){
      // do something and then add routing
      browser.addRoute( fromNode, "isActive", myself, "clicked");
    }
    function clicked(value){
      // do something
    }"
}
```

The following example illustrates assigning with references and assigning by copying:

```
Script {
  eventIn  SFBool  eI
  eventOut SFVec3f eO
  field    MFVec3f f [ ]
  url "javascript:
    function eI() {
      eO = new SFVec3f(0,1,2); // 'eO' contains the value
                               // (0,1,2) which will be sent
                               // out when the function
                               // is complete.

      a = eO;                  // 'a' contains a SFVec3f
                               // object with the value (0,1,2)

      b = a;                   // 'b' references the same
                               // object as 'a'.

      a.x = 3;                 // 'a' and 'b' both contain
                               // (3,1,2). 'eO' is unchanged.
```

Example **461**

```
        f[1] = a;                       // 'f[1]' contains the value
                                        // (3,1,2).

        c = f[1];                       // 'b' contains a SFVec3f
                                        // object with the value (3,1,2)

        f[1].y = 4;                     // 'f[1]' contains the value
                                        // (3,4,2).  'c' is unchanged.
    }"
}
```

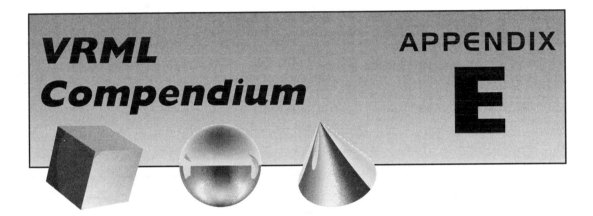

VRML Compendium

APPENDIX E

This chapter lists the URLs of a variety of interesting and useful VRML-related Web sites. Topics include browsers, general information guides, organizations, discussion groups, and technical documents on VRML 2.0.

E.1 VRML Browsers

Table E-1 contains known VRML 2.0 browsers as of January 1997. See the information site for more current listings.

TABLE E-1 *VRML 2.0 browsers*

Browser	Company	URL
Heat	Newfire, Inc.	http://www.newfire.com/
Community Place	Sony Corporation	http://vs.spiw.com/vs/
Cosmo Player	Silicon Graphics, Inc.	http://vrml.sgi.com/

TABLE E-I *VRML 2.0 browsers (Continued)*

Browser	Company	URL
GLview	EMD Enterprises	`http://www.glview.com/`
Live3D	Netscape Communication, Inc.	`http://home.netscape.com/eng/live3d/`
Liquid Reality	Dimension X, Inc.	`http://www.dimensionx.com/`
Oz Virtual	Oz Interactive, Inc.	`http://www.oz-inc.com/`
WorldView	Intervista, Inc.	`http://www.intervista.com/`

E.2 VRML Information Sites

The URLs in Table E-2 refer to Web sites that contain general and specific information on VRML. This includes introductory tutorials, history, frequently asked questions (FAQs), lists of VRML worlds, and references to relevant information:

TABLE E-2 *VRML 2.0 information sites*

Site	Who	URL
Browser Comparison	Greg Seidman	`http://zing.ncsl.nist.gov/~gseidman/` `vrml/comparison.html`
VRML Repository	SDSC	`http://www.sdsc.edu/vrml`
VRML Site	Bob Crispen	`http://hiwaay.net/~crispen/vrml`
SGI's VRML Site	Silicon Graphics, Inc.	`http://vrml.sgi.com/`
VRMLSite Magazine	Adrian Scott	`http://www.vrmlsite.com/`
VRML Forum	IAT	`http://www.iat.unc.edu/technology/vrml/`
VRML from Hell	Jim Race	`http://www.well.com/user/caferace/` `vrml.html`
VRML Test Suite	NIST	`http://www.itl.nist.gov/div897/ctg/vrml/` `vrml.htm`
VRML Update	Richard Tilmann	`http://cedar.cic.net/~rtilmann/mm/` `vrmlup.htm`

E.3 VRML Organizations

TABLE E-3 *Table E-3 VRML organizations*

Organization	URL
The VRML Architecture Group (VAG)	`http://vag.vrml.org/`
The VRML Consortium	`http://vag.vrml.org/consort/`

E.4 VRML Email Lists and Newsgroups

TABLE E-4 *VRML email lists and newsgroups*

Name	Description
`comp.lang.vrml`	Discussion of VRML language issues (technical)
`news.livingworlds.com`	Living Worlds newsgroups (see `http://www.livingworlds.com/`)
`secnews.netscape.com/netscape.live3d`	Netscape's live 3D newsgroup
`vrml-java`	VRML discussion group on Java scripting
`vrml.sgi.com/sgi.cosmoplayer`	Silicon Graphics, Inc.'s, Cosmo Player newsgroup
`vrml.sgi.com/sgi.cosmoworlds`	Silicon Graphics, Inc.'s, Cosmo Worlds newsgroup
`www-vrml@vag.vrml.org`	Primary VRML discussion group (see `http://vag.vrml.org/www-vrml/`)

E.5 VRML Technical Documents

Document	URL
Proposal for External Authoring Interface	`http://vrml.sgi.com/moving-worlds/spec/ExternalInterface.html`
Proposal for VRML 2.0 Compressed Binary Format	`http://www.rs6000.ibm.com/vrml/binary/`
The VRML 1.0 Specification	`http://vag.vrml.org/www-vrml/vrml10c.html`
The VRML 2.0 Specification	`http://vag.vrml.org/VRML2.0/FINAL/` and `http://vrml.sgi.com/moving-worlds/`

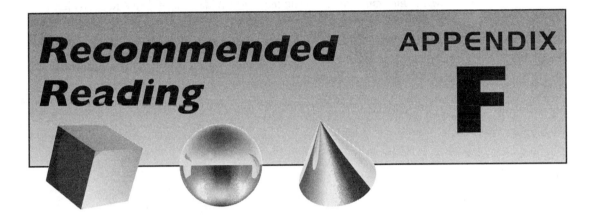

Recommended Reading

APPENDIX F

The following books provide an excellent background on computer graphics:

- *Computer Graphics Principles and Practice* by J. D. Foley, A. van Dam, S. Feiner, and J. F. Hughes (Addison-Wesley, 1990)
- *OpenGL Programming Guide* by Mason Woo, Jackie Neider, and Tom Davis (Addison-Wesley, 1997)
- *The Inventor Mentor* by Josie Wernecke (Addison-Wesley, 1994)

The following books provide complementary reading on VRML:

- *The VRML Handbook* by Jed Hartman and Josie Wernecke (Addison-Wesley, 1996)
- *The VRML 2.0 Sourcebook* by Andrea Ames, David R. Nadeau, and John L. Moreland (Wiley Computer Publishing, 1996)
- *Teach Yourself VRML 2.0 in 21 Days* by Chris Marrin and Bruce Campbell (Macmillan Computer Publishing, 1997)

The following books provide general information on the WWW and the Internet:

- *How to Set Up and Maintain a Web Site* by Lincoln D. Stein (Addison-Welsey, 1997)

- *Web Weaving: Designing and Managing an Effective Web Site* by Eric Tilton, Carl Steadman, and Tyler Jones (Addison-Wesley, 1996)

- *HTML for the World Wide Web: Visual QuickStart Guide* by Elizabeth Castro (Peachpit Press, 1996)

- *HTML 3: Electronic Publishing on the World Wide Web* by Dave Raggett, Jenny Lam, and Ian Alexander (Addison-Wesley, 1996)

- *Java in a Nutshell* by David Flanagan (O'Reilly and Associates, Inc., 1996)

- The *Java Series* of books (Addison-Wesley, 1996), `http://www.aw.com/com/cp/javaseries.html`.

- *JavaScript for the World Wide Web: Visual QuickStart Guide* by Ted Gesing and Jeremy Schneider (Peachpit Press, 1996)

Summary of Java Scripting API

APPENDIX

G

TABLE G-1 *Summary of Java classes, methods, and exceptions*

Class. .Method	<- Superclasses (argument types)	Return type
BaseNode.	<- Object	
.getType	()	String
.getBrowser	()	Browser
Browser.	<- Object	
.addRoute	(BaseNode, String, BaseNode, String)	void
.createVrmlFromString	(String vrmlSyntax)	BaseNode[]
.createVrmlFromURL	(String[] url, BaseNode, String eventIn)	void
.deleteRoute	(BaseNode, String, BaseNode, String)	void
.getName	()	String
.getVersion	()	String

TABLE G-I *Summary of Java classes, methods, and exceptions (Continued)*

Class. .Method	<- Superclasses (argument types)	Return type
.getCurrentSpeed	( )	float
.getCurrentFrameRate	( )	float
.getWorldURL	( )	String
.loadURL	(String url, String[] params)	void
.replaceWorld	(MFNode)	void
.setDescription	(String description)	void
ConstField.	**<- Field <- Object**	
Note: All ConstSF fields ...	**... unless otherwise noted:**	
ConstSF{type}.	**<- ConstField <- Field <- Object**	
ConstSF{type}	({javatype})	ConstSF{type}
.getValue	( )	{javatype}
ConstSFBool.	**javatype is boolean**	
ConstSFColor.	**<- ConstField <- Field <- Object**	
ConstSFColor	(float r, float g, float b)	ConstSFColor
.getBlue	( )	float
.getGreen	( )	float
.getRed	( )	float
.getValue	(float[] color)	void
ConstSFFloat.	**javatype is float**	
ConstSFImage.	**<- ConstField <- Field <- Object**	
ConstSFImage	(int w, int h, int nC, byte[] pixels)	ConstSFImage
.getComponents	( )	int
.getHeight	( )	int
.getPixels	(byte[] pixels)	void
.getWidth	( )	int
ConstSFInt32.	**javatype is int**	
ConstSFNode.	**javatype is BaseNode**	

TABLE G-I *Summary of Java classes, methods, and exceptions (Continued)*

Class. .Method	<- Superclasses (argument types)	Return type
ConstSFRotation.	<- ConstField <- Field <- Object	
ConstSFRotation	(float x, float y, float z, float angle)	ConstSFRotation
.getValue	(float[] xyza)	void
ConstSFString.	**javatype is ConstSFString**	
.getValue	()	String
ConstSFTime:	**javatype is double**	
ConstSFVec2f.	<- ConstField <- Field <- Object	
ConstSFVec2f	(float x, float y)	ConstSFVec2f
.getValue	(float[] xy)	void
.getX	()	float
.getY	()	float
ConstSFVec3f.	<- ConstField <- Field <- Object	
ConstSFVec3f	(float x, float y, float z)	ConstSFVec3f
.getValue	(float[] xyz)	void
.getX	()	float
.getY	()	float
.getZ	()	float
ConstMField.	<- ConstField <- Field <- Object	
Note: All ConstMF fields ...	**... unless otherwise noted:**	
ConstMF{type}.	<- ConstMField <- ConstField <- Field <- Object	
ConstMF{type}	({javatype}[])	ConstMF{type}
ConstMF{type}	(int size, {javatype}[])	ConstMF{type}
.get1Value	(int index)	{javatype}
.getValue	(float {javatype}[])	void
ConstMFColor.	<- ConstMField <- ConstField <- Field <- Object	
ConstMFColor	(float colors[][])	ConstMFColor

TABLE G-1 *Summary of Java classes, methods, and exceptions (Continued)*

Class. .Method	<- Superclasses (argument types)	Return type
ConstMFColor	(float colors[])	ConstMFColor
ConstMFColor	(int size, float color[])	ConstMFColor
.get1Value	(int index, float colors[])	void
.get1Value	(int index, SFColor color)	void
.getValue	(float colors[][])	void
.getValue	(float colors[])	void
ConstMFFloat.	**javatype is float**	
ConstMFInt32.	**javatype is int**	
ConstMFNode.	**<- ConstMField <- ConstField <- Field <- Object**	
ConstMFNode	(BaseNode node[])	ConstMFNode
ConstMFNode	(int size, BaseNode node[])	ConstMFNode
.get1Value	(int index)	BaseNode
.getValue	(BaseNode node[])	void
ConstMFRotation.	**<- ConstMField <- ConstField <- Field <- Object**	
ConstMFRotation	(float rots[][])	ConstMFRotation
ConstMFRotation	(float rots[])	ConstMFRotation
ConstMFRotation	(int size, float rot[s])	ConstMFRotation
.get1Value	(int index, float rots[])	void
.get1Value	(int index, SFRotation rots)	void
.getValue	(float rots[][])	void
.getValue	(float rots[])	void
ConstMFString.	**javatype is String**	
ConstMFTime.	**javatype is double**	
ConstMFVec2f.	**<- ConstMField <- ConstField <- Field <- Object**	
ConstMFVec2f	(float vec2[][])	ConstMFVec2f
ConstMFVec2f	(float vec2[])	ConstMFVec2f

TABLE G-I *Summary of Java classes, methods, and exceptions (Continued)*

Class. .Method	<- Superclasses (argument types)	Return type
ConstMFVec2f	(int size, float vec2[][])	ConstMFVec2f
.get1Value	(int index, float vec2[])	void
.get1Value	(int index, SFVec2f vec)	void
.getValue	(float vec2[][])	void
.getValue	(float vec2[])	void
ConstMFVec3f.	**<- ConstMField <- ConstField <- Field <- Object**	
ConstMFVec3f	(float vec3[][])	ConstMFVec3f
ConstMFVec3f	(float vec3[])	ConstMFVec3f
ConstMFVec3f	(int size, float vec2[][])	ConstMFVec3f
.get1Value	(int index, float vec2[])	void
.get1Value	(int index, SFVec3f vec)	void
.getValue	(float vec3[][])	void
.getValue	(float vec3[])	void
Event.	**<- Object**	
.clone	()	Object
.getName	()	String
.getTimeStamp	()	double
.getValue	()	ConstField
Field.	**<- Object**	
.clone	()	Object
MField.	**<- Field <- Object**	
.clear	()	void
.delete	(int index)	void
.getSize	()	int
Note: All MF fields . . .	**. . . unless otherwise noted:**	
MF{type}.	**<- MField <- Field <- Object**	
MF{type}	()	MF{type}

TABLE G-1 *Summary of Java classes, methods, and exceptions (Continued)*

Class. .Method	<- Superclasses (argument types)	Return type
MF{type}	({javatype}[])	MF{type}
MF{type}	(int size, {javatype}[])	MF{type}
.addValue	({javatype})	void
.addValue	(ConstSF{type})	void
.addValue	(SF{type})	void
.get1Value	(int index)	{javatype}
.getValue	({javatype}[])	void
.insertValue	(int index, {javatype})	void
.insertValue	(int index, ConstSF{type})	void
.insertValue	(int index, SF{type})	void
.set1Value	(int index, {javatype})	void
.set1Value	(int index, ConstSF{type})	void
.set1Value	(int index, SF{type})	void
.setValue	({javatype}[])	void
.setValue	(ConstMF{type})	void
.setValue	(MF{type})	void
MFColor.		
MFColor	()	MFColor
MFColor	(float[])	MFColor
MFColor	(int size, float[])	MFColor
MFColor	(float[][])	MFColor
.addValue	(float r, float g, float b)	void
.addValue	(ConstSFColor)	void
.addValue	(SFColor)	void
.get1Value	(int index, float[])	void
.get1Value	(int index, SFColor)	void
.getValue	(float[][])	void

TABLE G-1 *Summary of Java classes, methods, and exceptions (Continued)*

Class. .Method	<- Superclasses (argument types)	Return type
.getValue	(float[])	void
.insertValue	(int index, float r, float g, float b)	void
.insertValue	(int index, ConstSFColor)	void
.insertValue	(int index, SFColor)	void
.set1Value	(int index, float r, float g, float b)	void
.set1Value	(int index, ConstSFColor)	void
.set1Value	(int index, SFColor)	void
.setValue	(float[])	void
.setValue	(float[][])	void
.setValue	(ConstMFColor)	void
.setValue	(int size, float[])	void
.setValue	(MFColor)	void
MFFloat.	**javatype is float**	
MFInt32.	**javatype is int**	
MFNode.	**javatype is BaseNode**	
MFRotation.		
MFRotation	()	MFRotation
MFRotation	(float[])	MFRotation
MFRotation	(int size, float[])	MFRotation
MFRotation	(float[][])	MFRotation
.addValue	(float x, float y, float z, float angle)	void
.addValue	(ConstSFRotation)	void
.addValue	(SFRotation)	void
.get1Value	(int index, float[])	void
.get1Value	(int index, SFRotation)	void
.getValue	(float[][])	void
.getValue	(float[])	void

TABLE G-1 *Summary of Java classes, methods, and exceptions (Continued)*

Class. .Method	<- Superclasses (argument types)	Return type
.insertValue	(int index, float, float, float, float a)	void
.insertValue	(int index, ConstSFRotation)	void
.insertValue	(int index, SFRotation)	void
.set1Value	(int index, float, float, float, float a)	void
.set1Value	(int index, ConstSFRotation)	void
.set1Value	(int index, SFRotation)	void
.setValue	(float[])	void
.setValue	(float[][])	void
.setValue	(ConstMFRotation)	void
.setValue	(int size, float[])	void
.setValue	(MFRotation)	void
MFString.	**javatype is String**	
MFTime.	**javatype is double**	
MFVec2f.		
MFVec2f	()	MFVec2f
MFVec2f	(float[])	MFVec2f
MFVec2f	(int size, float[])	MFVec2f
MFVec2f	(float[][])	MFVec2f
.addValue	(float x, float y)	void
.addValue	(ConstSFVec2f)	void
.addValue	(SFVec2f)	void
.get1Value	(int index, float[])	void
.get1Value	(int index, SFVec2f)	void
.getValue	(float[][])	void
.getValue	(float[])	void
.insertValue	(int index, float x, float y)	void
.insertValue	(int index, ConstSFVec2f)	void

TABLE G-1 *Summary of Java classes, methods, and exceptions (Continued)*

Class. .Method	<- Superclasses (argument types)	Return type
.insertValue	(int index, SFVec2f)	void
.set1Value	(int index, float x, float y)	void
.set1Value	(int index, ConstSFVec2f)	void
.set1Value	(int index, SFVec2f)	void
.setValue	(float[])	void
.setValue	(float[][])	void
.setValue	(ConstMFVec2f)	void
.setValue	(int size, float[])	void
.setValue	(MFVec2f)	void
MFVec3f.		
MFVec3f	()	MFVec3f
MFVec3f	(float[])	MFVec3f
MFVec3f	(int size, float[])	MFVec3f
MFVec3f	(float[][])	MFVec3f
.addValue	(float x, float y)	void
.addValue	(ConstSFVec3f)	void
.addValue	(SFVec3f)	void
.get1Value	(int index, float[])	void
.get1Value	(int index, SFVec3f)	void
.getValue	(float[][])	void
.getValue	(float[])	void
.insertValue	(int index, float x, float y)	void
.insertValue	(int index, ConstSFVec3f)	void
.insertValue	(int index, SFVec3f)	void
.set1Value	(int index, float x, float y)	void
.set1Value	(int index, ConstSFVec3f)	void
.set1Value	(int index, SFVec3f)	void

TABLE G-I *Summary of Java classes, methods, and exceptions (Continued)*

Class. .Method	<- Superclasses (argument types)	Return type
.setValue	(float[])	void
.setValue	(float[][])	void
.setValue	(ConstMFVec3f)	void
.setValue	(int size, float[])	void
.setValue	(MFVec3f)	void
Node.	**<- BaseNode <- Object**	
.getEventIn	(String name)	Field
.getEventOut	(String name)	ConstField
.getExposedField	(String name)	Field
Script.	**<- BaseNode <- Object**	
.eventsProcessed	()	void
.getField	(String name)	Field
.getEventOut	(String name)	Field
.getEventIn	(String name)	Field
.initialize	()	void
.processEvent	(Event)	void
.processEvents	(int count, Event[])	void
.shutdown	()	void
Note: All SF field types . . .	**. . . unless otherwise noted:**	
SF{type}.	**<- Field <- Object**	
SF{type}	()	SF{type}
SF{type}	({javatype})	SF{type}
.getValue	()	{javatype}
.setValue	({javatype})	void
.setValue	(ConstSF{type})	void
.setValue	(SF{type})	void
SFBool.	**javatype is boolean**	

TABLE G-1 *Summary of Java classes, methods, and exceptions (Continued)*

Class. .Method	<- Superclasses (argument types)	Return type
SFColor.	<- Field <- Object	
SFColor	( )	SFColor
SFColor	(float r, float g, float b)	SFColor
.getBlue	( )	float
.getGreen	( )	float
.getRed	( )	float
.getValue	(float[] color)	void
.setValue	(float color[])	void
.setValue	(ConstSFColor)	void
.setValue	(SFColor)	void
SFFloat.	javatype is float	
SFImage.	<- Field <- Object	
SFImage	( )	SFImage
SFImage	(int w, int h, int nC, byte[] pixels)	SFImage
.getComponents	( )	int
.getHeight	( )	int
.getPixels	(byte[] pixels)	void
.getWidth	( )	int
.setValue	(int w, int h, int nC, byte[] pixels)	void
.setValue	(ConstSFImage)	void
.setValue	(SFImage)	void
SFInt32.	javatype is int	
SFNode.	javatype is BaseNode	
SFRotation.	<- Field <- Object	
SFRotation	( )	SFRotation
SFRotation	(float x, float y, float z, float angle)	SFRotation
.getValue	(float[] xyza)	void

TABLE G-1 *Summary of Java classes, methods, and exceptions (Continued)*

Class. .Method	<- Superclasses (argument types)	Return type
.setValue	(float[] xyza)	void
.setValue	(ConstSFRotation)	void
.setValue	(SFRotation)	void
SFString.	**javatype is String**	
SFTime.	**javatype is double**	
SFVec2f.	**<- Field <- Object**	
SFVec2f	( )	SFVec2f
SFVec2f	(float x, float y)	SFVec2f
.getValue	(float[] xy)	void
.getX	( )	float
.getY	( )	float
.setValue	(float[])	void
.setValue	(floatx, float y)	void
.setValue	(ConstSFVec2f)	void
.setValue	(SFVec2f)	void
SFVec3f.	**<- Field <- Object**	
SFVec3f	( )	SFVec3f
SFVec2f	(float x, float y)	SFVec2f
.getValue	(float[] xy)	void
.getX	( )	float
.getY	( )	float
.getZ	( )	float
.setValue	(float[])	void
.setValue	(floatx, float y, float z)	void
.setValue	(ConstSFVec3f)	void
.setValue	(SFVec3f)	void

G.1 Summary of Exception Classes

- ArrayIndexOutOfBoundsException
- InvalidEventInException
- InvalidEventOutException
- InvalidExposedFieldException
- InvalidFieldChangeException
- InvalidFieldException
- InvalidRouteException
- InvalidVrmlSyntaxException

Summary of JavaScript Scripting API

APPENDIX H

TABLE H-I *Summary of JavaScript functions, objects, methods, and properties*

Function
Object.
  .Method
  . Property
	(argument types)
	
	(argument types)
	[index, if any]
		Return type
		
		Return type
		Property type

Browser.		
.addRoute	(SFNode, String, SFNode, String)	–void–
.createVrmlFromString	(String vrmlSyntax)	MFNode
.createVrmlFromURL	(MFString url, Node, String event)	–void–
.deleteRoute	(SFNode, String, SFNode, String)	–void–
.getName	()	String
.getVersion	()	String
.getCurrentSpeed	()	numeric

TABLE H-I *Summary of JavaScript functions, objects, methods, and properties* (*Continued*)

Function
Object.
  .Method
  . Property
	(argument types)
	
	(argument types)
	[index, if any]
		Return type
		
		Return type
		Property type

.getCurrentFrameRate	( )	numeric
.getWorldURL	( )	String
.loadURL	(MFString url, MFString params)	-void-
.replaceWorld	(MFNode)	-void-
.setDescription	(String description)	-void-
parseInt	(String, [radix])	numeric
parseFloat	(String)	numeric
For all MF field types:		
new MF{type}	(SF{type} ...)	MF{type}
MF{type}.		
.length	numeric	
.toString	( )	String
new SFColor	(r, g, b)	SFColor
SFColor.		
.b	[2]	numeric
.g	[1]	numeric
.getHSV	( )	numeric array
.r	[0]	numeric
.setHSV	(numeric h, numeric s, numeric v)	-void-
.toString	( )	String
new SFImage	(x, y, z, comp, array)	SFImage

TABLE H-1 *Summary of JavaScript functions, objects, methods, and properties (Continued)*

Function
Object.
  .Method
  . Property
	(argument types)
	
	(argument types)
	[index, if any]
		Return type
		
		Return type
		Property type

SFImage.		
.array	MFInt32	
.comp	numeric (1-4)	
.toString	()	String
.x	numeric	
.y	numeric	
new SFNode	(string vrmlsyntax)	SFNode
SFNode.		
.toString	()	String
new SFRotation	(SFVec3f axis, angle)	SFRotation
new SFRotation	(SFVec3f from, SFVec3f to)	SFRotation
new SFRotation	(x, y, z, angle)	SFRotation
SFRotation.		
.angle	[3]	numeric
.getAxis	()	SFVec3f
.inverse	()	SFRotation
.multiply	(SFRotation)	SFRotation
.multVec	(SFVec3f)	SFVec3f
.setAxis	(SFVec3f)	-void-
.slerp	(SFRotation to, numeric t)	SFRotation
.toString	()	String
.x	[0]	numeric
.y	[1]	numeric

TABLE H-I *Summary of JavaScript functions, objects, methods, and properties (Continued)*

Function
Object.
  .Method
  . Property
	(argument types)
	
	(argument types)
	[index, if any]
		Return type
		
		Return type
		Property type

.z	[2]	numeric
new SFVec2f	(x, y)	SFVec2f
SFVec2f.		
.add	(SFVec2f)	SFVec2f
.divide	(numeric)	SFVec2f
.dot	(SFVec2f)	numeric
.length	( )	numeric
.multiply	(numeric)	SFVec2f
.negate	( )	SFVec2f
.normalize	( )	SFVec2f
.subtract	(SFVec2f)	SFVec2f
.toString	( )	String
.x	[0]	
.y	[1]	
new SFVec3f	(x, y, z)	SFVec3f
SFVec3f.		
.add	(SFVec3f)	SFVec3f
.cross	(SFVec3f)	SFVec3f
.divide	(numeric)	SFVec3f
.dot	(SFVec3f)	numeric
.length	( )	numeric
.multiply	(numeric)	SFVec3f
.negate	( )	SFVec3f
.normalize	( )	SFVec3f

TABLE H-I *Summary of JavaScript functions, objects, methods, and properties* (*Continued*)

Function
Object.
  .Method
  . Property
	(argument types)
	
	(argument types)
	[index, if any]
		Return type
		
		Return type
		Property type

.subtract	(SFVec3f)	SFVec3f
.toString	( )	String
.x		
.y		
.z		
new VrmlMatrix	(f11, f12, ..., f44)	VrmlMatrix
new VrmlMatrix	( )	VrmlMatrix
VrmlMatrix.		
.setTransform	(t, r, s, sO, c)	-void-
.getTransform	(t, r, s)	-void-
.inverse	( )	VrmlMatrix
.multLeft	(VrmlMatrix)	VrmlMatrix
.multMatrixVec	(SFVec3f)	SFVec3f
.multRight	(VrmlMatrix)	VrmlMatrix
.multVecMatrix	(SFVec3f)	SFVec3f
.toString	( )	String
.transpose	( )	VrmlMatrix

Index

The VRML Quick Reference

Illegal first characters: + - 0-9 " ' # , . []
\ {} 0x0-0x20

Illegal characters: " ' # , . [] \ {}
0x0-0x20

Reserved keywords: DEF EXTERNPROTO FALSE
IS NULL PROTO ROUTE TO TRUE USE eventIn eventOut exposedField field

PROTO syntax:

```
PROTO PrototypeName [
  eventIn       eventtype name
  eventOut      eventtype name
  exposedField fieldtype name defaultValue
  field         fieldtype name defaultValue
  ... ]
{
# Zero or more routes and prototypes
# First node (defines node type of this prototype)
# Zero or more nodes (any type), routes, and protos
}
```

EXTERNPROTO syntax:

```
EXTERNPROTO ExternPrototypeName [
  eventIn   eventtype name
  eventOut  eventtype name
  field     fieldtype name
  exposedField fieldtypename name
  ... ]
"URL/URN" or [ "URL/URN", "URL/URN", ... ]
```

Node summary:

```
Anchor {
  eventIn       MFNode    addChildren
  eventIn       MFNode    removeChildren
  exposedField MFNode    children          []
  exposedField SFString  description       ""
  exposedField MFString  parameter         []
  exposedField MFString  url               []
  field         SFVec3f   bboxCenter        0 0 0
  field         SFVec3f   bboxSize          -1 -1 -1
}
Appearance {
  exposedField SFNode material          NULL
  exposedField SFNode texture           NULL
  exposedField SFNode textureTransform  NULL
}
```

```
AudioClip {
  exposedField SFString description       ""
  exposedField SFBool   loop              FALSE
  exposedField SFFloat  pitch             1.0
  exposedField SFTime   startTime         0
  exposedField SFTime   stopTime          0
  exposedField MFString url               []
  eventOut      SFTime   duration_changed
  eventOut      SFBool   isActive
}
Background {
  eventIn       SFBool    set_bind
  exposedField MFFloat  groundAngle   []
  exposedField MFColor  groundColor   []
  exposedField MFString backUrl       []
  exposedField MFString bottomUrl     []
  exposedField MFString frontUrl      []
  exposedField MFString leftUrl       []
  exposedField MFString rightUrl      []
  exposedField MFString topUrl        []
  exposedField MFFloat  skyAngle      []
  exposedField MFColor  skyColor      [ 0 0 0 ]
  eventOut      SFBool   isBound
}
Billboard {
  eventIn       MFNode    addChildren
  eventIn       MFNode    removeChildren
  exposedField SFVec3f  axisOfRotation  0 1 0
  exposedField MFNode   children         []
  field         SFVec3f  bboxCenter       0 0 0
  field         SFVec3f  bboxSize         -1 -1 -1
}
Box {
  field    SFVec3f size  2 2 2
}
Collision {
  eventIn       MFNode    addChildren
  eventIn       MFNode    removeChildren
  exposedField MFNode   children         []
  exposedField SFBool   collide          TRUE
  field         SFVec3f  bboxCenter       0 0 0
  field         SFVec3f  bboxSize         -1 -1 -1
  field         SFNode   proxy            NULL
  eventOut      SFTime   collideTime
}
Color {
  exposedField MFColor color  []
}
ColorInterpolator {
  eventIn       SFFloat set_fraction
  exposedField MFFloat key            []
  exposedField MFColor keyValue       []
  eventOut      SFColor value_changed
}
```

```
Cone {
    field       SFBool      bottom          TRUE
    field       SFFloat     bottomRadius 1
    field       SFFloat     height          2
    field       SFBool      side            TRUE
}
Coordinate {
    exposedField MFVec3f point   []
}
CoordinateInterpolator {
    eventIn         SFFloat set_fraction
    exposedField MFFloat key                 []
    exposedField MFVec3f keyValue            []
    eventOut        MFVec3f value_changed
}
Cylinder {
    field       SFBool      bottom          TRUE
    field       SFFloat     height          2
    field       SFFloat     radius          1
    field       SFBool      side            TRUE
    field       SFBool      top             TRUE
}
CylinderSensor {
    exposedField SFBool     autoOffset      TRUE
    exposedField SFFloat    diskAngle       0.262
    exposedField SFBool     enabled         TRUE
    exposedField SFFloat    maxAngle        -1
    exposedField SFFloat    minAngle        0
    exposedField SFFloat    offset          0
    eventOut        SFBool      isActive
    eventOut        SFRotation  rotation_changed
    eventOut        SFVec3f     trackPoint_changed
}
DirectionalLight {
    exposedField SFFloat    ambientIntensity 0
    exposedField SFColor    color           1 1 1
    exposedField SFVec3f    direction       0 0 -1
    exposedField SFFloat    intensity       1
    exposedField SFBool     on              TRUE
}
ElevationGrid {
    eventIn         MFFloat set_height
    exposedField SFNode     color           NULL
    exposedField SFNode     normal          NULL
    exposedField SFNode     texCoord        NULL
    field       MFFloat     height          []
    field       SFBool      ccw             TRUE
    field       SFBool      colorPerVertex  TRUE
    field       SFFloat     creaseAngle     0
    field       SFBool      normalPerVertex TRUE
    field       SFBool      solid           TRUE
    field       SFInt32     xDimension      0
    field       SFFloat     xSpacing        0.0
    field       SFInt32     zDimension      0
    field       SFFloat     zSpacing        0.0
}
Extrusion {
    eventIn     MFVec2f     set_crossSection
    eventIn     MFRotation  set_orientation
    eventIn     MFVec2f     set_scale
    eventIn     MFVec3f     set_spine
    field       SFBool      beginCap        TRUE
    field       SFBool      ccw             TRUE
    field       SFBool      convex          TRUE
    field       SFFloat     creaseAngle     0
    field       MFVec2f     crossSection    [ 1 1, 1 -1,
    -1 -1, -1 1, 1 1 ]
    field       SFBool      endCap          TRUE
    field       MFRotation  orientation     0 0 1 0
    field       MFVec2f     scale           1 1
    field       SFBool      solid           TRUE
    field       MFVec3f     spine           [ 0 0 0, 0 1 0 ]
}
Fog {
    exposedField SFColor    color           1 1 1
    exposedField SFString   fogType         "LINEAR"
    exposedField SFFloat    visibilityRange 0
    eventIn     SFBool      set_bind
    eventOut    SFBool      isBound
}
```

```
FontStyle {
    field MFString family        "SERIF"
    field SFBool   horizontal    TRUE
    field MFString justify       "BEGIN"
    field SFString language      ""
    field SFBool   leftToRight   TRUE
    field SFFloat  size          1.0
    field SFFloat  spacing       1.0
    field SFString style         "PLAIN"
    field SFBool   topToBottom   TRUE
}
Group {
    eventIn         MFNode      addChildren
    eventIn         MFNode      removeChildren
    exposedField MFNode      children        []
    field       SFVec3f     bboxCenter      0 0 0
    field       SFVec3f     bboxSize        -1 -1 -1
}
ImageTexture {
    exposedField MFString url                 []
    field       SFBool      repeatS TRUE
    field       SFBool      repeatT TRUE
}
IndexedFaceSet {
    eventIn         MFInt32 set_colorIndex
    eventIn         MFInt32 set_coordIndex
    eventIn         MFInt32 set_normalIndex
    eventIn         MFInt32 set_texCoordIndex
    exposedField SFNode      color           NULL
    exposedField SFNode      coord           NULL
    exposedField SFNode      normal          NULL
    exposedField SFNode      texCoord        NULL
    field       SFBool      ccw             TRUE
    field       MFInt32     colorIndex      []
    field       SFBool      colorPerVertex  TRUE
    field       SFBool      convex          TRUE
    field       MFInt32     coordIndex      []
    field       SFFloat     creaseAngle     0
    field       MFInt32     normalIndex     []
    field       SFBool      normalPerVertex TRUE
    field       SFBool      solid           TRUE
    field       MFInt32     texCoordIndex   []
}
IndexedLineSet {
    eventIn         MFInt32 set_colorIndex
    eventIn         MFInt32 set_coordIndex
    exposedField SFNode      color           NULL
    exposedField SFNode      coord           NULL
    field       MFInt32     colorIndex      []
    field       SFBool      colorPerVertex  TRUE
    field       MFInt32     coordIndex      []
}
Inline {
    exposedField MFString url                 []
    field       SFVec3f     bboxCenter 0 0 0
    field       SFVec3f     bboxSize    -1 -1 -1
}
LOD {
    exposedField MFNode  level       []
    field       SFVec3f center      0 0 0
    field       MFFloat range       []
}
Material {
    exposedField SFFloat ambientIntensity 0.2
    exposedField SFColor diffuseColor    0.8 0.8 0.8
    exposedField SFColor emissiveColor   0 0 0
    exposedField SFFloat shininess       0.2
    exposedField SFColor specularColor   0 0 0
    exposedField SFFloat transparency    0
}
MovieTexture {
    exposedField SFBool      loop            FALSE
    exposedField SFFloat     speed           1
    exposedField SFTime      startTime       0
    exposedField SFTime      stopTime        0
    exposedField MFString    url             []
    field       SFBool      repeatS         TRUE
    field       SFBool      repeatT         TRUE
    eventOut        SFTime      duration_changed
    eventOut        SFBool      isActive
}
```

```
NavigationInfo {
    eventIn      SFBool     set_bind
    exposedField MFFloat    avatarSize    [ 0.25, 1.6, 0.75 ]
    exposedField SFBool     headlight     TRUE
    exposedField SFFloat    speed         1.0
    exposedField MFString   type          "WALK"
    exposedField SFFloat    visibilityLimit 0.0
    eventOut     SFBool     isBound
}
Normal {
    exposedField MFVec3f vector  []
}
NormalInterpolator {
    eventIn      SFFloat set_fraction
    exposedField MFFloat key          []
    exposedField MFVec3f keyValue     []
    eventOut     MFVec3f value_changed
}
OrientationInterpolator {
    eventIn      SFFloat    set_fraction
    exposedField MFFloat    key          []
    exposedField MFRotation keyValue     []
    eventOut     SFRotation value_changed
}
PixelTexture {
    exposedField SFImage image   0 0 0
    field        SFBool  repeatS TRUE
    field        SFBool  repeatT TRUE
}
PlaneSensor {
    exposedField SFBool  autoOffset        TRUE
    exposedField SFBool  enabled           TRUE
    exposedField SFVec2f maxPosition       -1 -1
    exposedField SFVec2f minPosition       0 0
    exposedField SFVec3f offset            0 0 0
    eventOut     SFBool  isActive
    eventOut     SFVec3f trackPoint_changed
    eventOut     SFVec3f translation_changed
}
PointLight {
    exposedField SFFloat ambientIntensity 0
    exposedField SFVec3f attenuation      1 0 0
    exposedField SFColor color            1 1 1
    exposedField SFFloat intensity        1
    exposedField SFVec3f location         0 0 0
    exposedField SFBool  on               TRUE
    exposedField SFFloat radius           100
}
PointSet {
    exposedField SFNode color NULL
    exposedField SFNode coord NULL
}
PositionInterpolator {
    eventIn      SFFloat set_fraction
    exposedField MFFloat key          []
    exposedField MFVec3f keyValue     []
    eventOut     SFVec3f value_changed
}
ProximitySensor {
    exposedField SFVec3f    center       0 0 0
    exposedField SFVec3f    size         0 0 0
    exposedField SFBool     enabled      TRUE
    eventOut     SFBool     isActive
    eventOut     SFVec3f    position_changed
    eventOut     SFRotation orientation_changed
    eventOut     SFTime     enterTime
    eventOut     SFTime     exitTime
}
ScalarInterpolator {
    eventIn      SFFloat set_fraction
    exposedField MFFloat key          []
    exposedField MFFloat keyValue     []
    eventOut     SFFloat value_changed
}
```

```
Script {
    exposedField MFString url           []
    field        SFBool   directOutput  FALSE
    field        SFBool   mustEvaluate  FALSE
    # And any number of:
    eventIn      eventType eventName
    field        fieldType fieldName initialValue
    eventOut     eventType eventName
}
Shape {
    exposedField SFNode appearance NULL
    exposedField SFNode geometry   NULL
}
Sound {
    exposedField SFVec3f direction   0 0 1
    exposedField SFFloat intensity   1
    exposedField SFVec3f location    0 0 0
    exposedField SFFloat maxBack     10
    exposedField SFFloat maxFront    10
    exposedField SFFloat minBack     1
    exposedField SFFloat minFront    1
    exposedField SFFloat priority    0
    exposedField SFNode  source      NULL
    field        SFBool  spatialize  TRUE
}
Sphere {
    field SFFloat radius  1
}
SphereSensor {
    exposedField SFBool     autoOffset        TRUE
    exposedField SFBool     enabled           TRUE
    exposedField SFRotation offset            0 1 0 0
    eventOut     SFBool     isActive
    eventOut     SFRotation rotation_changed
    eventOut     SFVec3f    trackPoint_changed
}
SpotLight {
    exposedField SFFloat ambientIntensity 0
    exposedField SFVec3f attenuation      1 0 0
    exposedField SFFloat beamWidth        1.570796
    exposedField SFColor color            1 1 1
    exposedField SFFloat cutOffAngle      0.785398
    exposedField SFVec3f direction        0 0 -1
    exposedField SFFloat intensity        1
    exposedField SFVec3f location         0 0 0
    exposedField SFBool  on               TRUE
    exposedField SFFloat radius           100
}
Switch {
    exposedField MFNode  choice      []
    exposedField SFInt32 whichChoice -1
}
Text {
    exposedField MFString string   []
    exposedField SFNode   fontStyle NULL
    exposedField MFFloat  length    []
    exposedField SFFloat  maxExtent 0.0
}
TextureCoordinate {
    exposedField MFVec2f point  []
}
TextureTransform {
    exposedField SFVec2f center      0 0
    exposedField SFFloat rotation    0
    exposedField SFVec2f scale       1 1
    exposedField SFVec2f translation 0 0
}
TimeSensor {
    exposedField SFTime  cycleInterval 1
    exposedField SFBool  enabled       TRUE
    exposedField SFBool  loop          FALSE
    exposedField SFTime  startTime     0
    exposedField SFTime  stopTime      0
    eventOut     SFTime  cycleTime
    eventOut     SFFloat fraction_changed
    eventOut     SFBool  isActive
    eventOut     SFTime  time
}
```

```
TouchSensor {                                          Viewpoint {
   exposedField SFBool   enabled TRUE                     eventIn      SFBool     set_bind
   eventOut     SFVec3f  hitNormal_changed                exposedField SFFloat    fieldOfView    0.785398
   eventOut     SFVec3f  hitPoint_changed                 exposedField SFBool     jump           TRUE
   eventOut     SFVec2f  hitTexCoord_changed              exposedField SFRotation orientation    0 0 1 0
   eventOut     SFBool   isActive                         exposedField SFVec3f    position       0 0 10
   eventOut     SFBool   isOver                           field        SFString   description    ""
   eventOut     SFTime   touchTime                        eventOut     SFTime     bindTime
}                                                         eventOut     SFBool     isBound
Transform {                                            }
   eventIn      MFNode      addChildren               VisibilitySensor {
   eventIn      MFNode      removeChildren                exposedField SFVec3f center   0 0 0
   exposedField SFVec3f     center           0 0 0        exposedField SFBool  enabled  TRUE
   exposedField MFNode      children         []           exposedField SFVec3f size     0 0 0
   exposedField SFRotation  rotation         0 0 1 0      eventOut     SFTime  enterTime
   exposedField SFVec3f     scale            1 1 1        eventOut     SFTime  exitTime
   exposedField SFRotation  scaleOrientation 0 0 1 0      eventOut     SFBool  isActive
   exposedField SFVec3f     translation      0 0 0     }
   field        SFVec3f     bboxCenter       0 0 0     WorldInfo {
   field        SFVec3f     bboxSize         -1 -1 -1     field MFString info  []
}                                                         field SFString title ""
                                                       }
```

Addison-Wesley Developers Press

Addison-Wesley Developers Press publishes high-quality, practical books and software for programmers, developers, and system administrators.

Here are some additional titles from A-W Developers Press that might interest you. If you'd like to order any of these books, please visit your local bookstore or:

 FAX us at (800) 367-7198 (24 hours a day)

 CALL us at (800) 822-6339 (8:30 AM to 6:00 PM eastern time, Monday-Friday)

 WRITE to us at Addison-Wesley Developers Press
One Jacob Way
Reading, MA 01867

 REACH us online at http://www.aw.com/devpress/

For international orders, contact one of the following Addison-Wesley subsidiaries or call (617) 944-3700 x5190:

Australia/New Zealand
Addison-Wesley Publishing Co.
6 Byfield Street
North Ryde, N.S.W. 2113
Australia
Tel: 61 2 878 5411
Fax: 61 2 878 5830

Latin America
Addison-Wesley Iberoamericana S.A.
Blvd. de las Cataratas #3
Col. Jardines del Pedregal
01900 Mexico D.F., Mexico
Tel: (52 5) 568-36-18
Fax: (52 5) 568-53-32
e-mail: ordenes@ibero.aw.com
    or: informacion@ibero.aw.com

United Kingdom and Africa
Addison Wesley Longman Group
Limited
P.O. Box 77
Harlow, Essex CM 19 5BQ
United Kingdom
Tel: 44 1279 623 923
Fax: 44 1279 453 450

Southeast Asia
Addison-Wesley
(Singapore) Pte. Ltd.
11 Cantonment Road
Singapore 089736
Tel: 65 223 8155
Fax: 65 223 7155

Europe and the Middle East
Addison-Wesley Publishers B.V.
Concertgebouwplein 25
1071 LM Amsterdam
The Netherlands
Tel: 31 20 671 7296
Fax: 31 20 675 2141

All other countries:
Addison-Wesley Publishing Co.
Attn: International Order Dept.
One Jacob Way
Reading, MA 01867 U.S.A.
Tel: (617) 944-3700 x5190
Fax: (617) 942-2829

If you would like a free copy of our Developers Press catalog, contact us at elizabs@aw.com